Using the Maps

Here are some important details about the walkthrough maps:

- **Moving platforms are usually shown in their starting positions.**
- **Areas that undergo significant changes through the course of a level are shown in the state that offers the most information. If, for example, a platform must be moved to reveal a door, that platform may not appear on the map.**
- **Invisible Blocks are indicated by the used Blocks that appear after you've found them.**
- **P Switches and ? Switches always appear on the maps, even if they're contained within Blocks.**
- **Temporary platforms and walkways are almost always indicated on a map. This includes platforms and Blocks that only appear while a P Switch or ? Switch is active.**

Tip, Note, and Caution Boxes

As you flip through the guide, you'll notice a variety of informative boxes. Different boxes serve different purposes, but they all contain useful information.

TIP

Tip boxes indicate recommended actions. Whether they detail unique opportunities or amusing tricks, Tip boxes are meant to improve your overall experience.

NOTE

Note boxes provide additional information without recommending a course of action. These boxes are usually used to detail available options, or to explain some of the game's basic elements or mechanics.

CAUTION

Caution boxes are meant to relay urgent information. These boxes often warn of dangerous situations, but they're also used to point out any unexpected consequences a particular course of action might have.

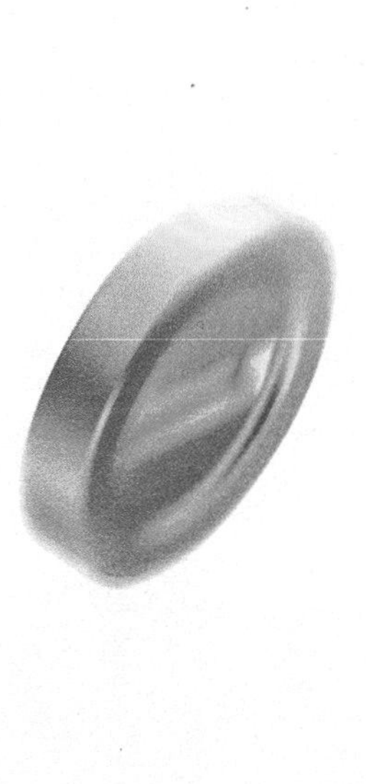

THE BASICS

Using the Touch Screen

While in a Level

The action may take place on the 3D Screen, but the Touch Screen is a very important tool. While you're in a level, the Touch Screen allows you to access your Stored Item. When you tap the stored item, the item will then appear on the 3D screen and fall from the top of the screen.

The Touch Screen also displays a variety of important information. While you're in a level, use the Touch Screen to keep track of your remaining lives, your approximate position, which Star Coins you've collected, and more.

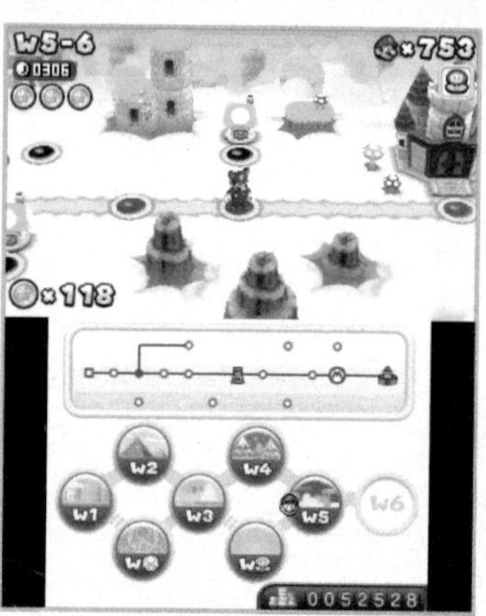

On the Map Screen

While on the Map Screen, the Touch Screen serves as an important navigational tool. Use the map at the top of the Touch Screen to review which paths and locations you've managed to unlock within your current World.

The Touch Screen also displays an icon for each World you've unlocked. To move to a different World, simply tap the corresponding icon.

NOTE

When you start a new game, only World One's icon is active. As you progress through the game, additional icons will be displayed on the Touch Screen.

Fire Mario

When Mario uses a Fire Flower, he transforms into Fire Mario. Fire Mario has all of Super Mario's abilities, but this transformation includes a special attack. While in this form, Mario can use fireballs to attack enemies from a distance. If Fire Mario takes damage, he transforms into Super Mario.

 TIP

While playing as Fire Mario, press the Dash button to throw a fireball.

Gold Mario

When Mario uses a Gold Flower, he transforms into Gold Mario. Gold Mario is an extremely powerful transformation. While in this form, Mario can throw explosive gold fireballs that are not only capable of defeating nearly any foe, they're also able to transform Blocks into coins. If Gold Mario takes damage, he reverts to his previous form.

 TIP

While playing as Gold Mario, press the Dash button to throw a gold fireball. If you complete a level as Gold Mario, this transformation will be removed. Enemies hit by the explosion from the Gold Fireball will give coins in the amounts of 5, 10, 15, and so on, but they have to be with in range. If they are not in range then the counter resets.

Raccoon Mario

When Mario uses a Super Leaf, he transforms into Raccoon Mario. Raccoon Mario is a very useful transformation. When in this form, Mario can attack enemies with his tail, glide over long distances, and even fly for a few seconds at a time! If Raccoon Mario takes damage, he transforms into Super Mario.

 TIP

While playing as Raccoon Mario, press the Dash button to perform a tail whip. To glide, press and hold the Jump button while you're falling. To fly, dash along the ground until your Power Meter is full, then press and hold the Jump button.

White Raccoon Mario

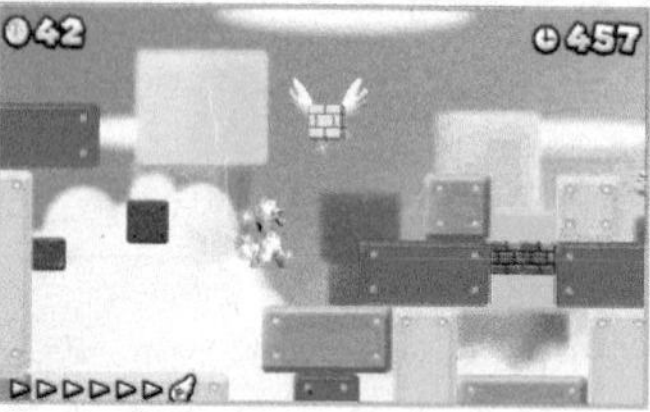

When Mario uses an Invincibility Leaf, he transforms into White Raccoon Mario. White Raccoon Mario has all of Raccoon Mario's abilities, but this transformation has the added benefit of damage immunity! This powerful form does have a couple of drawbacks, however. To start with, this transformation is only made available when you lose several lives while attempting to complete a single level. More importantly, levels you complete while using this transformation do not count toward your star rating!

Mega Mario

When Mario collects a Mega Mushroom, he transforms into Mega Mario. Mega Mario is a very powerful form—unfortunately this power doesn't last long. While in this form, Mario is immune to damage, and he can smash a path right through most obstacles.

 TIP

When the Mega Mario form wears off, Mario transforms into Super Mario.

 NOTE

During Co-op Play, Luigi has personalized versions of Mario's forms. The differences, however, are purely cosmetic.

Common Power-Ups and Items

1-Up Mushroom

When collected, a 1-Up Mushroom rewards you with an extra life.

Super Mushroom

When used, a Super Mushroom transforms Mario into Super Mario.

Gold Mushroom

In the Coin Rush Game Mode, all 1-Up Mushrooms are replaced by Gold Mushrooms. Gold Mushrooms provide bonus coins.

Fire Flower

When used, a Fire Flower transforms Mario into Fire Mario.

Super Leaf

When used, a Super Leaf transforms Mario into Raccoon Mario.

Mini Mushroom

When used, a Mini Mushroom transforms Mario into Mini Mario.

Mega Mushroom

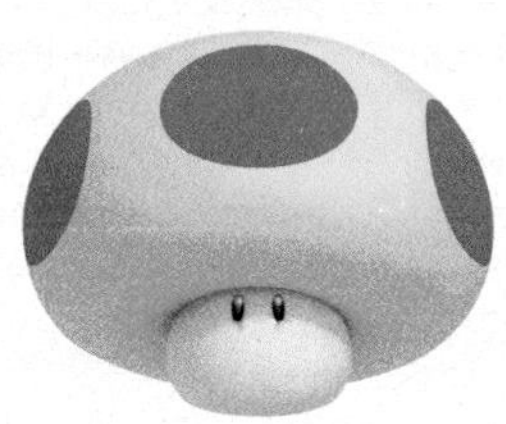

When collected, a Mega Mushroom transforms Mario into Mega Mario.

Gold Flower

When used, a Gold Flower transforms Mario into Gold Mario.

Invincibility Leaf

When collected, an Invincibility Leaf transforms Mario into White Raccoon Mario.

Super Star

When collected, a Super Star grants Mario temporary invincibility. While this power-up is active, Mario also has the ability to defeat virtually any creature simply by touching it.

If you defeat eight enemies while a Super Star is active, you'll be awarded an extra life. You'll then be rewarded for each additional enemy you defeat until the power-up wears off.

If you hit a ? Block while a Super Star is active, you'll generally receive a fresh Super Star. Depending on the specific level, this can allow you to maintain your invincibility for quite a long time!

Coin

You'll find coins scattered throughout the game. Each time you collect 100 coins, you're rewarded with an extra life.

Star Coin

Most hostile levels contain three Star Coins. Collect these valuable items and use them to open locked paths.

Moon Coin

All of the hostile levels within Star World contain three Moon Coins.

Red Ring

Pass through a Red Ring to initiate a brief challenge. For a short time after you activate a Red Ring, eight red coins appear in the area. If you manage to collect all eight red coins before they vanish, you'll be rewarded with a power-up.

The power-up granted by a Red Ring is almost always the same as the first available power-up in the level. If you complete a Red Ring challenge while you have an active power-up, you will receive a 1-Up Mushroom instead of the original reward.

Gold Ring

When you pass through a Gold Ring, enemies within the area transform into gold versions of themselves. While a Gold Ring is active, you earn coins for each enemy you defeat.

Many gold enemies offer ways to generate extra coins!

Block

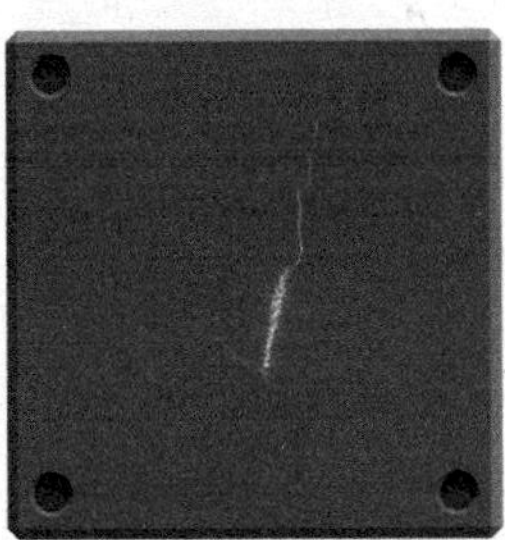

Blocks can serve a variety of purposes. Some Blocks act as platforms, while other Blocks act as obstacles. Many Blocks contain hidden items such as coins, power-ups, and switches.

NOTE

Not all Blocks can be seen. Most levels contain at least a few Invisible Blocks. To reveal an Invisible Block, you must jump up and hit it from below.

? Block

? Blocks always contain some sort of item. These useful objects are a common source of power-ups.

10-Coin Block

10-Coin Blocks may look like common Blocks, but they're potentially much more valuable. After you hit a 10-Coin Block, you have a short time in which you'll earn one coin for each additional hit. If you manage to collect at least 10 coins within the time limit, it transforms into a Gold Block!

TIP

To ensure you collect at least 10 coins, ground pound a 10-Coin Block and hold Down on the +Control Pad.

Gold Block

Hit a Gold Block from above or below to equip it. After you do, you'll generate coins as you move around the level.

The Gold Block lasts until you take damage, complete the level, or use it to generate 100 coins—whichever comes first.

NOTE

If you hit a Gold Block from the side (or if you already have one equipped), it erupts coins for a few seconds.

NOTE

Each time you earn 500 coins, a Flying Gold Block appears on the Map Screen. The next time you enter a level, this reward will be waiting for you.

POW Block

When you hit a POW Block, it sends a shock wave through the immediate area. The blast generally affects all nearby Blocks and enemies.

Roulette Coin Block

Roulette Coin Blocks cycle through a series of coin values. When you hit a Roulette Coin Block, you receive the displayed amount of coins.

Assist Block

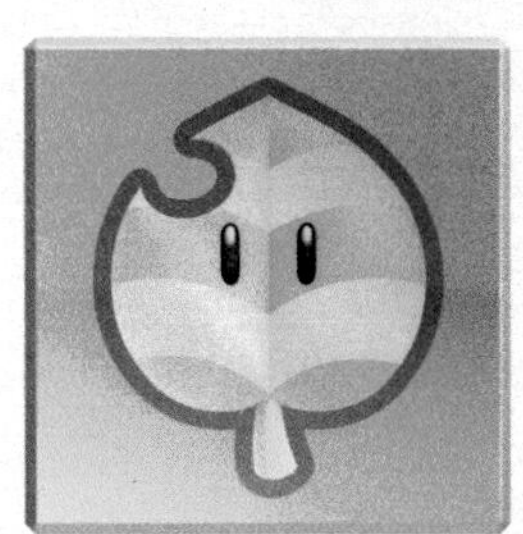

An Assist Block appears if you lose fives lives within a single level without completing it. When this happens, you can hit it to reveal an Invincibility Leaf.

ENEMIES

Common Critters

Goomba

Goombas are one of the most common enemies encountered. To defeat them, simply jump onto their heads.

Goomba Tower

Goomba Towers behave just like regular Goombas, but they're a bit tougher to stomp. Get to higher ground, hop onto the Goomba Tower, and stomp each enemy on your way down. If you line up your jump well, you can take out the whole stack before you hit the ground again!

You will earn a 1-Up if you Ground Pound a stack of 8 Goombas.

Paragoomba

These flying foes take two hits to take out. Jump on it once to knock it out of the air, then stomp it a second time to finish it off.

Bone Goomba

Don't be fooled by their eerie appearance—Bone Goombas aren't any tougher than their other varieties. You'll find these fellows patrolling Towers and Castles. Just stomp them and move on.

Mini Goomba

These pint-sized pests may not deal damage, but they just might be the most dangerous variety of Goomba! When a Mini Goomba climbs onto you, it severely limits your mobility. Perform a ground pound to shake these pests loose.

NOTE

Tail whip can also be used to shake them off.

Koopa

When you jump on a Koopa Troopa, it tucks into its shell. At this point you can either kick the shell, or pick it up to throw at Blocks, coins, or enemies. As you approach a Koopa, note the color of its shell. Green-shelled Koopas will walk right off of ledges, while red-shelled Koopas have the sense to turn back.

CAUTION

If you don't follow up after stomping a Koopa, it eventually gets the courage to emerge from its shell. Make sure you aren't holding it when it does!

Koopa Paratroopa

These enemies will take more than one jump to take out. Stomp them once to remove their wings, and then one more time to make them hide in their shell.

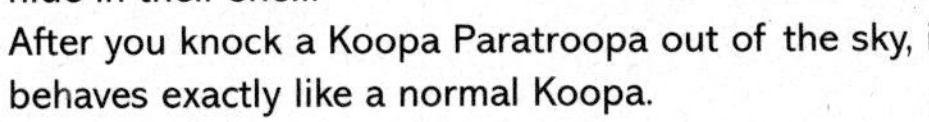

After you knock a Koopa Paratroopa out of the sky, it behaves exactly like a normal Koopa.

The Bros.

The Bros. are considerably more threatening than their Koopa counterparts. Most Bros. throw projectiles, making it fairly difficult to stomp their heads. It's usually best to blast these baddies with your own projectiles. If find yourself without a suitable power-up, however, try to slip under them as they jump in the air. If the Bro happens to be standing on a Block, smash the Block to knock the Bro off its perch.

Piranha Plant

Don't try to stomp these pipe-dwelling plants! Use a tail whip or fireball to knock a Piranha Plant out of its pipe—or simply wait for the creature to pull back into its pipe before you approach.

Sumo Bro

In addition to their projectile attacks, Sumo Bros. like to throw their weight around. Keep your eyes on a Sumo Bro when it jumps into the air—there's a good chance it will slam down with a powerful ground pound. To avoid getting stunned, jump into the air just before the Sumo Bro lands.

Big Piranha Plant

Big Piranha plants behave similarly to the smaller variety, but they're not nearly as easy to slip past. If you don't have a power-up capable of destroying one, look for a nearby Koopa. Even a Big Piranha Plant can't stand up against a thrown shell.

NOTE

Use the Fire Flower as a backup to defeat the Big Piranha Plant.

Venus Fire Trap

These aggressive enemies spit fireballs at you, and the fact that they tend to reside in pipes means they usually have the high ground! Your best bet is to dodge incoming fireballs as you close in on their position, then surprise them with a fireball of your own.

Bone Piranha Plant

Bone Piranha Plants are immune to fireballs, but tail whips and thrown shells will clear them out in no time.

Big Venus Fire Trap

Once you've faced the smaller variety, you know what to expect from a Big Venus Fire Trap. To clear one from your path, shoot it with a few fireballs or toss a shell at it.

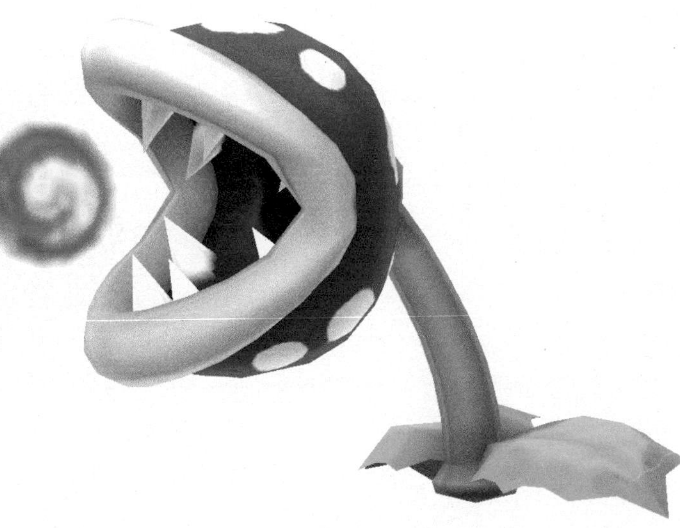

Big Bone Piranha Plant

It can be difficult to gauge the range of a Big Bone Piranha Plant. Whenever possible, use a thrown shell to take them out from a distance.

Cheep Cheep

While underwater, Cheep Cheeps are slow moving and fairly passive. Clear them out with fireballs, or simply avoid swimming into them. When Cheep Cheeps breach the water's surface, however, it can be difficult to predict when and where they'll emerge. In these cases, stick to higher ground and stomp them as they leap up at you.

Deep Cheep

While a Deep Cheep may look similar to a Cheep Cheep, it actually has quite the temper and will swim after you. Use a fireball or tail whip to take care of this enemy, or swim away as fast as possible!

Big Cheep Cheep

These oversized fish are like normal Cheep Cheeps—just bigger! Leave a little more space to get by them due to their size.

Big Deep Cheep

This nasty character behaves like normal Deep Cheep, but its larger size makes it much harder to dodge. Defeat them with a fireball, or avoid them all together.

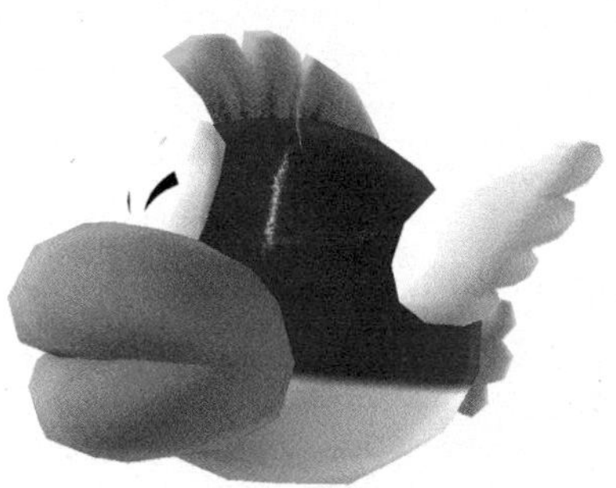

Cheep Chomp

Keep away from this enemy. If you get too close it will swallow you whole and you'll be defeated. Whenever possible, use a Fire Flower to take him out as he approaches.

Fishbones

When a Fishbones spots you, it becomes enraged and charges you. It's often best to turn its temper to your advantage! Wait near a wall until the Fishbones charges you, then dart out of its path just before it reaches you. You can even coax two different Fishbones to crash into each other.

Spiny Cheep Cheep

Like the Deep Cheep, this enemy will chase you around. The spikes on its back make it even more deadly, making it risky to try to use a tail whip against it. Swim away from this enemy or take it out with a fireball.

Urchin

This enemy usually just stays in the same place, bobbing up and down. Don't get too close to them though! Their spines will hurt you. Just swim by them carefully.

Porcupuffer

The Porcupuffer is one persistent enemy! These large fish swim along the water's surface, snapping at you each time they pass by. You can defeat this enemy with a well-timed fireball, but it won't be long before a new Porcupuffer takes its place.

A Koopa Shell can also be used to defeat this enemy.

Small Urchin

These little guys are just like their bigger cousins, but tend to appear in clusters. Swim around them and make sure not to get too close—those spines hurt!

Use a fireball to take out the Urchin and Small Urchin.

Blooper

From a distance, Bloopers seem to be fairly passive. You'll often spot these underwater creatures peeking out of pipes or floating aimlessly around the area. When you're within range, however, a Blooper lunges toward you with a surprising burst of speed. These troublesome enemies swim around erratically, making it hard to avoid them in tight spaces. Keep your distance, or use a power-up to take them out.

Dry Bones

You can jump on a Dry Bones to make it crumble into a pile of bones, but this resilient enemy will reassemble itself in a matter of seconds. Make sure to jump on one if it is in your way, then move along before it gets back up!

Blooper Nanny

These Bloopers act similar to a normal Blooper, but have a small group of tiny Bloopers following them. The tiny Bloopers will latch on to you, slowing you down and making it difficult to get away. Take out the Blooper Nanny with a fireball or a tail whip, and the tiny Bloopers will go down with it.

Big Dry Bones

Big Dry Bones are formidable foes! When you stomp one, the impact does little more than rattle its teeth. Since they're able to endure unlimited stomps, Big Dry Bones can sometimes be used to reach hidden objects. However, unless you have cause to linger, it's usually best to hurry past these enemies. They can be knocked down to a pile of bones by a ground pound.

Boo

Boos are very sneaky, trying to catch up to you once your back is turned. To stop them from approaching you, simply turn towards them. They'll cover their eyes and stay there until you turn your back to them again. You can clear them out if you happen to have a Super Star or Gold Flower, but it's generally best to move along.

Big Boo

Big Boos act exactly the same as Boos, but being that they are so much bigger they are very hard to avoid! Your best bet is to just run away and face them when you need to stop moving.

Boohemoth

At first glance, the Boohemoth seems to behave much like a Boo, but this massive enemy is much braver. When you turn to face a Boohemoth, it covers its eyes. After a moment, however, it shuffles toward you.

Peepa

Peepa aren't particularly aggressive, but they can certainly be a nuisance. You'll often see these grinning ghosts carrying platforms or spinning in circles. Unless you have a Super Star or a Gold Flower, it's best to consider Peepa as moving obstacles.

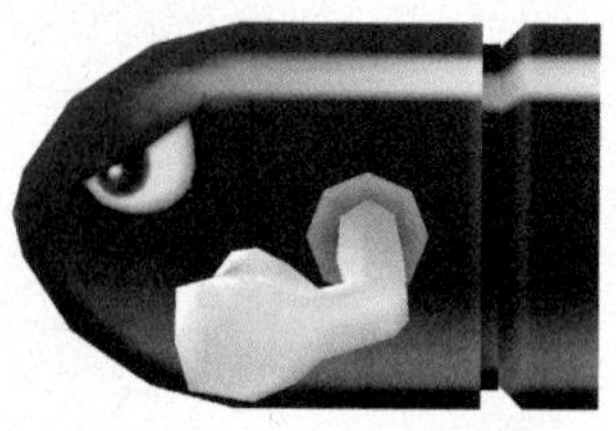

Bullet Bill

These enemies fly in a straight line across the area. Avoid them completely, or jump on top of them to take them out.

Banzai Bill

Banzai Bills are fairly similar to Bullet Bills, but their increased size makes them much more difficult to dodge. Banzai Bills are powerful enough to destroy any Blocks in their path, but a single stomp will knock them out of the sky.

Bob-omb

These explosive little enemies pack quite a wallop. Stomp a Bob-omb to light its fuse, then throw it at your intended target. When it explodes, the blast will deliver heavy damage to nearby enemies and objects.

Buzzy Beetle

This is one tough enemy! Fireballs will not work at all against it; the best bet is to jump on it once, causing it to hide in its shell. Once it goes into hiding, kick the shell away.

Para-bomb

Para-bombs are Bob-ombs that parachute down to the ground. Stomp these enemies to remove their parachutes, but be careful! These enemies drift back and forth as they fall, which can make it difficult to time your jump.

Red Spike Buzzy

Red Spike Buzzies are very similar to the Buzzy Beetle, but due to the large spike on their back you can't jump on them. Luckily, when you spot one of these enemies, there's usually a Buzzy Beetle nearby. If you find one, stomp it and use its shell to clear out this enemy. If not, a well-timed tail-whip may be your best option.

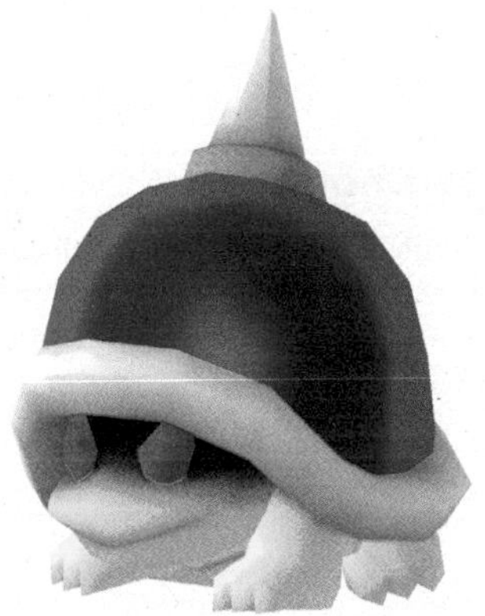

Chain Chomp

When you approach a Chain Chomp, it lunges at you. Luckily its chain limits the range of its attacks. Coax a Chain Chomp into attacking, then move out of its range. As it recovers from the lunge, slip past it or ground pound the stake that anchors it to the ground. If you drive the stake all the way into the ground, the Chain Chomp lunges away, destroying any Blocks or enemies along its path.

Amp

Unless you have a Gold Flower or a Super Star, it's best to stay clear of an Amp. These creatures typically move along tracks, so just slip past them while the path is clear.

A Koopa Shell can take out an Amp.

Flame Chomp

Flame Chomps aren't nearly as tough as Chain Chomps, but they're much more mobile. When a Flame Chomp attacks, dodge its fiery tail and stomp it out of the sky.

Fire Snake

Once a Fire Snake spots you, it follows you around the area. Fireballs have no effect, and you certainly wouldn't want to stomp one, but one tail whip is enough to send a Fire Snake packing.

Fuzzy

These wild-eyed enemies race back and forth along special tracks, so it's fairly easy to anticipate their movements. Fuzzies generally appear in clusters. If there's a POW Block nearby, try to activate it when several Fuzzies are in range. If not, use a Fire Flower to deal with one enemy at a time, or simply avoid them.

NOTE

Tail whip can also be used to take out the Fuzzies.

Thwomp

Thwomps slam into the ground as you get near them. As they rise back up to their starting positions, slip under them. Keep moving! Once the Thwomp reaches its original position, it slams back down to the ground.

Big Fuzzy

Big Fuzzies are essentially the same as their smaller counterparts, but their increased size makes it a bit trickier to slip past them. Whenever possible, use a POW Block or a suitable power-up to clear these enemies from your path.

NOTE

Big Fuzzy can be dealt with by a Fire Flower as well.

Big Thwomp

A Big Thwomp behaves much like a smaller Thwomp. Use the same tactics to get past one.

Whomp

When you approach a Whomp, it leaps in the air and slams down on its own face. When it does, make sure you're not in its way! After a Whomp slams down, hop onto its back and perform a ground pound.

Pokey

Pokeys may look friendly, but these prickly creatures are far from it. You can't stomp a Pokey, so use a suitable power-up to deal with these enemies. Use a fireball or a tail whip to hit a Pokey's head. If you attack anywhere else, this segmented enemy can survive multiple hits.

Big Whomp

Big Whomps are very similar to the smaller variety, so it's best to use the same strategy. Bait the Big Whomp into attacking, then hop on its back and shatter it with a ground pound.

Wiggler

Wigglers are happy creatures as long as you leave them alone. If you stomp Wiggler, however, it becomes enraged. Use a tail whip or a thrown shell to defeat this enemy, or simply leave the area.

Swooper

When you approach a Swooper, it drops down from its roost and swoops toward you. Once a Swooper begins its attack, however, it maintains its course. Dodge this enemy as it flies past you, or stomp it as it moves into range.

Lava Bubble

These creatures often jump out of lava areas, usually in timed increments. Once you have a sense of a Lava Bubble's rhythm, it's fairly easy to slip past it.

Crow

When a Crow spots you, it slowly circles the area above you, then it picks up its speed and dives right toward you. Stomp a Crow while it attacks, or jump out of the way and allow it to fly away.

Coin Coffer

Occasionally, passing through a Red Ring causes a Coin Coffer to appear. When this happens, allow this strange creature to hop away, then scoop up the red coins it leaves in its path. You can also get all 8 red coins by defeating the Coin Coffer.

Lakitu

A Lakitu generally uses its cloud to stay out of reach, which can make it very difficult to land a successful attack—especially while you're dodging the Spiny Eggs it throws at you! When a Lakitu attacks, head over to higher ground. If it follows you, stomp its head to knock it off of its cloud.

TIP

Shortly after you defeat a Lakitu, its cloud disappears. Until it does, however, use the cloud to fly around the area!

Spiny Egg

When a Spiny Egg lands on the ground, it hatches to reveal a Spiny. It's usually best to stay clear of these spiky hazards.

Spiny

It won't do you any good to stomp a Spiny. If you don't have a suitable power-up, it's best to avoid them. Fireball or Tail Whip is suitable to defeat Spinys

Spider

These dangling enemies can often be used to reach hidden areas and objects. Sometimes, however, they're simply in the way. If a Spider is proving to be a pest, stomp it and knock it loose from its web.

Reznor

Each time you climb to the top of a Tower, you'll find some fire-breathing Reznors in the final chamber. These creatures are always perched on ? Blocks. To defeat one, simply hit its ? Block and knock it out of the area.

Gold Creatures

Gold Goombas

All varieties of Gold Goombas behave exactly as they do in their normal forms. Aside from its appearance, the only difference is the coin reward you receive for stomping the gold enemy.

Gold Koopas

After you stomp a Gold Koopa, throw its shell to generate additional coins. A Gold Shell not only earns a coin bonus for each enemy it knocks out of its way, it also leaves a coin trail as it moves through the area.

Gold Bros.

Instead of throwing their weapons at you, Gold Bros. throw coins.

Gold Cheep Cheep

As it moves through the area, a gold Cheep Cheep drags a trail of coins behind it.

Gold Piranha Plant

When you defeat a Gold Piranha plant, a fountain of coins erupts from the vacant pipe.

Gold Boo

Gold Boos turn and flee from you, leaving coin trails behind them.

Gold Big Boo

Gold Big Boos turn and flee, leaving massive coin trails behind them.

Gold Banzai Bill

As a Gold Banzai Bill flies through the area, it creates a massive trail of coins.

Gold Bullet Bill

As a Gold Bullet Bill flies through the area, it creates a trail of coins.

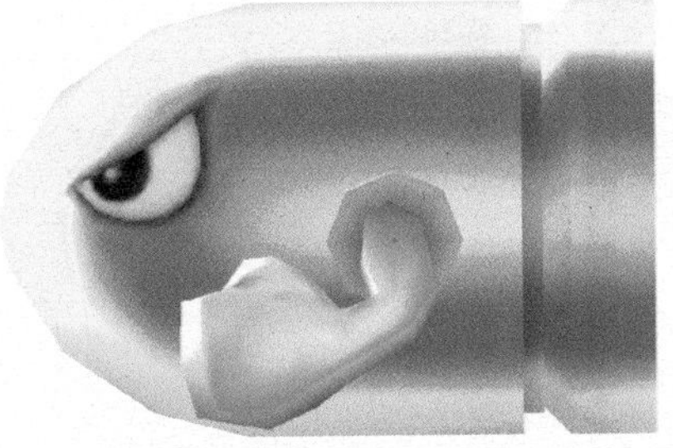

Gold Lakitu

Instead of throwing Spiny Eggs, a Gold Lakitu throws coins. When you commandeer a Gold Lakitu's cloud, it generates coins as you move through the area.

WORLD ONE

WORLD LOCATIONS				
Hostile Levels	Toad Houses	Boo Houses	Warp Cannons	Boss
9	4	0	1	Roy Koopa

Main Path Levels:

- World 1-1
- World 1-2
- World 1-3
- World 1-Tower
- World 1-4
- World 1-5
- World 1-Castle

Alternate Path Levels:

- World 1-A
- World 1-Warp Cannon

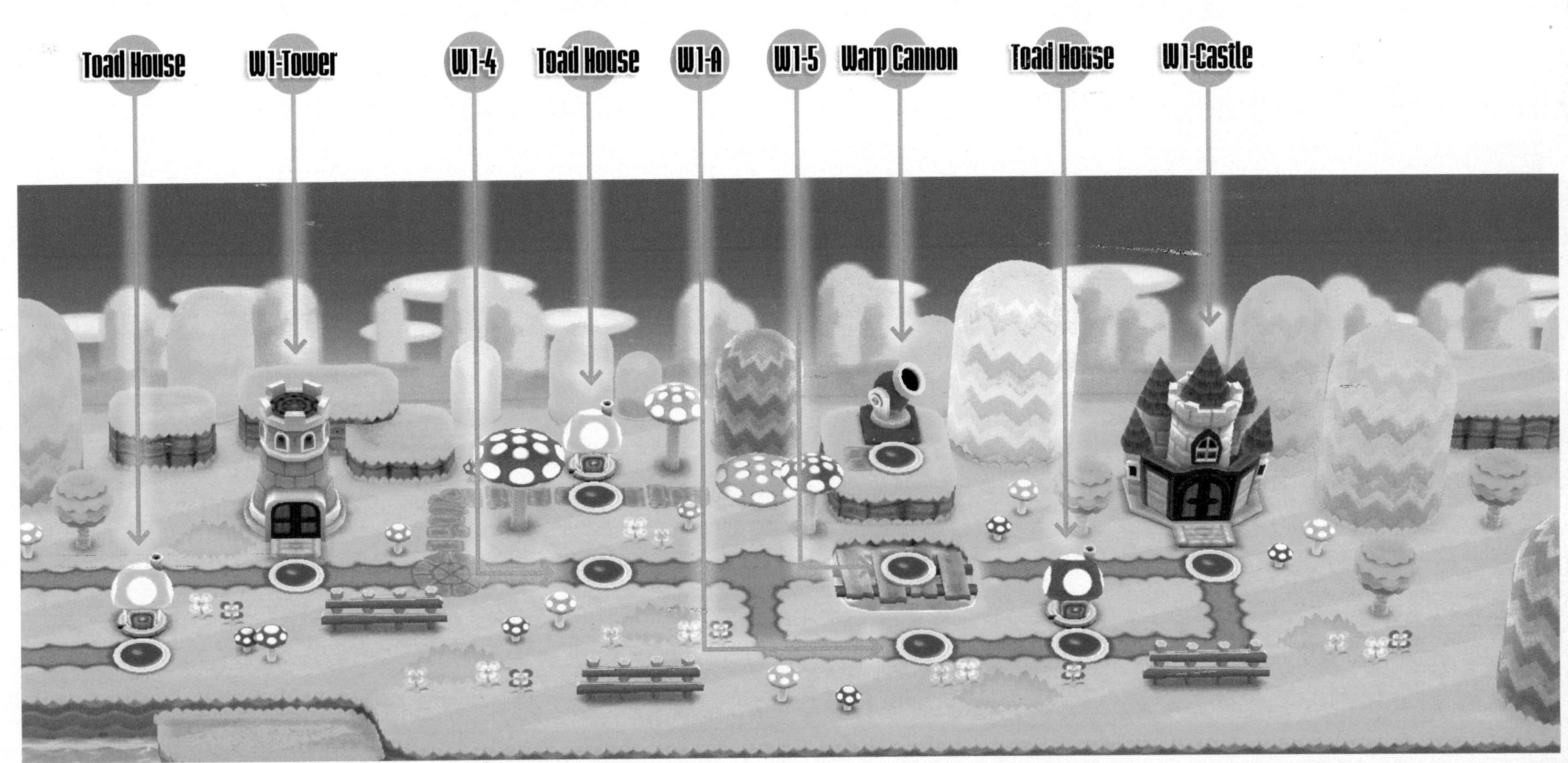

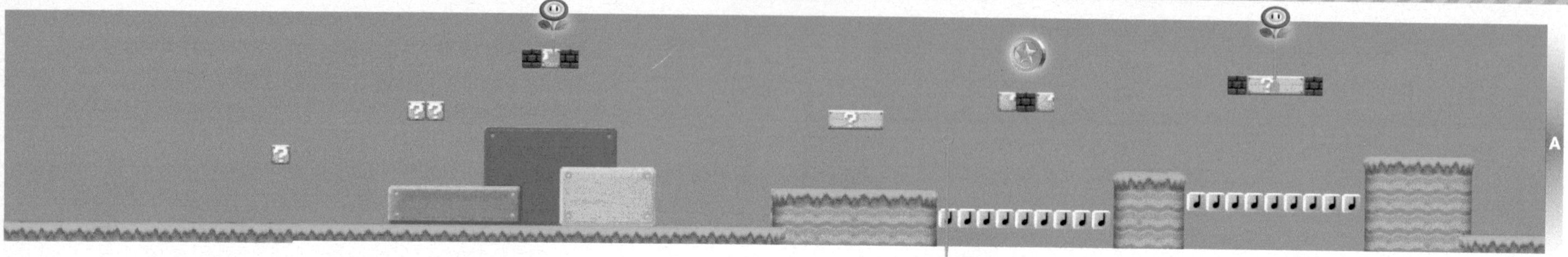

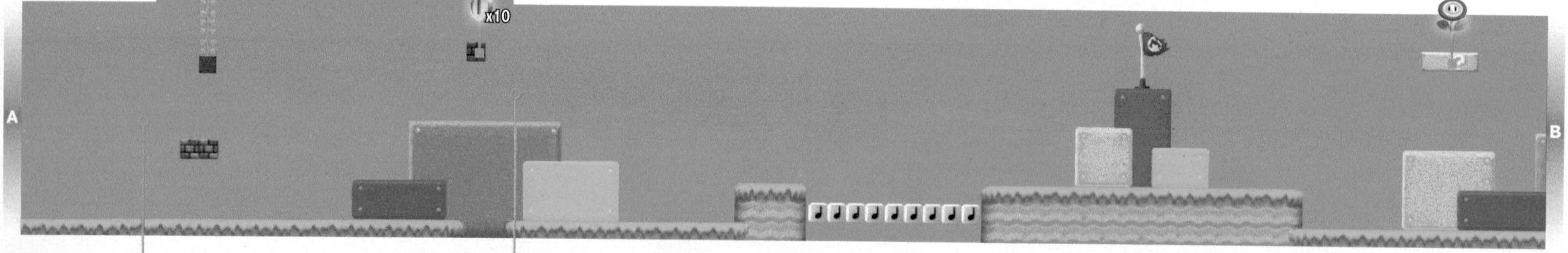

1

The first Star Coin is easy to spot. When you reach the Note Blocks, use a well-timed jump to bounce up to the Star Coin.

2

Hop onto the Blocks at Point 2 and jump up to reveal a Beanstalk hidden inside of an Invisible Block.

Climb up the Beanstalk to find a hidden area. Grab the nearby coins, then hit the Block to the right to reveal a 1-Up Mushroom.

3

This level contains several 10-Coin Blocks, and you can earn a lot of extra coins if you convert all of them into Gold Blocks.

TIP

It's best to stand on a 10-Coin Block and perform an extended ground pound attack. If you hit one of these special Blocks from below, however, keep jumping!

4

The second Star Coin is high above the Note Blocks at Point 4. Use the Note Blocks to bounce up and clear a path through the Blocks above you.

WORLD 1-1

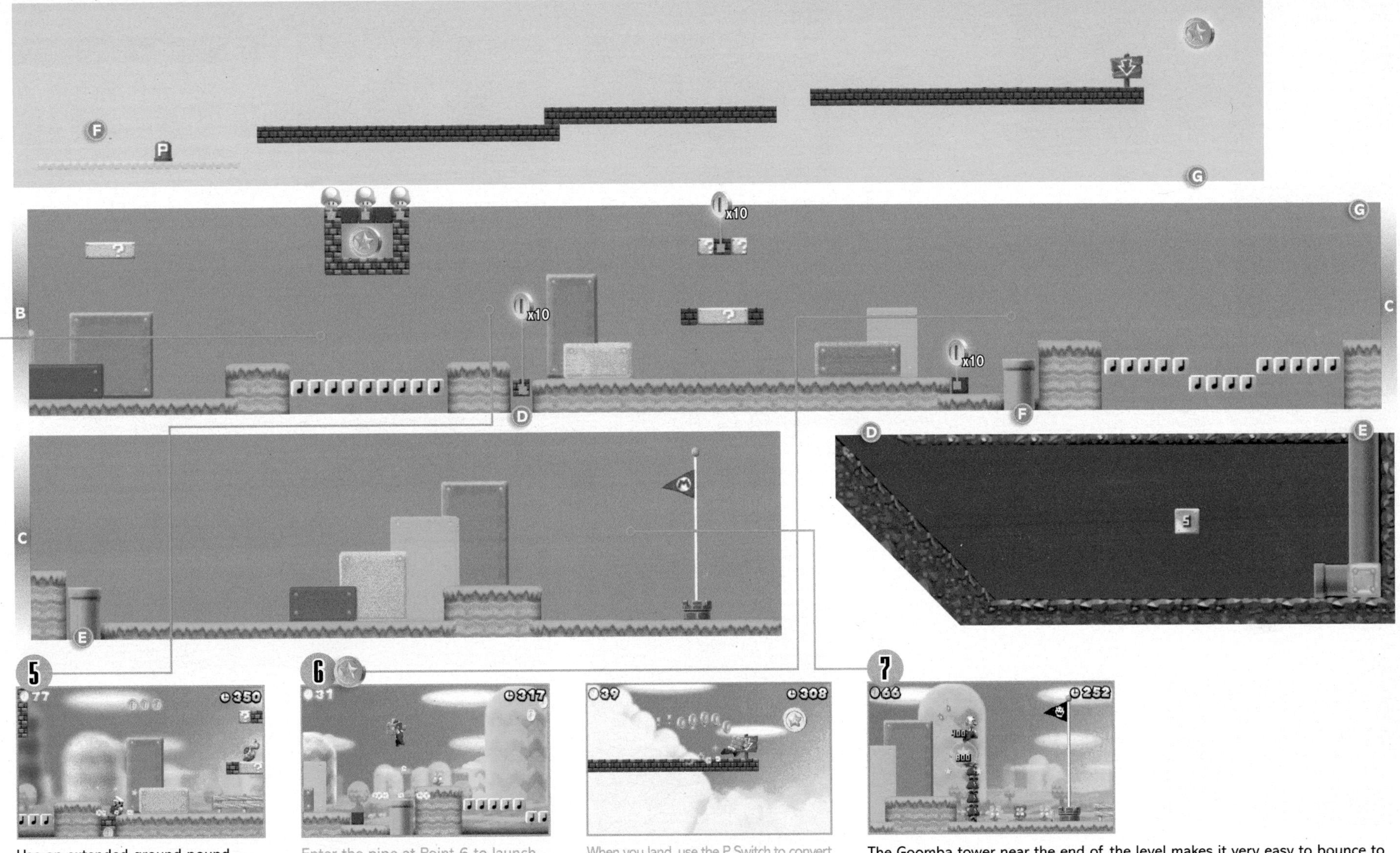

Use an extended ground pound attack on the 10-Coin Block at Point 5. If you extract at least 10 coins, you create a Gold Block and clear the path down to a hidden area.

Enter the pipe at Point 6 to launch yourself up to a hidden area.

When you land, use the P Switch to convert the nearby coins into a long row of Blocks. Follow the trail of blue coins to the right, then jump through the Star Coin to grab it on your way back down to the ground. You only have a few seconds before the Blocks turn back into coins, so move quickly!

The Goomba tower near the end of the level makes it very easy to bounce to the top of the Goal Pole. However, you can earn an extra life if you stomp on all eight Goombas without touching the ground. If you do this, you can still reach the top of the Goal Pole—move back to the left, build up some speed, and jump along the colorful platforms. It takes precision timing, but it's an important skill to learn.

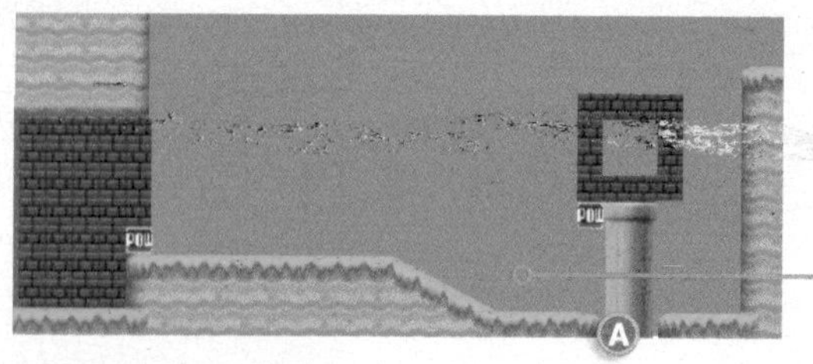

When the level starts, hit the POW Block at Point 1 to shatter the nearby Blocks and stun the Koopa.

Before you enter the pipe, grab the Green Shell and throw it at the POW Block to the left. The impact shatters the nearby Blocks and reveals a stash of coins.

CAUTION

Green Shells are very useful, but they're also very dangerous! The Green Shell will bounce back and forth between the used Block and the pipe, so make sure you jump over it whenever it approaches.

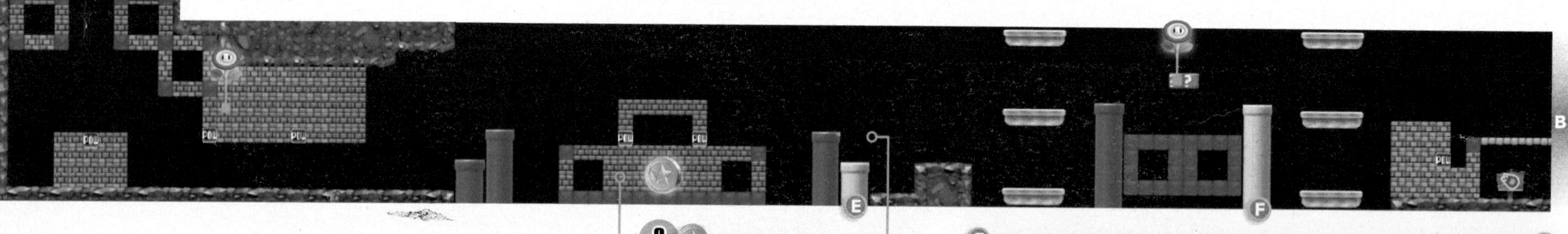

TIP

POW Blocks play an important role in this level. Each time you see one, look for a way to activate it. If you can't reach it from below, you may be able to hit it with a ground pound or Koopa shell.

The level's first Star Coin is hidden behind the Blocks at Point 2. Ground pound down to each of the POW Blocks, or use a Koopa shell to hit them from the side.

After you clear away all of the Blocks, drop down and grab the Star Coin below you.

To collect the second Star Coin, enter the yellow pipe at Point 3.

When you exit the pipe, use the P Switch to temporarily transform all of the Blocks into coins. Dash to the right, then jump to the upper

platform. Dash back to the left to reach the Star Coin before the P Switch deactivates. If you dodge the Koopas, you should make it in time. If not, use a Green Shell to clear a path through the remaining Blocks.

If you've managed to hang on to at least one Fire Flower, you can use the special ! Pipe at Point 4. Stomp the Koopa patrolling the area, then toss its shell into the POW Block to clear a path to the ! Pipe.

WORLD 1-2

Toss fireballs into the pipe's lower opening until a Mega Mushroom pops out of the top. Move quickly to grab the power-up before it falls down the nearby hole. When you become Mega Mario, use the powerful form to smash your way to the end of the level.

TIP

You'll need the Mega Mario form if you hope to collect the level's last Star Coin. Make sure you have a Fire Flower when you reach the ! Pipe.

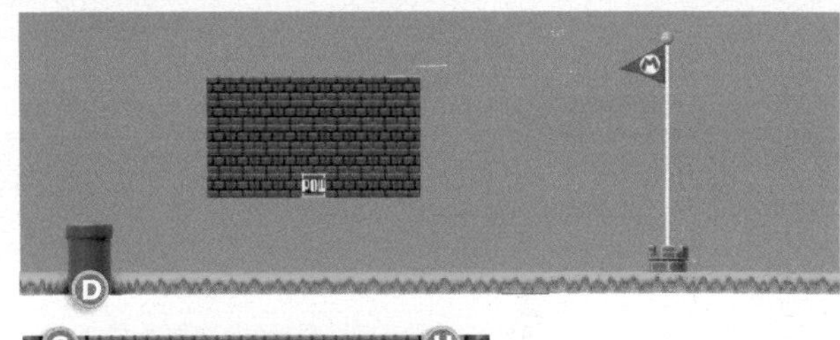

5

If you collected the Mega Mushroom, you should smash a path to the end of the area. If not, use the yellow pipe at Point 5 to enter a secret area. Stomp the Koopa patrolling the area above the pipe, then grab its shell and hop onto the blocks to the left. Toss the shell down through the gap in the Blocks. After several bounces, the shell hits the POW Block near the yellow pipe.

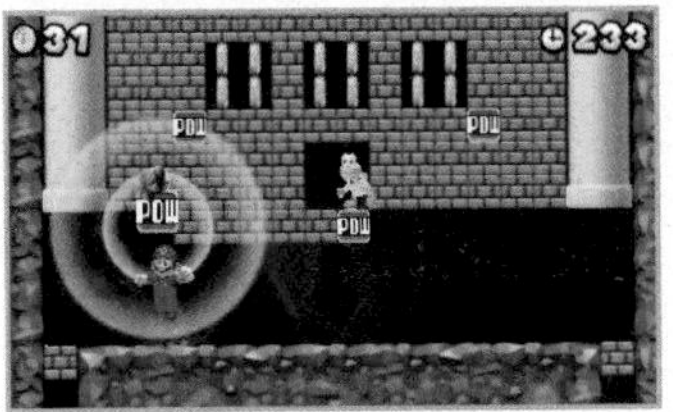

Pass through the yellow pipe to find a hidden area. Two POW Blocks are sliding back and forth across the room. Wait for the POW Block on the left to reach the left side of the room, then jump up to hit it. The shock wave causes a 1-Up Mushroom to emerge from the Block near the wall. Repeat the process on the right side of the room for a second 1-Up Mushroom!

6

To collect the level's third Star Coin, use the Mega Mario form to smash through the enclosure at Point 6. If you didn't collect the Mega Mushroom at Point 4—or if the Mega Mario form wears off before you reach the enclosure—you must revisit the level to collect this Star Coin.

7

If you want to collect the 1-Up Mushroom at Point 7, don't approach the area until the Mega Mario form wears off. Hop onto the second ? Block from the end, then jump up to reveal the 1-Up Mushroom. Jump up along the moving platforms to the left, and then leap onto the Blocks to collect it.

8

To collect the 1-Up Mushroom at the end of the path, you must approach the Block from above. Perform a series of wall jumps between the exit pipe and the nearby Blocks, then watch the Koopas below you.

Use one big ground pound to smash through the Blocks on the left half of the enclosure. If you time it properly, you should be able to clear out all three Koopas with one attempt. After you land, move right and jump up to reveal a well-earned 1-Up Mushroom.

1

To collect all of the Star Coins in this level, you'll need to find a Super Leaf. Two of these power-ups are located near the start of the level, so make sure you grab at least one of them.

2

After you clear out the enemies near Point 2, use the area to charge your Power Meter. Dash along the ground until the meter is full, then fly up to the treetops.

Don't forget to search the treetops to the left. A little exploration yields a 1-Up Mushroom and some 10-Coin Blocks! Use a Koopa shell to claim it all qucikly.

3

The first Star Coin is located on the treetop at Point 3. Use Raccoon Mario to fly up and collect it.

4

The second Star Coin is located high above the treetops. Use Raccoon Mario to fly up to Point 4, then hop into the pipe to launch yourself up to a hidden area.

When you land, move left until you reach the edge of the screen. Dash to the right to fill the Power Meter before you reach the edge of the platform, then fly up to collect the Star Coin before you drop back down to the ground.

WORLD 1-3

5

When you pass through the Red Ring at Point 5, the red coins appear to the right.

The parachutes keep the coins from dropping too fast, but it is still important to move quickly. Collect all of the coins before time runs out to earn a Super Leaf or a 1-Up Mushroom.

6

The last Star Coin is located at Point 6. Use Raccoon Mario's tail whip to clear the Blocks out of your path. If you lost your Super Leaf, stomp a nearby Koopa and use its shell to smash the Block at the bottom of the stack. Dash toward the Blocks, then crouch down to slide through the opening.

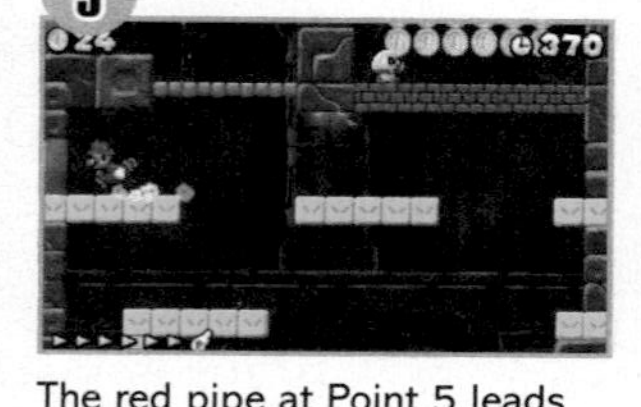

5 The red pipe at Point 5 leads to another hidden area. If you want to collect the level's second Star Coin, make sure you take this route.

6 After you pass through the red pipe, hit the P Switch in the hidden room. Try to collect the blue coins that appear, but move quickly! You must collect the Star Coin before the P Switch deactivates. Jump onto the aas to the right, then hop up to the platform above you.

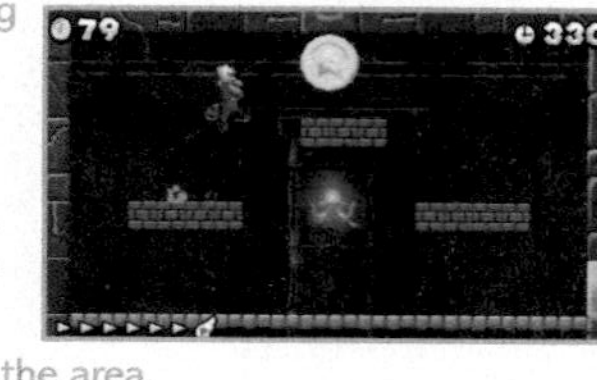

Jump up along the Blocks to grab the Star Coin before time runs out. Use the green pipe to the right to leave the area.

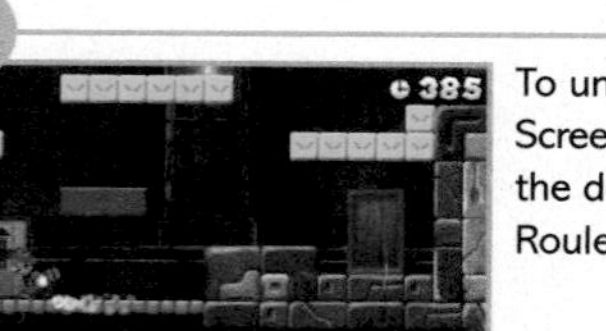

4 To unlock the secret path on the World One Map Screen, you must find this Tower's secret exit. Enter the door at Point 4 to find a hidden room containing a Roulette Coin Block.

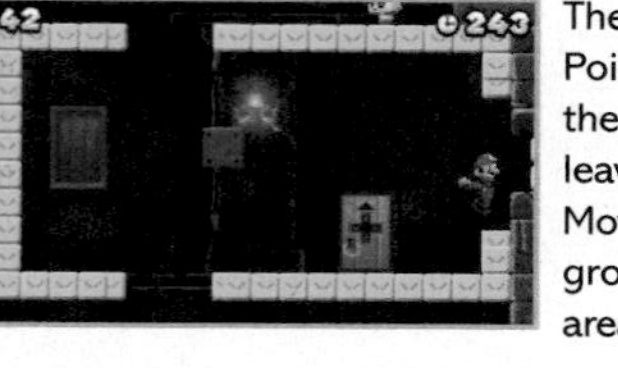

The door near the Roulette Coin Block leads back to Point 4, but the hole in the room's right wall leads to the secret exit! Wait for a group of Snake Blocks to leave the room, then follow them through the hole. Move quickly to avoid being crushed by the next group of Snake Blocks! When you reach the next area, follow the path to the Goal Pole.

There are some coins hidden at the top of the room. To collect them, jump onto the Roulette Coin Block, then hop through one of the gaps between the Snake Blocks. Just watch out for the Bone Goombas emerging from the red pipe!

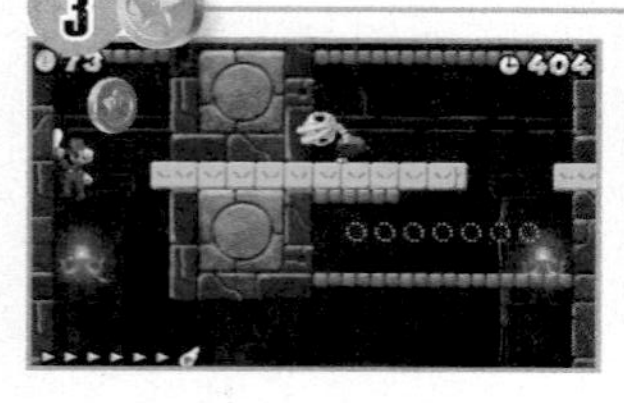

3 To collect the first Star Coin, make sure you're on the left side of the Tower when you reach Point 3. Wait for the Snake Blocks to move out of your path, then wall jump up to the Star Coin.

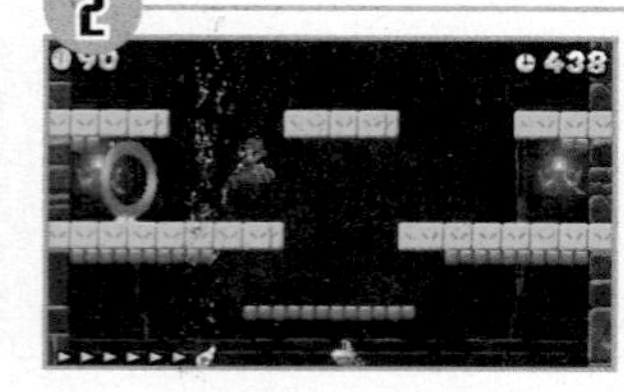

2 *Pass through the Red Ring at Point 2 to reveal the red coins scattered around the area.*

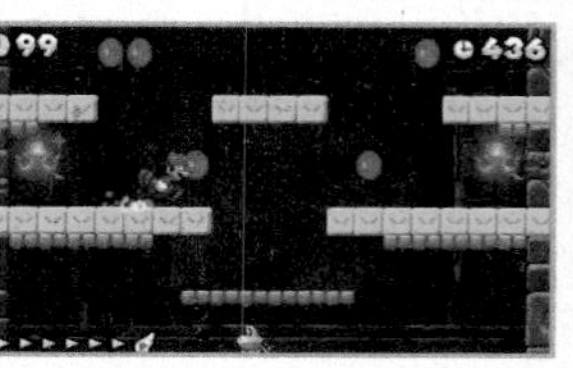

Circle the area to collect all eight red coins before time runs out. The Snake Blocks can make it difficult to find a clear path through the area, so time each jump carefully.

1 To reach the top of this Tower, you must take advantage of the Snake Blocks moving throughout the level. The area also contains several power-ups. Try to collect at least one Super Leaf, then use Raccoon Mario's tail whip to deal with troublesome Bone Piranha Plants.

NOTE

To reveal the path to World 1-Warp Cannon, you must find this level's secret exit.

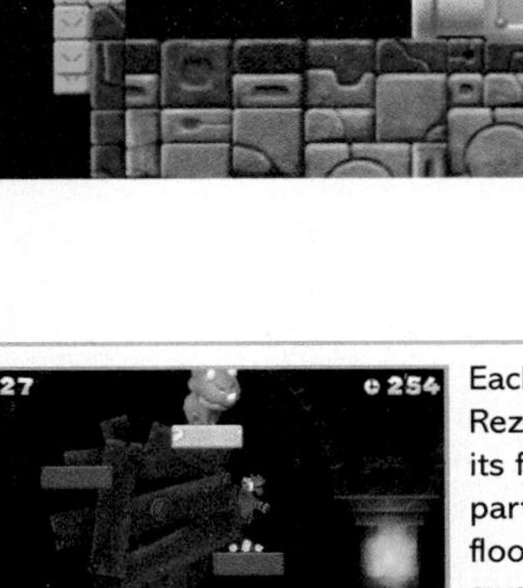

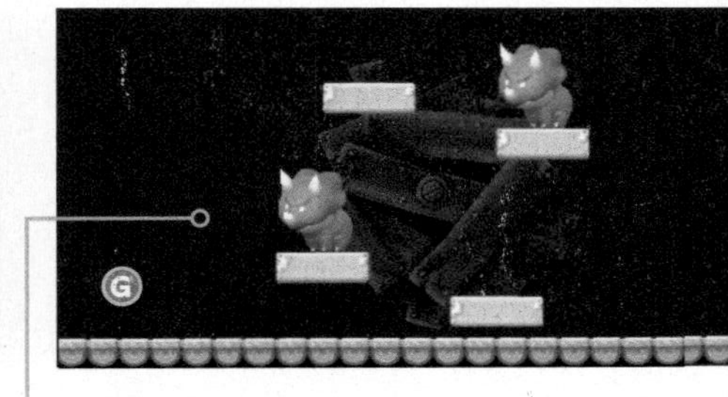

8

When you reach the top of the Tower, you must defeat two Reznors on a spinning wheel. As the wheel spins, slip under the nearest Reznor and jump up to knock it off of its ? Block. If you move quickly, you can repeat the process with the second Reznor before it has time to attack. If you fail to finish off both enemies, you must adjust your tactics to survive the encounter.

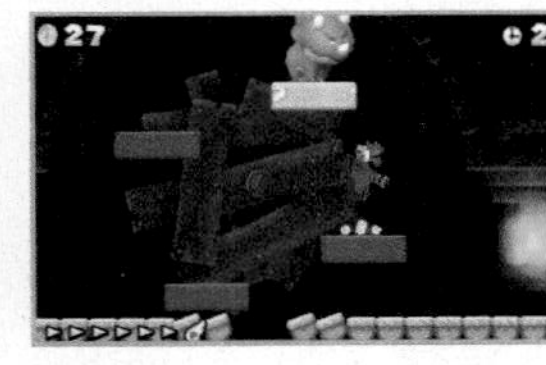

Each time a Reznor slams its feet down, part of the floor falls away. If this happens, hop onto a vacant ? Block. Reznors can also spit fireballs, so take care to avoid any incoming attacks. As the wheel spins, hop between the ? Blocks to maneuver yourself under each enemy. Knock both Reznors off of their ? Blocks to complete the level.

NOTE

Each Tower contains a similar area, so it's important to master the basics of these Reznors encounters.

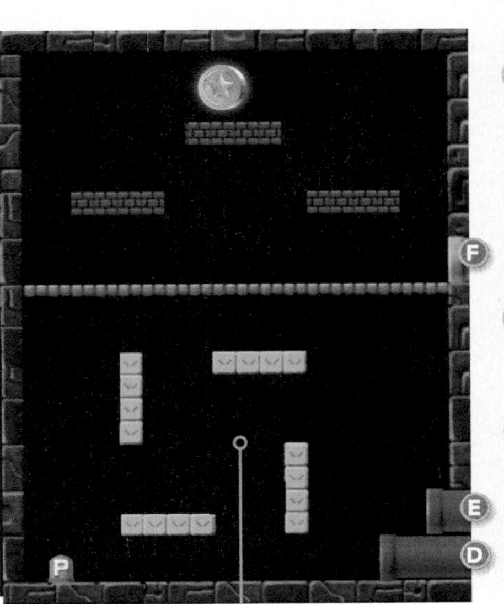

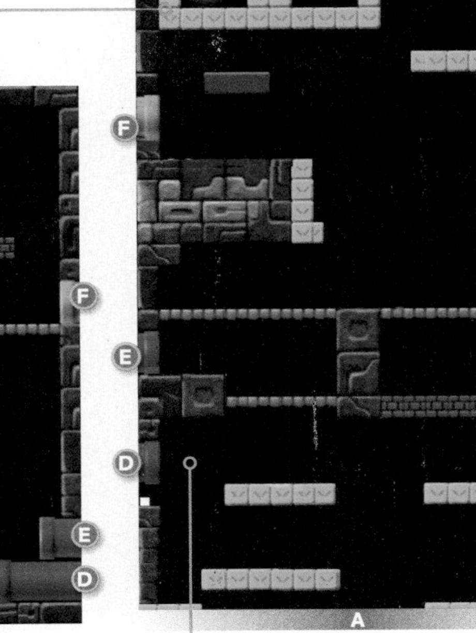

7

The last Star Coin is located at Point 7. If you managed to hang on to a Super Leaf, use a tail whip to clear away the Bone Piranha Plant before you grab the Star Coin.

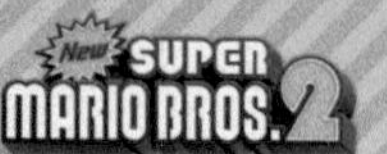

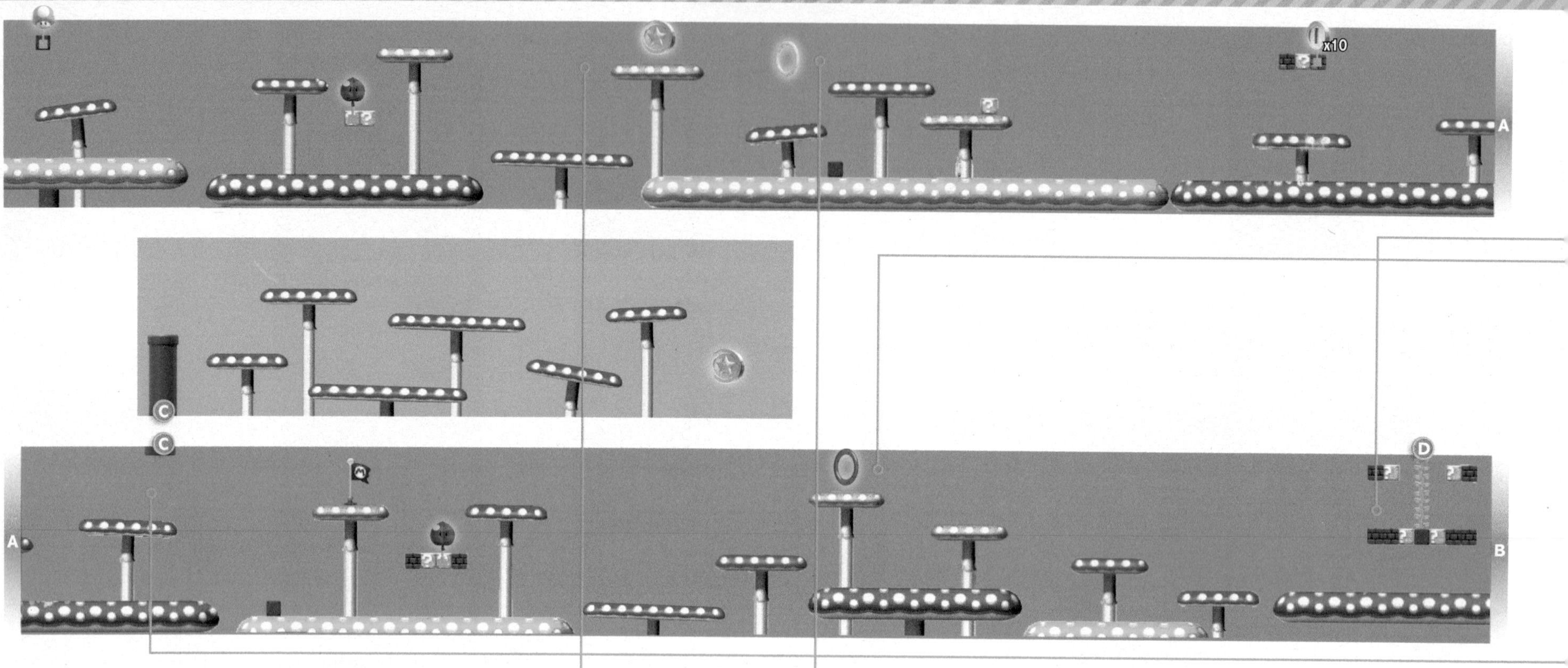

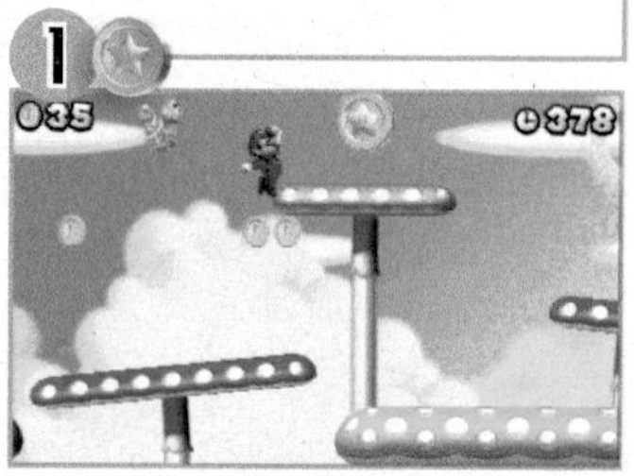

1

2

The first Star Coin is located at Point 1. Wait for the pink toadstool to tilt up toward the orange toadstool, then make a running leap to the Star Coin.

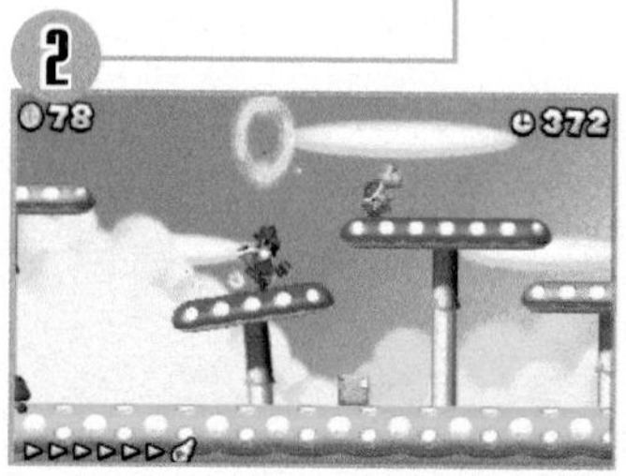

This level contains two Gold Rings. Before you approach a Gold Ring, it's usually best to stomp a Koopa and grab its shell.

Pass through the Gold Ring to transform all of the enemies in the area—including any Koopas tucked inside of their shells! When you throw a Gold Shell, it leaves a trail of coins while it moves through the area.

WORLD 1-4

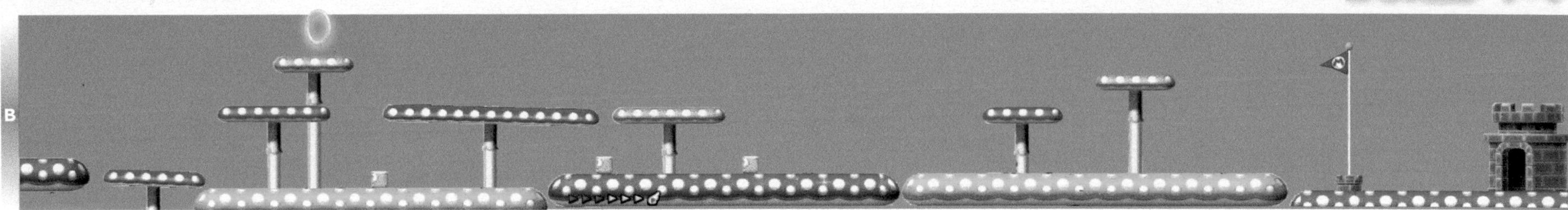

3

The second Star Coin is located in a hidden area. When you reach Point 3, enter the blue pipe near the top of the screen.

Move across the toadstools to the right. When you reach the last platform, jump through the Star Coin and exit the area.

4

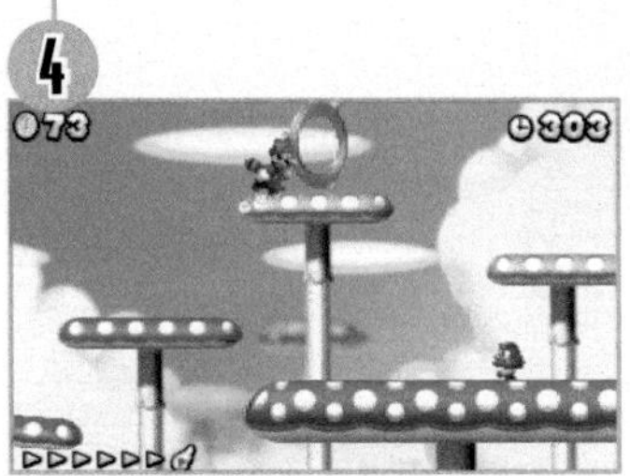

Pass through the Red Ring at Point 4, then grab the red coins that appear to the right.

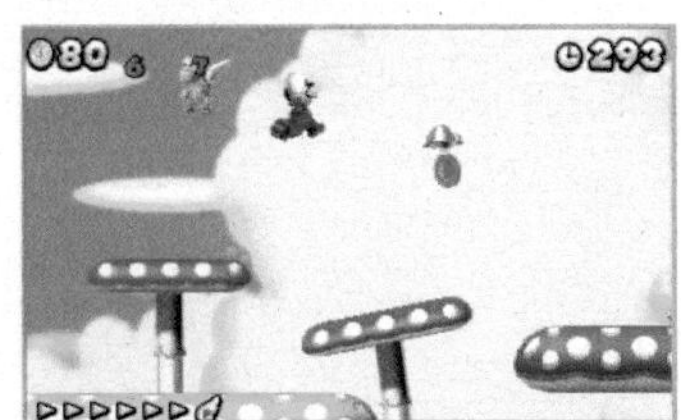

The last red coin is hanging from a parachute, so make sure you grab it before it drifts out of reach.

5

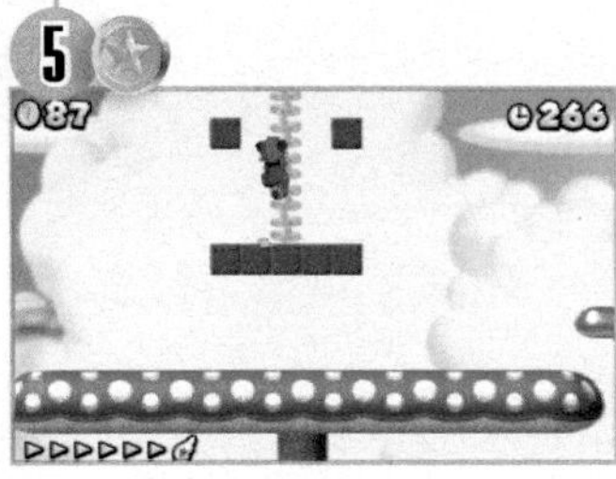

The last Star Coin is located in another hidden area. Stand in the center of the large red toadstool at Point 5, then jump up to hit the Invisible Block above you. Wait for the Beanstalk to grow, then climb up to the hidden area.

Hit the P Switch at the top of the Beanstalk, then follow the trail of blue coins as it zigzags inside of the Block enclosure. As you approach the top of the enclosure, wall jump up to the last ledge. Grab the Star Coin before the P Switch deactivates.

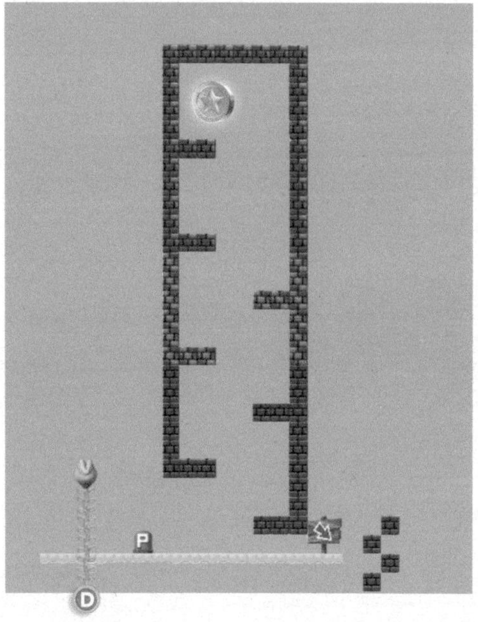

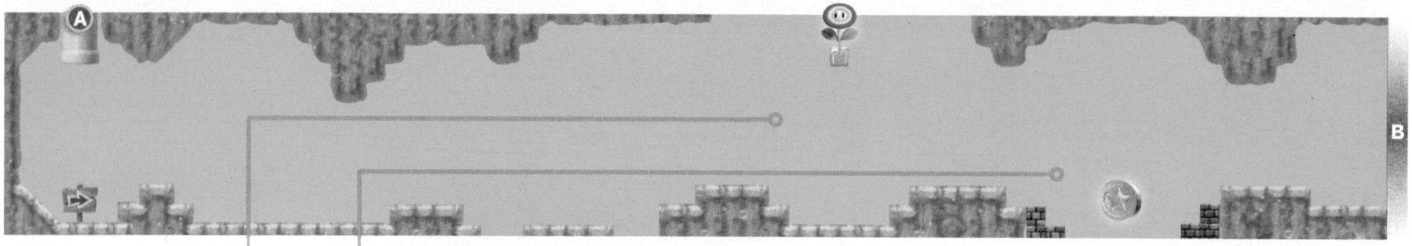

TIP

Under the first Star Coin is a stash of blocks for when the player has a Gold Flower.

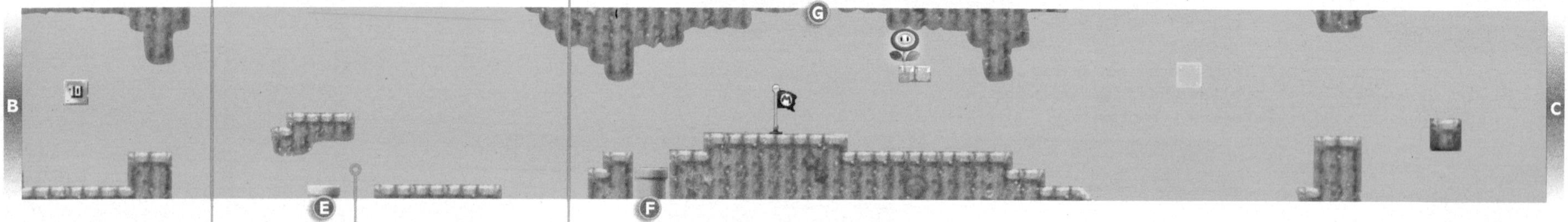

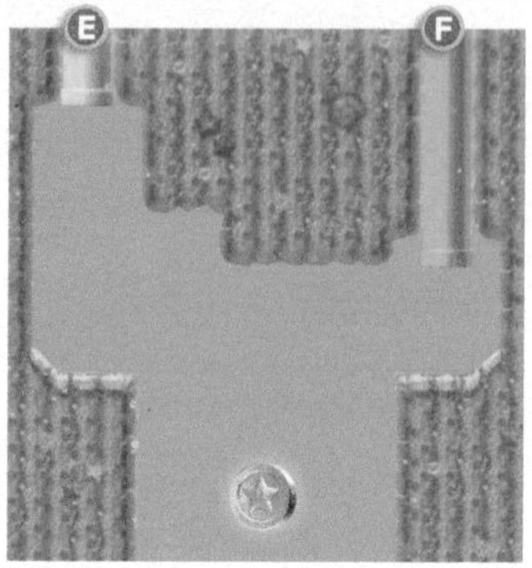

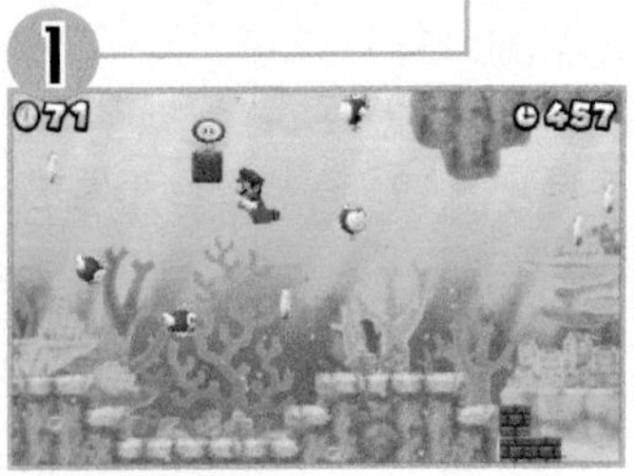

1

It's much easier to swim through the area when you're able to clear enemies out of your way. Make sure you grab at least one of the available Fire Flowers.

2

The first Star Coin is located at Point 2. The Spiny Cheep Cheep can be fairly aggressive, so use your fireballs to deal with this enemy before you sink down to the Star Coin.

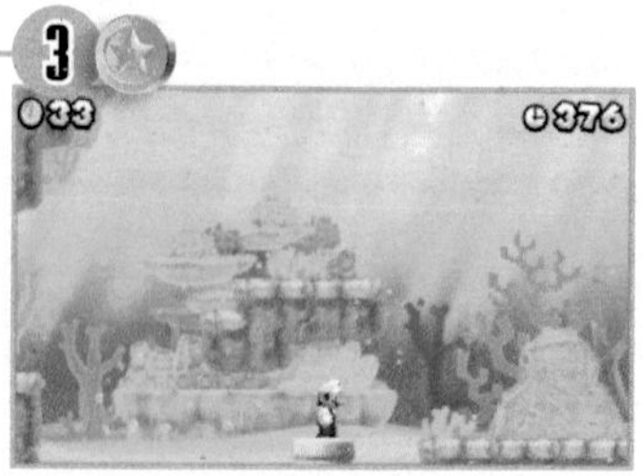

3

Swim over the platform at Point 3, then circle back and enter the yellow pipe at the bottom of the screen.

After you pass through the pipe, sink down toward the Star Coin. Swim against the current to avoid being pulled off of the screen, but allow yourself to drop low enough to collect the Star Coin. As you fight your way back out of the current, watch out for the Cheep Cheeps swimming through the area.

WORLD 1-5

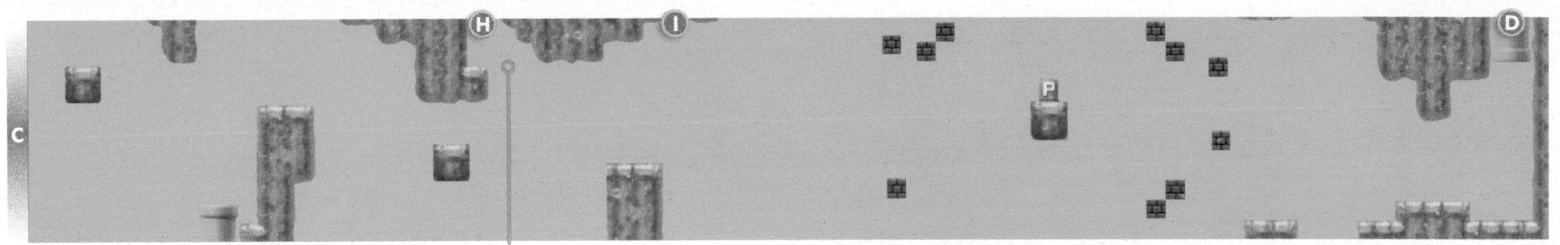

4

The last Star Coin is located in a hidden area near Point 4. When you reach this spot, swim up through the narrow opening along the top of the passage.

Swim up to the water's surface, then leap up to grab the Star Coin.

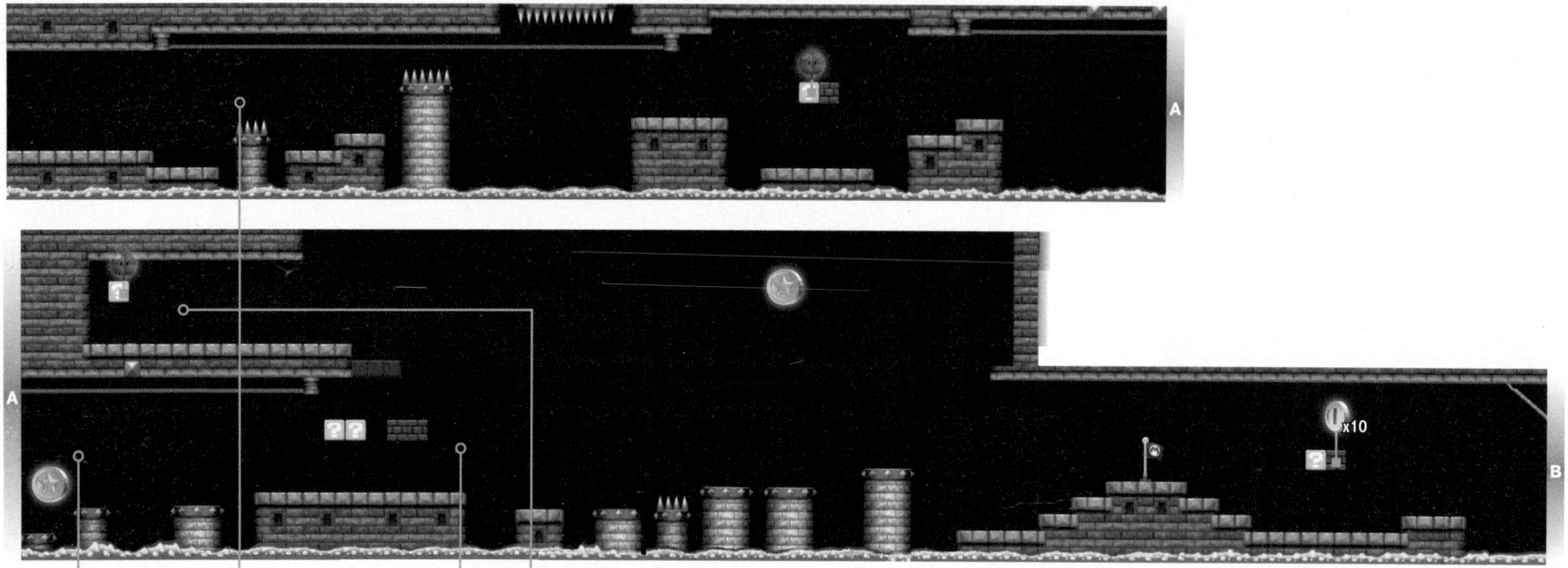

1

Use the ropes at the start of the level to move through the area. As you do, watch out for the spikes and Lava Bubbles that move in and out of your path.

2

The first Star Coin is floating just above the lava at Point 2. Wait for the platforms to emerge from the lava, then drop down and collect the Star Coin. Move quickly to return to the rope before the platforms vanish.

3

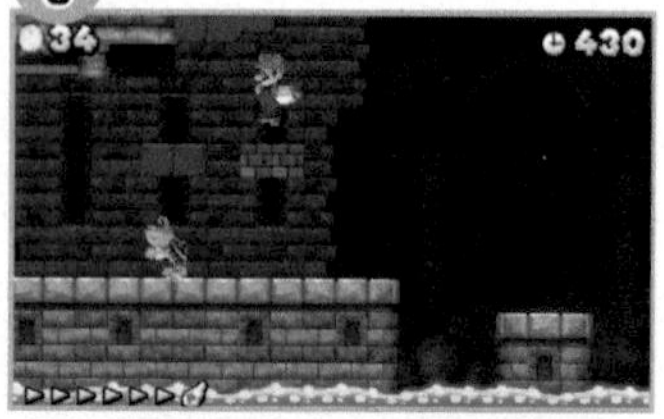

Hop onto the Blocks at Point 3, then jump up to reveal the Invisible Blocks above you—this creates a new platform that leads to a hidden ledge. Jump up to explore the area above you.

4

To collect the second Star Coin, you need the Raccoon Mario form. Dash along the ledge to fill your Power Meter, then fly to the right.

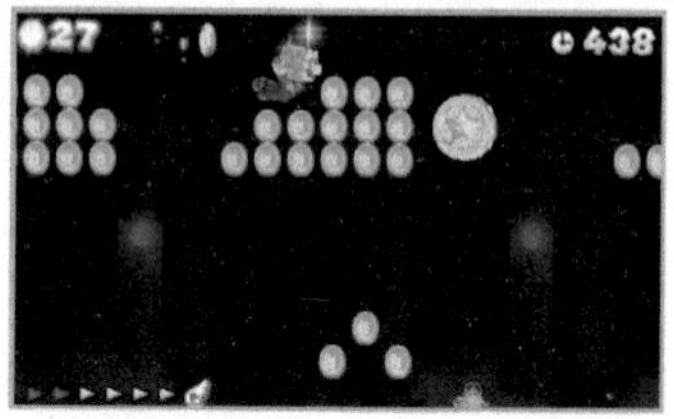

Follow the coins to the right and grab the Star Coin floating high above the lava.

WORLD 1-CASTLE

5

Watch out for the Thwomps near the end of the level. You can dash right under the first Thwomp, but the uneven platforms make it much more difficult to pass under the second one. Jump over the Thwomp when it slams down, or wait for it to move back toward the ceiling before you attempt to slip past it.

6

When you reach Point 6, coax the Big Thwomp into attacking two times. As it recovers from its second attack, slip past the Big Thwomp and grab the Star Coin.

7

To defeat Roy Koopa, you must stomp his head three times. You can attack any time his head is exposed, but it's best to do so while he's stunned. Dodge his fireball attacks until he dashes toward you, then jump over him. When Roy charges into the wall, the impact leaves him temporarily stunned. Jump on his head before he recovers.

Each time you damage Roy, the walls move slightly closer together. When he recovers, Roy tucks into his shell and bounces around the room. Dodge the shell until Roy emerges from his shell, then repeat the process to stomp him again. Land three successful attacks to defeat Roy and unlock World Two.

1

The level's first power-up is located at Point 1. To collect it, stomp the Koopa patrolling the Blocks, then throw its shell to the right. After a few bounces, the shell hits the Block below you to reveal the power-up.

2

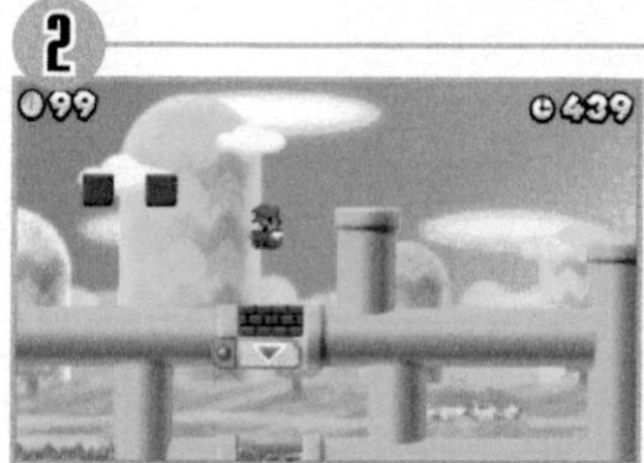

Perform a ground pound at Point 2 to slam through the Blocks and drop down to a hidden area. This route contains one of the level's Star Coins, so make sure you explore it!

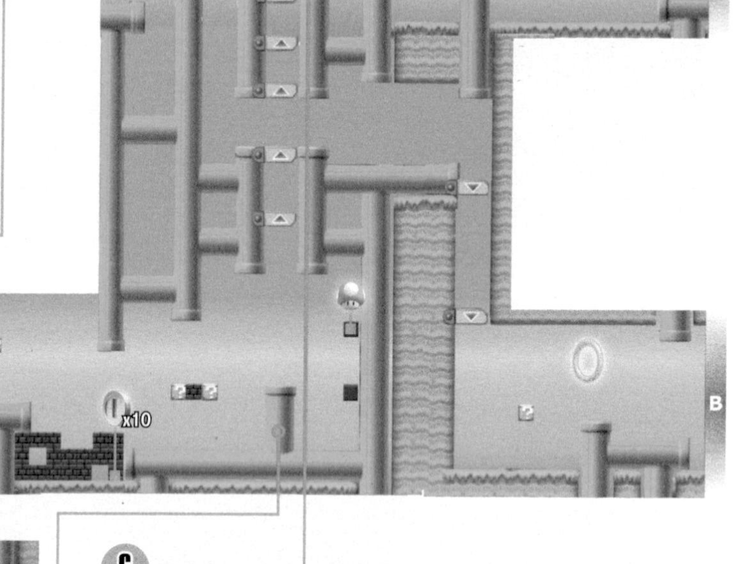

3

After you drop through the hidden area, jump onto the Blocks and grab the Star Coin. Stomp the Koopa if it approaches you, but avoid kicking or throwing its shell within the enclosure.

6

There's a hidden path near the Checkpoint Flag! Wall jump between the pipes at Point 6, then drop down between the pipes to the left.

4

When you're finished exploring the hidden area, enter the pipe at Point 4 to launch yourself back up to the surface.

5

When you reach Point 5, enter the pipe to launch yourself through the coins and into the next area.

WORLD 1-A

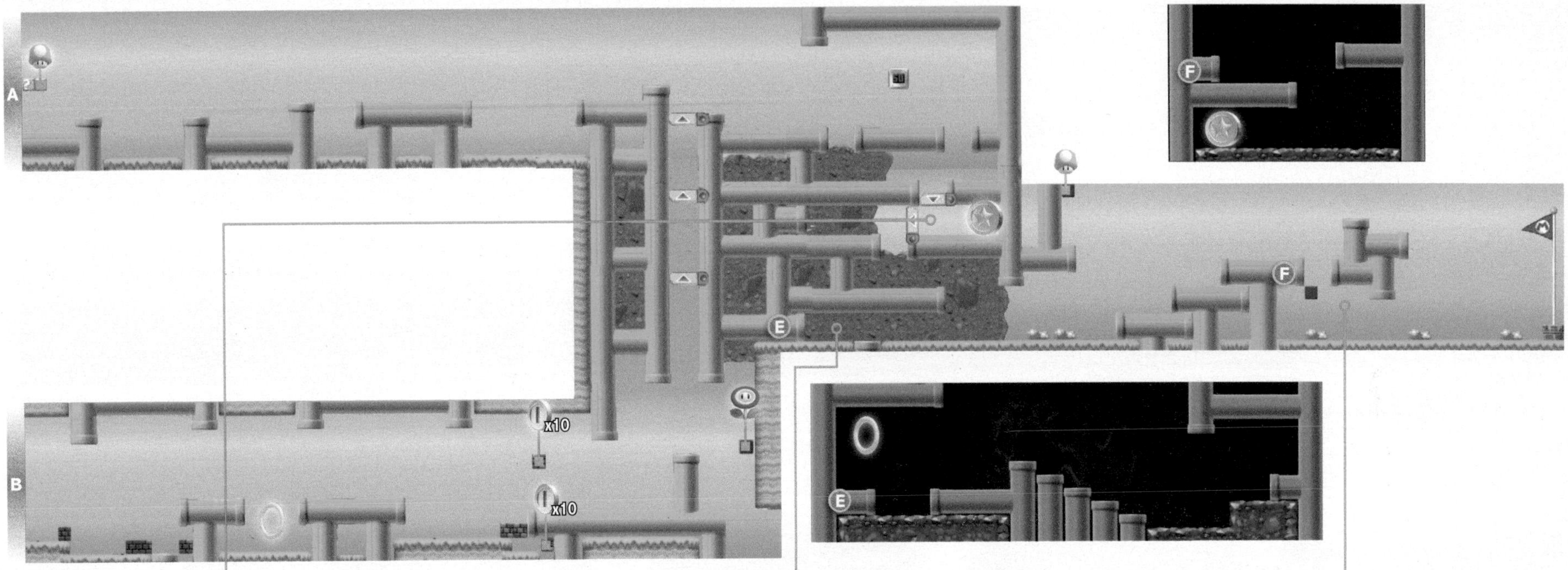

The second Star Coin is in a small enclosure at Point 7. Drop through the hinged panel, then move left just far enough for the panel to snap back in place. If you move too far, you'll be locked out of the enclosure, so make sure you grab the Star Coin before you leave the area.

One of the pipes at Point 8 leads to a hidden area.

After you pass through the pipe, stomp the Koopa and grab its shell. Leap through the Gold Ring, then toss the shell through the Gold Piranha Plants to the right.

The last Star Coin is hidden in a secret area. When you reach Point 9, drop to the ground and locate the Invisible Block above you. When you find it, jump onto the used Block and enter the pipe to the left.

After you pass through the pipe, stomp the Koopa and toss its shell down to the Big Piranha Plant. The shell not only defeats this imposing enemy, it bounces back to the left and collects the Star Coin.

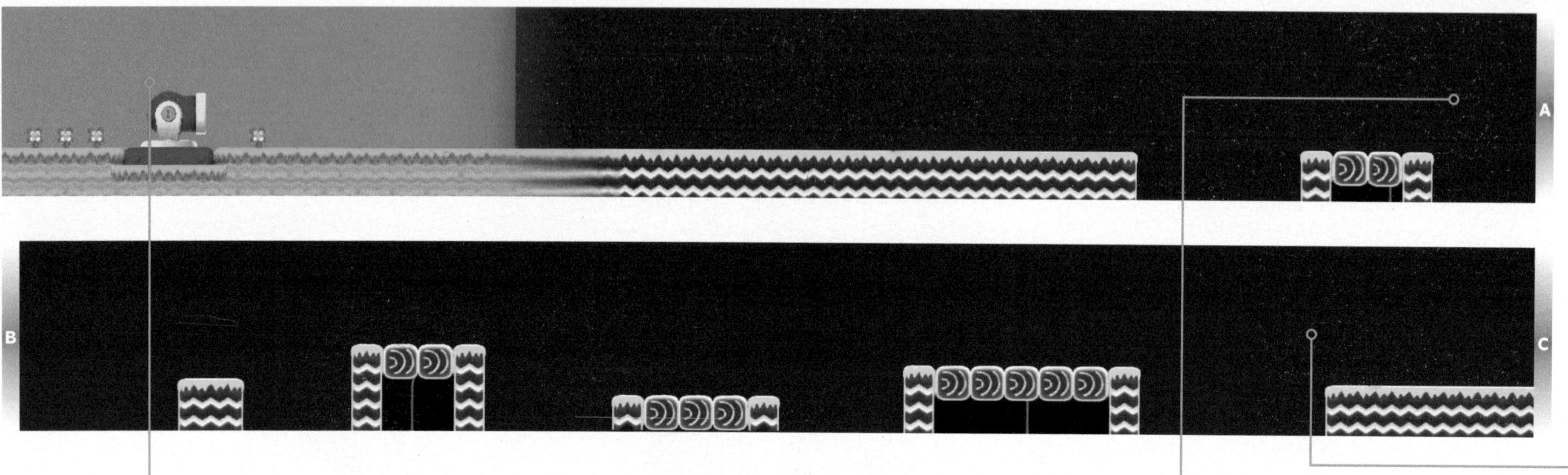

NOTE

Before you can access this level, you must find the secret exit in World 1-Tower.

While you traverse this level, you have no control over your speed or the direction in which you travel. To survive the trip, you must make a series of precision jumps. When you're ready to begin the challenge, enter the Warp Cannon at Point 1.

Use the coins to help gauge each jump. A long coin trail indicates an extended leap, while a short coin trail indicates a slight hop or bounce. Many coin trails lead to a Parakoopa—when this happens, follow the coins to land safely on the enemy.

TIP

Before you stomp on a Parakoopa, take note of the next coin trail. If it's a short trail, just allow yourself to bounce off of the enemy. If it's a long coin trail, you must hit the Jump button the instant you touch the Parakoopa. This gives your leap the extra height you need and ensures you make a safe landing.

A B C

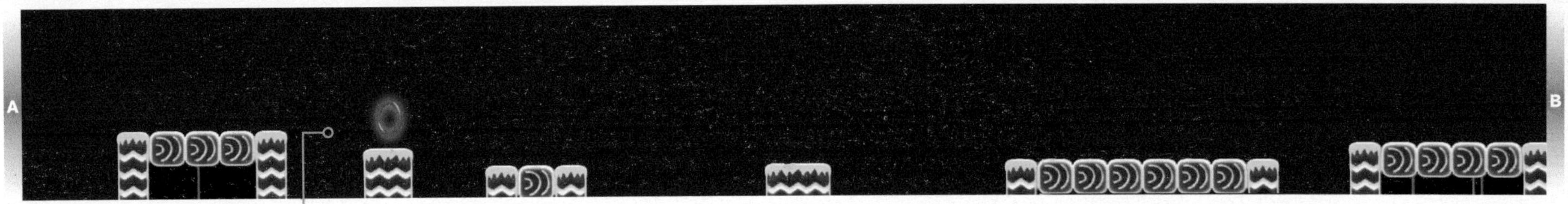

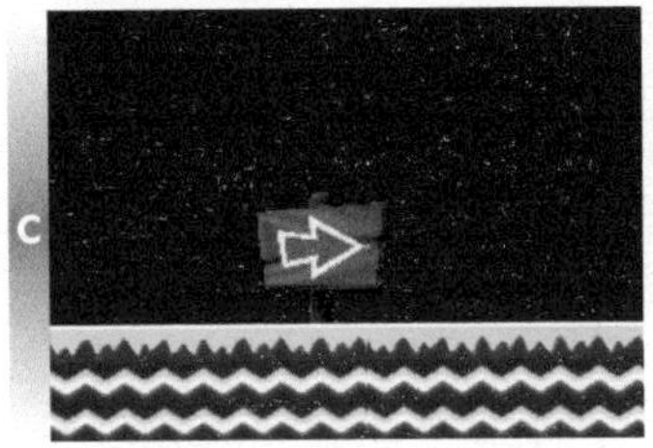

3

There's a Red Ring located at Point 3. Instead of leaping through the long coin trail, hop across the small gaps to pass through the Red Ring. When you do, eight red coins appear. As you follow the remaining coin trails, collect all eight red coins to earn a Gold Flower!

4

Follow the coins across each gap to survive each jump. Reach the end of the level to unlock Mushroom World!

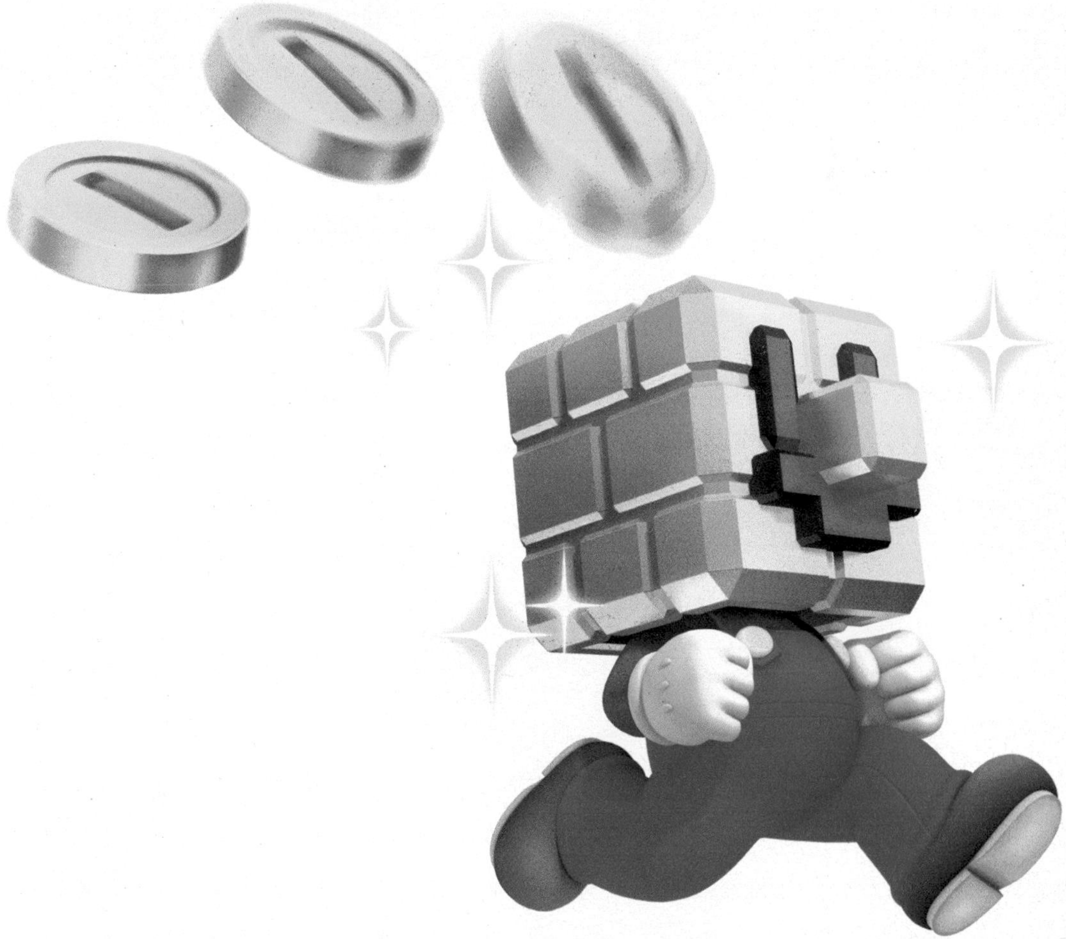

WORLD TWO

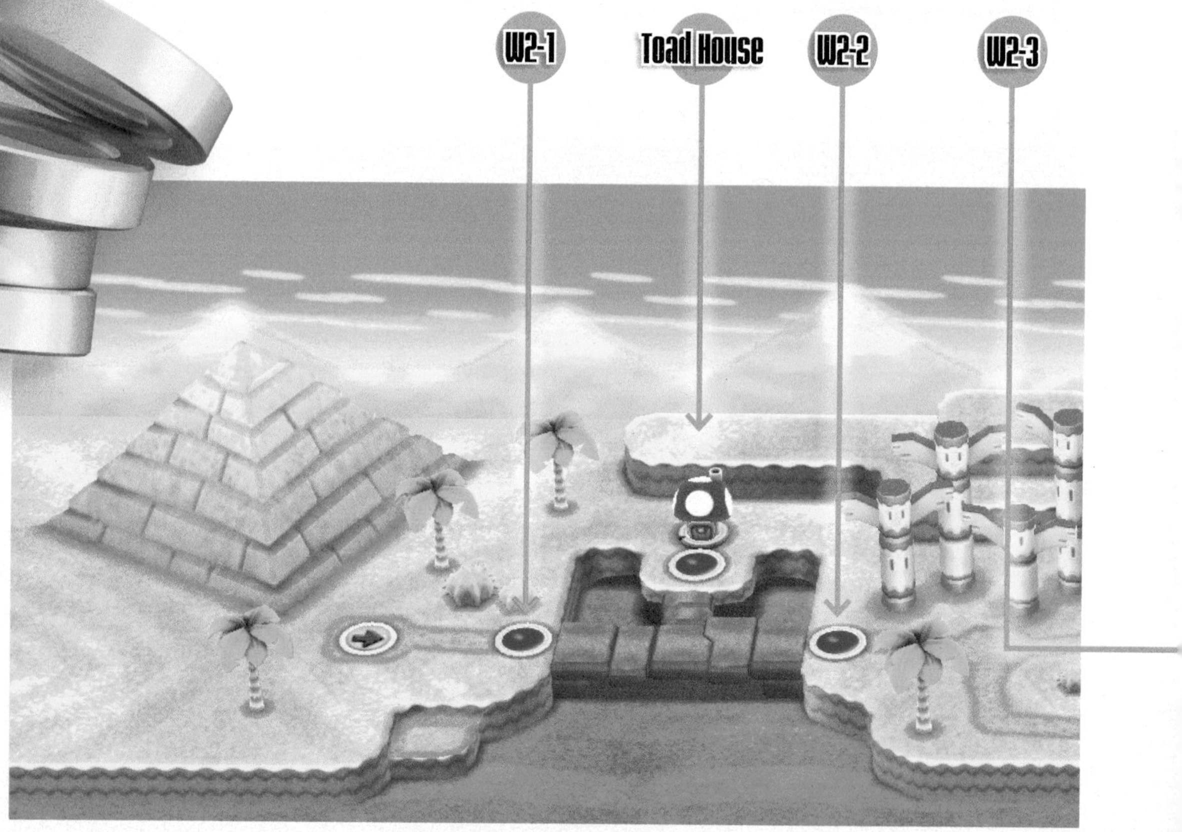

W2-1

Toad House

W2-2

W2-3

WORLD LOCATIONS				
Hostile Levels	Toad Houses	Boo Houses	Warp Cannons	Boss
10	4	1	0	Larry Koopa

Main Path Levels:

- World 2-1
- World 2-2
- World 2-3
- World 2-Tower
- World 2-Boo House
- World 2-4
- World 2-5
- World 2-Castle

Alternate Path Levels:

- World 2-A
- World 2-B

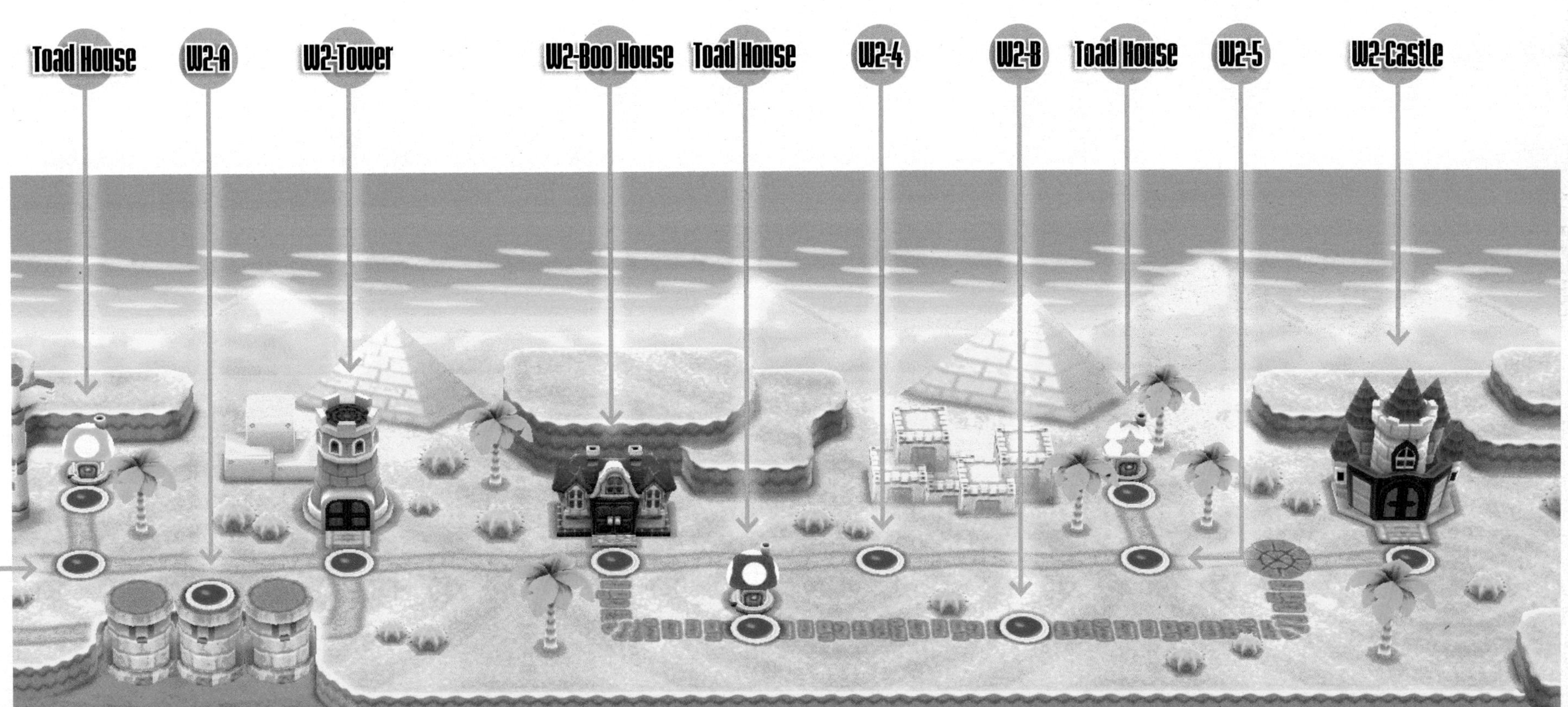

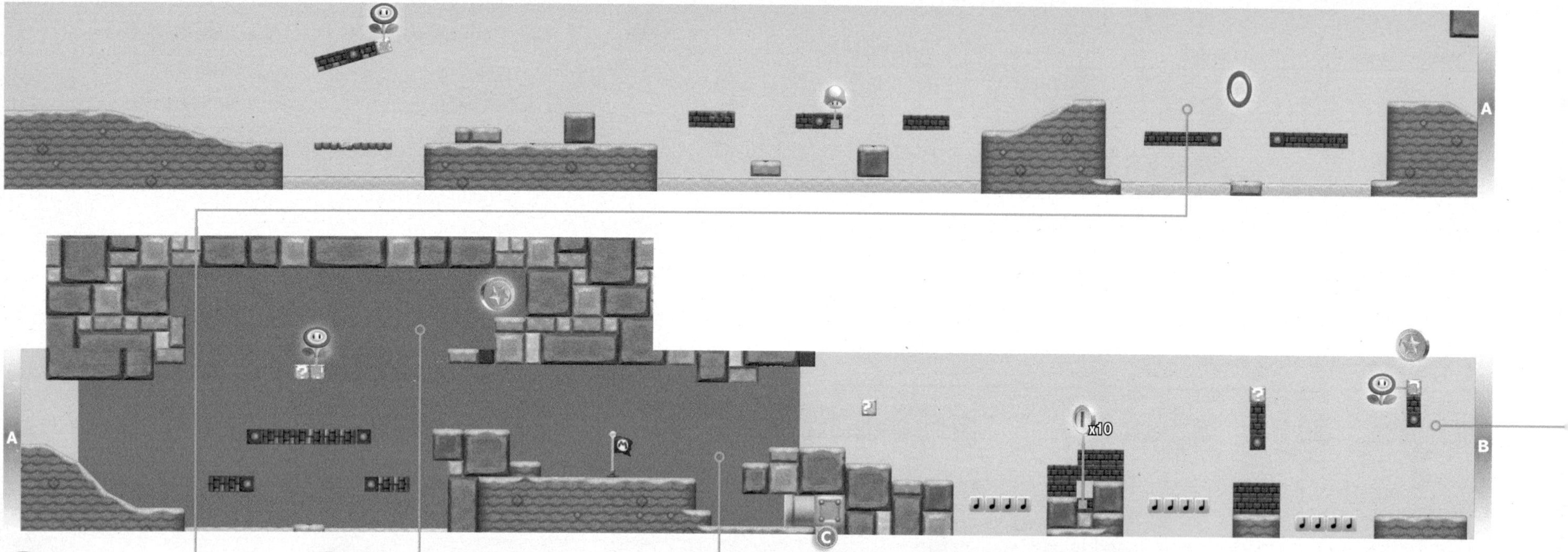

1

When you pass through the Red Ring at Point 1, eight red coins drop down from above you. Jump between the swiveling platforms to collect the coins as they approach.

2

The first Star Coin is hidden in a nook above Point 2. Locate the ledge at the top of the screen, then wait for the nearest set of Blocks to swivel into place.

Make a running leap up to the ledge, then hop up to grab the Star Coin.

3

The path splits just past the Checkpoint Flag. Each path contains one of the remaining Star Coins. If you wish to collect them both, enter the yellow pipe to search the underground passage before you explore the upper path.

WORLD 2-1

4

Hit the ? Block at the start of the underground passage to collect a Gold Flower. Use your gold fireballs to blast a path to the Star Coin at Point 4.

TIP

It's much easier to reach the Star Coin's enclosure if the nearby Blocks are intact. If you've already cleared the area, however, use a triple jump to reach the ledge.

5

When you return to the surface, move left to find the Star Coin at Point 5. Use the Note Blocks to bounce up to the lower set of Blocks, then jump over and collect the Star Coin.

CAUTION

Watch out for the to Koopa Paratroopa flying near the Star Coin!

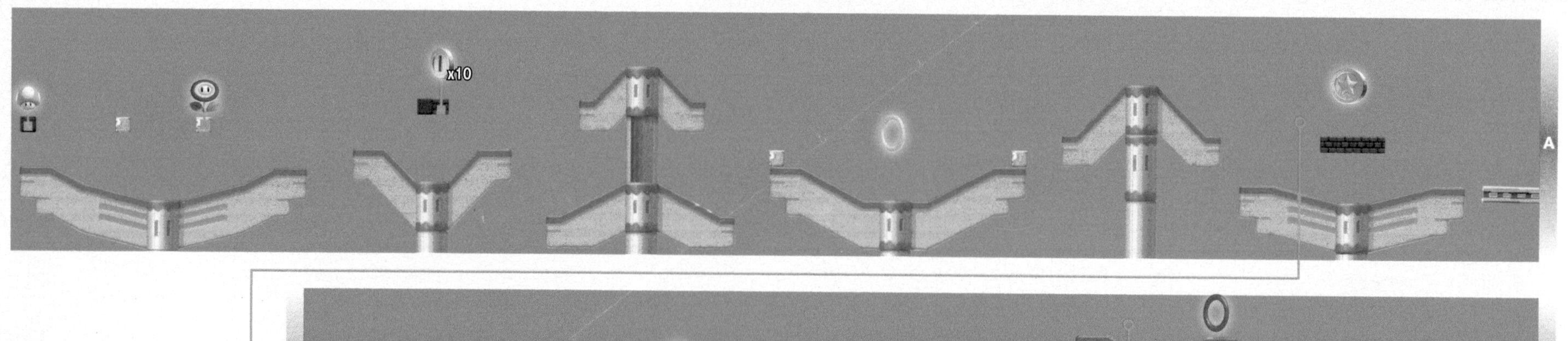

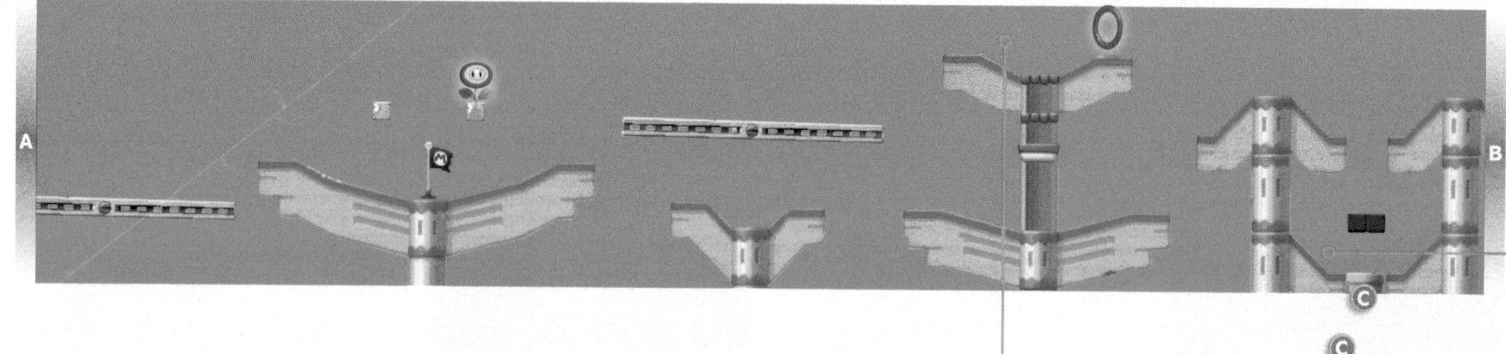

1

The first Star Coin is floating above the Hammer Bro at Point 1. Use a fireball or shell to defeat this enemy, then hop onto the Blocks and collect the Star Coin.

If you choose to attack the Hammer Bro from below, try to leave at least one of the Blocks intact. It's much easier to reach the Star Coin if you do.

2

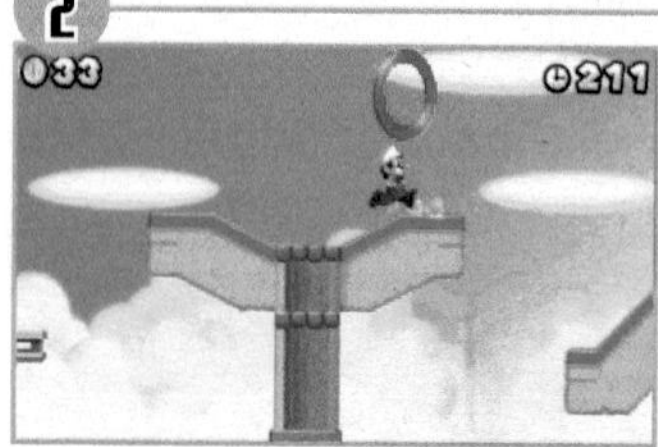

Pass through the Red Ring at Point 2, then collect the red coins that appear to the right.

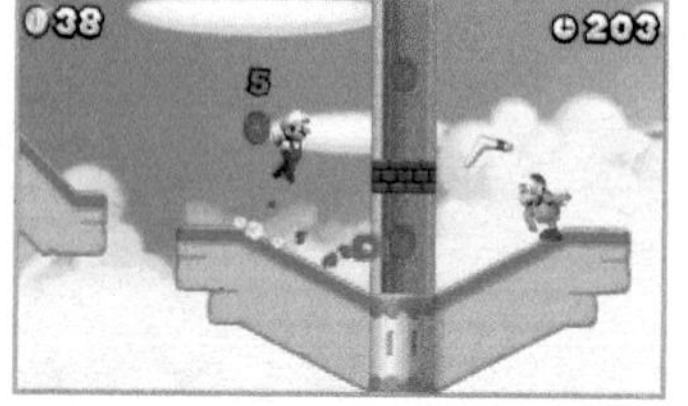

The last few red coins are near a Boomerang Bro. If possible, use a fireball to clear out this pesky enemy before you hop onto the Blocks to collect the last of the coins.

WORLD 2-2

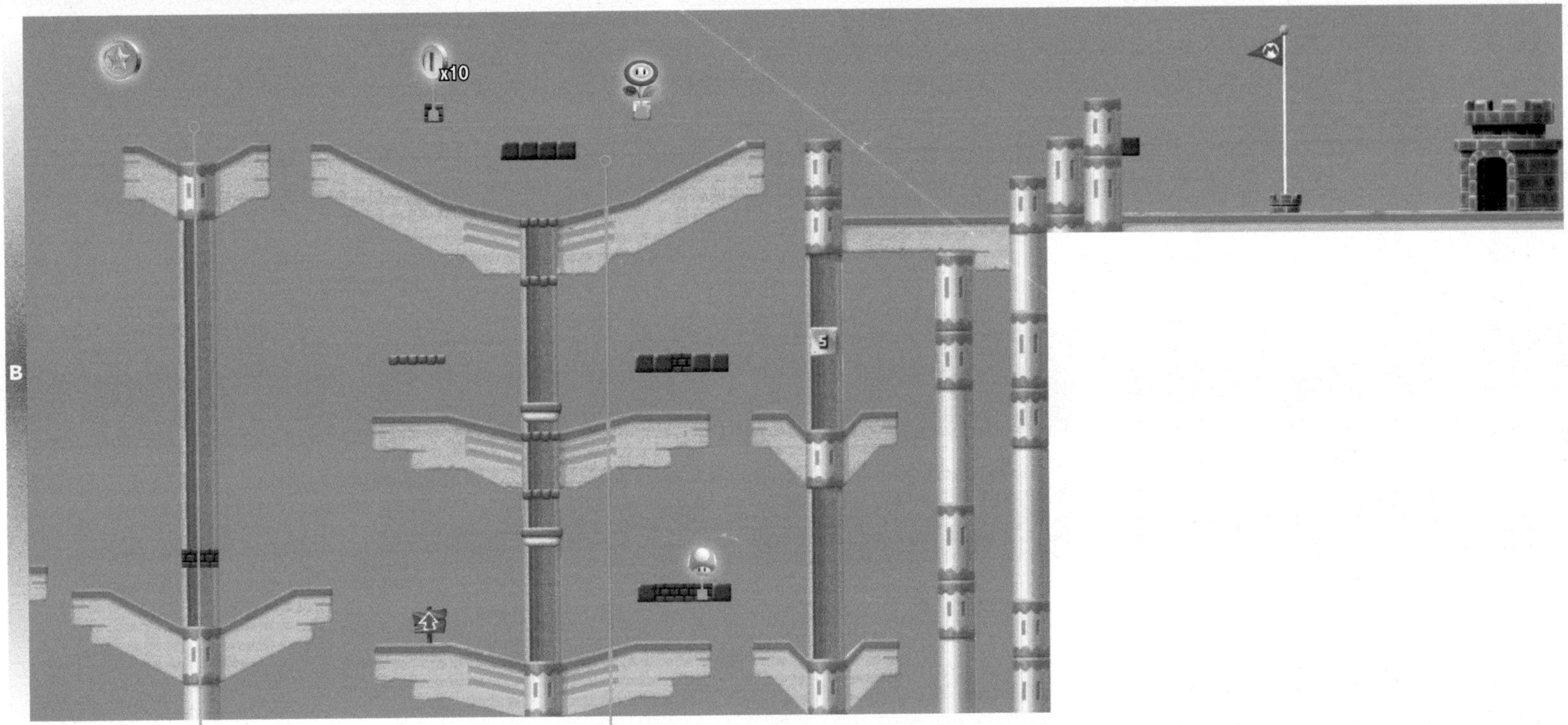

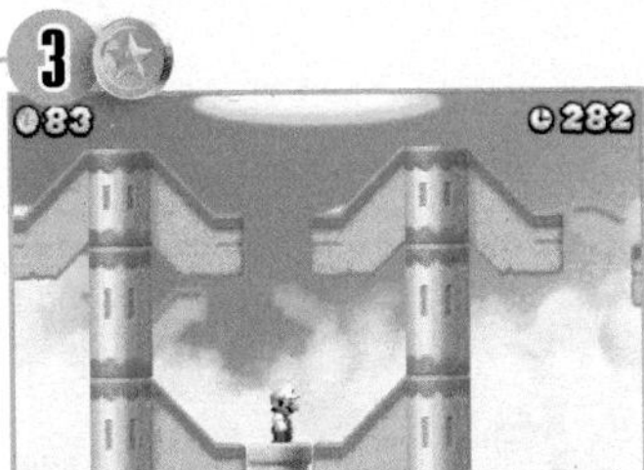

3

The second Star Coin is located in a hidden area. Enter the pipe at Point 3 to find it.

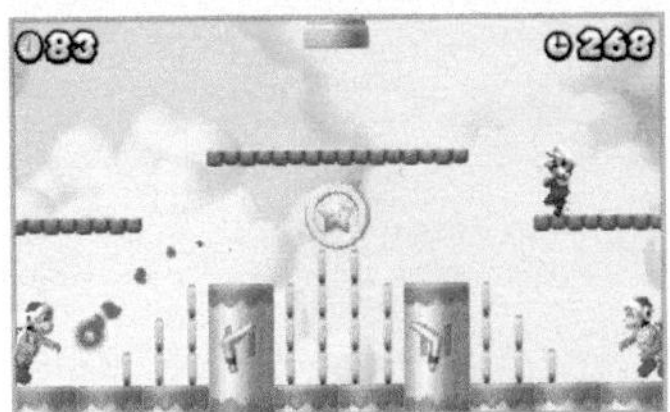

The Boomerang Bros. can make it difficult to collect the Star Coin. If you still have a Fire Flower power-up, use your fireballs to clear out both of the enemies before you drop down from the upper platforms.

4

The Big Bro at Point 4 is standing on a sturdy platform, so you can't attack from below. Avoid this enemy's hammers and powerful ground pound attacks, then jump up and clear it out with a fireball or stomp on its head.

5

After you deal with the Big Bro, move left to find the Star Coin floating at Point 5.

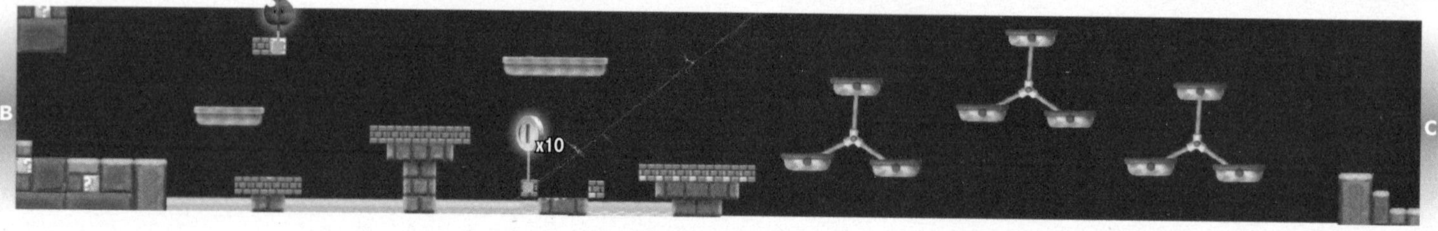

1

Use the Springboard to reach the Roulette Coin Blocks and the Roulette Block above the Checkpoint Flag. While you bounce, take care to avoid the Red Spike Buzzy patrolling each Block.

Use the Buzzy Beatle to take out the Pokey between the 10-Coin Block and the Brick Block to gain all the coins from the 10-Coin Block. This also gives you a 1-Up by destroying the Pokey.

2

The first Star Coin is located in a hidden area. To reach it, you must enter the lower pipe at Point 2. Stomp the Buzzy Beetle near the upper pipe, then toss its shell at the POW Block near the moving platforms. The chain reaction clears a path to the lower pipe.

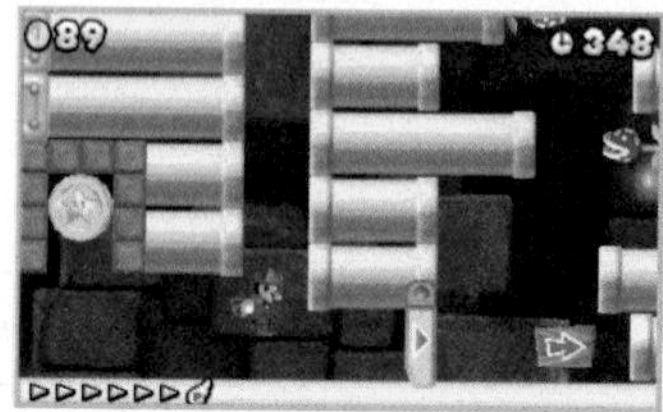

When you reach the hidden area, stomp the Buzzy Beetle and use its shell to clear the Piranha Plants on the left side of the room. Follow the shell down the passage to find the first Star Coin.

3

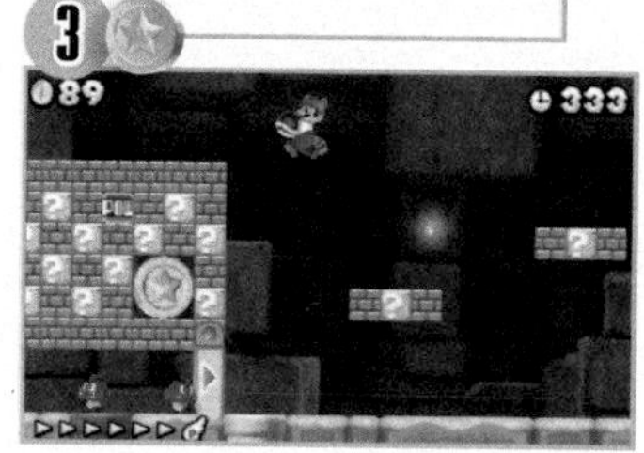

The second Star Coin is enclosed within the Blocks at Point 3. Stomp the nearby Buzzy Beetle, then carry its shell to the Blocks above the Star Coin.

Throw the shell to the left. When the shell strikes the POW Block, the impact clears a path to the Star Coin.

Watch out for the Goombas that emerge near the Star Coin! If you've managed to hang on to a Super Leaf, use Raccoon Mario's tail whip to clear the enemies from your path.

WORLD 2-3

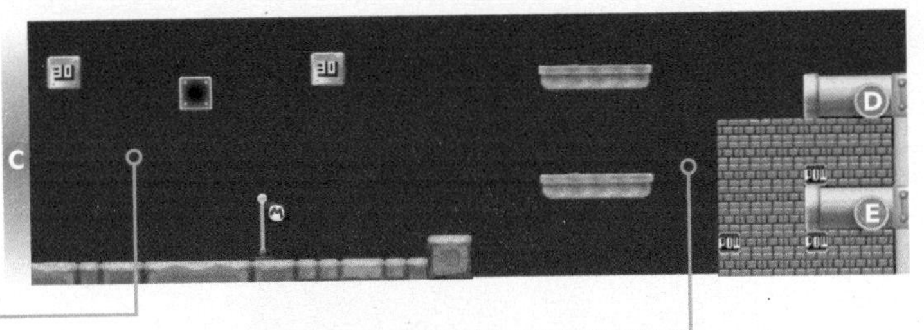

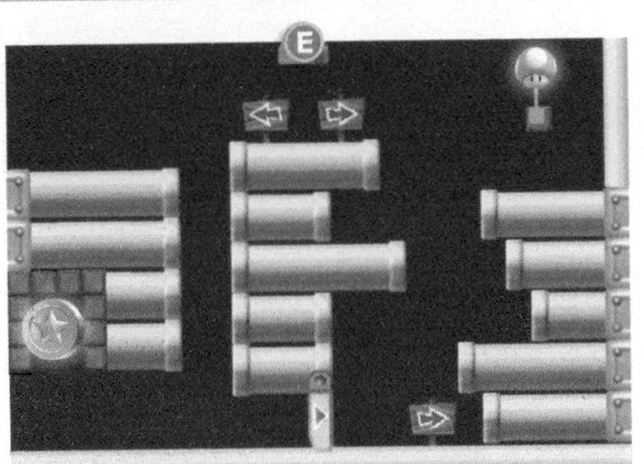

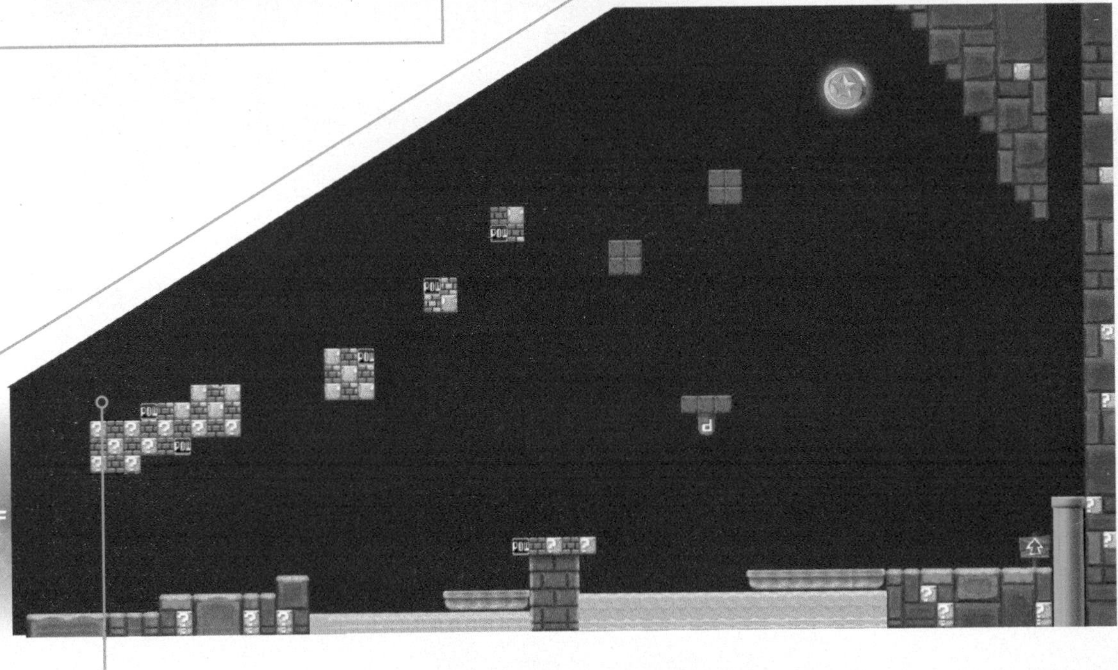

When you pass through the Red Ring at Point 4, red coins appear in a circle around you. Hop around the moving platforms to grab them before they vanish.

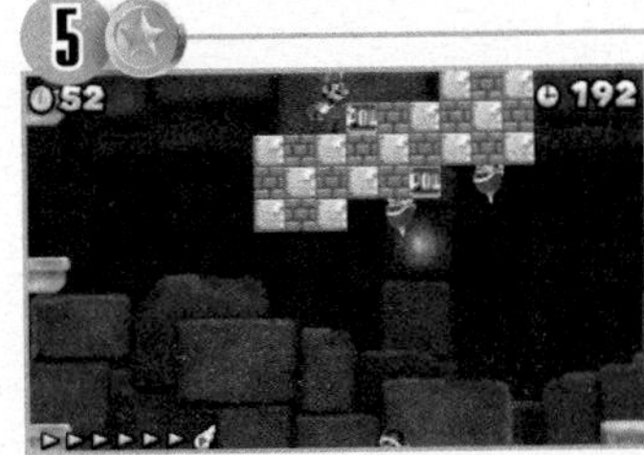

The third Star Coin is floating high above the ground. To find it, jump from the moving platforms to the Blocks at Point 5.

Jump along the Blocks as they lead you toward the cavern ceiling. Use the POW Blocks to defeat the Red Spike Buzzies along the way. When you reach the end of the Blocks, make a running leap to the Star Coin.

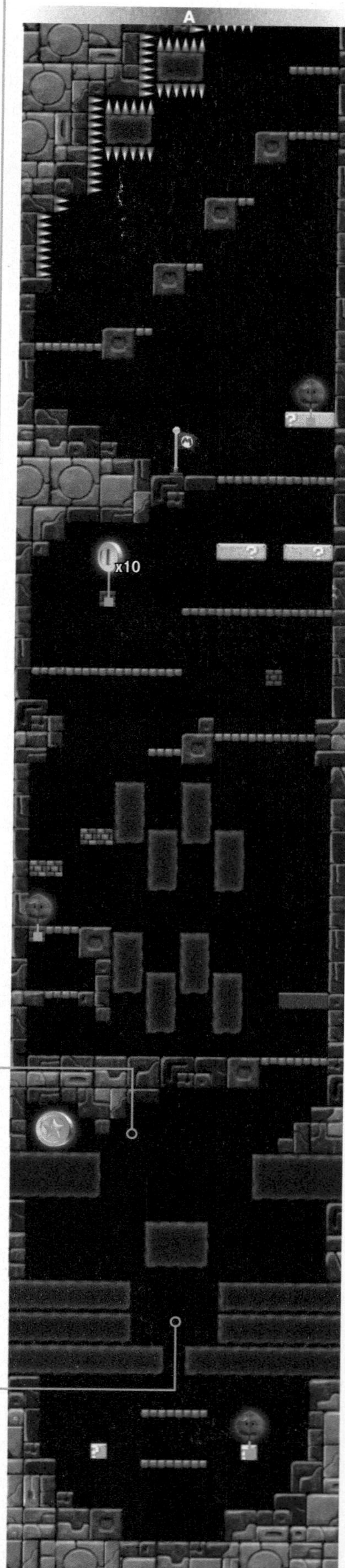

1

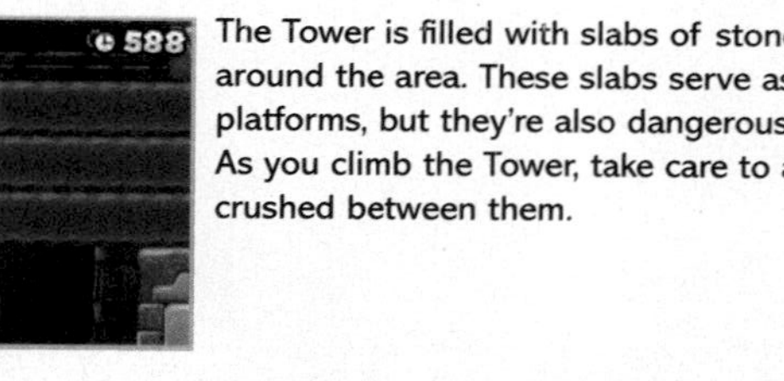

The Tower is filled with slabs of stone that move around the area. These slabs serve as essential platforms, but they're also dangerous hazards. As you climb the Tower, take care to avoid being crushed between them.

2

The first Star Coin is in a small nook at Point 2. Stand to the right of the Star Coin, then duck down and let the slab carry you into the nook.

3

The second Star Coin is located past the door at Point 3. Before you head through the door, collect the 1-Up Mushroom from the Invisible Block on the left side of the enclosure's entrance.

TIP

There's another Invisible Block on the right side of the entrance—avoid hitting it until after the 1-Up Mushroom drops into the enclosure.

4

After you pass through the door, jump up along the moving slabs until you reach the Star Coin at the top of the room.

CAUTION

The exit is located about halfway up the right wall. Don't leave the area before you collect the Star Coin.

WORLD 2-TOWER

5

The third Star Coin is floating at the top of the Tower. When you reach Point 5, wait for the slabs to drop down from the ceiling, then wall jump up along the wall to the left.

When you reach the small platform near the ceiling, wait for the slabs to drop out of your way, then dash under the spikes and jump to the Star Coin.

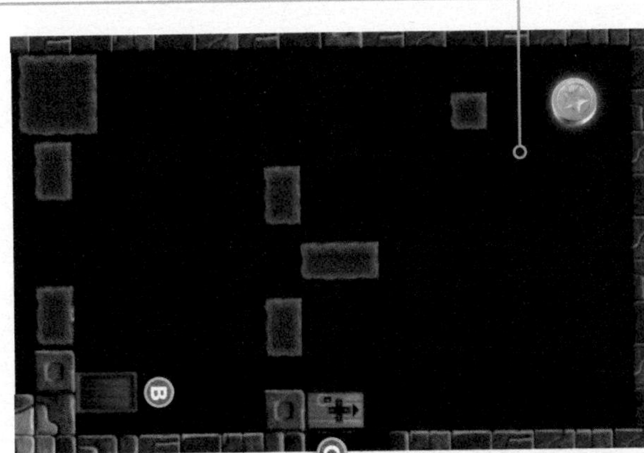

6

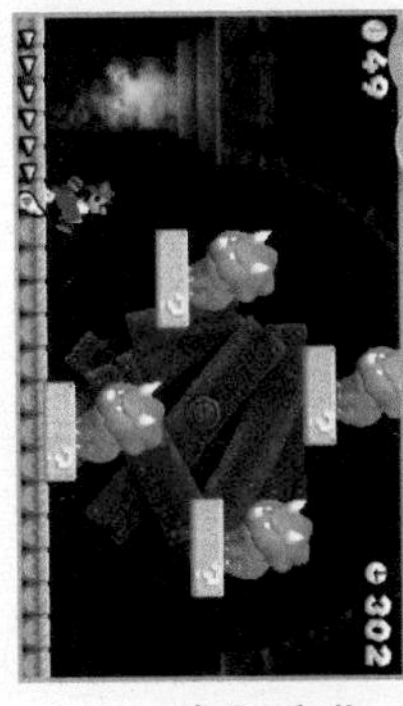

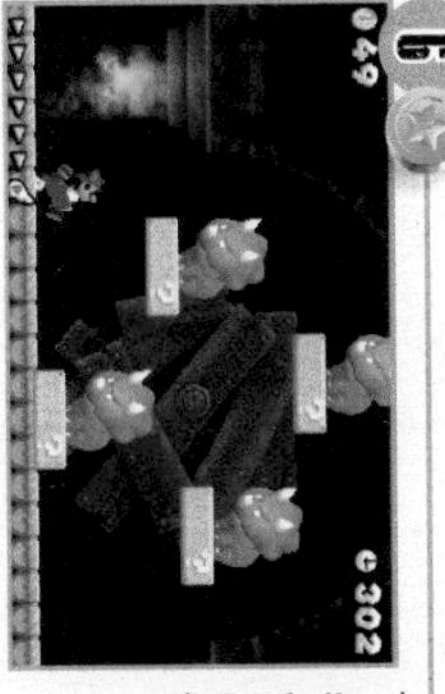

The final chamber contains four Reznors on one small wheel. There aren't any vacant ? Blocks when you enter the room, and after you clear out two Reznors the floor gives way. Defeat all four Reznors to complete the level.

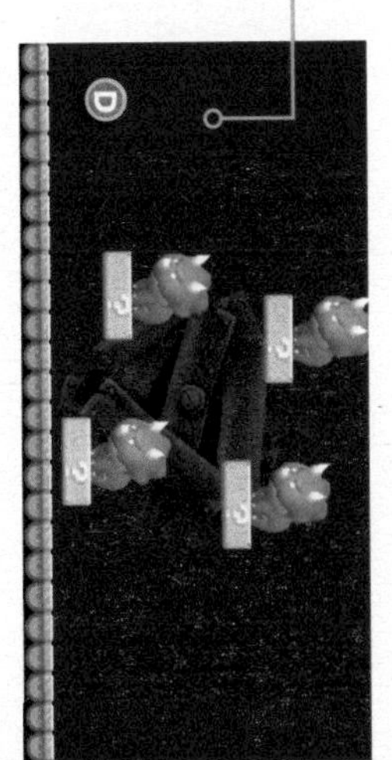

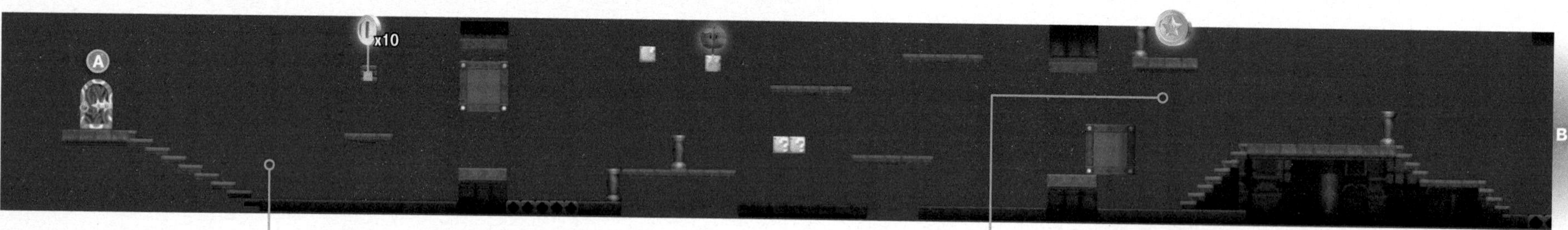

To unlock the path to World 2-B, you must find this level's secret exit.

When you pass through the first door, a Boohemoth appears to the left. The Boohemoth only moves at full speed when your back is turned, but unlike the Boo and Big Boo, the Boohemoth is brave enough to sneak toward you while you face it. Keep moving, and watch out for the Boos along the path to the right.

The first Star Coin is located on a platform at Point 2. If the moving platform is in position, wall jump up through the gap to the left of the Star Coin. If not, dash up the stairs, then make a running leap back to the left.

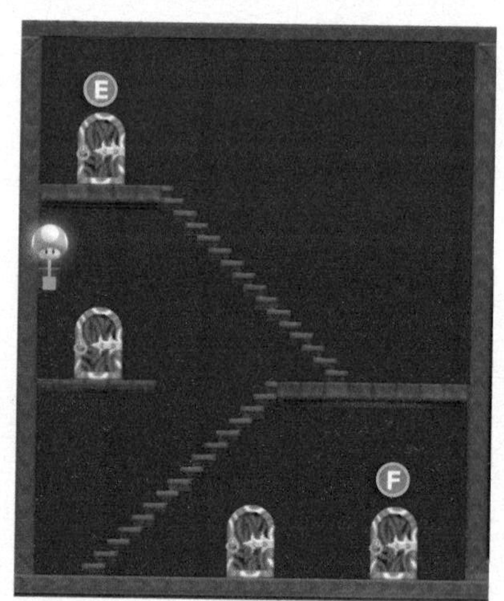

WORLD 2-BOO HOUSE

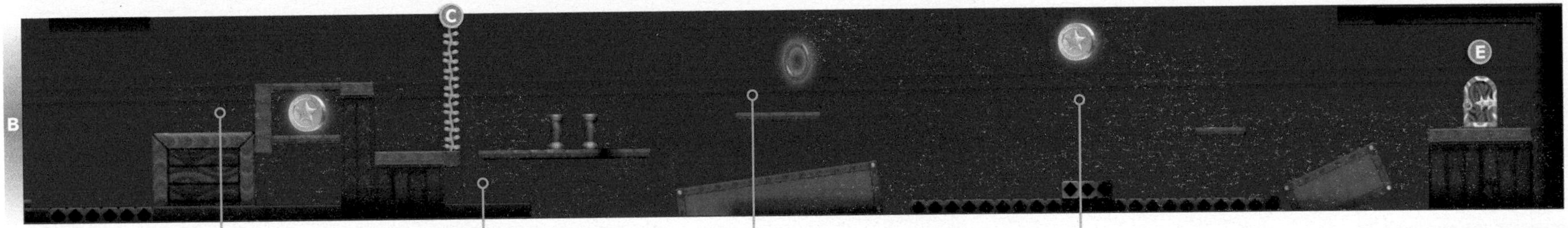

3

To reach the second Star Coin, stand on the large platform at Point 3. As the platform sinks into the floor, face the Boohemoth to slow its advance and draw the Boo away from the Star Coin. When the path is clear, move under the Star Coin and jump up along the platforms.

4

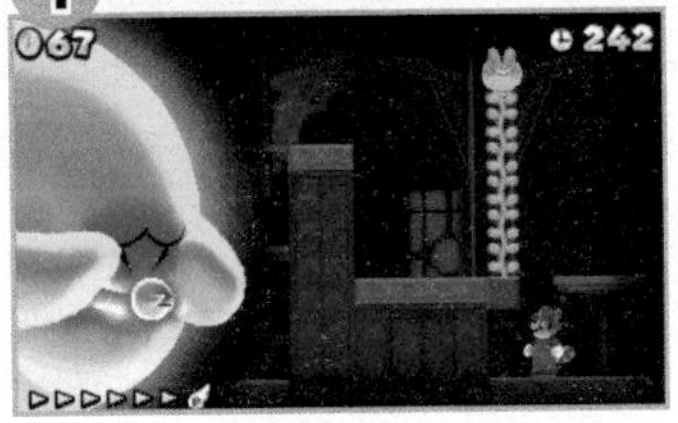

Hit the Invisible Block at Point 4 to reveal a Beanstalk. Climb up to the hidden area above you and follow the path to find this level's secret exit.

NOTE

Using the secret exit prevents you from collecting the third Star Coin, but it unlocks the secret path to World 2-B.

5

When you pass through the Red Ring at Point 5, a circle of red coins appears around you. Grab the coins closest to the Boohemoth before you collect the coins to the right.

6

As you move along the Trampoline Blocks at Point 6, look for the Star Coin swinging above you. Bounce up to grab it as it moves into range.

1

Stomp the Koopa at Point 1 and use its shell to smash the nearby Block. Slide through the gap and follow the path to find an Super Star hidden in a ? Block. Use this temporary power-up to defeat the Fire Snakes patrolling the platforms above you, then deal with other nearby enemies.

TIP

There are two more ? Blocks in the area. Hit them while you're invincible to collect fresh Super Stars.

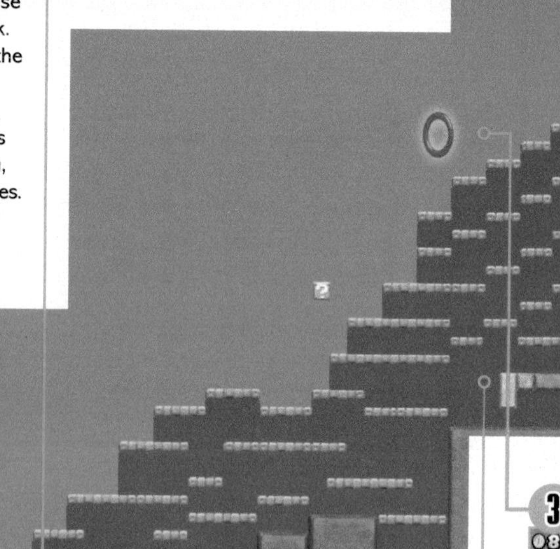

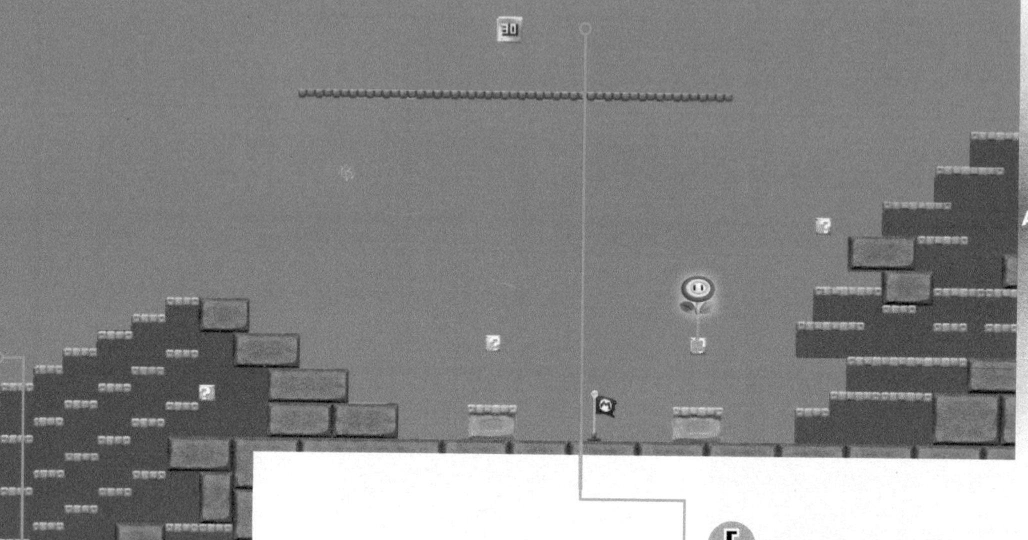

2

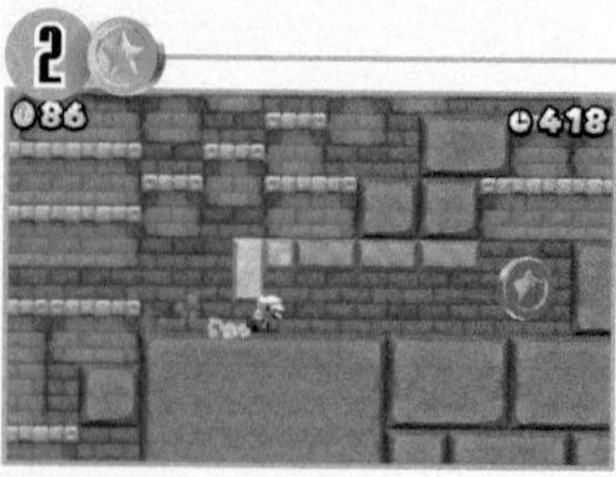

Slide under the platform at Point 2 to reach the level's first Star Coin.

3

When you jump through the Red Ring at Point 3, some red coins appear on the staggered platforms to the right. As you grab the red coins, try to keep your jumps relatively small. Leaping out of position can cost you valuable seconds!

4

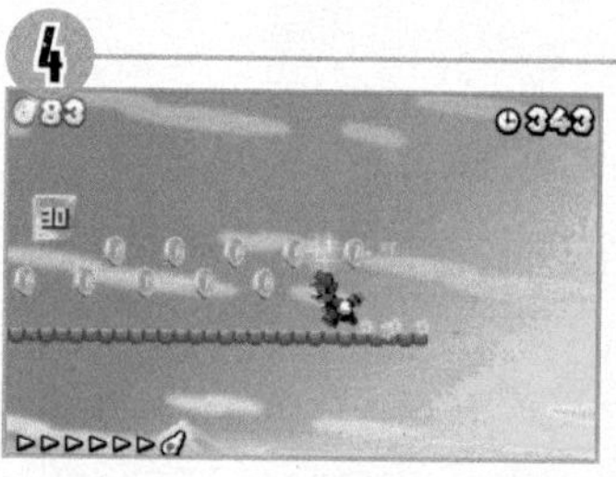

Use a Super Leaf to reach the Roulette Coin Block at Point 4. You can attempt to collect one of these power-ups from the Roulette Block at Point 1, but it's best to bring a Super Leaf into the level.

5

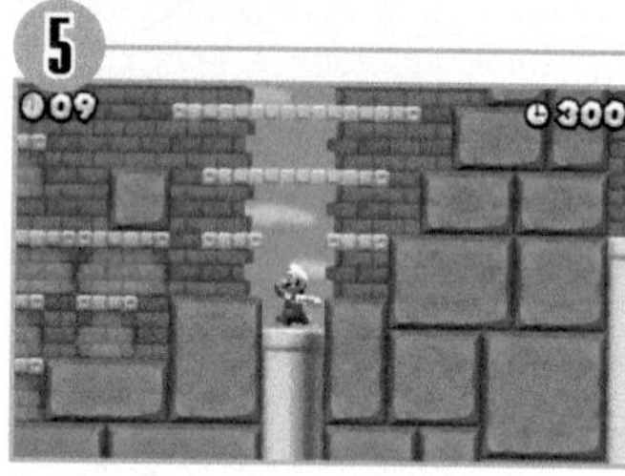

The pipe at Point 5 leads to a secret area.

After you pass through the pipe, wait for the room to fill with Goombas. When there are plenty of enemies in the area, stomp one and bounce up to the Gold Ring. Jump from Goomba to Goomba to earn coins until the Gold Ring wears off.

WORLD 2-4

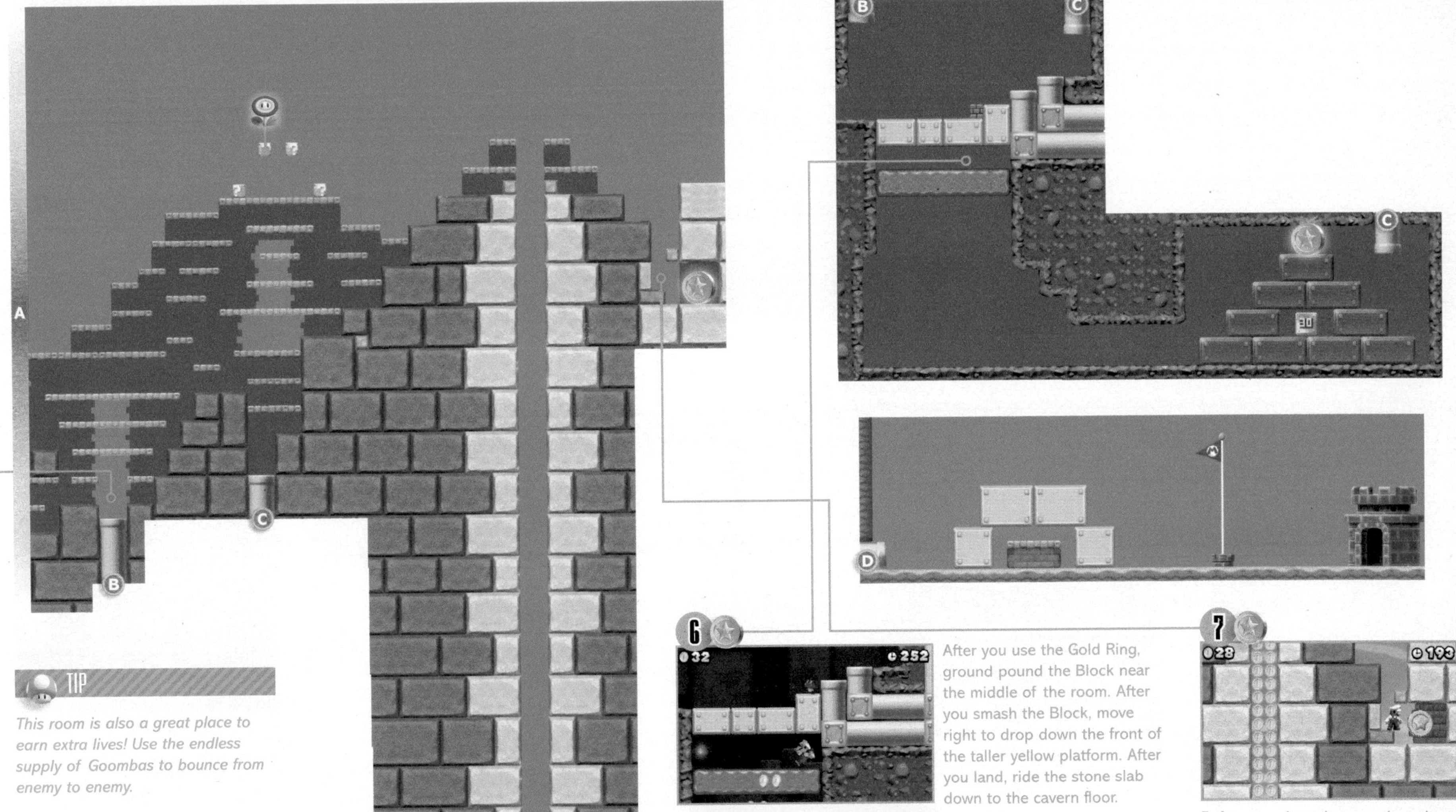

TIP

This room is also a great place to earn extra lives! Use the endless supply of Goombas to bounce from enemy to enemy.

After you use the Gold Ring, ground pound the Block near the middle of the room. After you smash the Block, move right to drop down the front of the taller yellow platform. After you land, ride the stone slab down to the cavern floor.

Follow the path to the right to find a Star Coin floating above a Roulette Coin Block.

Before you drop down to the exit, grab the Star Coin from the small nook at Point 7.

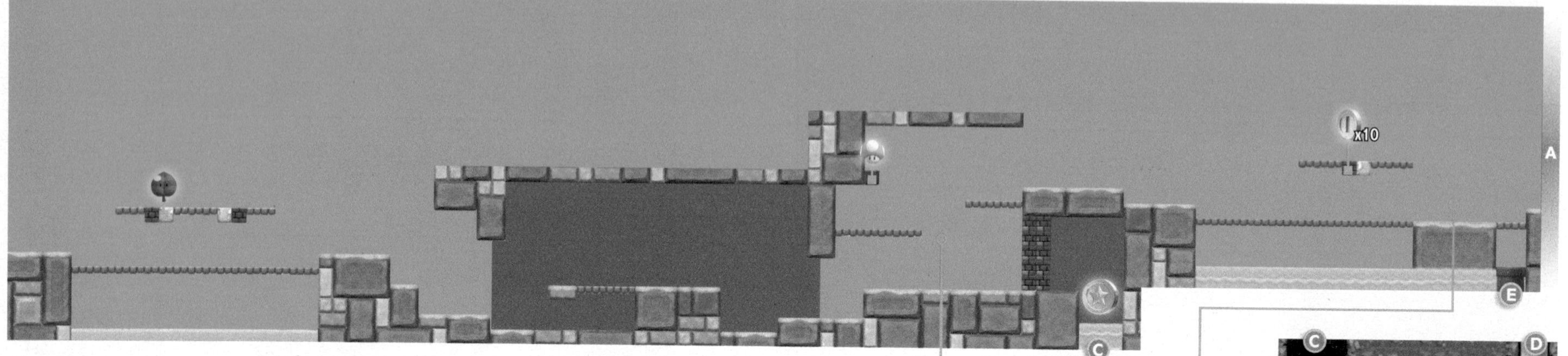

1

The first Star Coin is located in a small enclosure near a Chain Chomp at Point 1. Wait for the Chain Chomp to face the Blocks to the left, then ground pound its stake to set it free.

After the enemy smashes through the Blocks, grab the Star Coin floating above the small patch of quicksand.

If you fail to have the Chain Chomp destroy the Brick Blocks for you, you can use the Raccoon Mario to break the Brick Blocks.

2

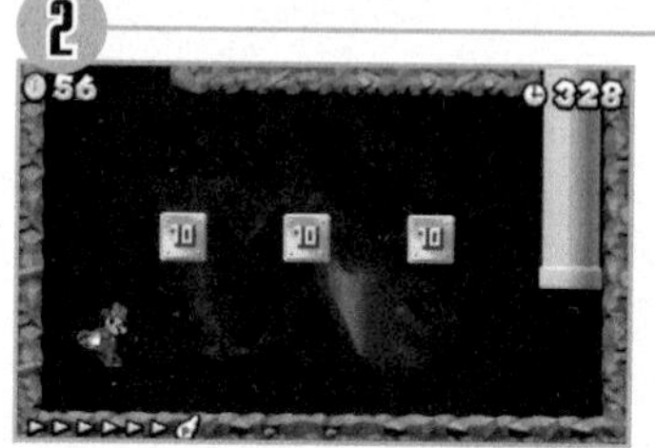

Sinking in quicksand usually costs Mario a life, but the quicksand below the first Star Coin actually leads to a secret area! This hidden cavern contains three Roulette Coin Blocks, and following this route allows you to bypass a large chunk of the level.

3

The second Star Coin is located in a hidden area. To reach it, you must free the Chain Chomp at Point 3. Ground pound the stake until the enemy hops away. After the platform sinks into the quicksand, enter the red pipe.

After you pass through the pipe, wait for the Chain Chomps to lunge, then jump up to the Star Coin before they recover.

WORLD 2-5

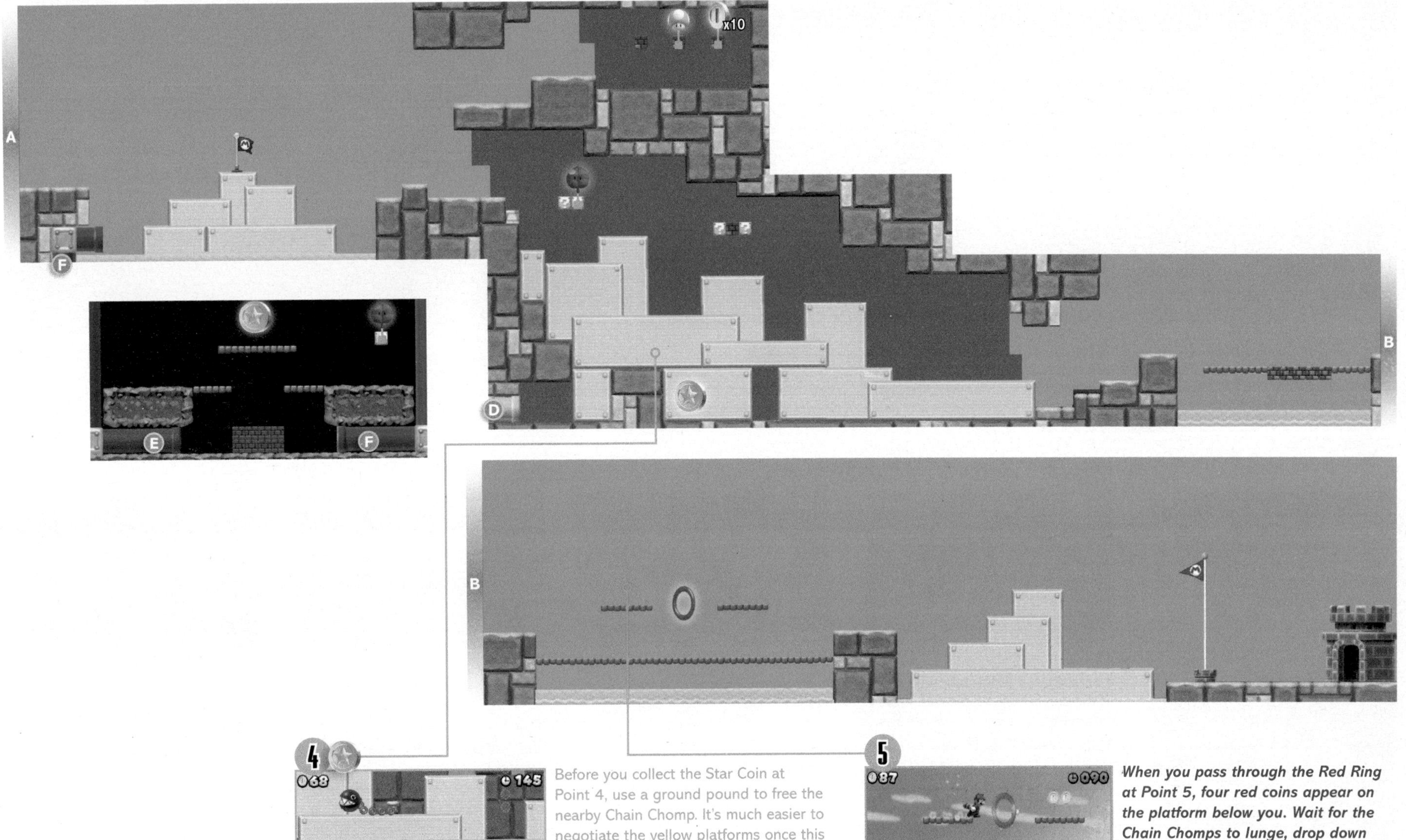

Before you collect the Star Coin at Point 4, use a ground pound to free the nearby Chain Chomp. It's much easier to negotiate the yellow platforms once this enemy is out of the area.

When you pass through the Red Ring at Point 5, four red coins appear on the platform below you. Wait for the Chain Chomps to lunge, drop down and grab the red coins, then hop back onto the higher platforms. Collect the remaining red coins as they parachute down from above you.

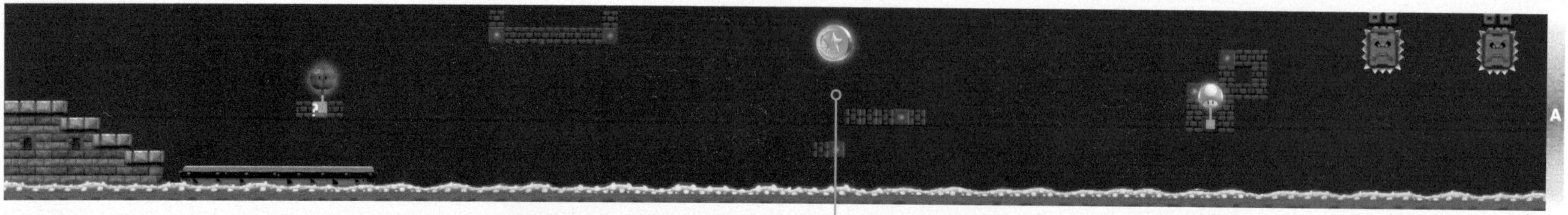

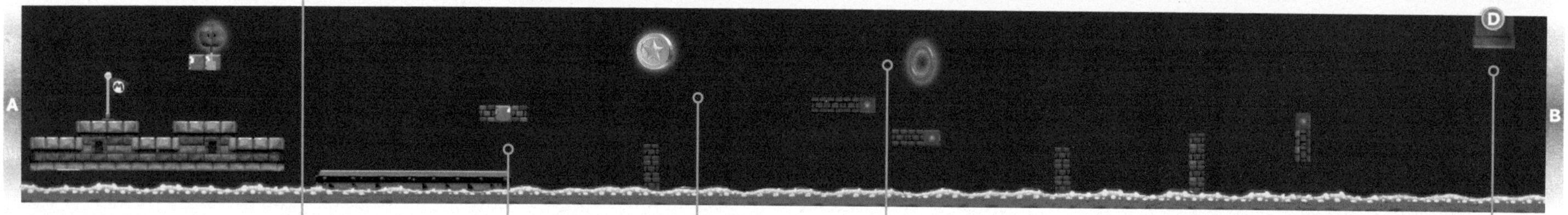

NOTE

Use the large rafts floating in the lava to traverse this level. When you stand on a raft, it moves to the right. When you jump off of a raft, it stops moving.

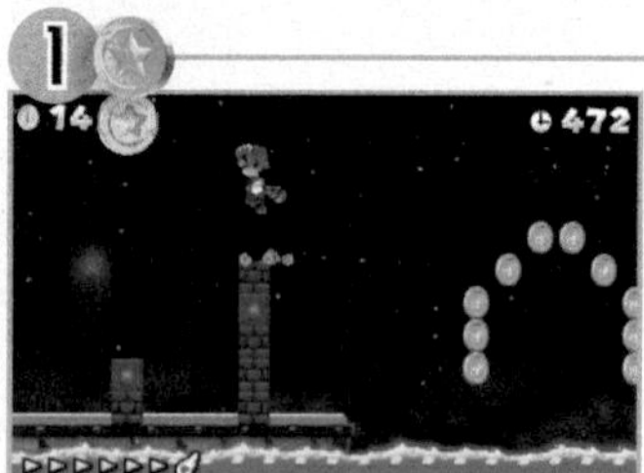

As you approach Point 1, the Blocks swivel down toward the lava. Position the raft under the Blocks, then use them to reach the Star Coin high above you.

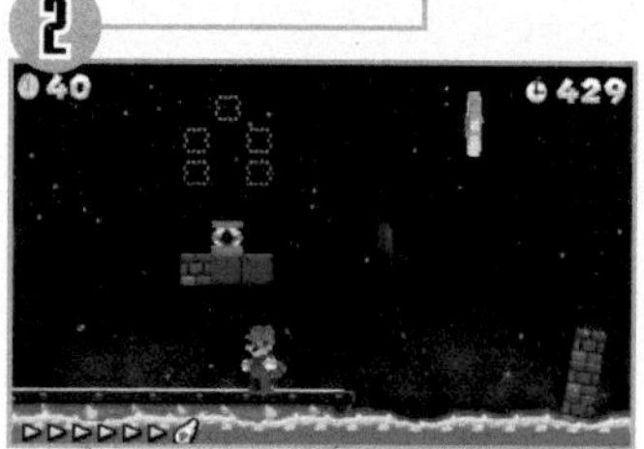

Hit the ? Block at Point 2 to reveal a Springboard. Hop up and grab it, then drop back to the raft. This valuable tool allows you to reach some important items, so try to keep it until you reach the end of the level.

TIP

When you're not using the Springboard, it's usually best to carry it. This prevents the level's many obstacles from knocking it into the lava.

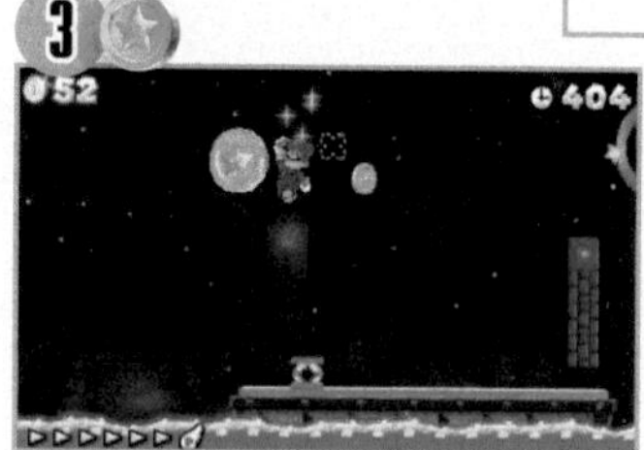

When you reach the coin outlines at Point 3, bounce on the Springboard to prevent the raft from moving. Watch for the Star Coin that swings through the area, then jump up and grab it.

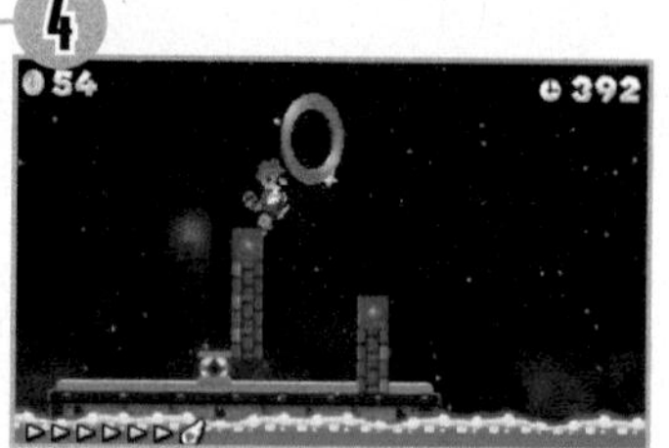

Bounce up to the Red Ring at Point 4, then drop back down to the raft. After the Springboard passes under the first set of Blocks, pick it up and collect the red coins to the right. When you reach the last group of red coins, use the Springboard to collect them.

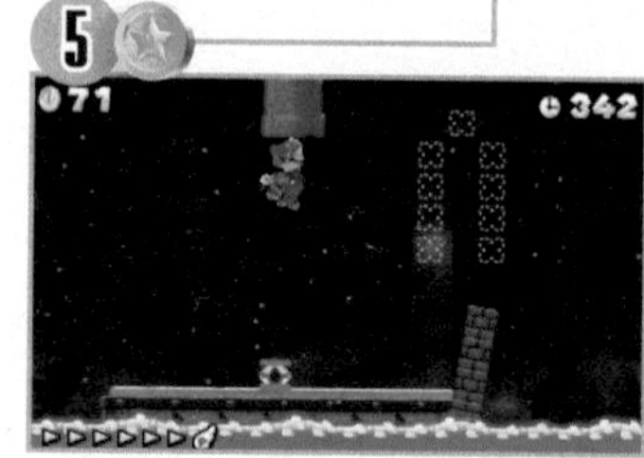

The last Star Coin is located in a hidden area. Use the Springboard to reach the red pipe at Point 5.

TIP

If the player loses the springboard, but has a super leaf, they can position the raft at the end of the level to get a running start and fly up to the pipe to acquire the third Star Coin.

WORLD 2-CASTLE

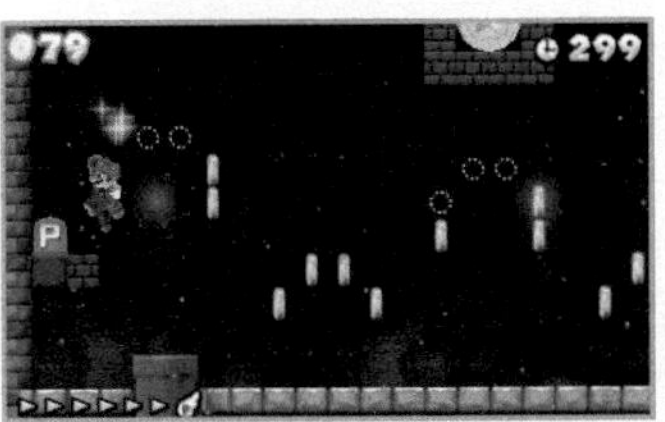

After you pass through the pipe, activate as many of the coin outlines as you can, but try not to collect the coins that appear. Hit the Block along the left wall to reveal a P Switch, then stomp it to transform all of the coins to Blocks. Use the Blocks to reach the Star Coin at the top of the room.

NOTE

While the P Switch is active, touching the remaining coin outlines causes additional Blocks to appear.

6

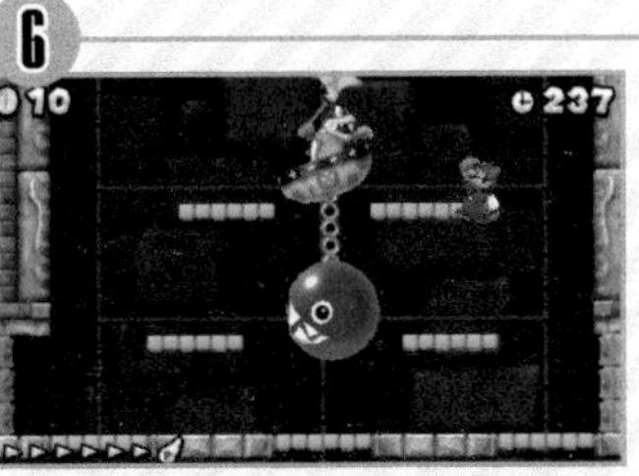

During the boss battle, a Chain Chomp pulls Larry Koopa around the room. Avoid the Chain Chomp and use the platforms to stomp on Larry's head.

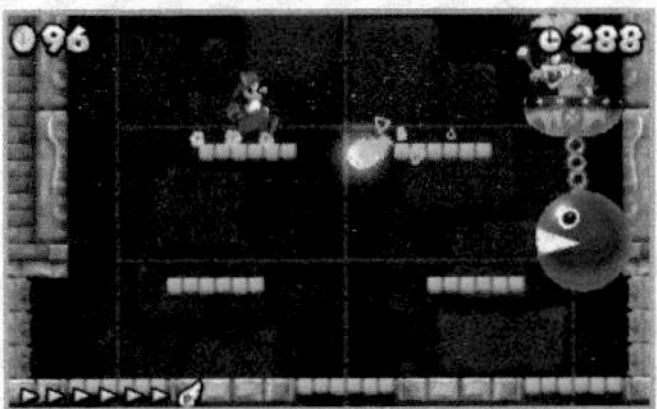

Larry uses his wand to shoot fireballs around the room. Dodge these attacks and position yourself to stomp him again. Jump on Larry Koopa three times to end the encounter and unlock World Three.

NOTE

Before you can visit this level, you must spend five Star Coins to unlock the appropriate path.

1

To collect the first Star Coin, you must leap to the platform at Point 1. When you do, the platform launches back to the left.

As you approach the next platform, make a running leap to the Star Coin.

2

To collect the second Star Coin, you need some help from the Koopa at Point 2. Stomp this enemy and quickly grab its shell. As you approach the Star Coin, leap to the stationary platforms.

Drop down to the lowest platform, then toss the shell into the Star Coin to collect it.

3

When you reach Point 3, look for a platform above you. The platforms to the right will carry you to the Goal Pole, but the upper path contains some valuable items. Wait for your current platform to land on the next track. As the platform you are on passes back through Point 3, make a running leap to the upper platform.

4

Search the Blocks at Point 4 to reveal a P Switch. When you're ready, stomp on the P Switch and hop onto the nearby platform.

Follow the blue coins to the next platform, then continue to the last Star Coin. Grab the Star Coin before the P Switch wears off and the Blocks disappear.

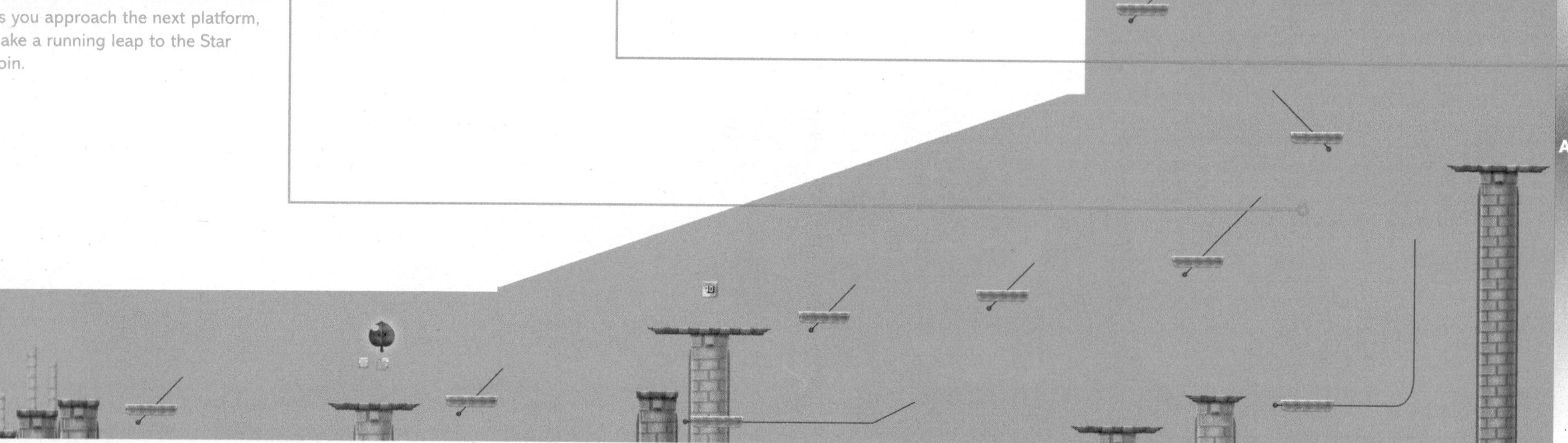

WORLD 2-A

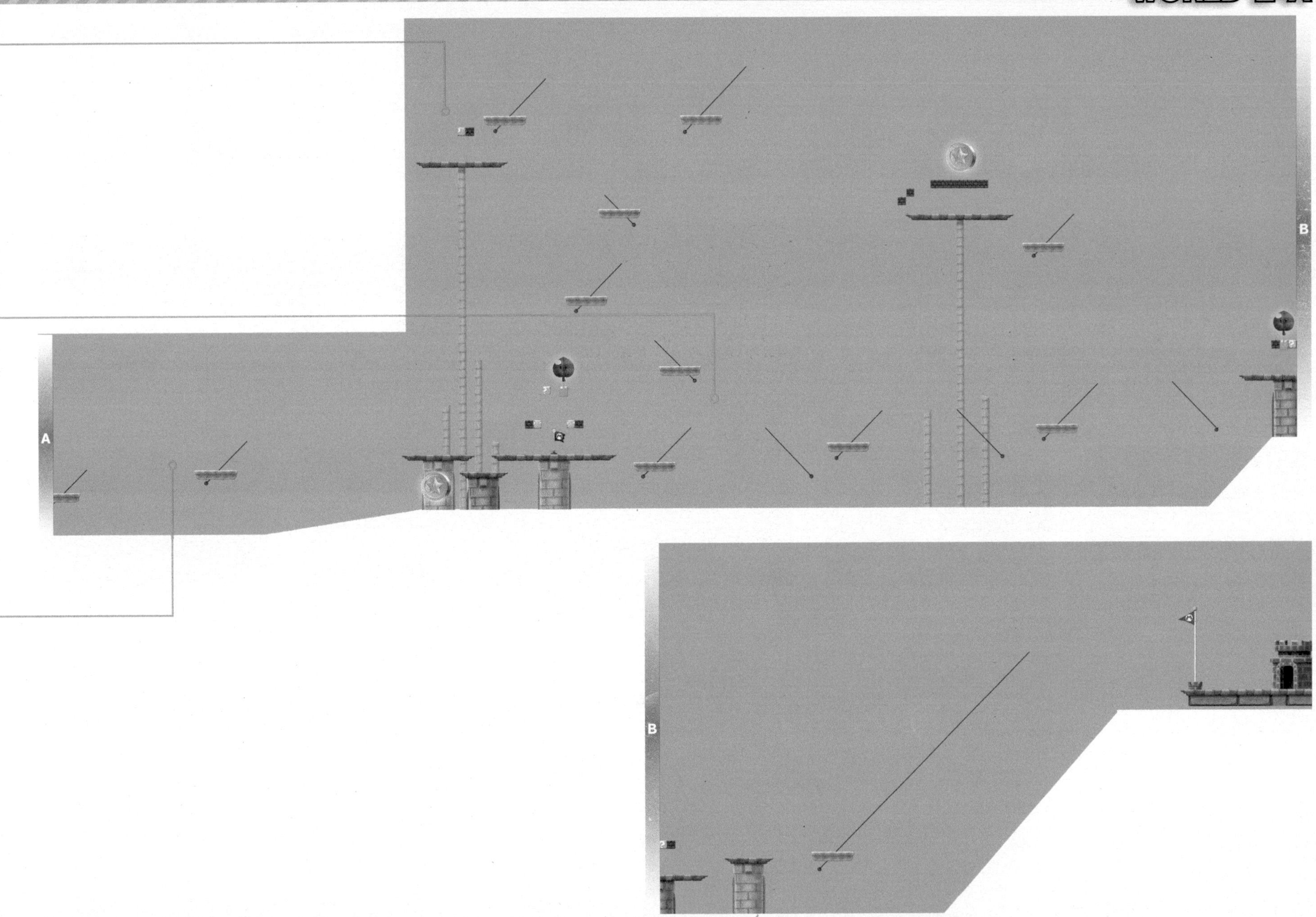

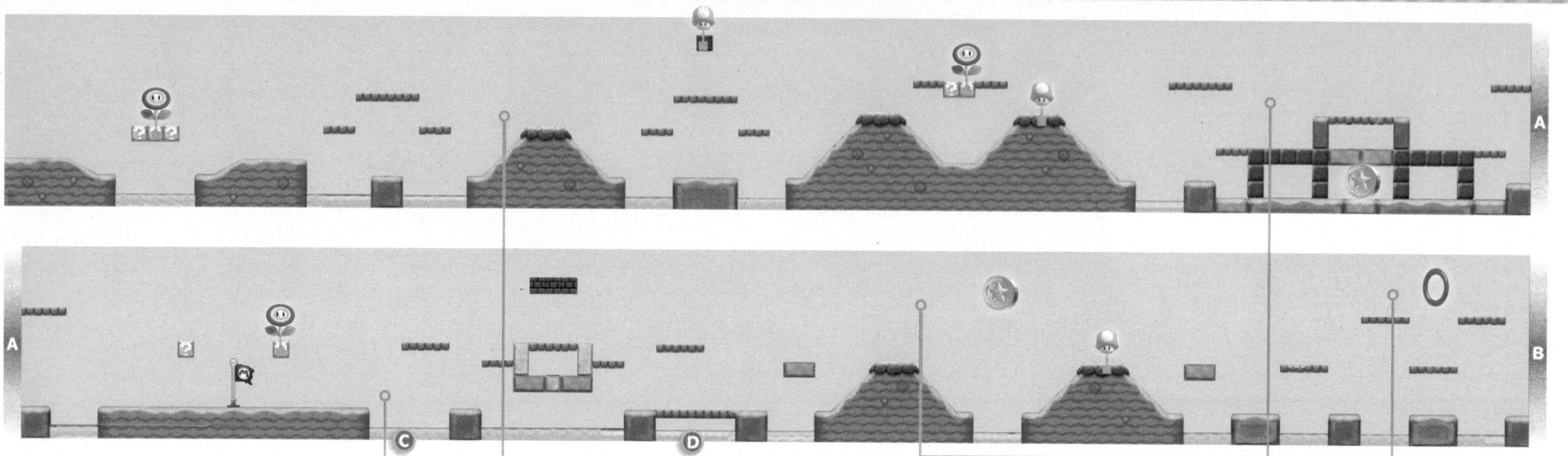

NOTE

To unlock this level, you must find the secret exit in World 2-Boo House.

CAUTION

This level contains an endless supply of Bob-ombs. Watch out for these enemies as they launch out of cannons or parachute down to the ground.

1

Bob-ombs are dangerous, but they're also very useful. Attack a Bob-omb to trigger its detonation sequence, then place it on the volcanoes scattered throughout the level. All volcanoes contain coins, but some also contain 1-Up Mushrooms.

2

When you reach Point 2, use the Bob-ombs to clear a path to the Star Coin. The nearby cannons provide a steady supply of these explosive enemies, so make sure you clear enough space to dodge new arrivals as you collect the Star Coin.

3

The second Star Coin is hidden below the quicksand at Point 3. Look for the coins that mark the secret entrance, then sink down to the hidden area.

When you reach the hidden area, use a Bob-omb to destroy the volcano's red crust. After the explosion, a Star Coin appears near the top of the cavern.

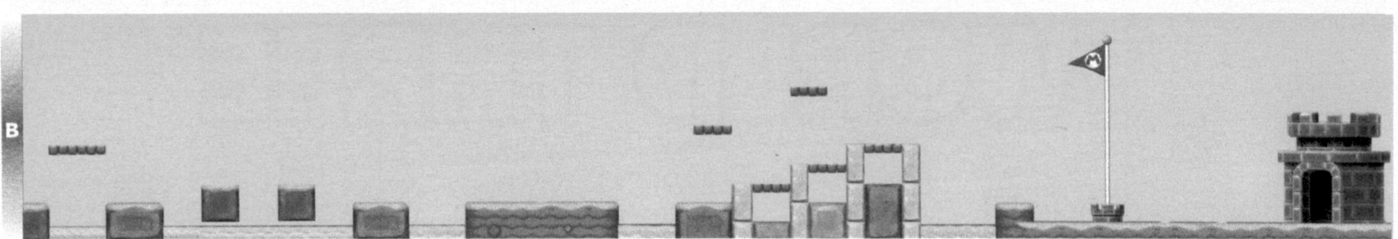

The level's last Star Coin is floating high above the ground. Stand on one of the nearby cannons and wait for it to fire a Bob-omb. Just after the Bob-omb deploys its parachute, make a running leap onto the enemy and bounce up to the Star Coin.

After you pass through the Red Ring at Point 5, collect the red coins to the right. Stomp on any Bob-ombs that drift into your path, and grab each red coin before it drifts out of reach.

WORLD THREE

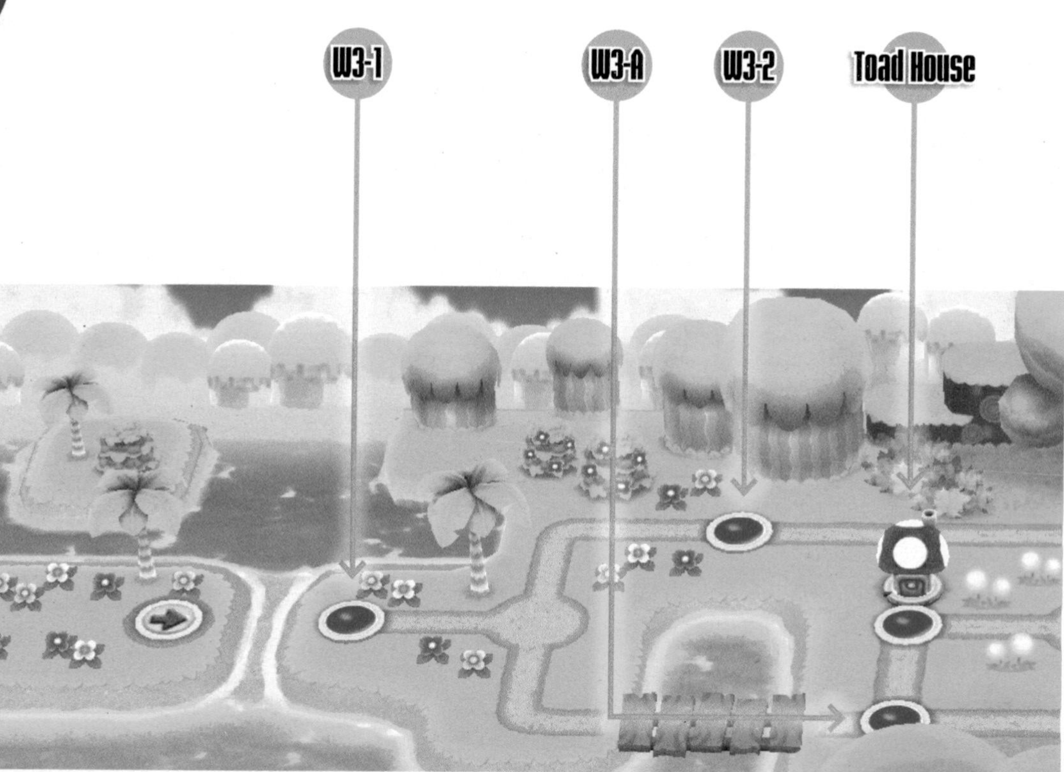

WORLD LOCATIONS				
Hostile Levels	Toad Houses	Boo Houses	Warp Cannons	Boss
11	3	1	1	Wendy Koopa

Main Path Levels:

- World 3-1
- World 3-2
- World 3-3
- World 3-Tower
- World 3-4
- World 3-Boo House
- World 3-5
- World 3-Castle

Alternate Path Levels:

- World 3-A
- World 3-B
- World 3-Warp Cannon

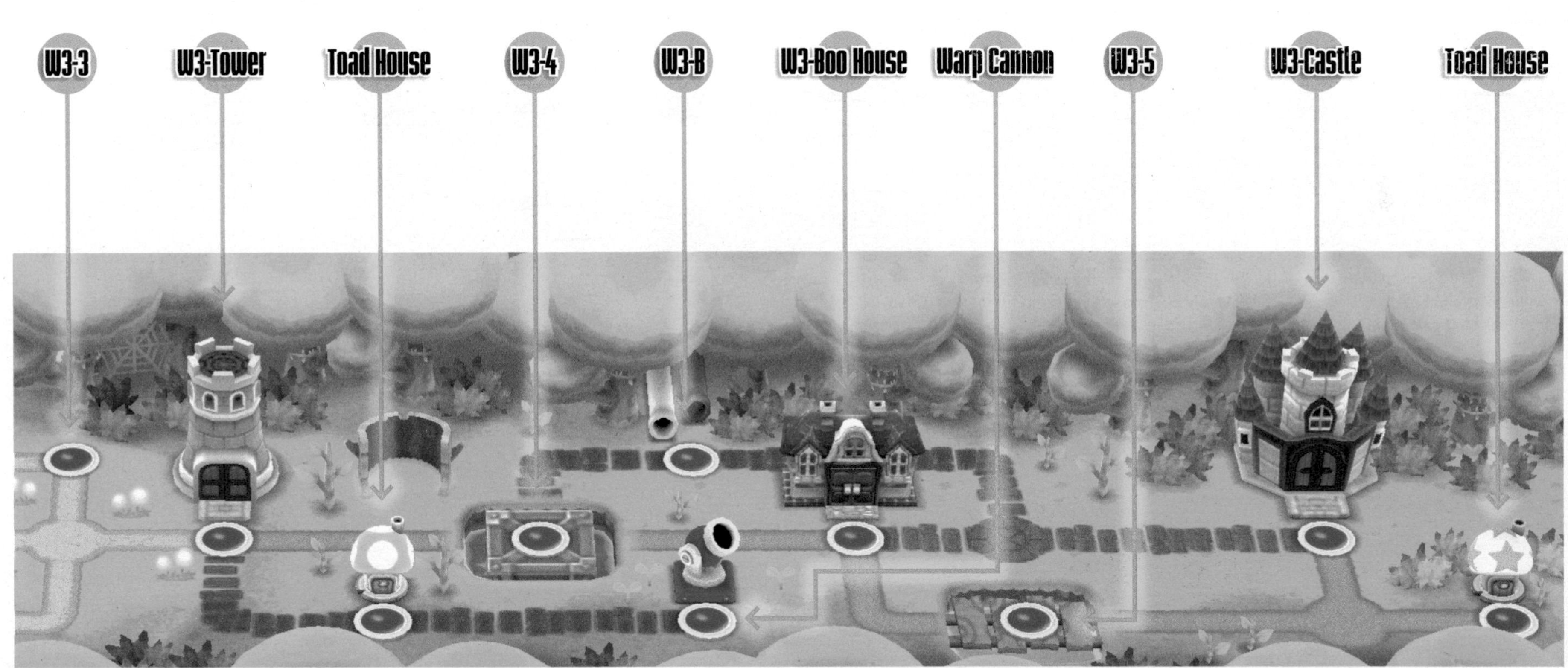

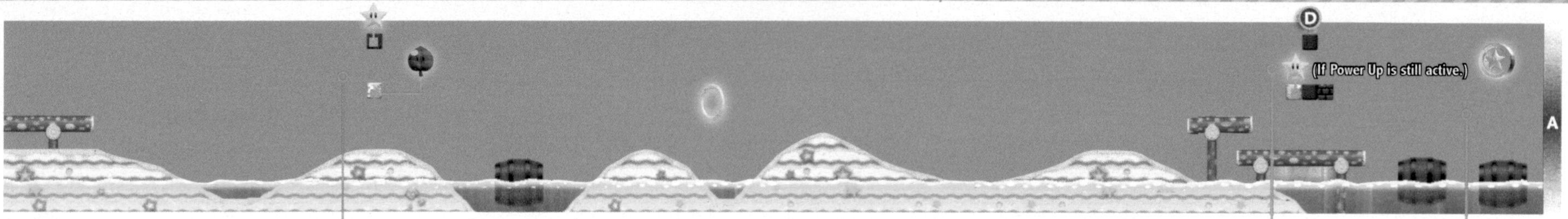

(If Power Up is still active.)

(If Power Up is still active.)

1

Hop onto the ? Block at Point 1, then jump straight up to find a Super Star hidden in an Invisible Block.

TIP

Once you collect the first Star Power Up you can collect three more throughout the level as long as you still have one activated. If you lose it the ? Blocks that contain them will be coins once again.

2

Hit the Invisible Blocks at Point 2 to reveal a Beanstalk, then climb up to find a hidden stash of coins!

3

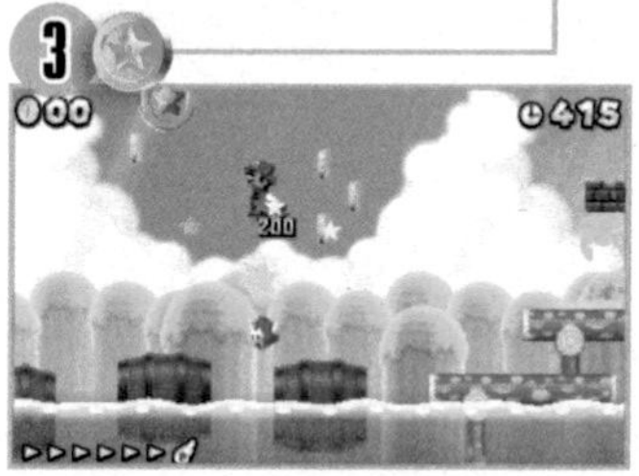

The first Star Coin is floating above the barrels at Point 3. Wait for a Cheep Cheep to pass through the area, then jump onto the enemy and bounce up to the Star Coin.

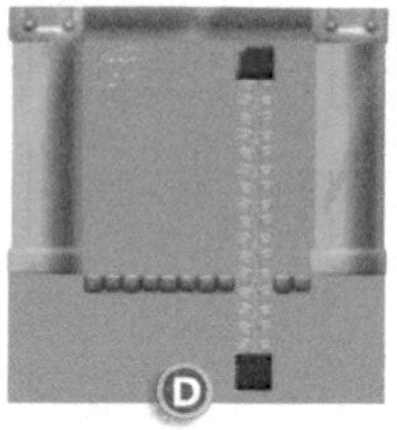

4

One of the Blocks at Point 4 contains a ? Switch. After you find it, activate the ? Switch to release a stash of coins from the nearby pipe.

WORLD 3-1

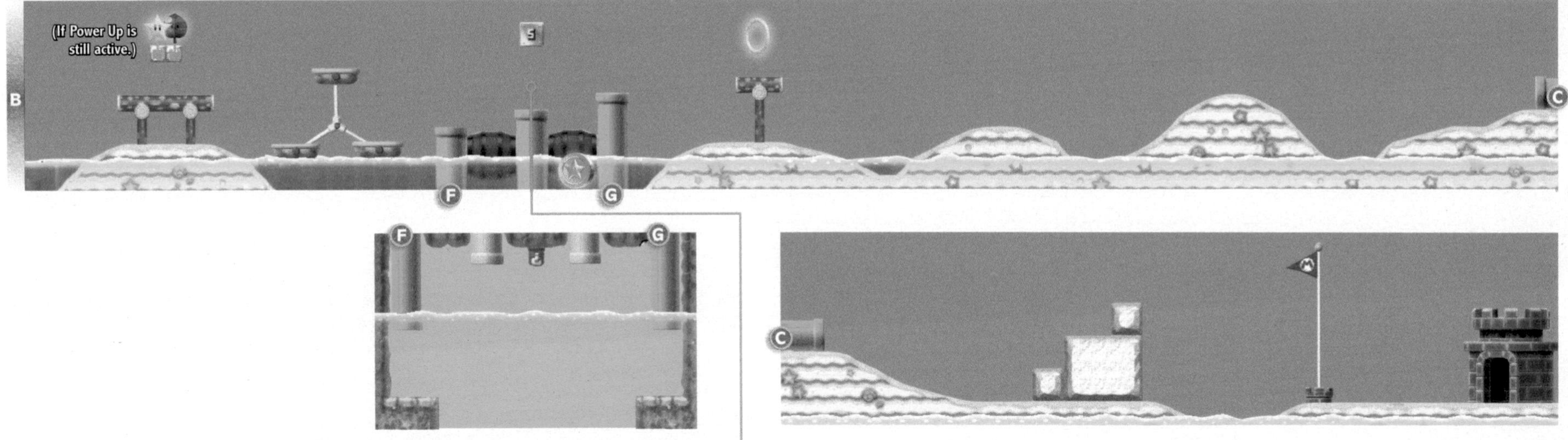

The second Star Coin is hidden above the rotating platforms at Point 5. Clear away the Piranha Plant at the top of the screen, or wait for it to pull into its pipe before you attempt to enter the hidden enclosure.

When the path is clear, wall jump off of the pipe entrance, then make a running leap up to the Star Coin.

The third Star Coin is hidden behind one of the barrels at Point 6. Jump onto the barrel to force it under the water's surface. Allow yourself to sink down until you collect the Star Coin.

If you fail to get the top of the Goal Pole, you can jump back to try again using the Cheep Cheep's that are coming out of the water.

1

Enter the green pipe at Point 1 to find a room with a Roulette Block.

2

The first Star Coin is located at Point 2. Swim through the gaps between the Caterpillar Blocks and grab it.

3

Toss fireballs into the ! Pipe at Point 3 to reveal a stash of coins and an Super Star.

4

If you have a Gold Flower power-up, use it to destroy the Blocks at Point 4. Enter the exposed pipe to find a room filled with Blocks, then use your gold fireballs to turn them all into coins!

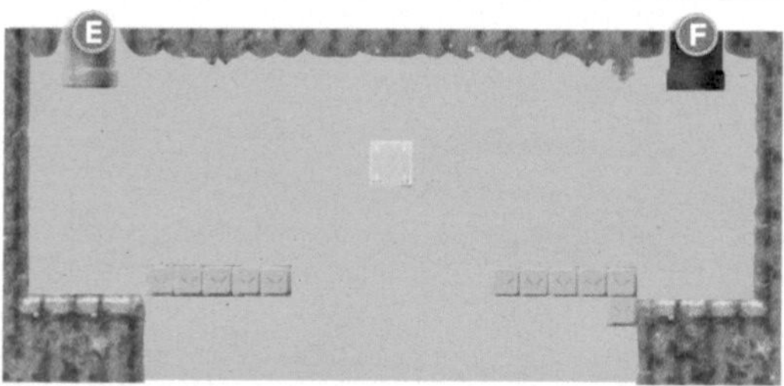

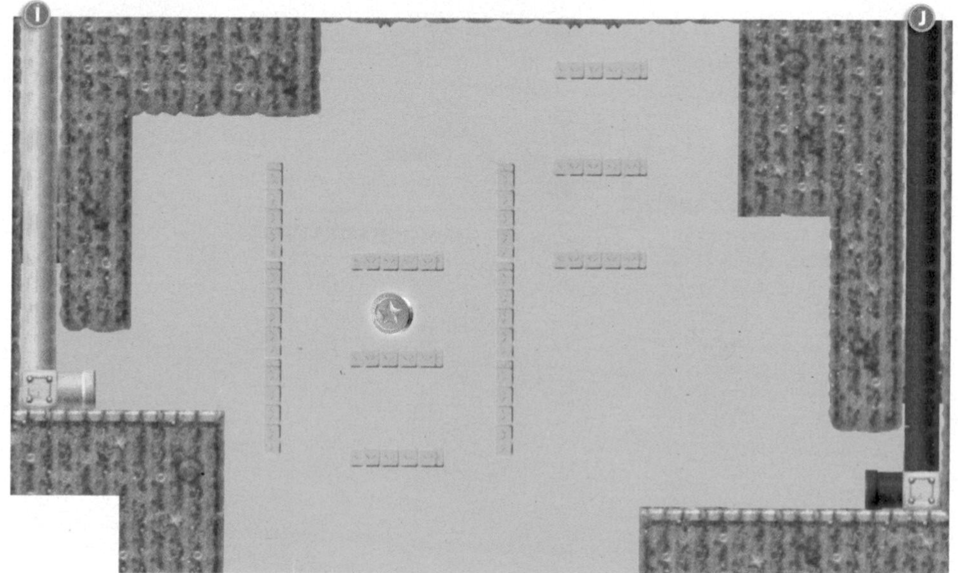

WORLD 3-2

5

The second Star Coin is located in a hidden room. To find it, enter the yellow pipe at Point 5.

There's a Spiny Cheep Cheep swimming near the Star Coin. If you managed to hang on to a Fire Flower power-up, use a fireball to clear out this pesky enemy before you collect the Star Coin.

6

The third Star Coin is floating at Point 6. Make sure you grab it as you weave through the Urchins and Caterpillar Blocks.

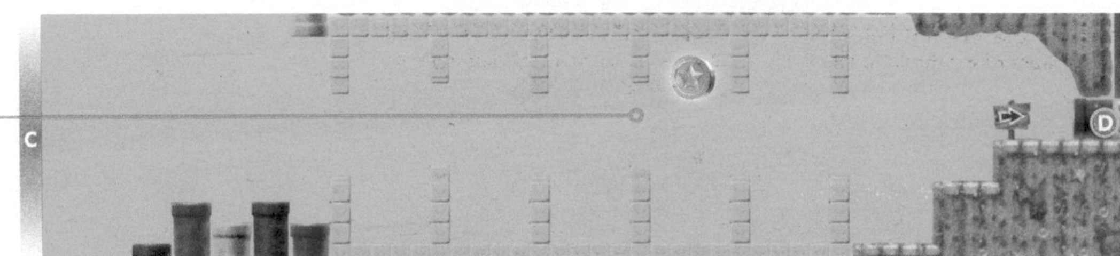

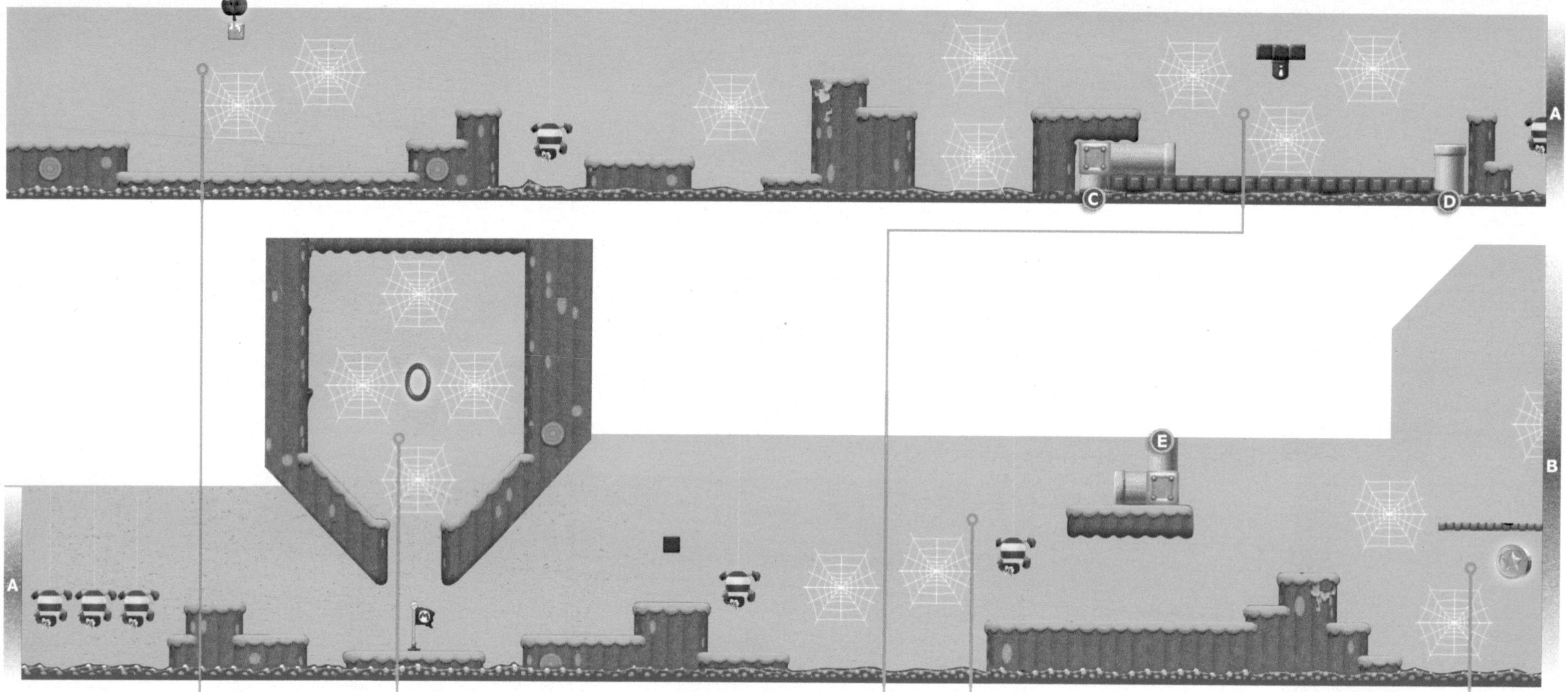

A

C

D

E

B

A

NOTE

To reach the Goal Pole, you must use the Spiders and webs scattered throughout the level. Bounce off of Spiders and climb webs to cross large gaps or reach high ledges.

1

To grab a web, press Up on the + Control Pad or Circle Pad. Webs eventually give way to Mario's weight, so watch each web for signs of wear. When you leave a web, it vanishes briefly—plan each jump before you make it.

2

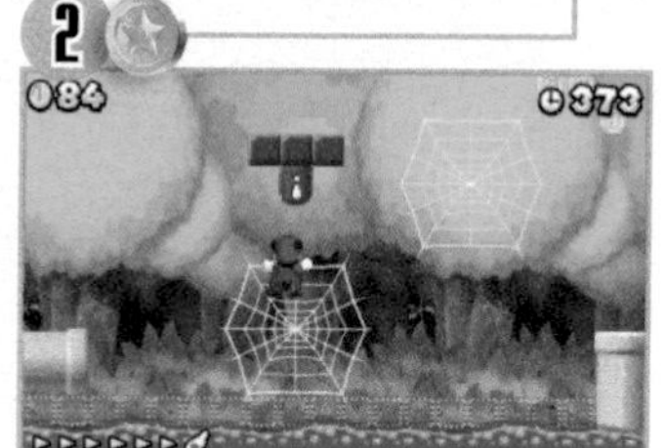

The first Star Coin is located in a hidden area. Hit the ! Switch at Point 2 to create temporary platform below you. Drop down and enter the pipe to the left.

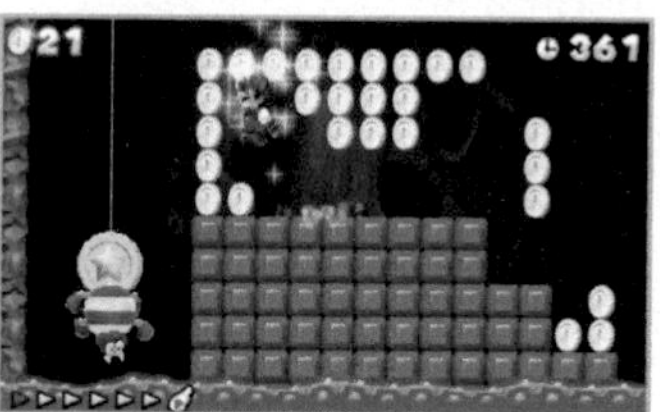

After you pass through the pipe, hit the nearby Blocks to reveal another ! Switch. Stomp the switch, then move across the temporary platforms to the left. When the Spider near the left wall approaches the Star Coin, jump onto its back. If you time it properly, you can grab the Star Coin and bounce back to the temporary platforms.

3

There's a Red Ring floating high above the Checkpoint Flag. Wall jump into the enclosure, then climb along the webs to reach Point 3. When you leap through the Red Ring, two red coins appear on each of the four webs.

WORLD 3-3

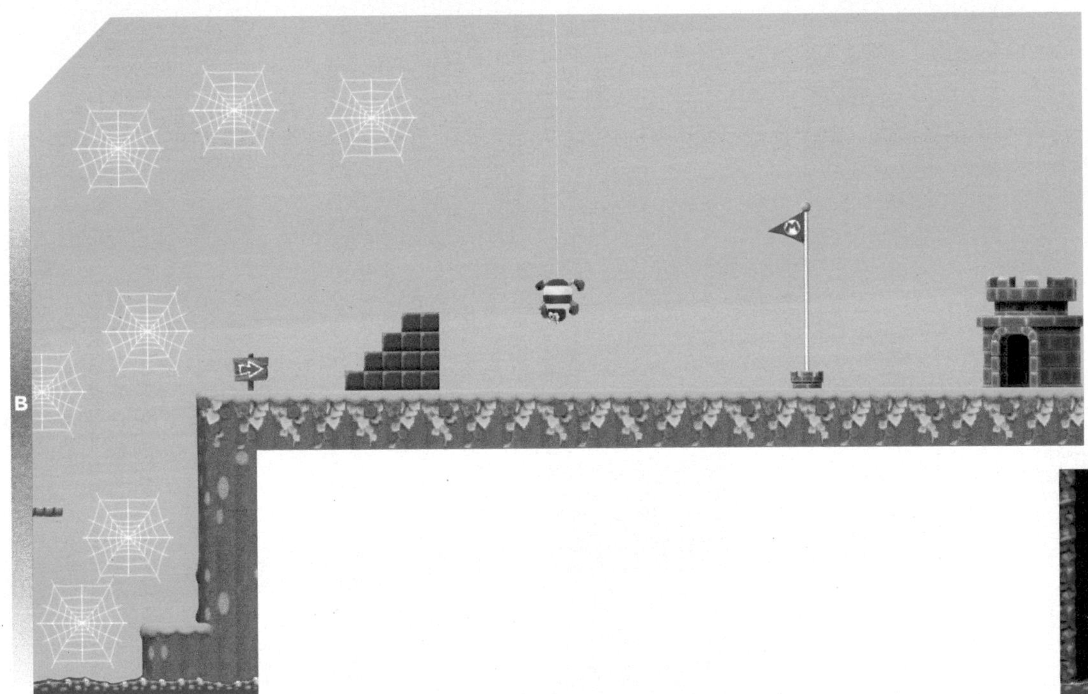

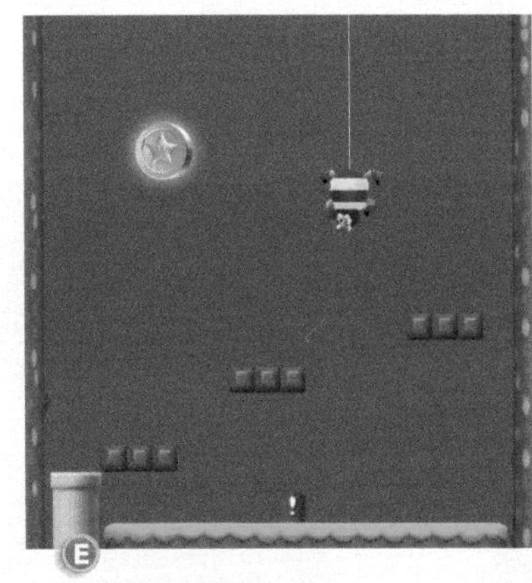

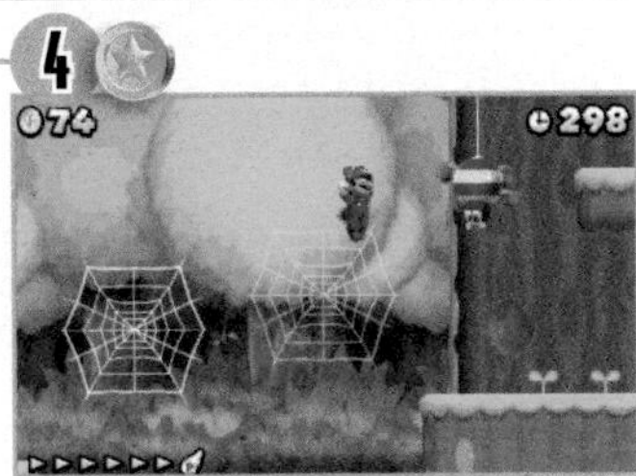

The second Star Coin is located in a hidden area. Climb the web at Point 4, then leap to the Spider and bounce to the nearby ledge. After you land, enter the pipe to the right.

After you pass through the pipe, stomp the ! Switch and jump along the temporary platforms. Avoid taking out the Spider until you reach the third platform, then use it to bounce up to the Star Coin.

TIP

At Point 4 if you fail to reach the second Star Coin after the time has expired, then you can use the Super Leaf to fly above the room and get the Star Coin.

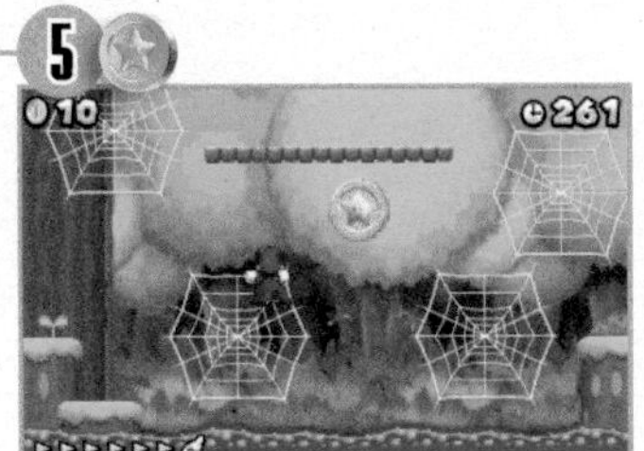

The third Star Coin is floating at Point 5. Move under the platform, then jump between the webs to grab the Star Coin.

4 *When you pass through the Red Ring at Point 4, red coins appear in the surrounding water currents. Move between the water currents to circle the room and collect all eight coins before they vanish.*

3 To use the secret exit, you must bring a Mini Mushroom into the level. Reach Point 3 as Mini Mario, then enter the small pipe to the right. Navigate the stone slabs and Fishbones along the alternate route to reach the secret Goal Pole.

NOTE

Using the secret exit prevents you from collecting the third Star Coin, but it unlocks the path to World 3-Warp Cannon.

2 The second Star Coin is located at Point 2. Wait for the Fishbones to swim to the left, then sneak up to the Star Coin. The enemies will attack when they turn around—draw them into one of the nearby slabs.

TIP

At the start of the climb up the Tower, swim up to get the Fishbones to attack you, then float down to have the two enemies collide into each other.

NOTE

To unlock the path to World 3-Warp Cannon, you must find this level's secret exit.

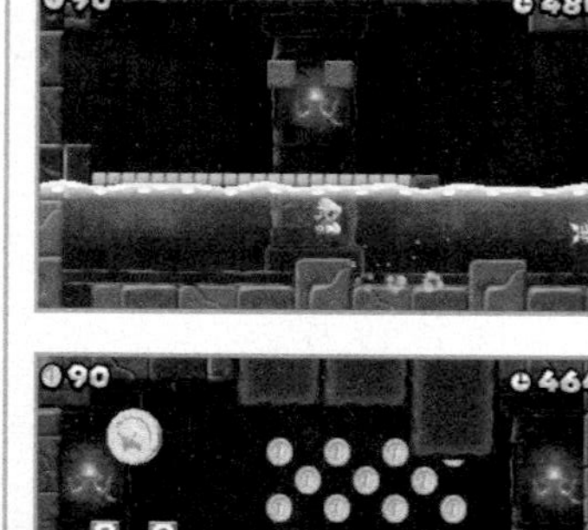

1 The first Star Coin is hidden in a secret room near the start of the level. Drop into the water to draw the Fishbones toward the right wall, then hop over the enemy and swim to the small hole on the left edge of the floor.

When you reach the next room, dodge the Fishbones and stone slabs to collect the Star Coin near the left wall.

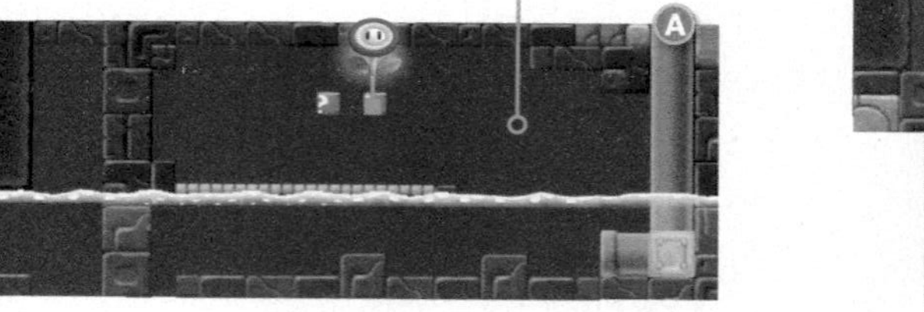

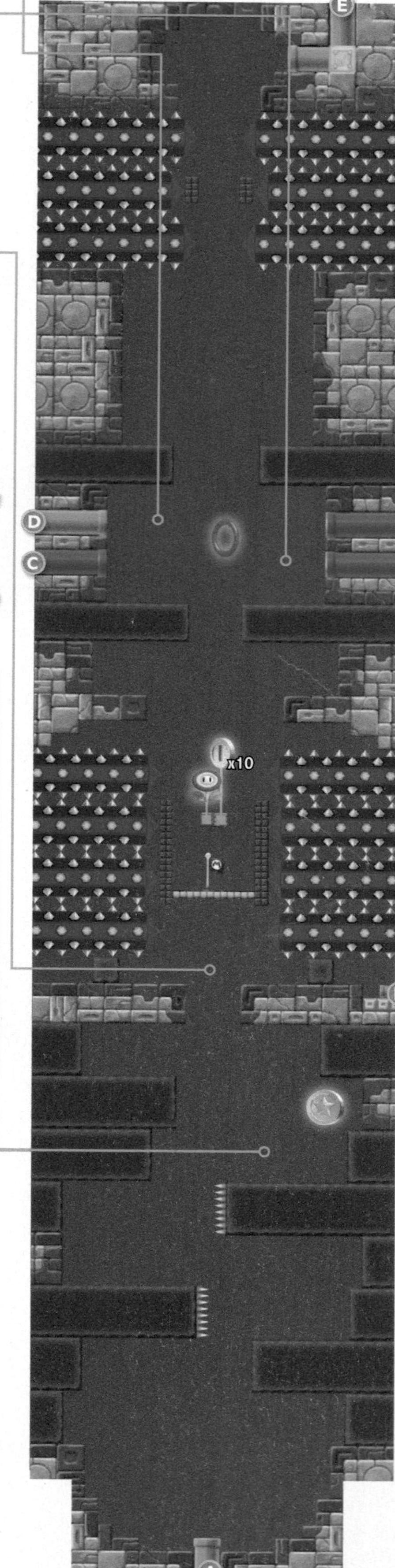

WORLD 3-TOWER

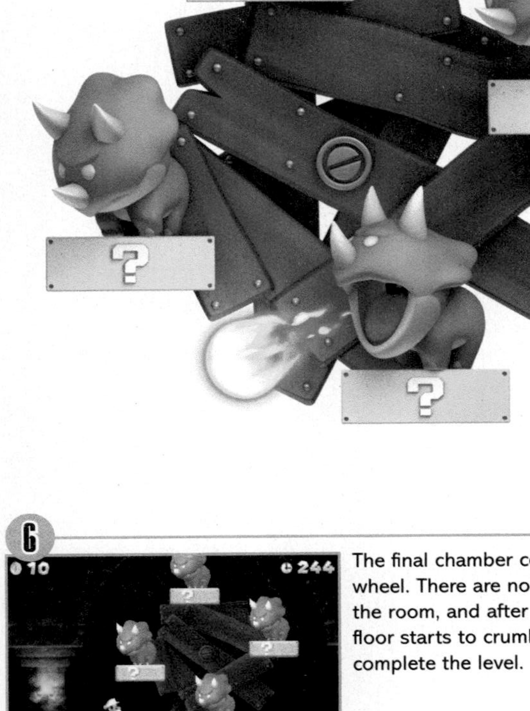

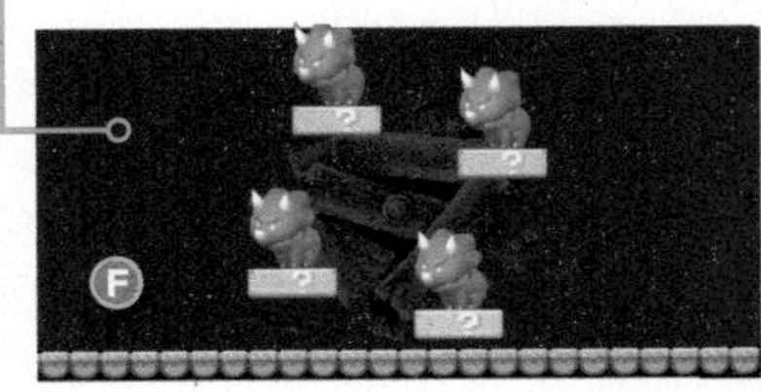

6

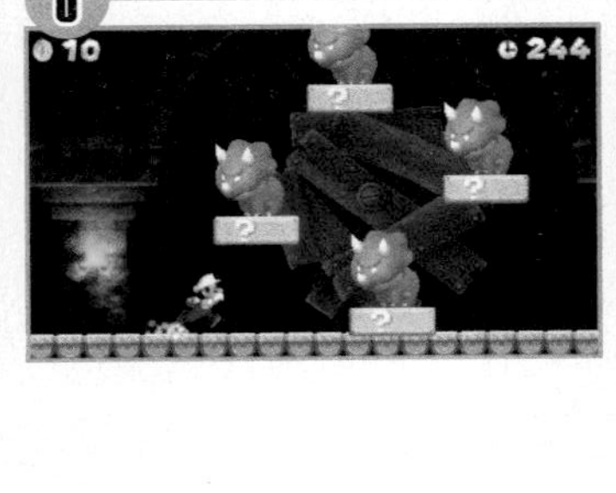

The final chamber contains four Reznors on a single wheel. There are no vacant ? Blocks when you enter the room, and after you defeat at two Reznors the floor starts to crumble. Clear out all four enemies to complete the level.

5

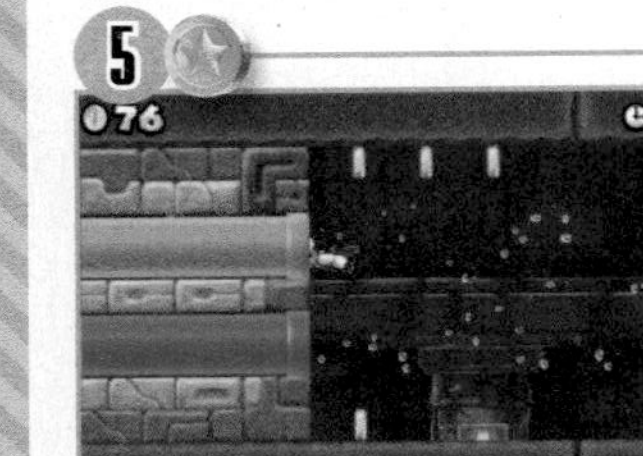

The third Star Coin is located in a hidden room. After you deal with the Red Ring, enter the green pipe to the left.

After you pass through the pipe, drop out of the water current and collect the Star Coin to the right.

NOTE

To unlock the path to World 3-B, you must find this level's secret exit.

CAUTION

The water in this level is toxic! As you move through the area, watch out for changing water levels and platforms that sink under Mario's weight.

1

As you play through this level, use the Wigglers to bounce up to otherwise unreachable objects.

2

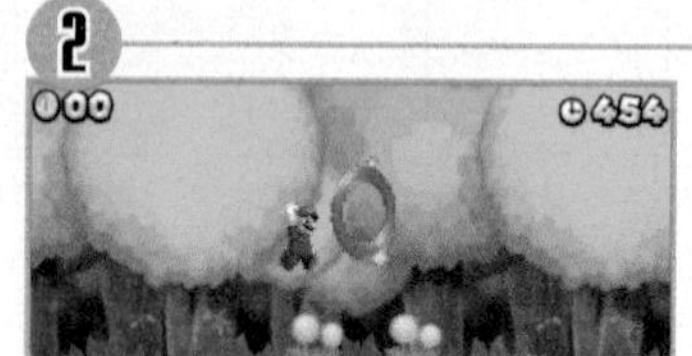

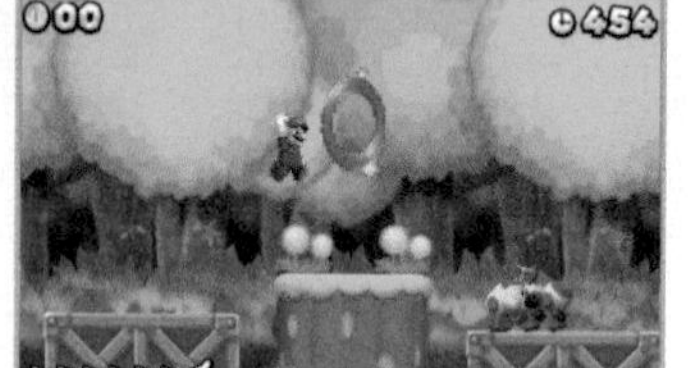

When you pass through the Red Ring at Point 2, the first four red coins appear on the crates to the left. Try to collect them before the remaining red coins parachute into the area.

3

The first Star Coin is floating above the Wiggler at Point 3. Hop onto the Wiggler and use a well-timed bounce to reach the Star Coin.

Just before the exit of this part of the level there is a ? Switch. Jump on the Wiggler to hit this switch to make it rain Coins from the Pipe above.

4

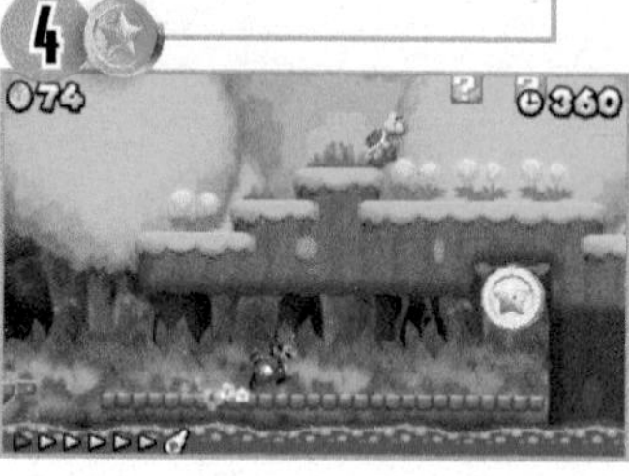

When you reach Point 4, wait for the water level to drop, then dash along the platform to grab the Star Coin. Move quickly to return to solid ground before the water rises back up.

5

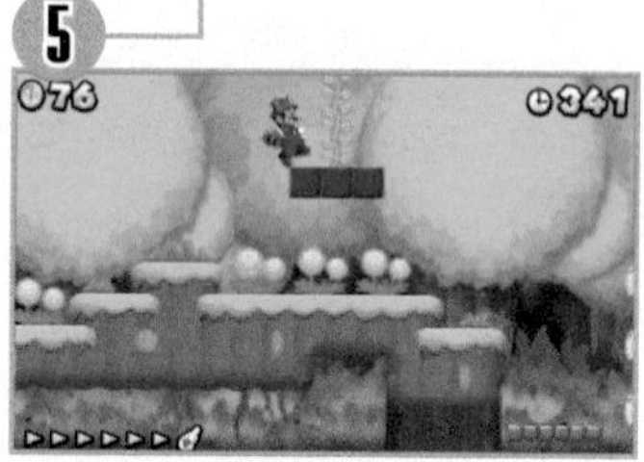

Hit the Invisible Block at Point 5 to reveal a Beanstalk. After it grows, climb up to find a hidden area with a Koopa, a Gold Ring, and plenty of space to bounce a Gold Shell!

WORLD 3-4

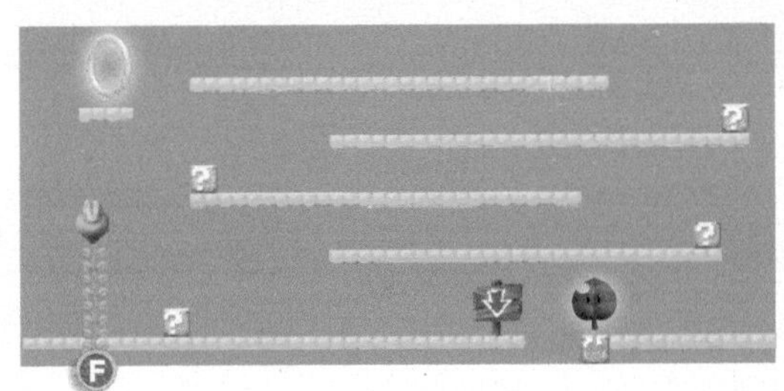

To collect the third Star Coin, stand on the crate until the water level begins to drop, then make a running leap toward the Star Coin. Perform a wall jump to gain a little extra height.

There's a shortcut located above Point 6. To use it, hop onto the small platform to the left of the Star Coin, then jump to the ledge above the Star Coin. A row of hidden coins is located up top.

To find the level's secret exit, stomp the Koopa at Point 7 and wait for the water level to drop. When it does, toss the shell into the Blocks to the right. Wait for the water to rise and drop one more time, then dash toward the remaining Block and slide through the gap. Follow the path through the pipe and touch the Goal Pole to unlock the path to World 3-B.

At Point 7 you can also just use a Raccoon tail whip to get rid of the Brick Blocks

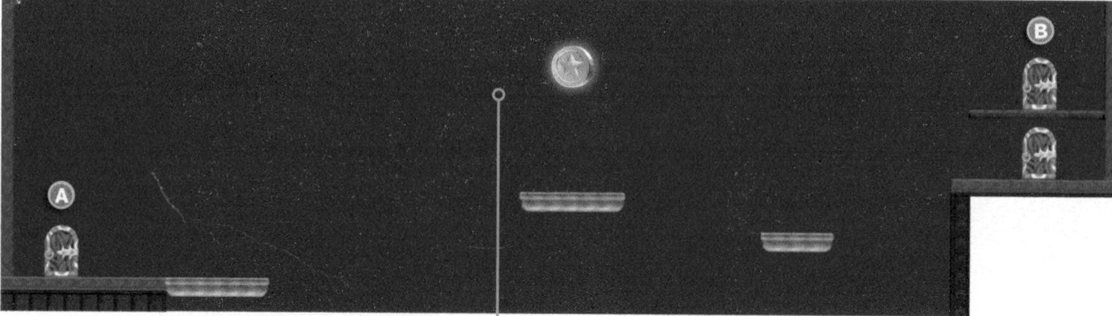

TIP

Locate this level's secret exit to unlock a shortcut to World 3-Castle!

CAUTION

This level contains several moving platforms. When the Peepas carrying a platform shake it back and forth, it means the mischievous ghosts are about to flip the platform or vanish completely, taking the platform with them!

2

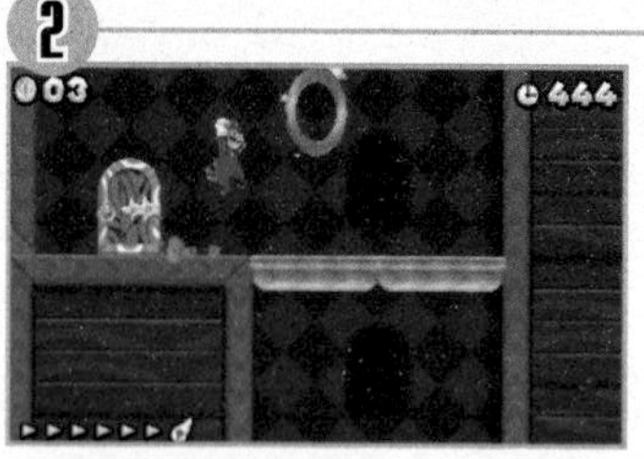

Jump through the Red Ring at Point 2 to reveal the red coins below you. Jump back and forth between the platforms as they move past each of the red coins.

1

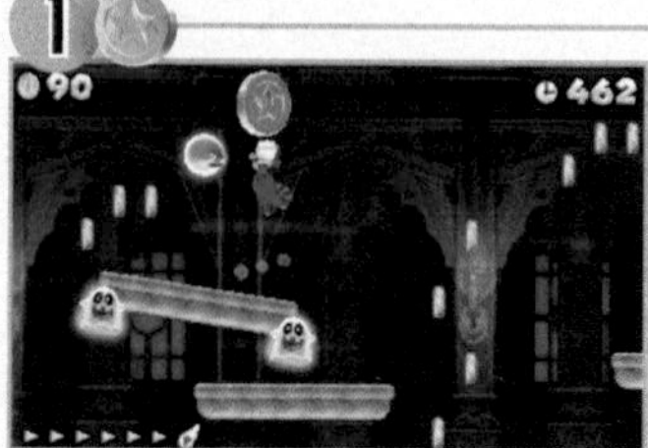

As you approach Point 1, turn your back to the Boo to draw it away from the Star Coin. When you have the Boo where you want it, face it to prevent it from moving. When the platform starts shaking, jump up to grab the Star Coin.

3

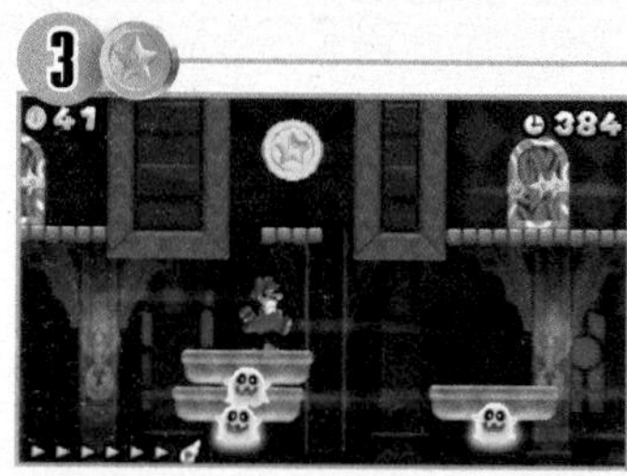

The second Star Coin is floating at Point 3. Hop on the platforms at the bottom of the room to ride up toward the ceiling, then leap up to grab the Star Coin.

4

There are three doors at the top of the room. To find the third Star Coin, enter the door near the right wall.

Jump on the platform and avoid the Boo as you ride around the room. When you reach the top of the room, jump up and grab the Star Coin.

WORLD 3-BOO HOUSE

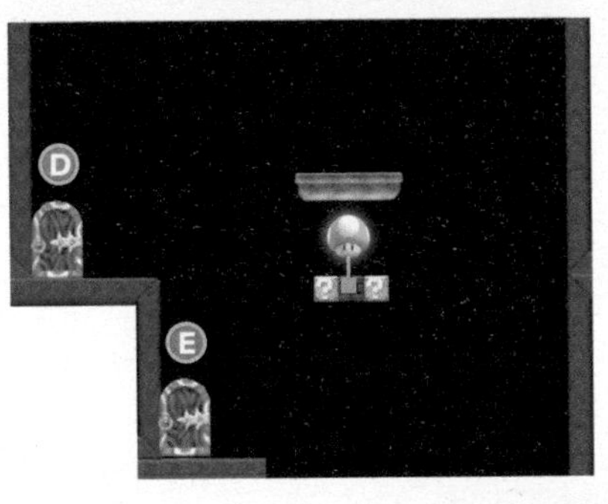

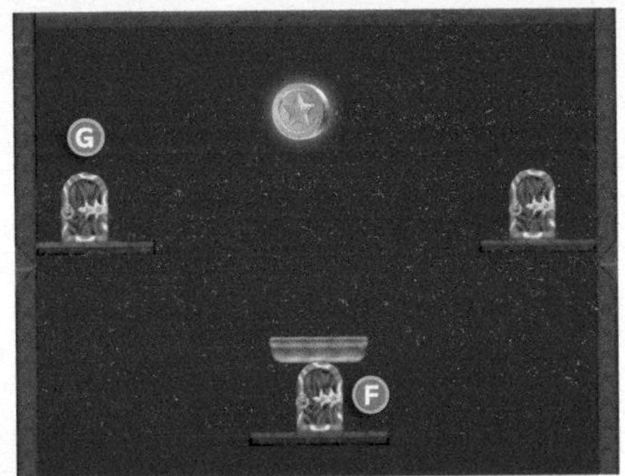

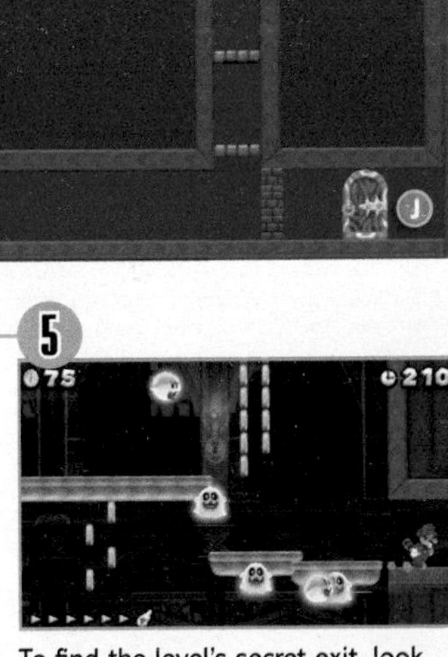

To find the level's secret exit, look for the passage at Point 5. Head through the opening to find a door behind some Blocks. If you have a Super Leaf, use Raccoon Mario to clear the Blocks from your path, then pass through the door. Grab the Goal Pole to reveal an alternate path to World 3-Castle.

At the top of this section the door is flanked by platforms on either side. Jump on these platforms to reveal hidden coins.

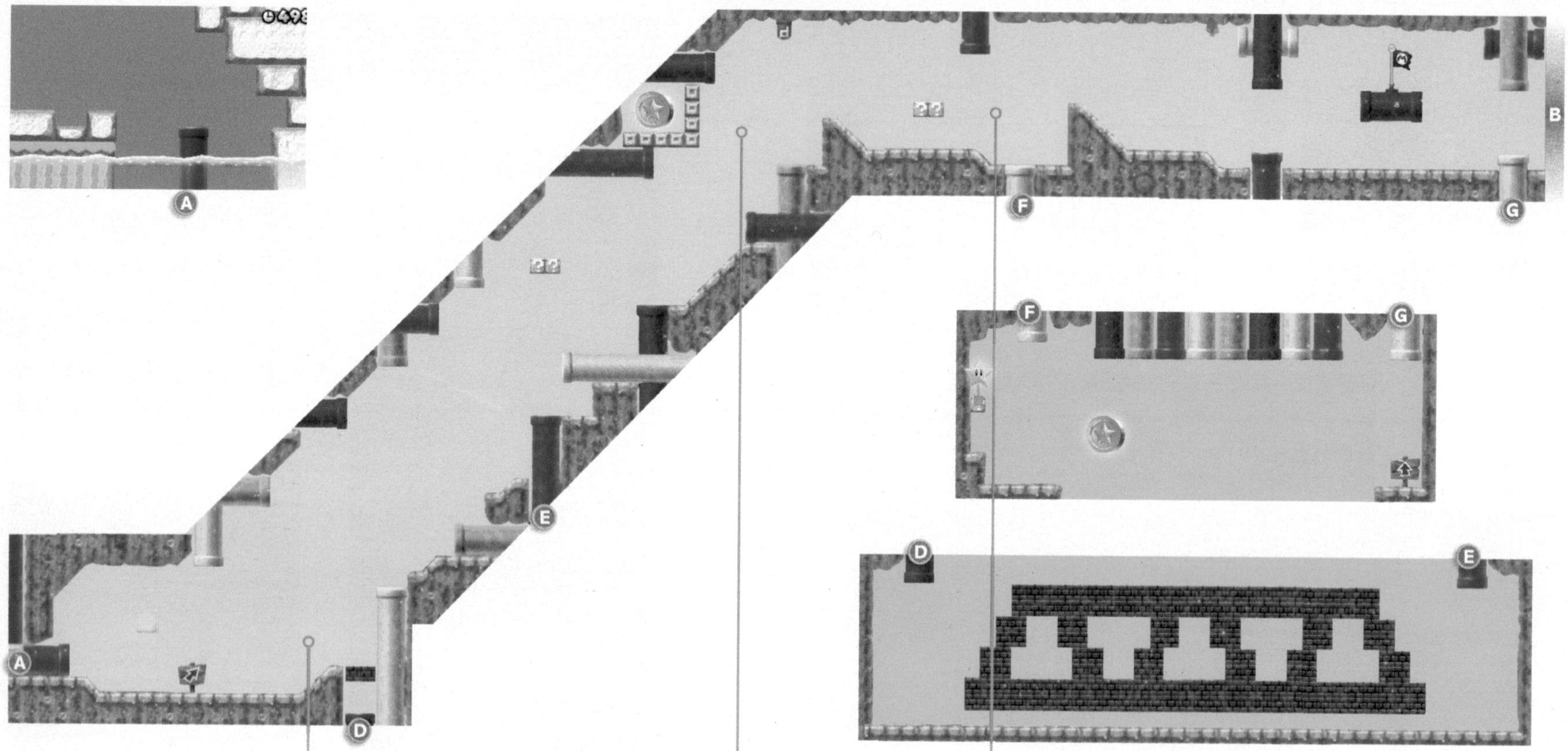

CAUTION

This level contains many unseen hazards. Watch out for Bloopers hidden in pipes, and be ready to dodge the boulders tumbling down the slopes!

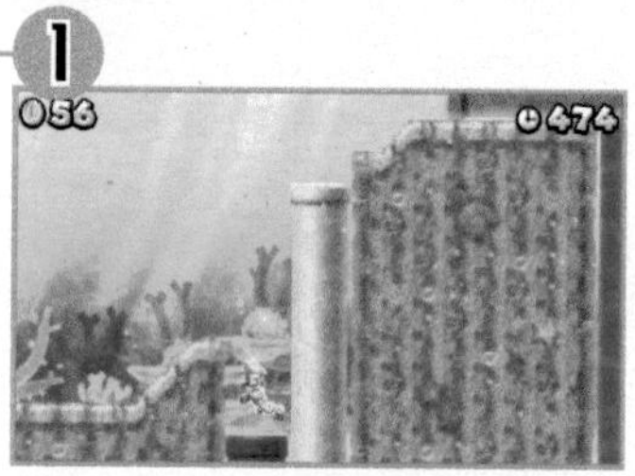

1

If you have a Gold Flower, use it to destroy the Blocks at Point 1. When the path is clear, enter the purple pipe to find a room filled with Blocks.

2

The first Star Coin is located at Point 2. Continue to the right until a boulder appears, then lead it back to the Star Coin. After the boulder destroys the enclosure, you're free to collect your prize.

3

The second Star Coin is located in a hidden area. Enter the yellow pipe at Point 3 to find it.

When you approach the Star Coin, it moves to the room's right wall. As you follow it, stay near the bottom of the area to avoid the Bloopers as they spring out of their pipes.

WORLD 3-5

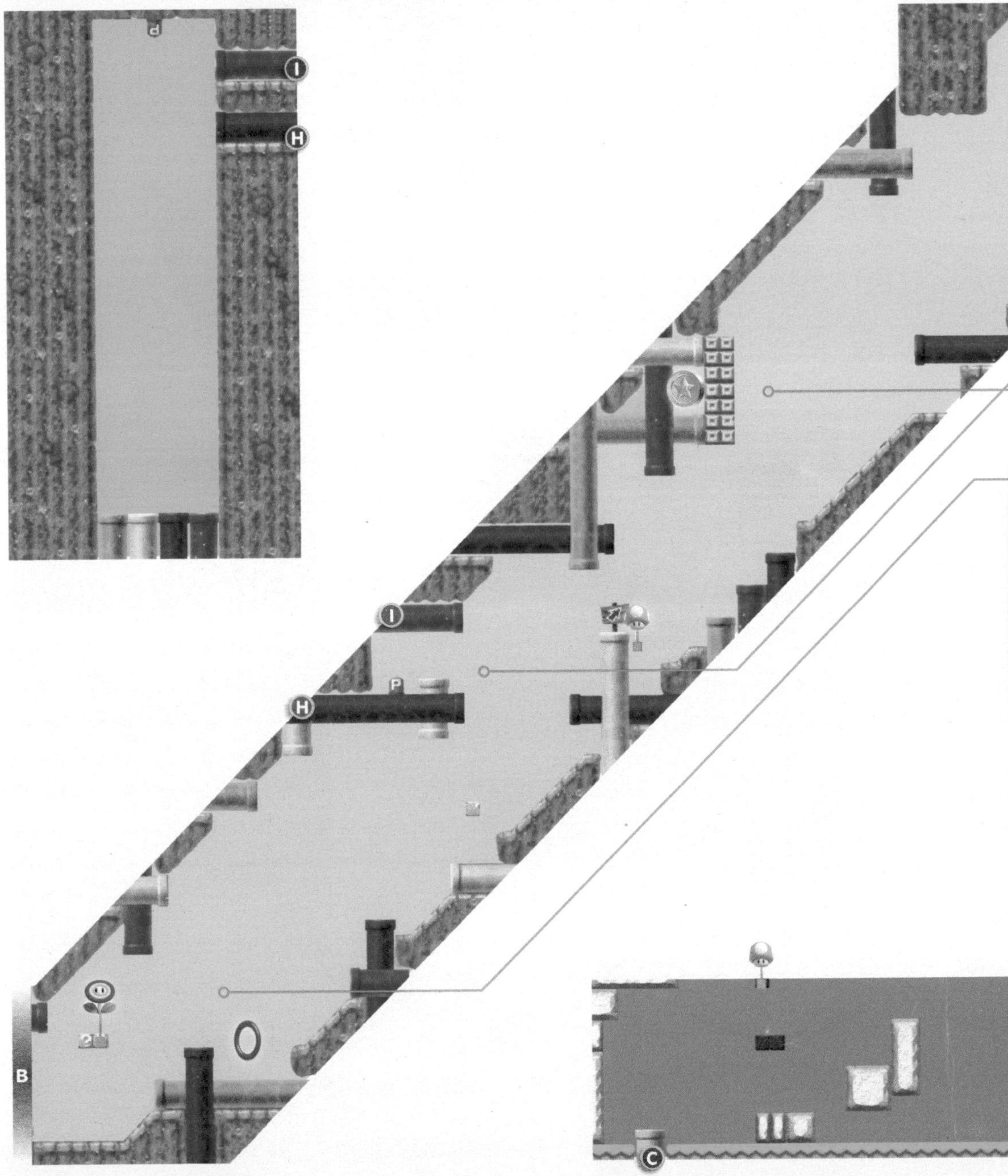

5

When you trigger the P Switch at Point 5, a trail of blue coins leads you into a nearby pipe. You can only enter the pipe while the P Switch is active, so move quickly!

4

If you've managed to hang on to a power-up, consider clearing the Bloopers out of the area before you pass through the Red Ring at Point 4. After you pass through the Red Ring, the red coins appear in two spinning clusters to the right.

6

The third Star Coin is located inside another enclosure. Swim near Point 6 until a large boulder tumbles toward you. When it does, take cover in the space below the pipe to the right. After the boulder destroys the enclosure, swim over and grab the Star Coin.

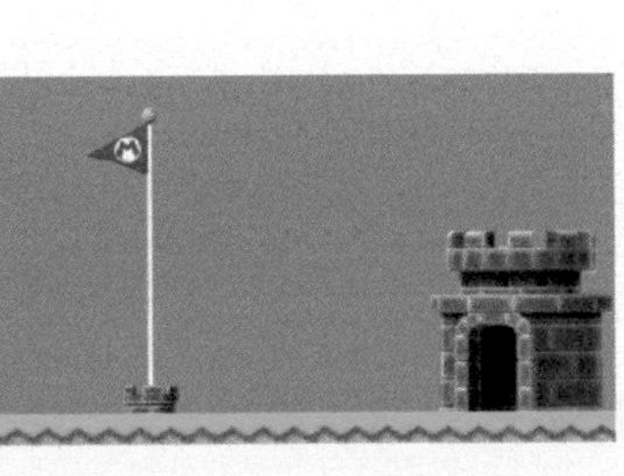

CAUTION

This level is filled with Grinders—circular saw blades that move along special tracks. Grinders tend to move in and out of sight, so stay alert when you're near one of their tracks.

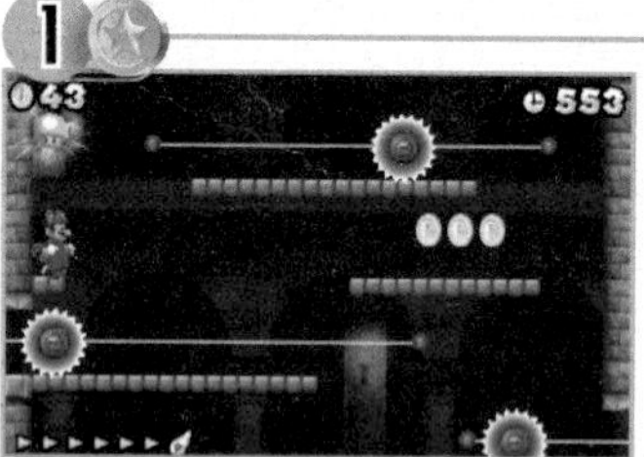

Hop onto the small platform at Point 1, then jump straight up to find an Invisible Block containing a 1-Up Mushroom.

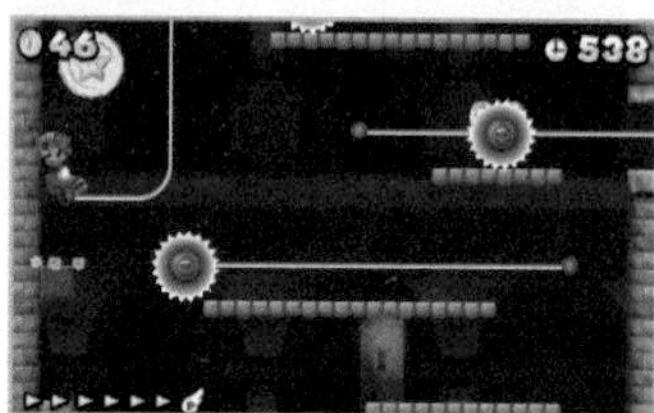

When the nearby Grinders move away from Point 1, hop onto the used Block and jump up to grab the Star Coin.

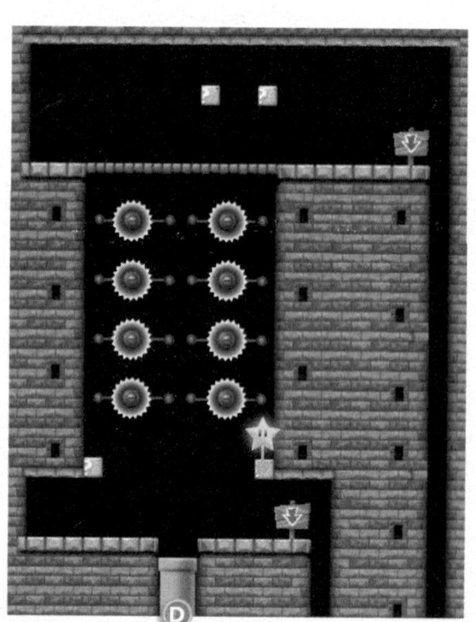

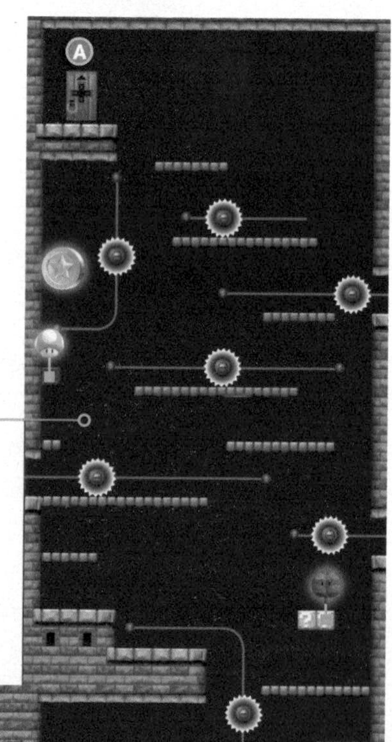

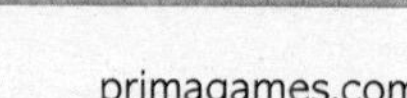

WORLD 3-A

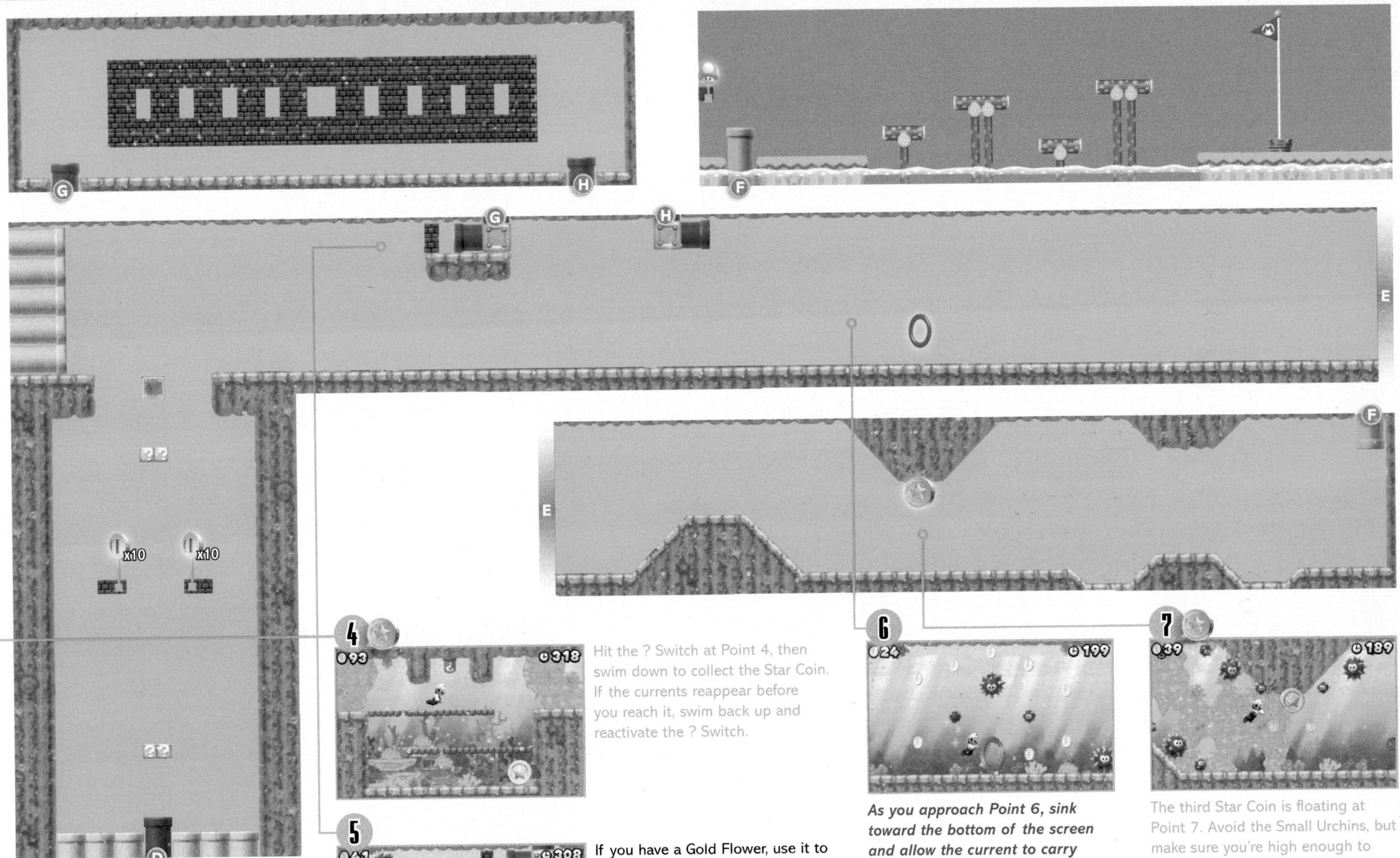

Hit the ? Switch at Point 4, then swim down to collect the Star Coin. If the currents reappear before you reach it, swim back up and reactivate the ? Switch.

If you have a Gold Flower, use it to clear the Blocks at Point 5. Enter the exposed pipe to find a hidden room filled with Blocks.

As you approach Point 6, sink toward the bottom of the screen and allow the current to carry you through the Red Ring. After it does, follow the trail of coins as it leads to the top of the screen and zigzags through the area. Doing this should keep you in position to collect all of the red coins.

The third Star Coin is floating at Point 7. Avoid the Small Urchins, but make sure you're high enough to collect the Star Coin as the current pushes you through the area.

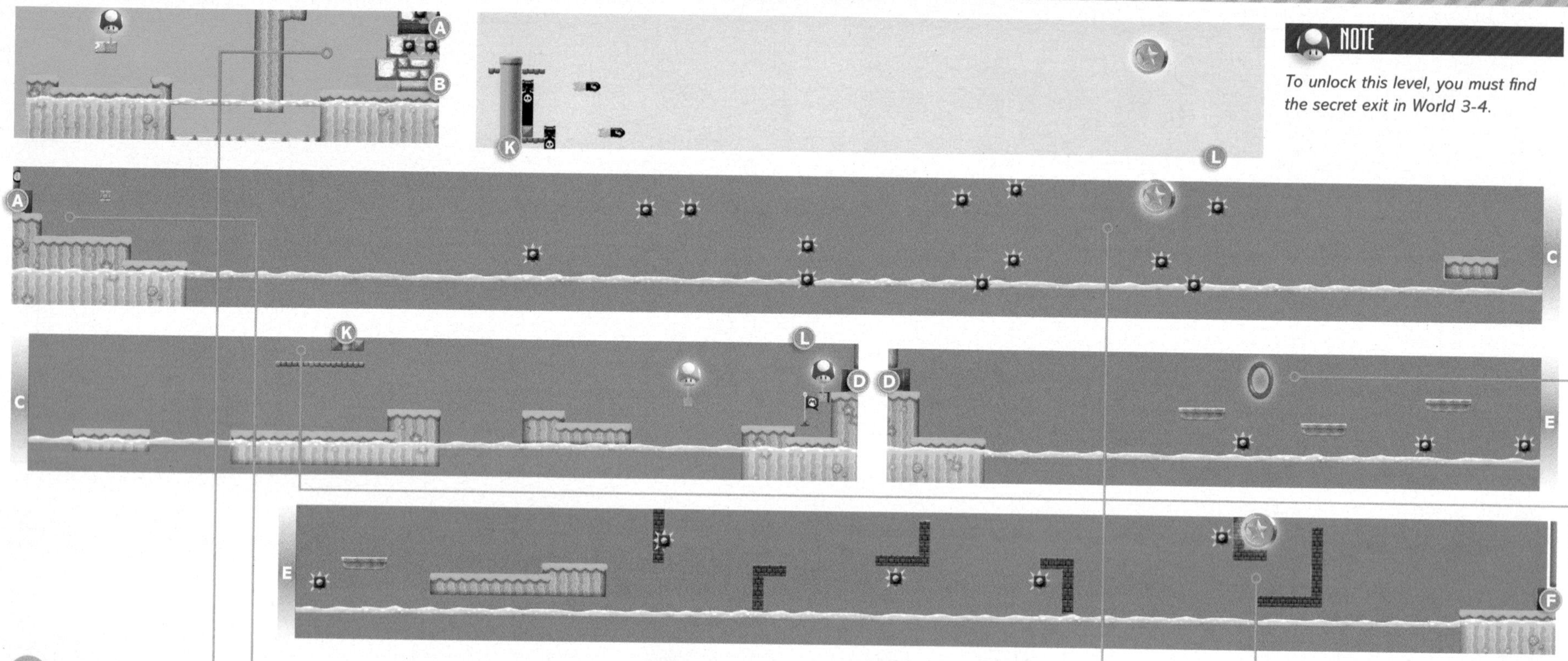

NOTE

To unlock this level, you must find the secret exit in World 3-4.

1

This level caters to the special abilities of Mini Mario. To reach the Goal Pole, you must pass through small pipes, run along the water's surface, and perform much bigger jumps than would otherwise be possible. Grab the Mini Mushroom from the ? Blocks at the start of the level, then head through the water and enter the small red pipe.

TIP

The red and yellow pipes lead to very similar areas, but the path through the red pipe contains all three of the level's Star Coins.

2

This level contains several Gold Blocks—make sure you hit each one you find. Aside from the coins generated by this temporary power-up, the Gold Block provides Mini Mario with some much-needed protection.

3

The first Star Coin is floating at Point 3. Jump onto the Koopa Paratroopa and bounce to the Star Coin.

WORLD 3-B

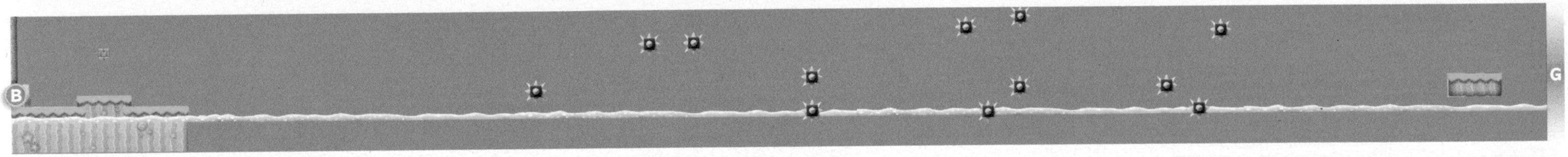

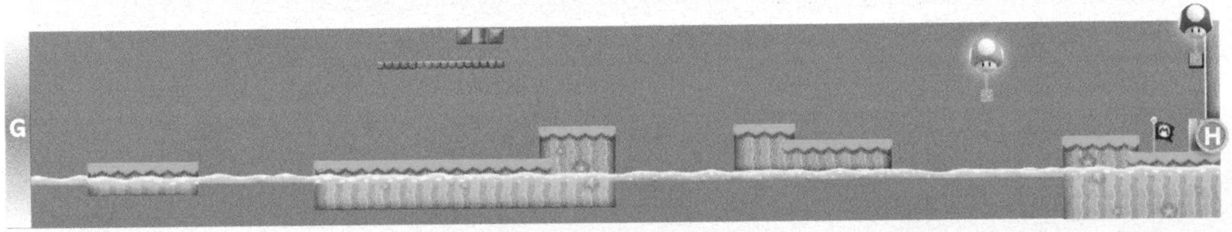

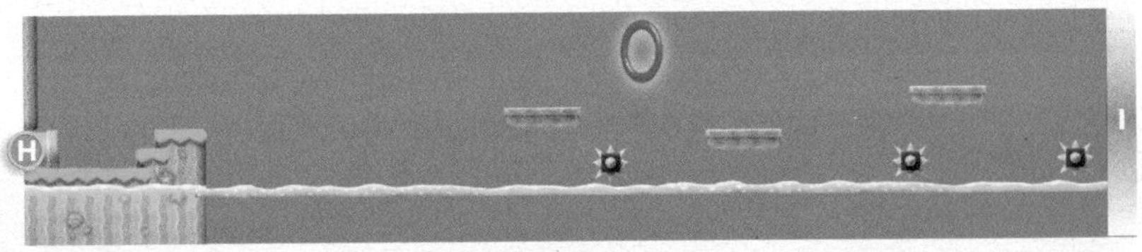

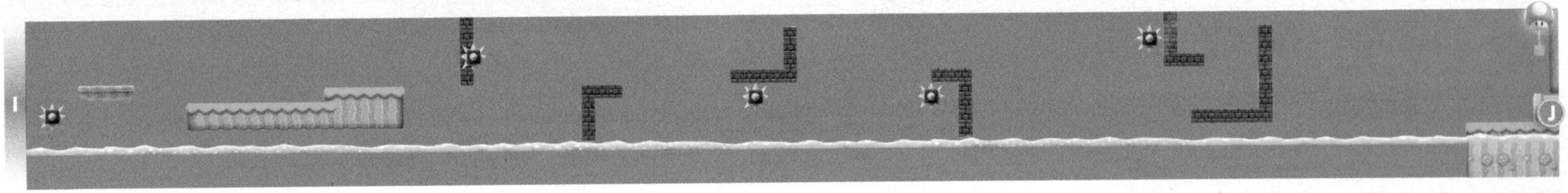

The second Star Coin is located in a hidden area. As you approach Point 4, jump onto the Koopa Paratroopa and bounce up to the platform. Enter the pipe at the top of the screen before it moves out of reach.

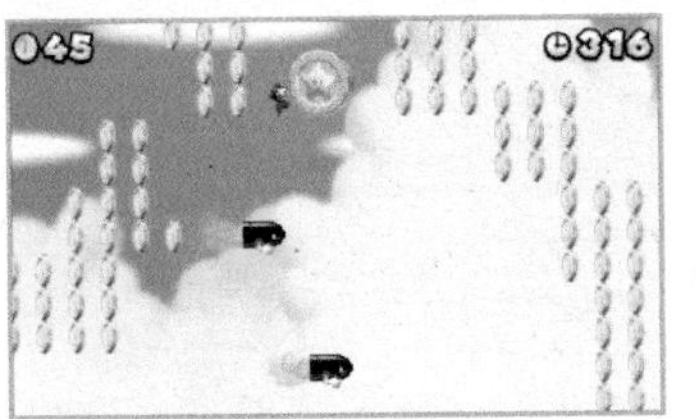

After you pass through the pipe, bounce on the Bullet Bills as they move through the area. Grab as many coins as you can, but make sure you're in position to collect the Star Coin near the end of the path.

Jump through the Red Ring at Point 5 to reveal the red coins to the right. To collect them, you must jump along the platforms and bounce off of one Koopa Paratroopa.

The third Star Coin is located at Point 6. Jump onto the nearby Blocks, then make a running leap to the Star Coin. Move quickly to make sure you reach it before it moves out of reach.

NOTE

The path through the yellow pipe is very similar to the path through the red pipe. It doesn't contain any Star Coins, but it's slightly shorter and it scrolls at a slower pace. It also contains a P Switch, which turns many of the obstacles into coins.

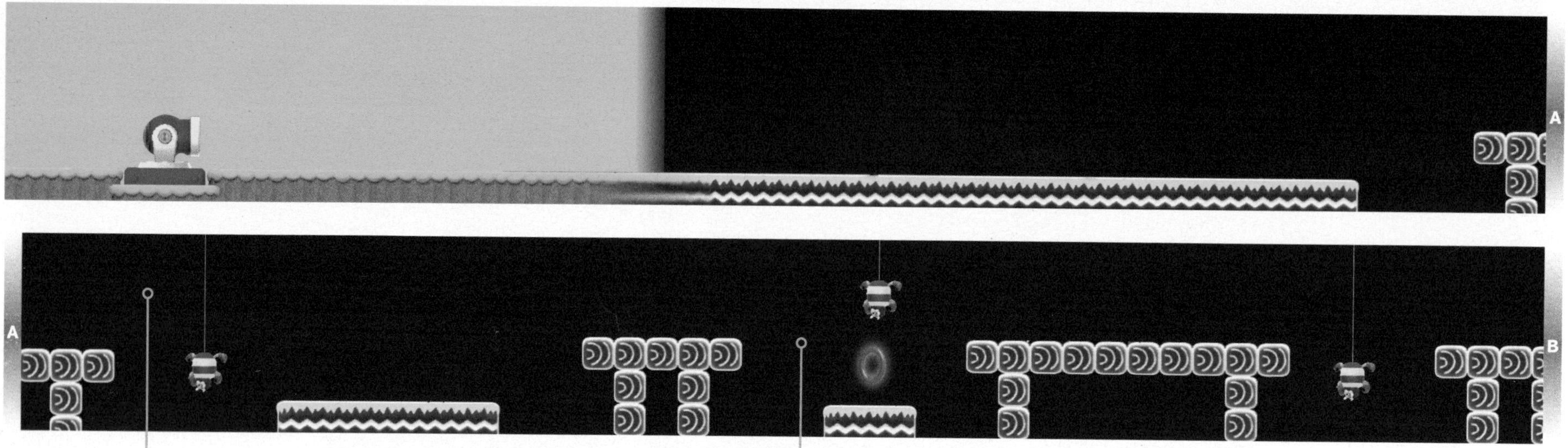

A

A

B

1

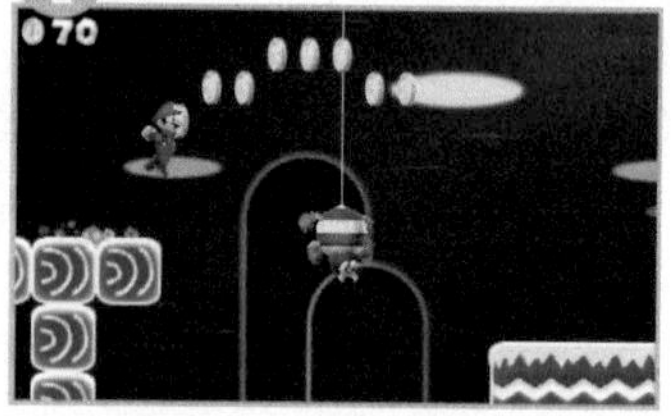

2

NOTE

To unlock this level, you must find the secret exit in World 3-Tower.

In this level, you must time your jumps to avoid (or utilize) Spiders and Wigglers. The coin trails indicate when you should jump, and how long each jump should be to ensure a safe landing. Do your best to follow them!

There's a Red Ring at Point 2. If you wish to activate it, ignore the coin trail and use a small hop to bounce off of the upcoming Wiggler.

After you pass through the Red Ring, the remaining coin trails change drastically. The course can be fairly difficult, but if you mange to collect all eight coins, you're rewarded with a Gold Flower.

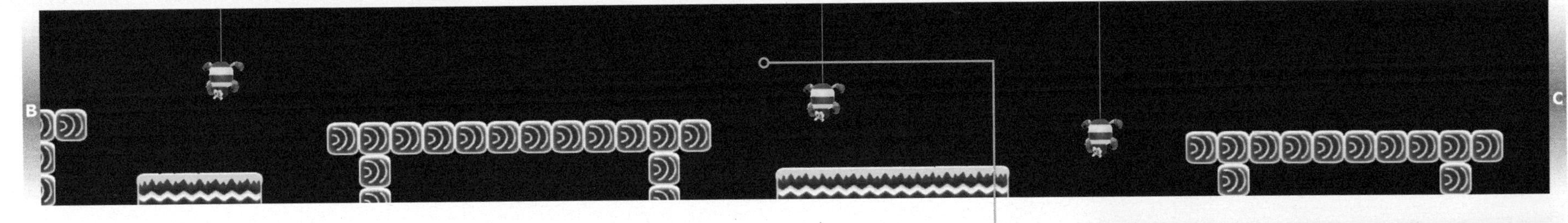

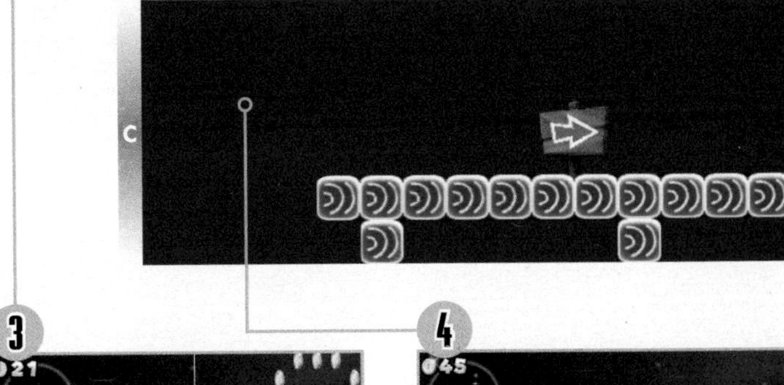

3

Each time a coin trail leads to an enemy, remember to look for the next coin trail. A longer, taller trail indicates that you must press the Jump button the moment you stomp the enemy. If you fail to do so, you're likely to wind up in a dangerous position.

4

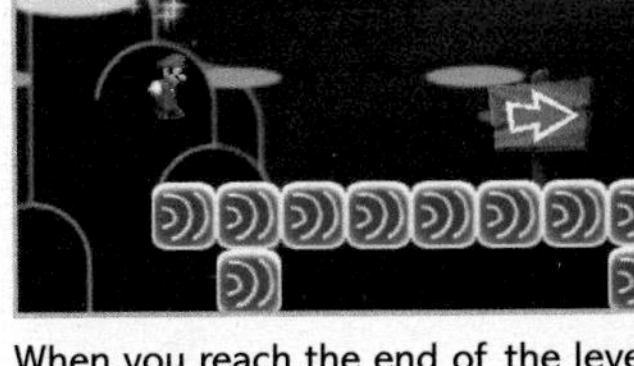

When you reach the end of the level, you gain access to Flower World!

WORLD FOUR

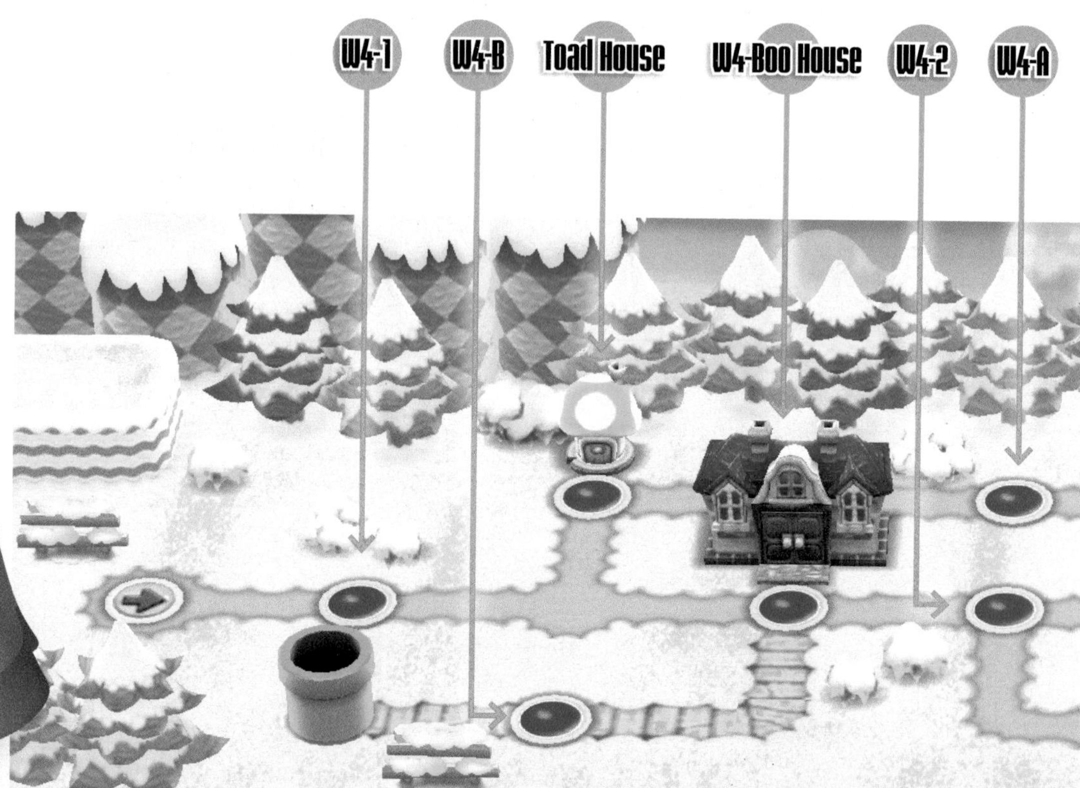

WORLD LOCATIONS				
Hostile Levels	Toad Houses	Boo Houses	Warp Cannons	Boss
11	5	1	0	Morton Koopa

Main Path Levels:

- World 4-1
- World 4-Boo House
- World 4-2
- World 4-Tower
- World 4-3
- World 4-4
- World 4-5
- World 4-Castle

Alternate Path Levels:

- World 4-A
- World 4-B
- World 4-C

Toad House

W4-Tower

Toad House

W4-3

Toad House

Toad House

W4-4

W4-5

W4-C

W4-Castle

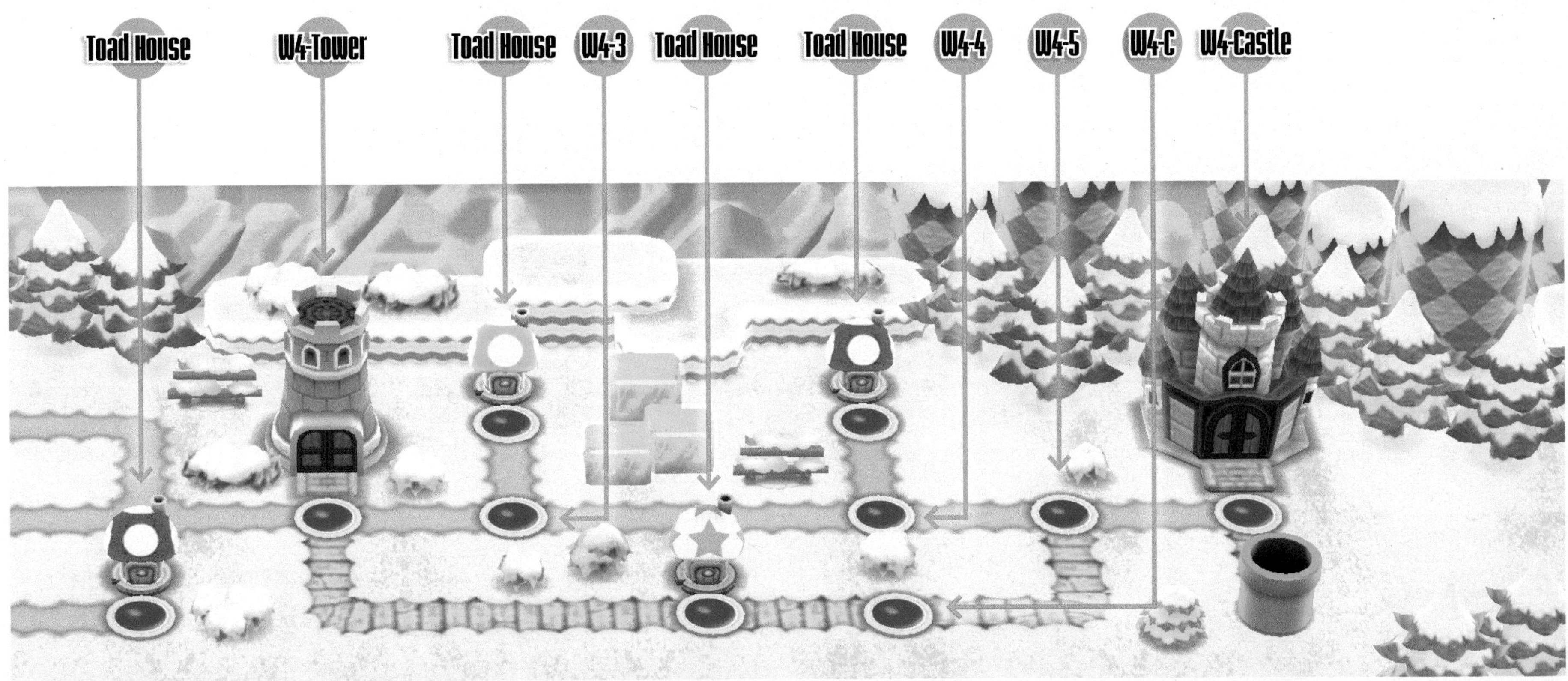

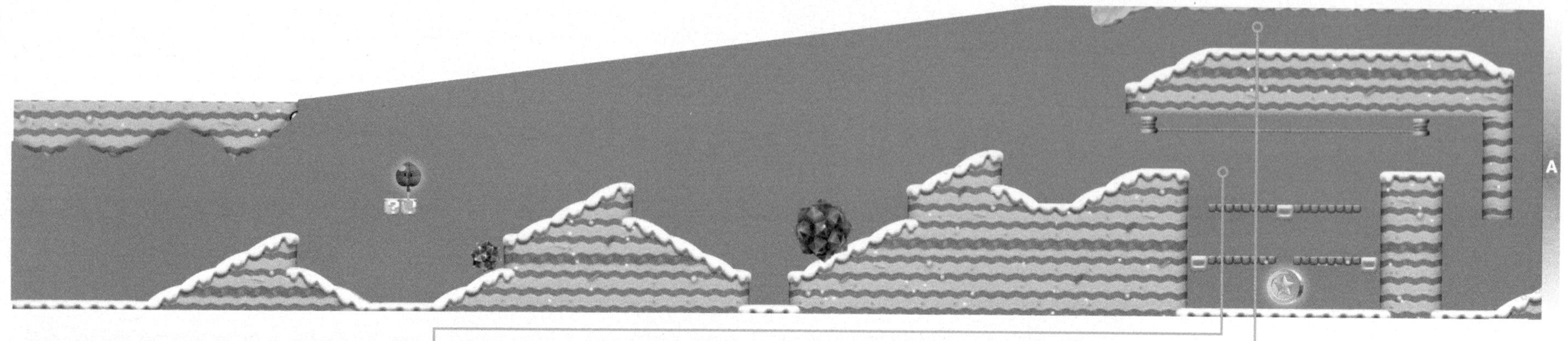

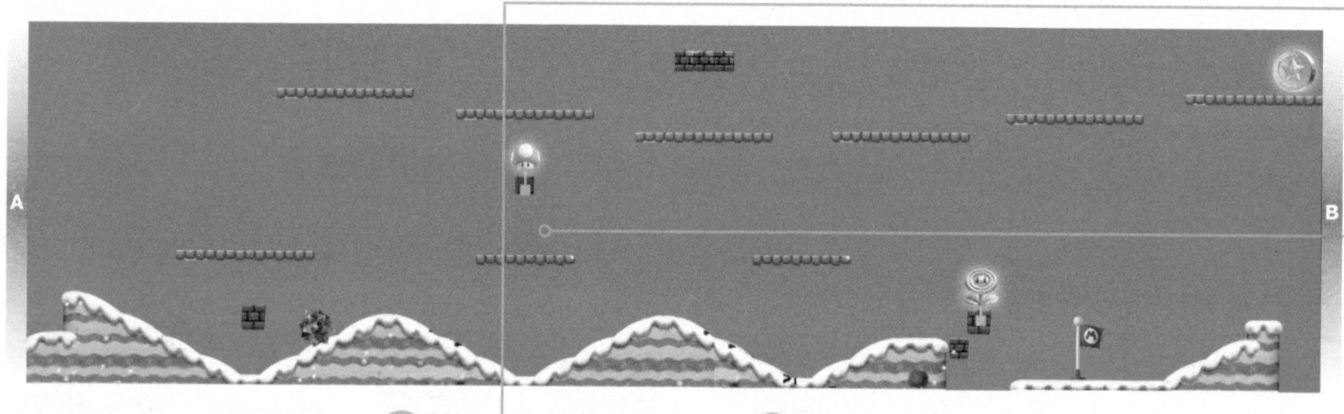

CAUTION

This level contains several Mini Goombas. When these pests climb onto Mario, they reduce his mobility. Before you attempt to hop over a rolling boulder or leap across a large gap, make sure you deal with any nearby Mini Goombas.

TIP

To deal with the Mini Goombas, do a Ground Pound attack to knock them off of you.

1

The first Star Coin is located beneath the boulders at Point 1. To collect it, drop down onto one of the Donut Blocks just as the boulders move away. If you time it properly, the Donut Block should drop down to the Star Coin before the boulders return.

2

To collect the second Star Coin, look for the hidden path at Point 2. Make a running leap up to the ledge, then dash through the coins to the right. If you're playing as Raccoon Mario, this should fill your Power Meter.

Fly to the right to find some platforms located high above the ground. Follow these platforms to find a Star Coin at the end of the path.

TIP

Search the Blocks on the way to the Star Coin to find a hidden P Switch.

3

There's a Gold Flower hidden in this level. To collect this valuable power-up, you must find it before the boulder rolling through the area destroys it! Stomp one of the nearby Koopas, grab its shell, and race along the platforms as the boulder rolls along the ground.

WORLD 4-1

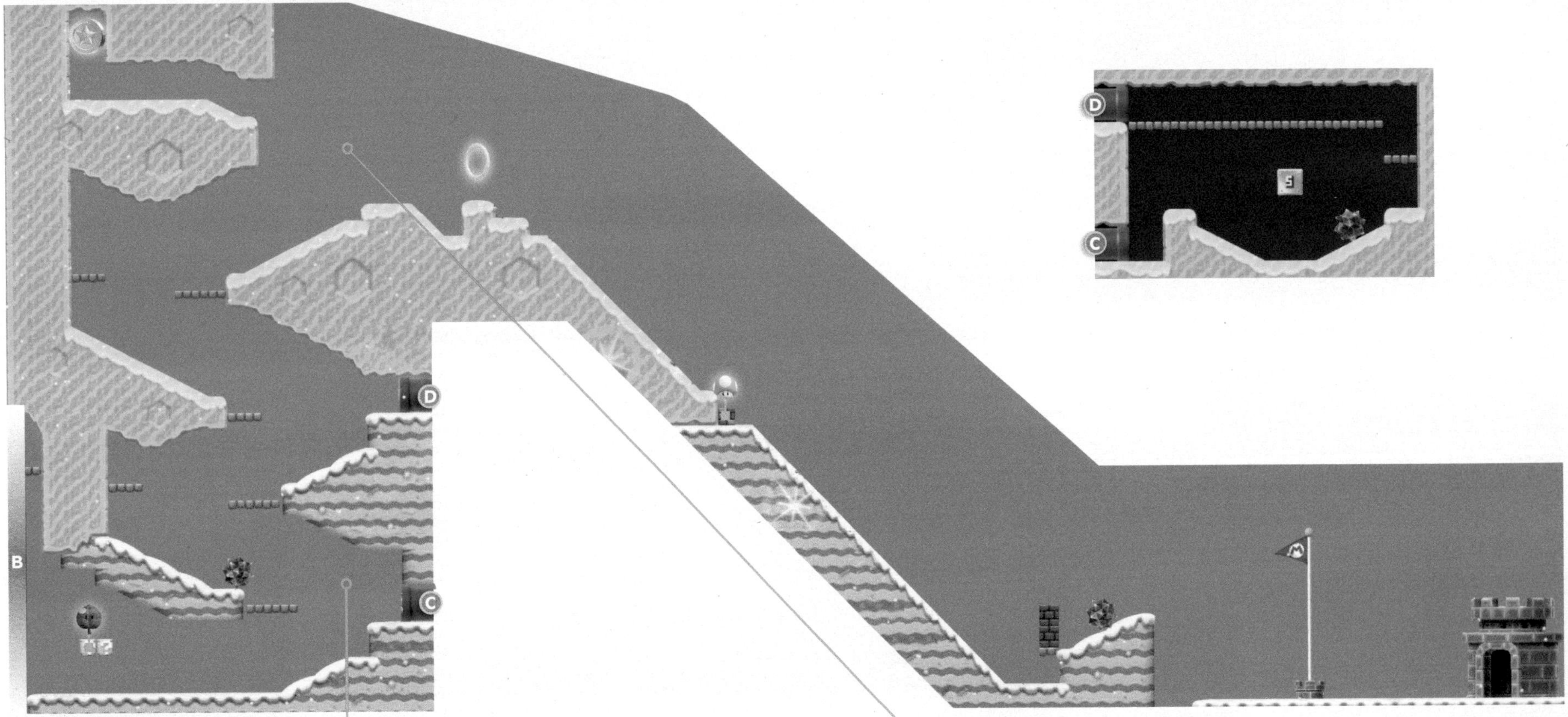

When you pull ahead of the boulder, throw the shell to the right and follow it. When the shell hits the Block near the Checkpoint Flag, jump down and grab the Gold Flower.

TIP

If you collect the Gold Flower, you can use gold fireballs to destroy the boulders in this level!

4

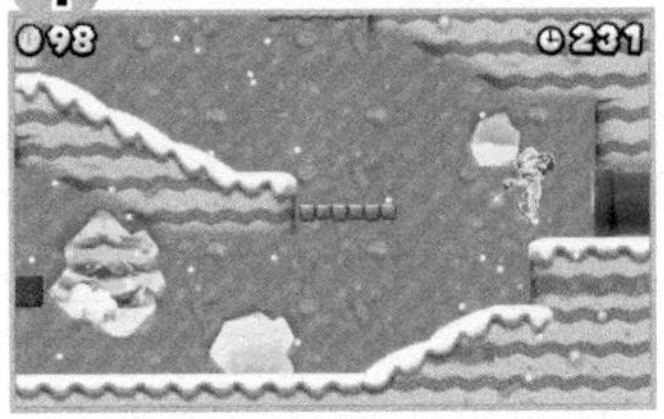

Enter the pipe at Point 4 to find a hidden room containing a Roulette Coin Block.

5

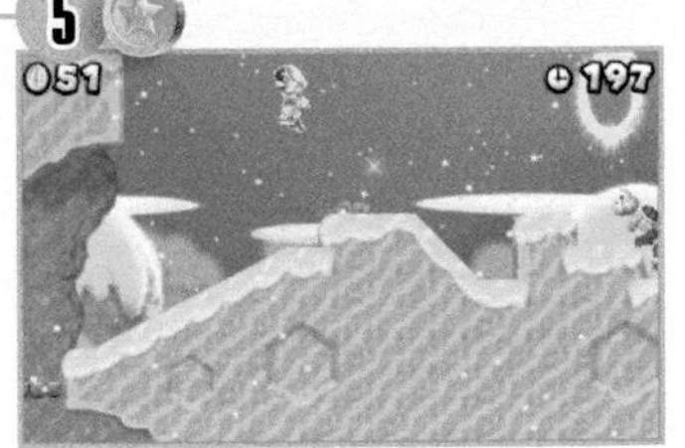

The third Star Coin is hidden near Point 5. When you spot the Gold Ring, turn back and make a running leap to the ledge in the upper-left corner of your screen.

After you land, move left to find the Star Coin floating at the end of the path.

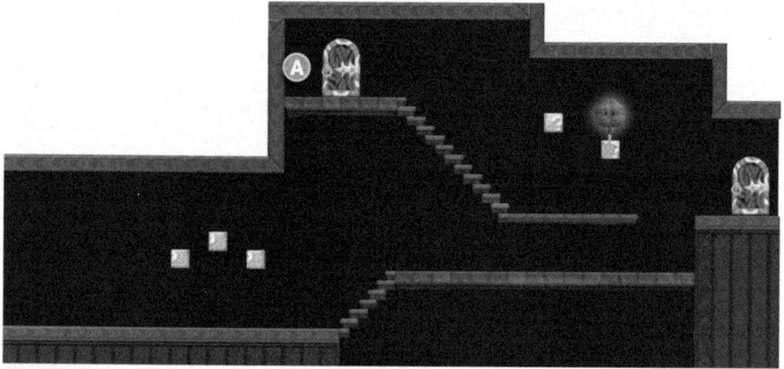

TIP

Stand on the triggered platform to make it easier to get the First Star Coin.

NOTE

Using the secret exit prevents you from collecting the level's remaining Star Coins, but it unlocks the path to World 4-B.

When you reach Point 3, draw the Boo up toward the Red Ring. Just before the enemy reaches you, jump up to trigger the Red Ring, then collect each of the red coins as they appear.

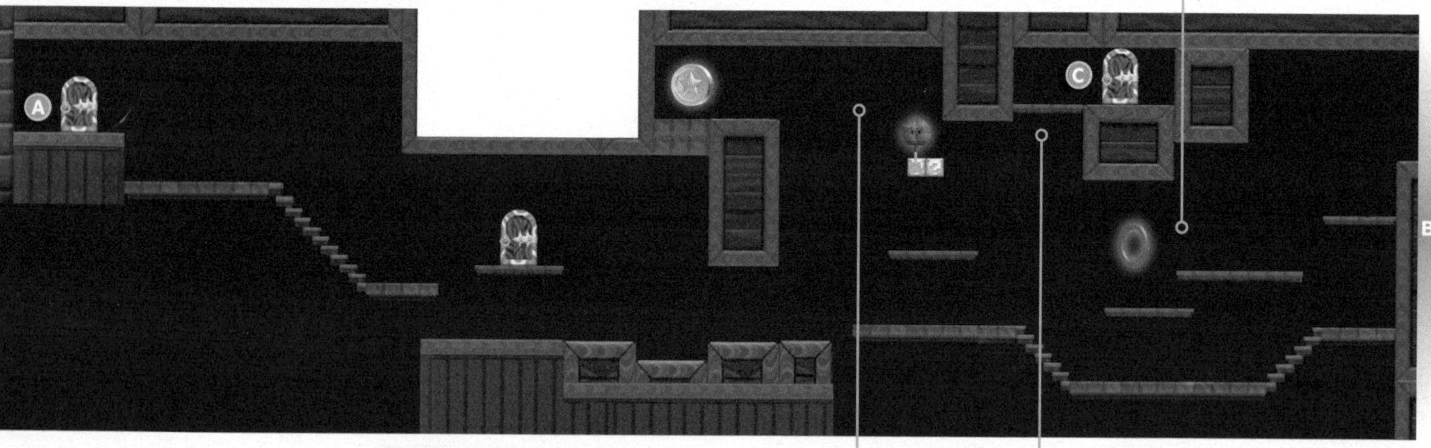

When you reach the ? Blocks near Point 4, wall jump up toward the ceiling to find the second Star Coin. Grab the Star Coin and drop to floor before you're pinned against the platforms to the right.

NOTE

To unlock the path to World 4-B, you must locate this level's secret exit.

CAUTION

As you play through this level, you spend most of your time trapped between two moving walls. These walls not only determine the speed at which you can move through the area, they can crush you against obstacles in the environment!

Soon after you reach the ? Blocks at Point 1, the moving walls slow down. Stand on the Blocks and look for the ledge near the upper-left corner of your screen—the first Star Coin is located on that platform.

When the walls move back to the left, wall jump up to the ledge and grab the Star Coin. As you do, the platform below you vanishes. Drop to the floor and avoid the nearby Boo until the walls force you out of the area.

To reach the secret exit, you must leave through the door at Point 2. As you approach this area, wall jump up to the ledge.

WORLD 4-BOO HOUSE

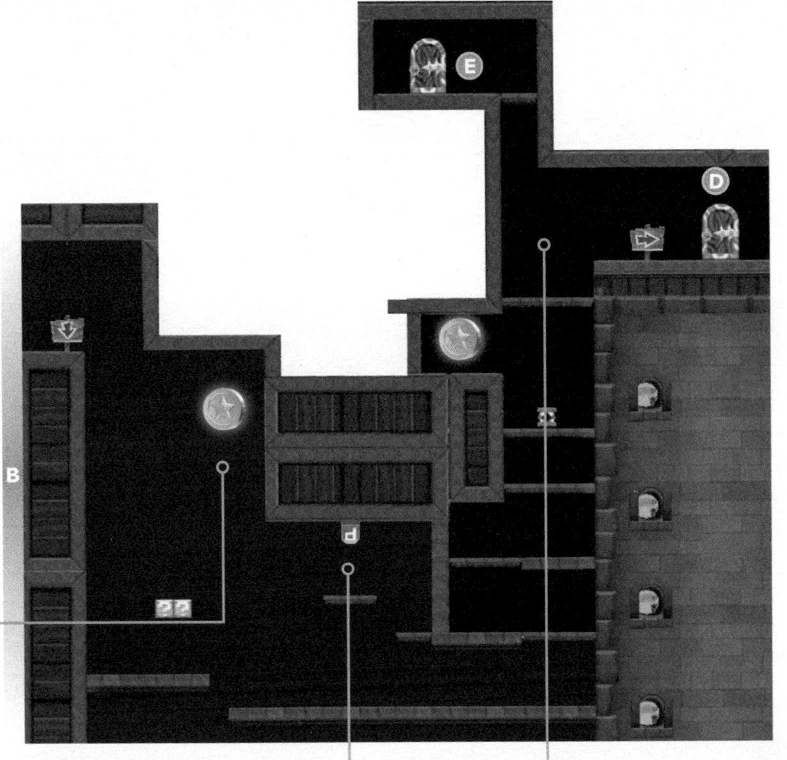

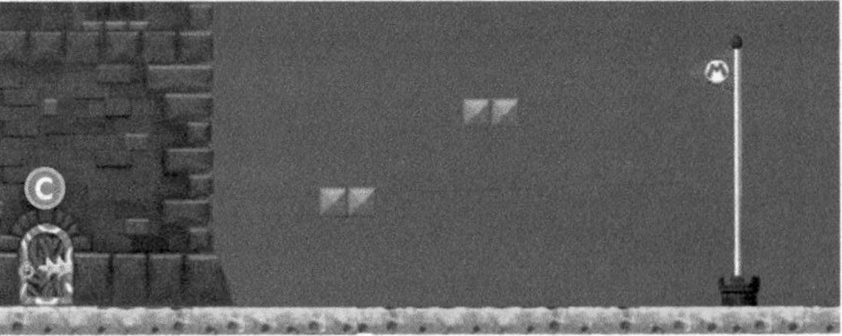

5

To collect the third Star Coin, you must move very quickly. After you hit the P Switch at Point 5, follow the blue coins as they lead you to the right and up a series of platforms.

Rather than collecting every blue coin, focus on climbing the platforms. As you approach the end of the trail, a Springboard drops down from the ceiling. Jump to the ledge on your left, then dash to the Star Coin before it disappears behind the wall.

6

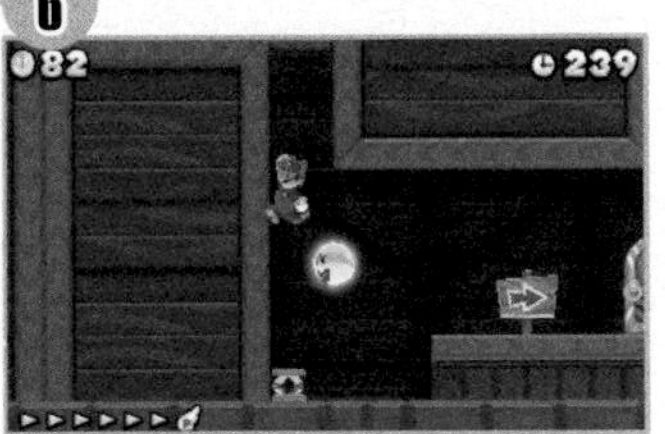

If you managed to catch the Springboard when it fell, use it to reach a hidden room near Point 6. Bounce up to the gap in the ceiling, then wall jump up to find another door. Soon after you enter the secret room, the walls begin closing in. Grab as many coins as you can, but make sure you climb to safety before you're crushed!

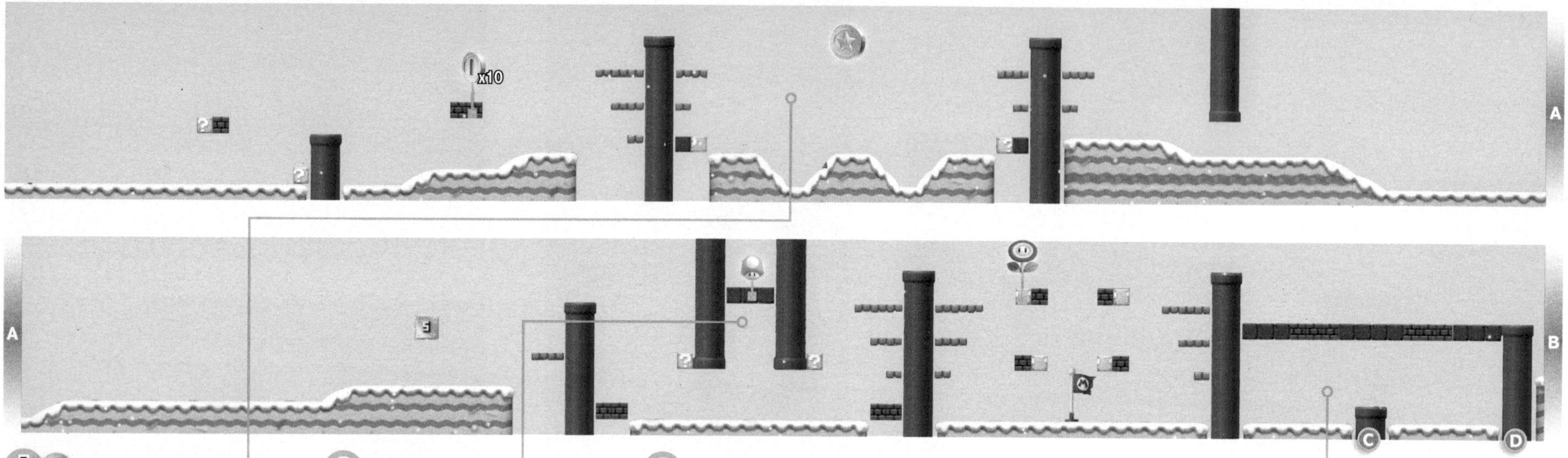

1

The first Star Coin is floating at Point 1. Stomp one of the nearby Koopas and bounce up to collect it.

2

There's a row of three Invisible Blocks located between the pipes at Point 2. Wall jump up to the Invisible Block in the center of the row to find a 1-Up Mushroom. Allow the 1-Up Mushroom to drop to the ground before you reveal the remaining Invisible Blocks.

3

The pipe at Point 3 leads to a hidden room. Drop down to the pipe, collect the coins from the Invisible Blocks above you, then enter the pipe to find the hidden room.

WORLD 4-2

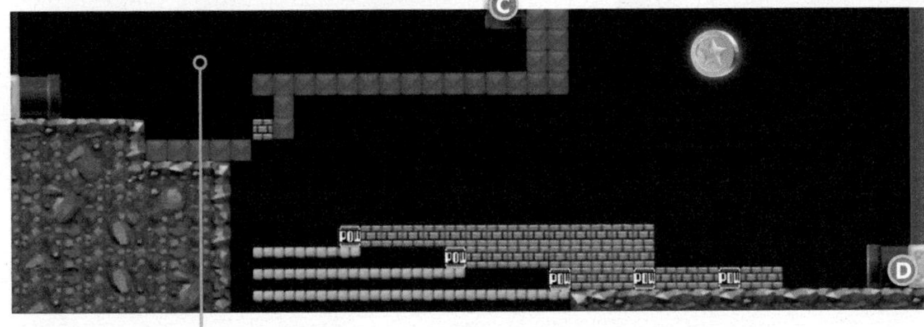

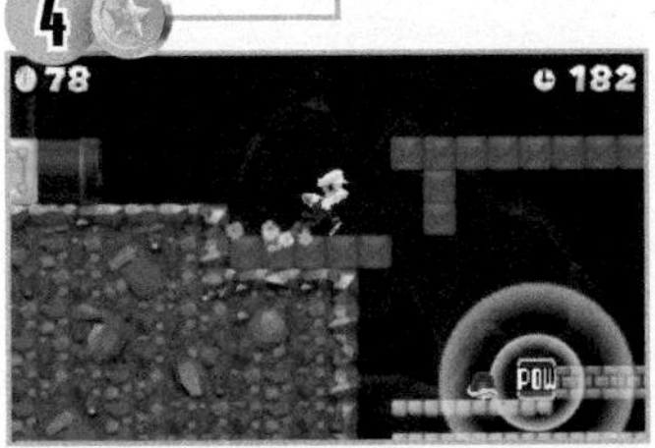

After you pass through the pipe, stomp the Buzzy Beetle and throw its shell into the Block at the top of the room. When the shell drops down to the first POW Block, follow it through the gap.

Dash along the Blocks to the right before the shell destroys them. As you approach the last group of Blocks, make a running leap up to the Star Coin.

The third Star Coin is located below the platforms at Point 5. Stomp the nearby Koopa and throw its shell at the Star Coin to collect it.

4

The second lift takes you past two ! Pipes. The first ! Pipe contains three 1-Up Mushrooms, but the ! Pipe at Point 4 contains a Super Star. The lift is about to pick up several enemies, so try to grab this power-up before it's too late!

NOTE

If you're fast enough you can collect all three of the 1-UP's and the Star power-up.

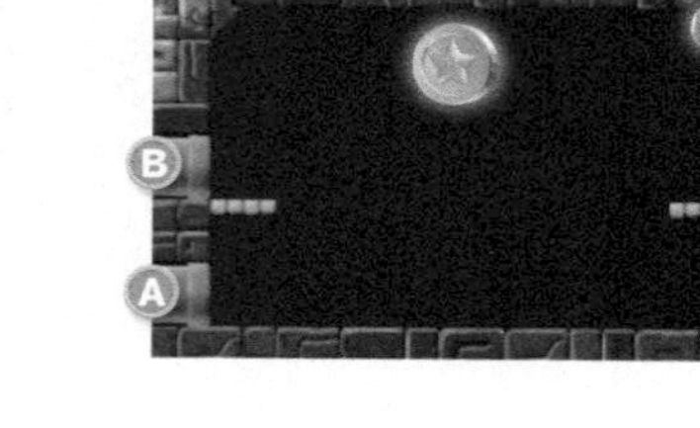

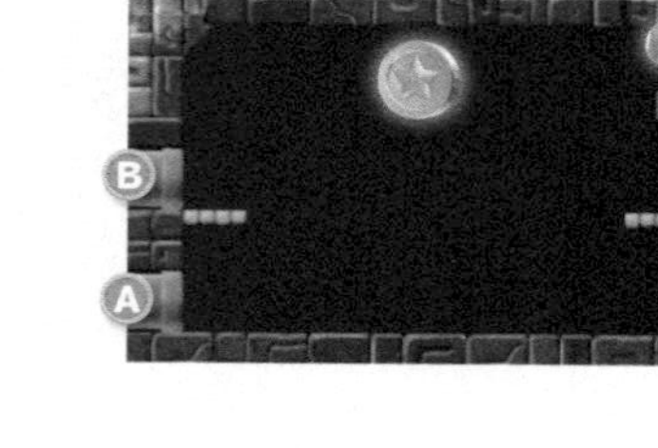

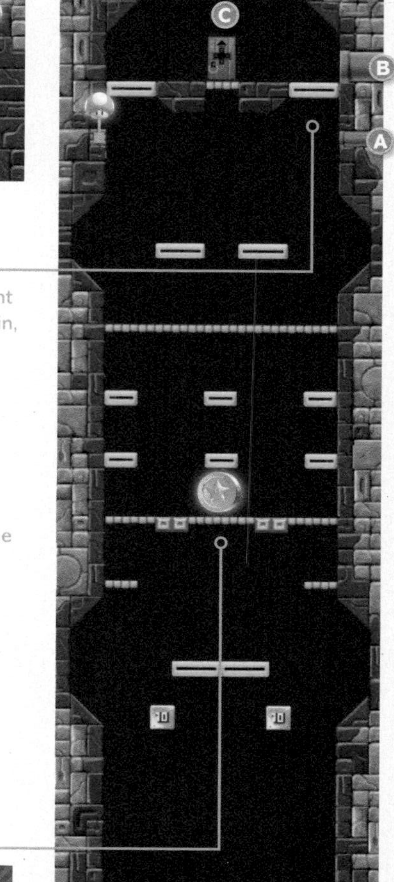

3

The second Star Coin is located through the small pipe at Point 3. Only Mini Mario can enter this pipe—to collect this Star Coin, you must bring a Mini Mushroom into the level.

After you pass through the pipe, make a running leap up to the Star Coin.

2

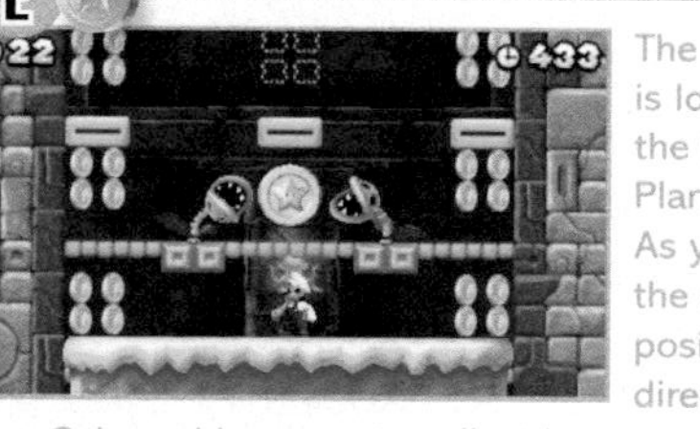

The first Star Coin is located between the Bone Piranha Plants at Point 2. As you approach the enemies, position yourself directly under the Star Coin and jump up to collect it.

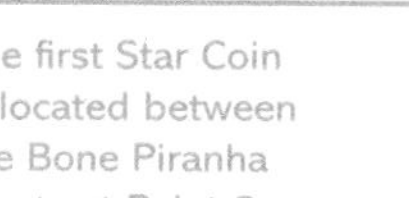

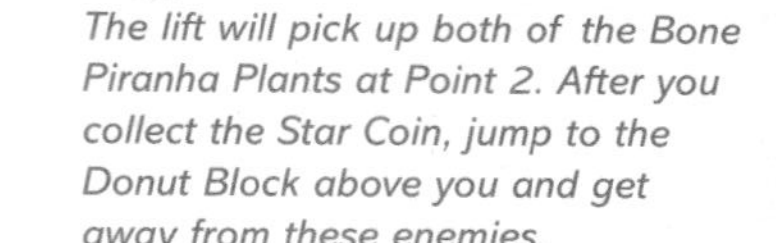

CAUTION

The lift will pick up both of the Bone Piranha Plants at Point 2. After you collect the Star Coin, jump to the Donut Block above you and get away from these enemies.

1

To traverse this level, you must ride the icy lifts contained in each half of the Tower. As one of these lifts moves through an area, it picks up some unwanted passengers. Stomp the Bone Goombas as they appear, and use Buzzy Beetle shells to defeat any Bone Piranha Plants that make it onto the lifts.

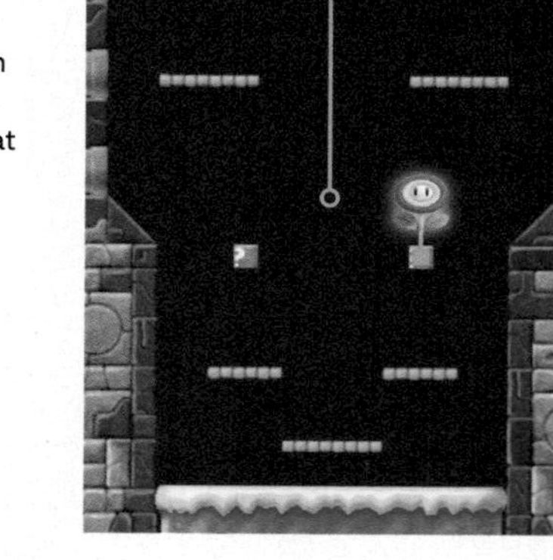

NOTE

To unlock the path to World 4-C, you must find this level's secret exit.

WORLD 4-TOWER

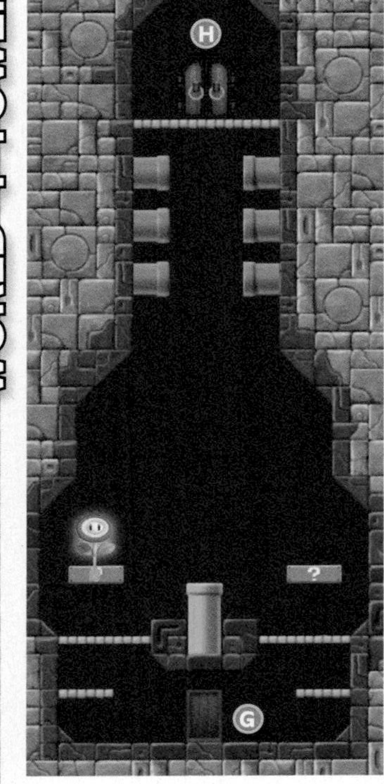

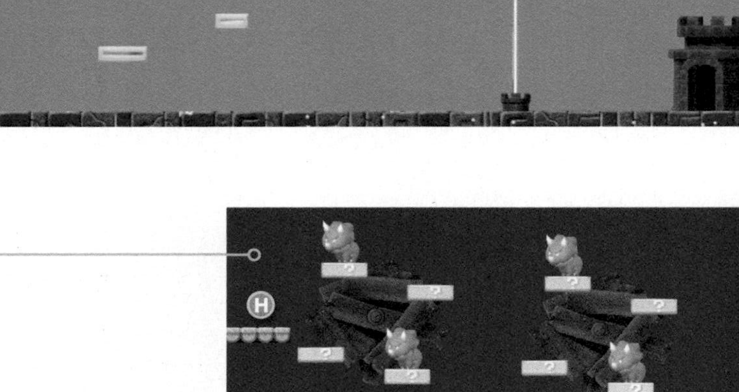

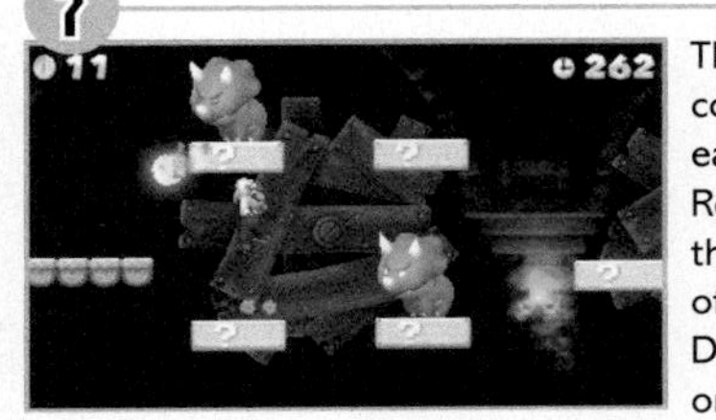

7

The final chamber contains two wheels, each of which holds two Reznors. After you enter the room, jump on one of the vacant ? Blocks. Deal with the Reznors on the first wheel, then jump across to the second wheel and repeat the process.

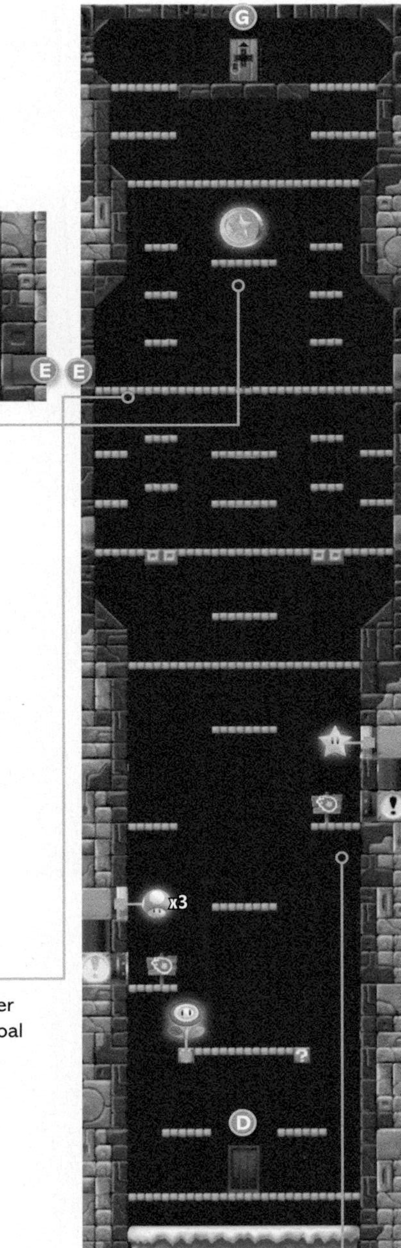

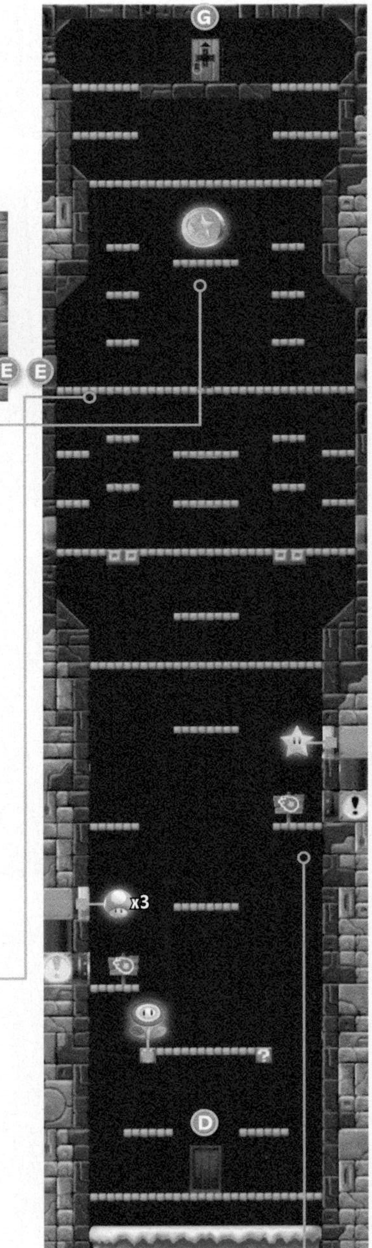

6

The third Star Coin is located at Point 6. Use the nearby platforms to reach the Star Coin before the lift carries troublesome enemies into the area.

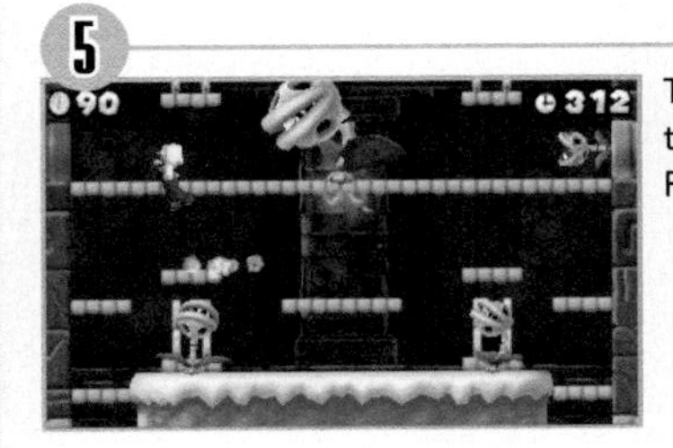

5

The blue pipe at Point 5 leads to the level's secret exit. Enter the pipe and follow the path out of the Tower. Reach the Goal Pole to unlock the path to World 4-C.

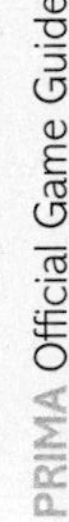

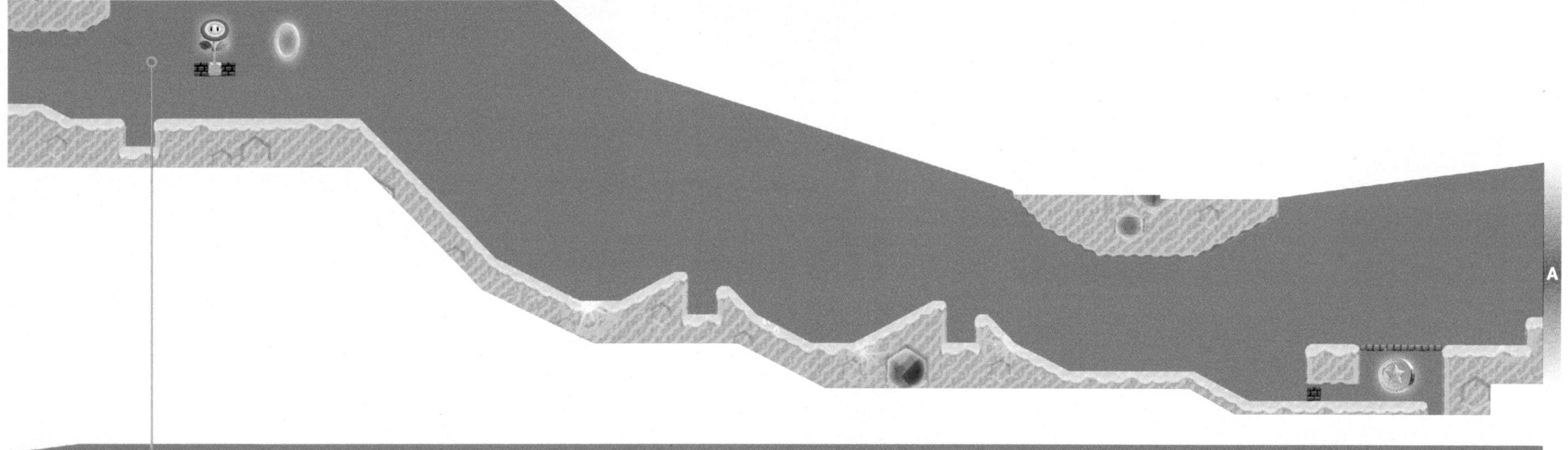

Unless you bring a Super Leaf into the level, you'll need some help to collect the first Star Coin. Stomp the Koopa at Point 1, jump through the Gold Ring, then toss the shell down the hill.

Slide down the hill to keep the Gold Shell in sight, but make sure you keep your distance. You need the shell to smash the Block at the bottom of the hill, so don't slide into the shell until it does. After the impact, the shell bounces back towards you. Slide through the shell, into the opening, and right to the Star Coin.

Pass through the Red Ring at Point 2, then collect the red coins as they parachute down along the path to the right.

After you collect the sixth red coin, slide down the hill and under the nearby platform to grab the last two coins before they drift out of reach.

The second Star Coin is floating above the Piranha Plants at Point 3. You must make a running leap to collect the Star Coin. If you've managed to hang on to a Fire Flower, clear the enemies from the area before you attempt your jump!

WORLD 4-3

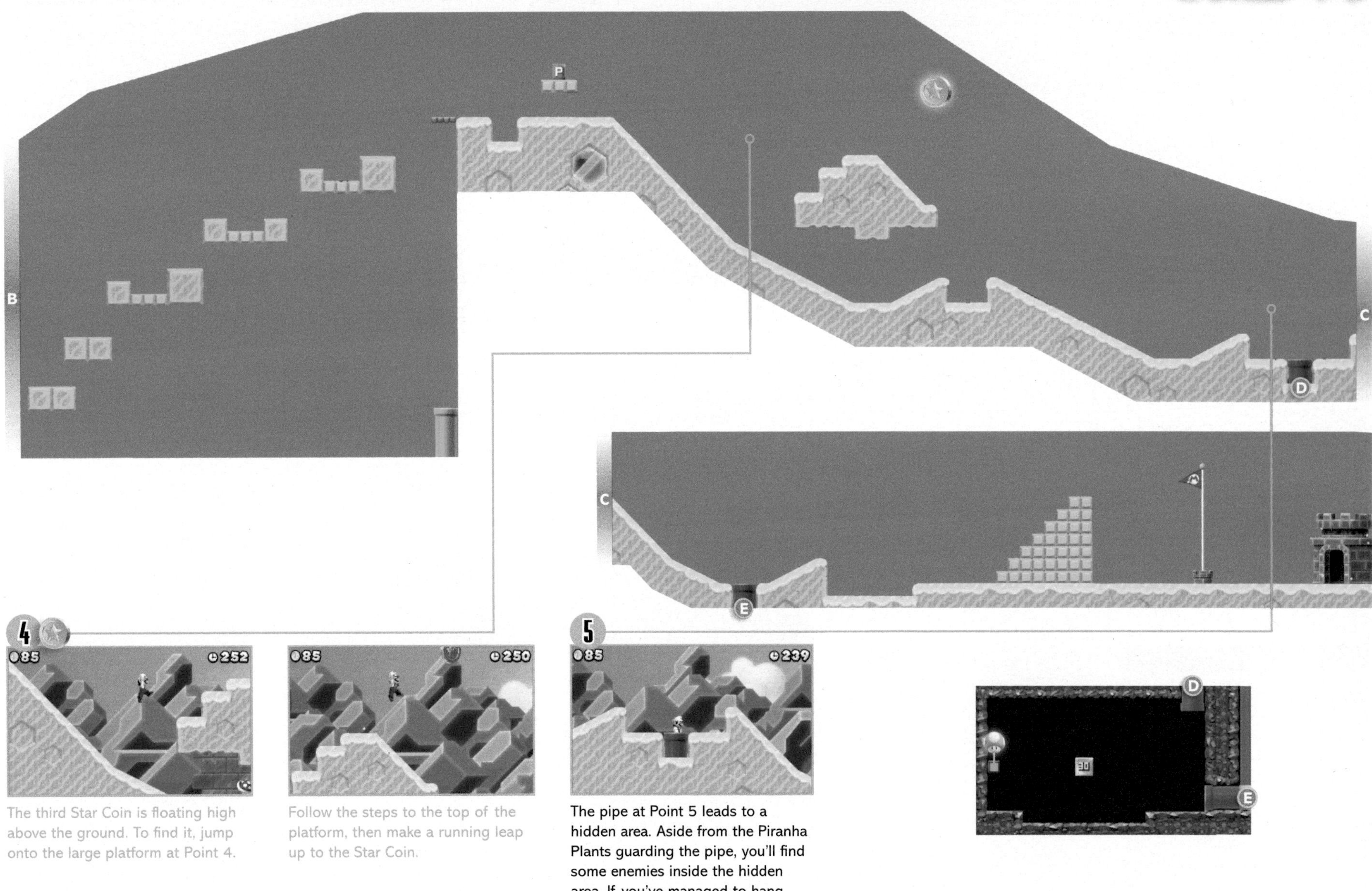

The third Star Coin is floating high above the ground. To find it, jump onto the large platform at Point 4.

Follow the steps to the top of the platform, then make a running leap up to the Star Coin.

The pipe at Point 5 leads to a hidden area. Aside from the Piranha Plants guarding the pipe, you'll find some enemies inside the hidden area. If you've managed to hang on to a Fire Flower, make sure you use it to clear out any problematic enemies.

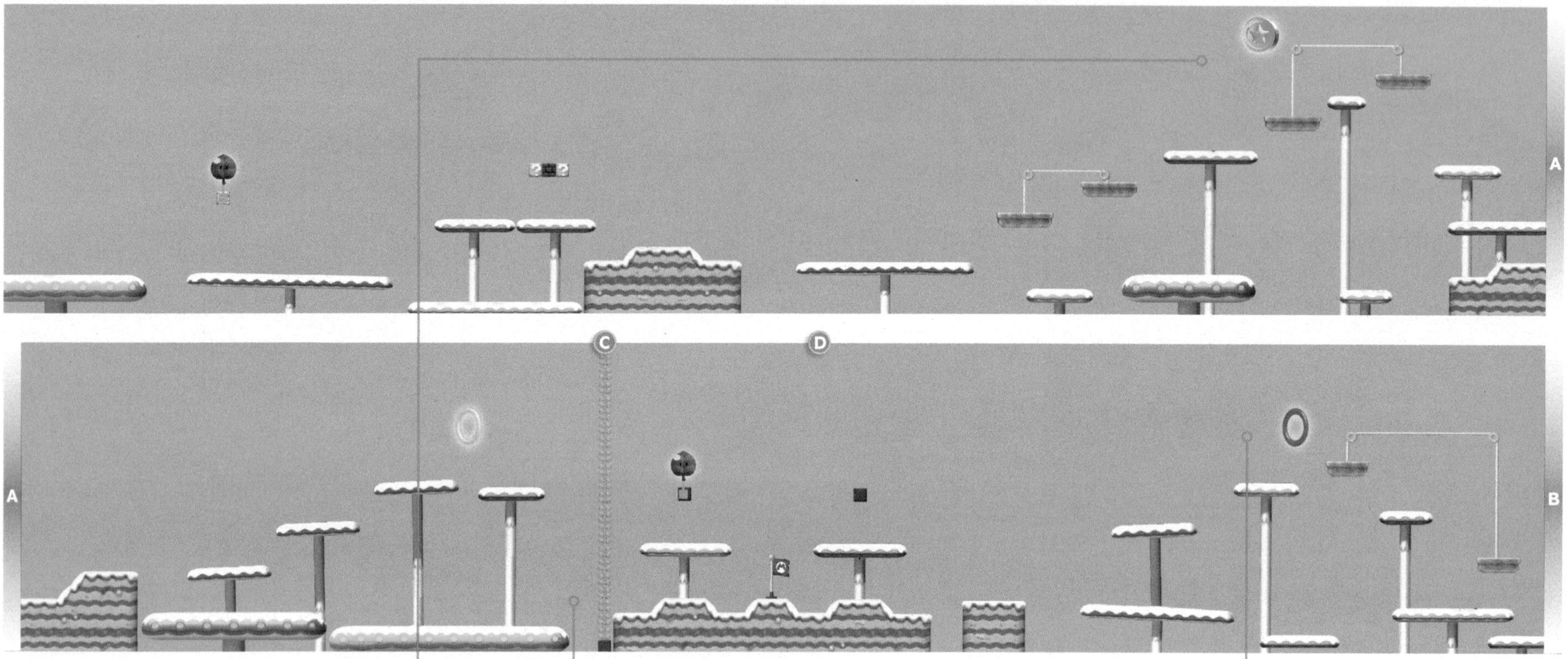

A

A

B

C

D

NOTE

This level contains several pulley platforms. Use Mario's weight to adjust the positions of two connected platforms, but be careful! If either platform touches a pulley, both platforms fall off of the rope.

1

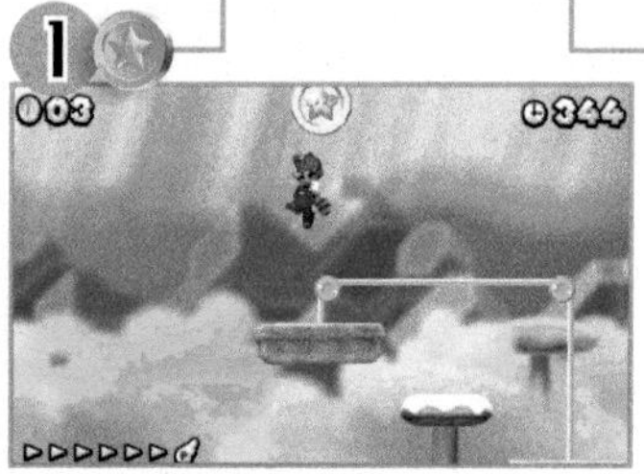

Use the pulley platforms at Point 1 to reach the first Star Coin. Stand on the right platform to raise the left platform into position. Hop up to the left platform, then jump straight up to collect the Star Coin.

2

The second Star Coin is located in a secret area. To reach it you must reveal the Beanstalk hidden in the Block at Point 2. Stomp the Koopa patrolling the platforms above this area, then throw its shell at the Block.

Climb the Beanstalk to reach the secret area, then jump up along the platforms. The Star Coin is floating at the top of the area.

3

When you jump through the Red Ring at Point 3, the red coins appear around the nearby pulley platforms. You must adjust these platforms to collect all of the coins, so make sure you don't break them! Any time wasted waiting for the platforms to reappear could prevent you from completing your task.

WORLD 4-4

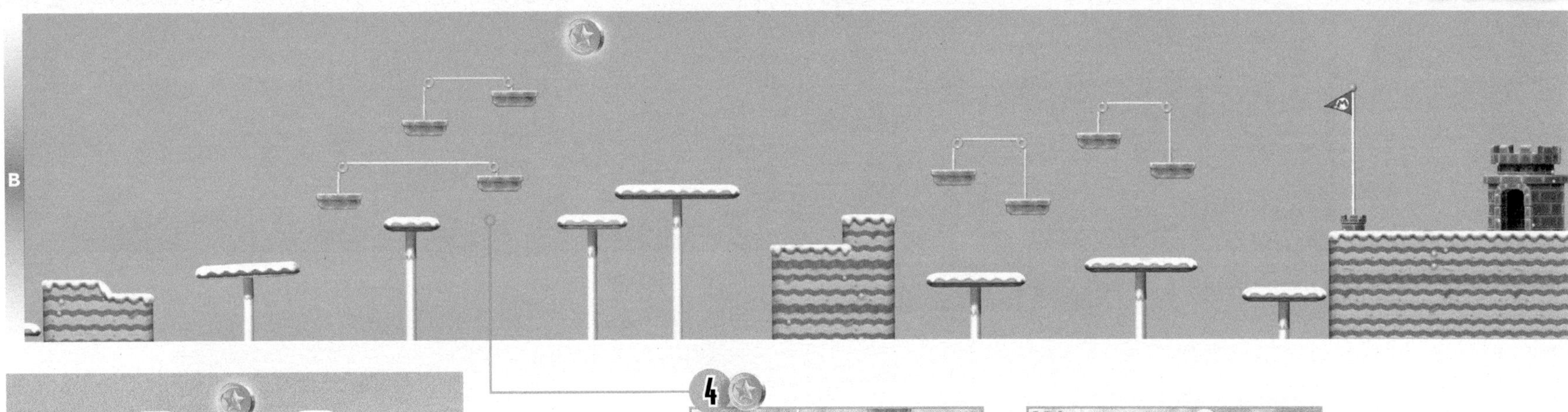

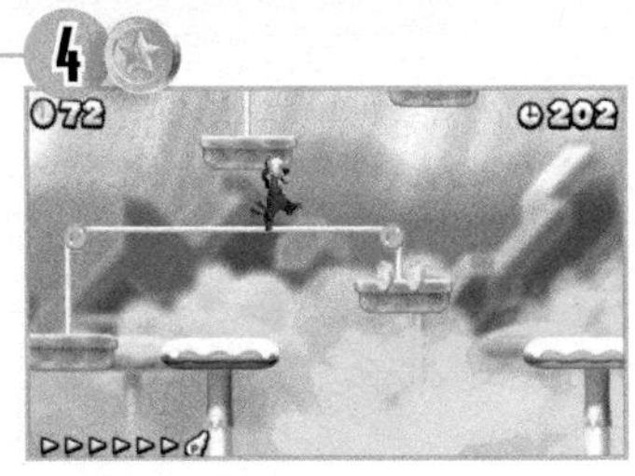

The third Star Coin is floating above the pulley platforms at Point 4. Use the lower set of pulley platforms to reach the upper set's left platform.

Stand on the left platform until the right platform is as high as it can safely go, then use it to reach the Star Coin.

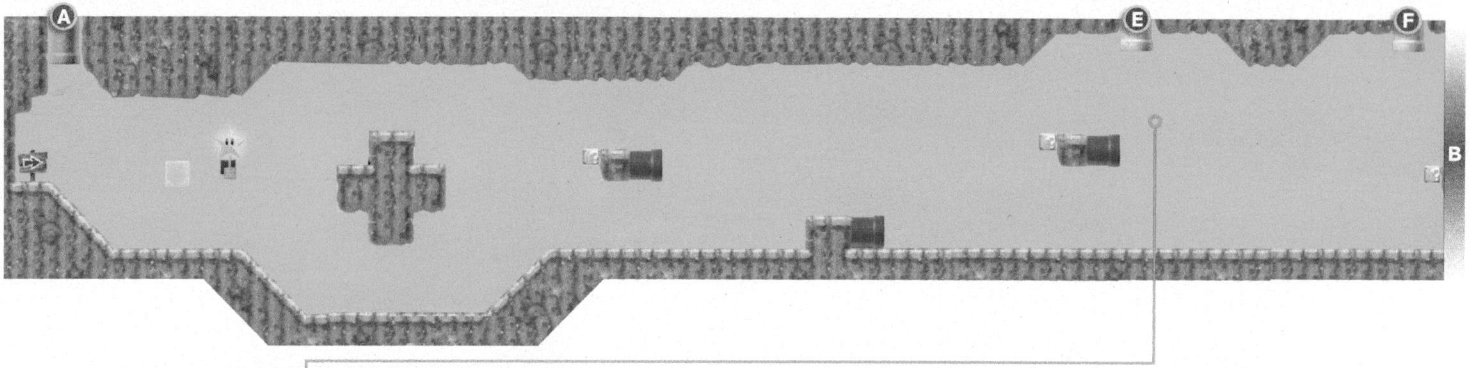

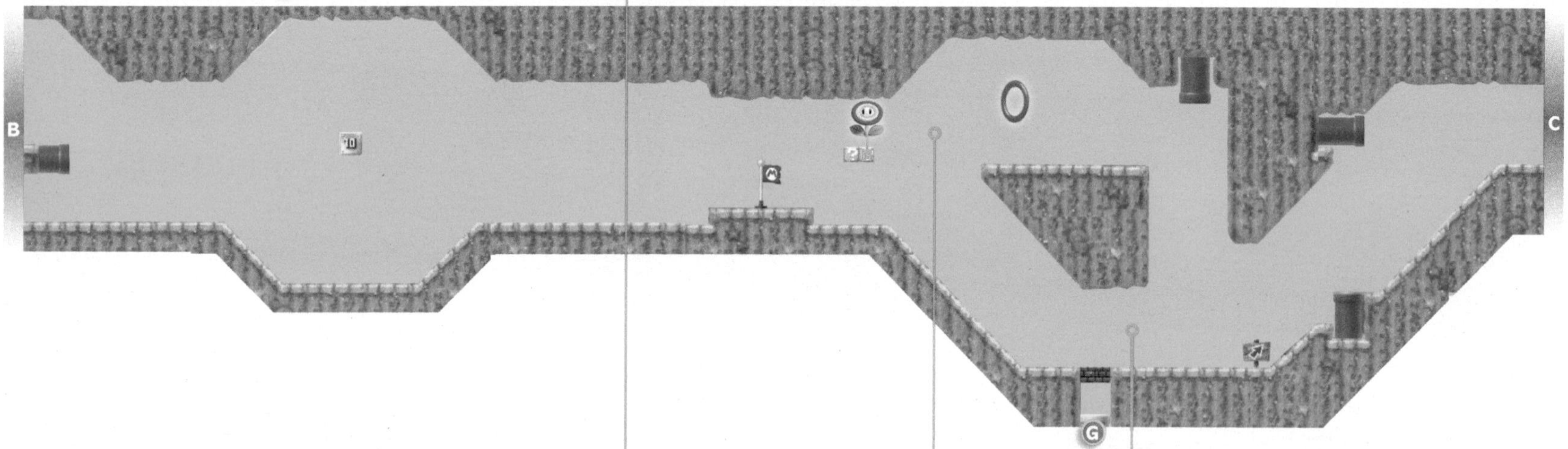

TIP

This level contains several Cheep Chomps. These enemies can be a lot to handle, particularly if you don't have an appropriate power-up. Consider bringing a Fire Flower into the level. The extra firepower should prove very useful until you find additional power-ups.

TIP

After collecting the Star power-up from the Hidden Block, the next three Coin Blocks will contain Star power ups to keep you going for a little while through the level.

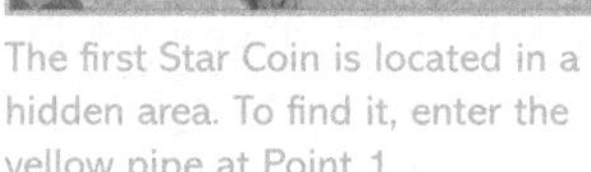

1

The first Star Coin is located in a hidden area. To find it, enter the yellow pipe at Point 1.

After you pass through the pipe, jump across the water in the center of the area. When you're directly above the Star Coin, perform a ground pound. This move allows you to overcome the water currents that would otherwise prevent you from reaching the Star Coin.

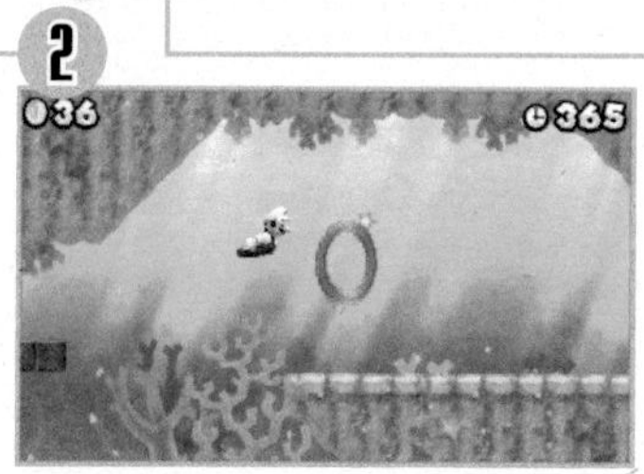

2

Pass through the Red Ring at Point 2 to reveal a trail of red coins to the right. Follow the coins down to the cavern floor and up through the passage to the right. The last red coin floats away as you approach it, so keep swimming until you catch it!

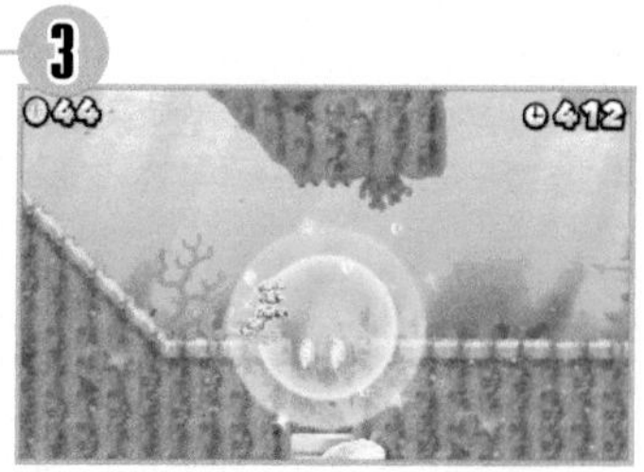

3

If you brought a Gold Flower (or received one from the Roulette Block near the start of the level), use a gold fireball to destroy the Blocks at Point 3. Enter the exposed pipe to find a room filled with Blocks.

WORLD 4-5

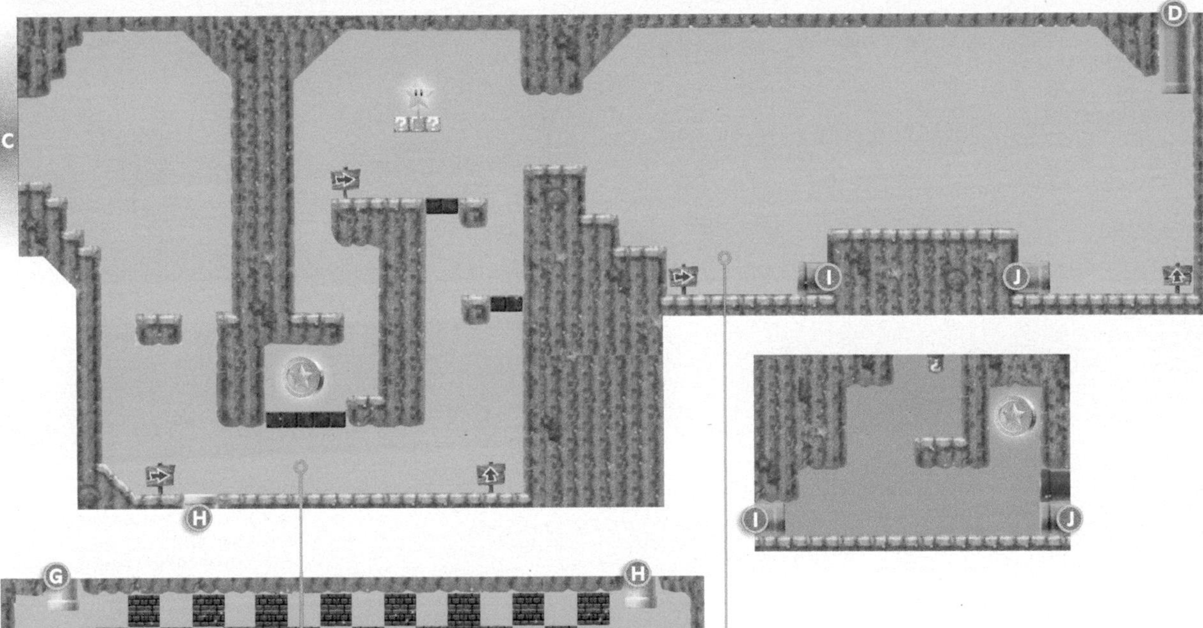

The second Star Coin is floating at Point 4, but a row of Invisible Blocks prevents you from reaching it. Continue to the right, then swim up to the cavern ceiling.

When you reach the row of ? Blocks, swim down through the opening to the left and approach the Star Coin from above.

TIP

After collecting the Star Coin head back up the way you came to collect a Star power up. This will help you take out the Cheep Chomp if you have lost your Fire Flower power up.

The third Star Coin is in a hidden area. To find it, enter the pipe at Point 5.

After you pass through the pipe, swim up and hit the ? Switch to deactivate the water currents flowing from the pipes across the room. Dodge the Cheep Cheeps swimming through the area, and grab the Star Coin before the ? Switch wears off.

CAUTION

This level contains several spiked balls. Whether they're dropping down from the ceiling or rolling across the floor, take care to avoid these hazards.

TIP

If the coins aren't in place when you activate the P Switch, you can use Raccoon Mario to wall jump or fly up to the Star Coin. These methods are much more difficult, however.

Avoid collecting the coins at Point 1. It's much easier to reach the first Star Coin if you leave them in place. Hit the P Switch to transform the coins into Blocks, then use the Blocks to climb up to the Star Coin.

The second Star Coin is near the spiked ball at Point 2. Wait for the spiked ball to roll away from the Star Coin, then hop down and grab it.

The third Star Coin is located in a hidden area. To find it, enter the red pipe at Point 3.

The Star Coin is floating near the green pipe at the top of the room. Jump along the Caterpillar Blocks as they move through the area. Avoid the spiked balls on your way to the Star Coin, then use the green pipe to leave the area.

WORLD 4-CASTLE

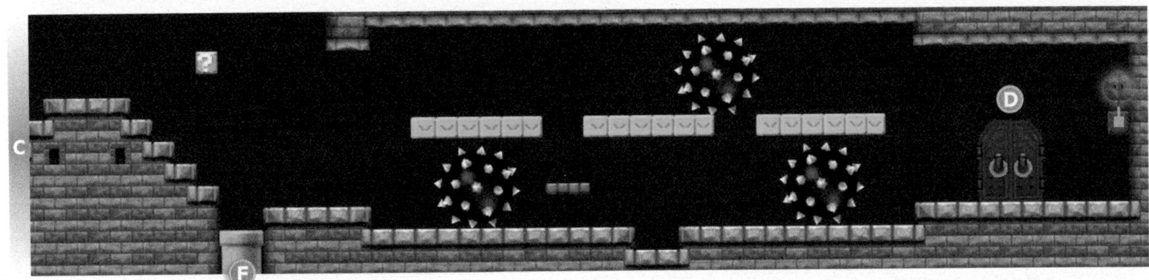

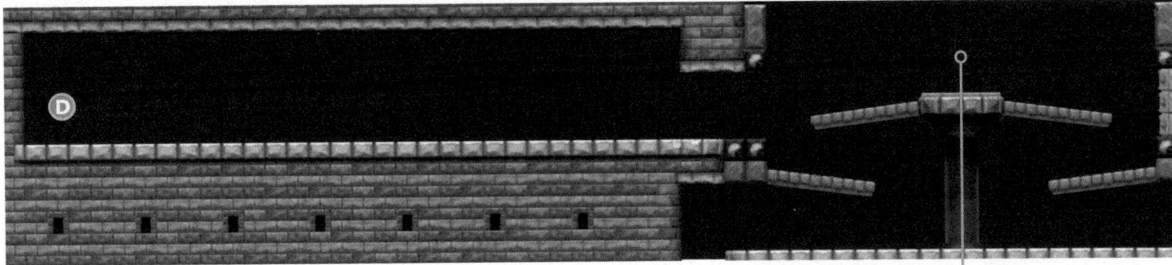

4

Morton Koopa uses his wand to conjure spiked balls, and his slam attack is powerful enough to stun you. Dodge the spiked balls and wait for Morton to perform his slam attack. Just before the impact, jump into the air to avoid its effects. After the slam attack, Morton starts to conjure another spiked ball. While he does, stomp on his head.

After you stomp Morton, he tucks into his shell and leaves the room. Dodge Morton on his way out and wait for his return. Repeat the process until you stomp Morton three times and unlock World Five.

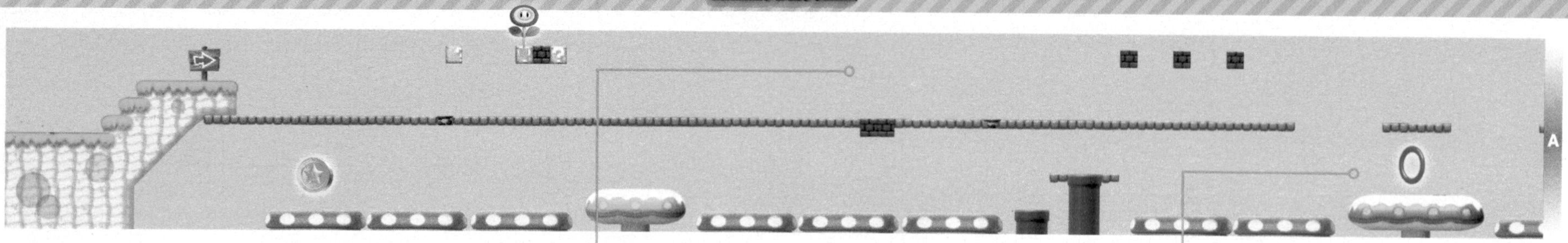

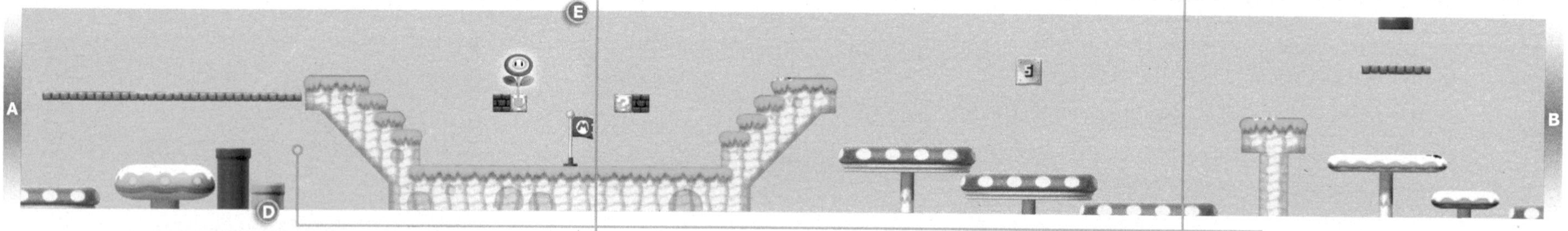

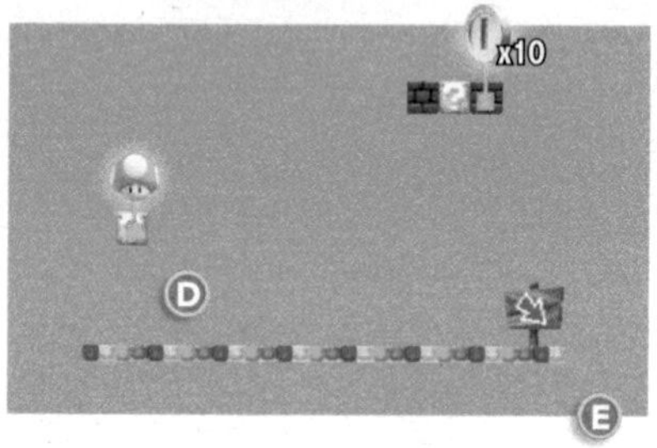

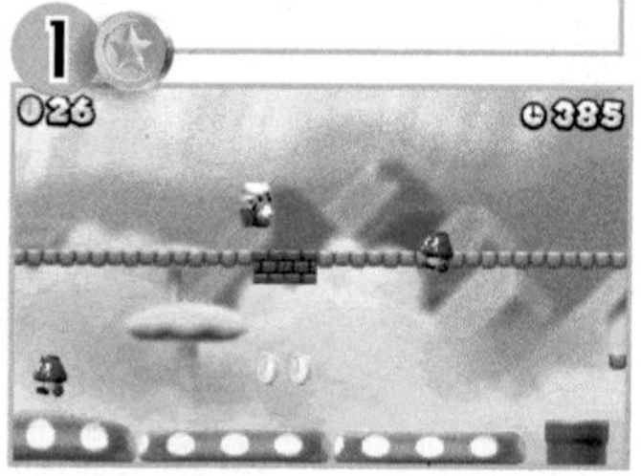

The first Star Coin is located near the start of the level, but the walkway prevents you from reaching it. Follow the path until you reach the Blocks at Point 1, then ground pound through the Block on the left.

The remaining Block should slow the Goombas bouncing in from the right. Bounce along the pink toadstools to the left, and use your fireballs to clear out the enemies on your way to the Star Coin.

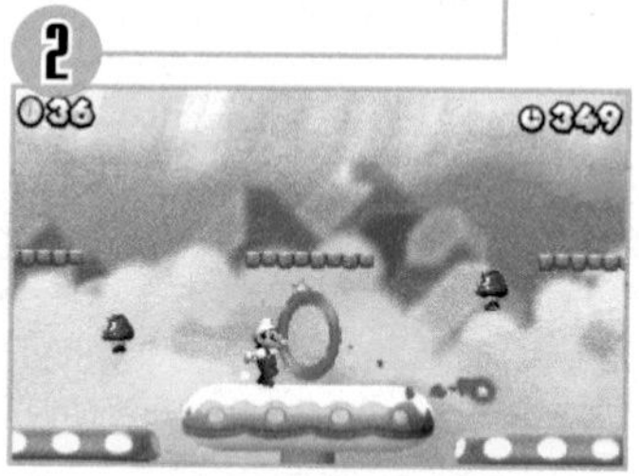

When you pass through the Red Ring at Point 2, eight red coins appear on the surrounding platforms. As you collect the coins, take care to avoid the Goombas as they bounce off of the nearby toadstools.

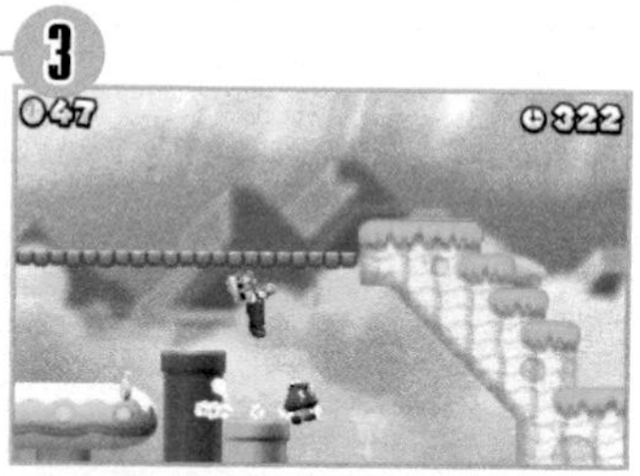

Enter the green pipe to reach a secret area high above the platforms.

NOTE

To access this level, you must pay five Star Coins to unlock the necessary path on the Map Screen.

WORLD 4-A

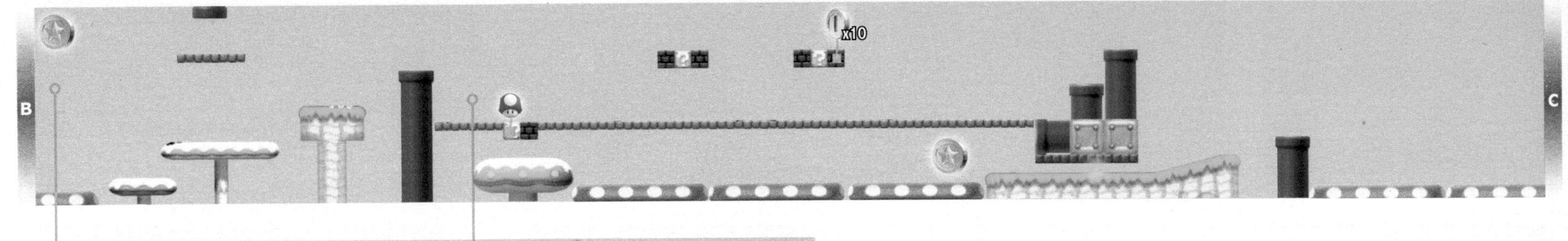

When you land, hit the ? Block to the left. When you do, it transforms into a Flying ? Block. Wait for it to move near the remaining Blocks, then hit it to lock it into place. The used Block can now serve as a platform, allowing you to reach the remaining Blocks.

The second Star Coin is located high above the pink toadstool at Point 4. Wait for a Goomba to step onto the toadstool, then stomp it as it's launched into the air. Use the extra height to bounce up to the Star Coin.

TIP

You can jump from the platform that the Goombas land on to collect the second Star Coin.

Only Mini Mario can reach the level's third Star Coin. Ground pound the ? Block at Point 5, then dash to the right as the Mini Mushroom drops to the platform below the walkway.

Hop over the pipes at the end of the walkway to catch the Mini Mushroom as it emerges from the tiny passage. As Mini Mario, head back to the left and collect the Star Coin under the walkway. When you do, take care to avoid the Goombas emerging from the nearby pipe and any enemies above you.

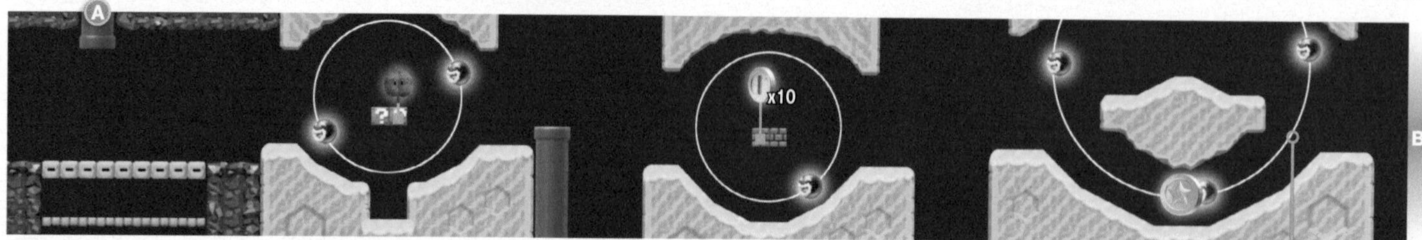

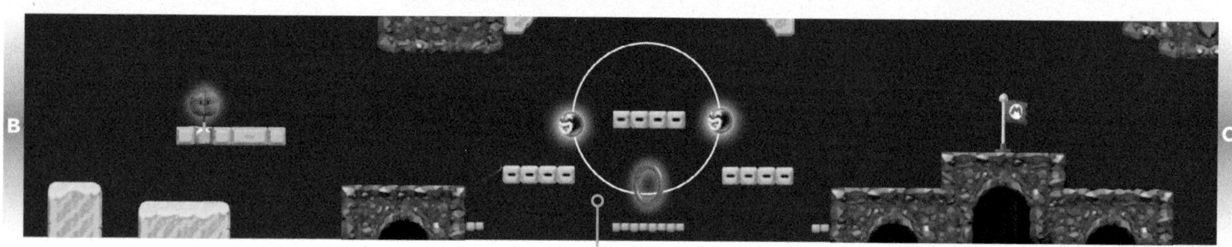

NOTE

To unlock this level, you must find the secret exit in World 4-Boo House.

CAUTION

This level is filled with Amps. These enemies are very predictable, but the icy environment makes it all too easy to slide right into them.

TIP

Compleating this level gains you access to the World 4 - Castle faster.

1

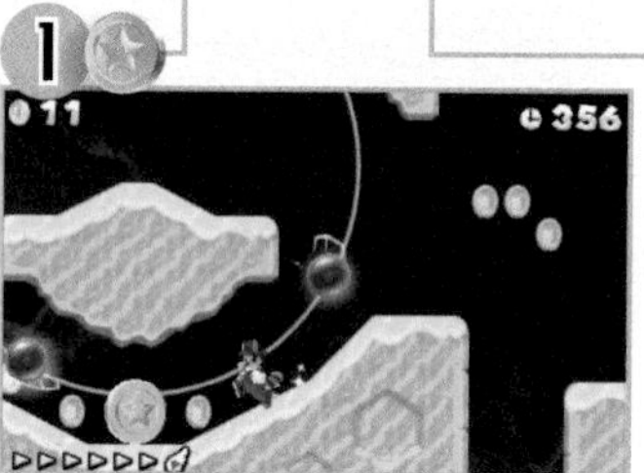

The first Star Coin is located along the Amp track at Point 1. Move past the Star Coin, then slip between two of the Amps and double back to collect it.

2

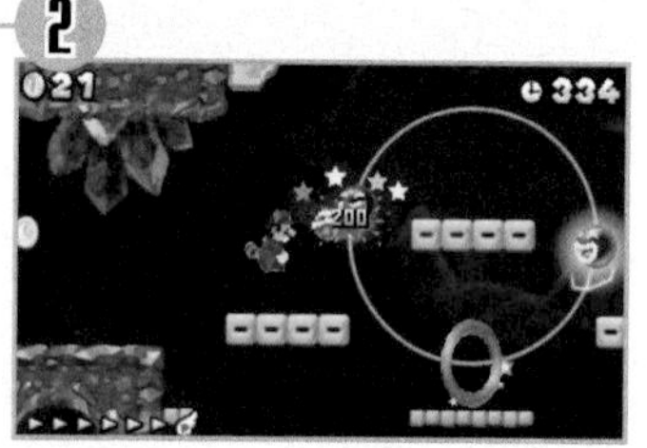

Before you touch the Red Ring, stomp the nearby Koopa and use its shell to dispatch one of the Amps at Point 2. With one less Amp in the area, you'll have a much easier time collecting the red coins.

3

There are three pipes just past the Checkpoint Flag. The first pipe leads to a hidden room.

WORLD 4-B

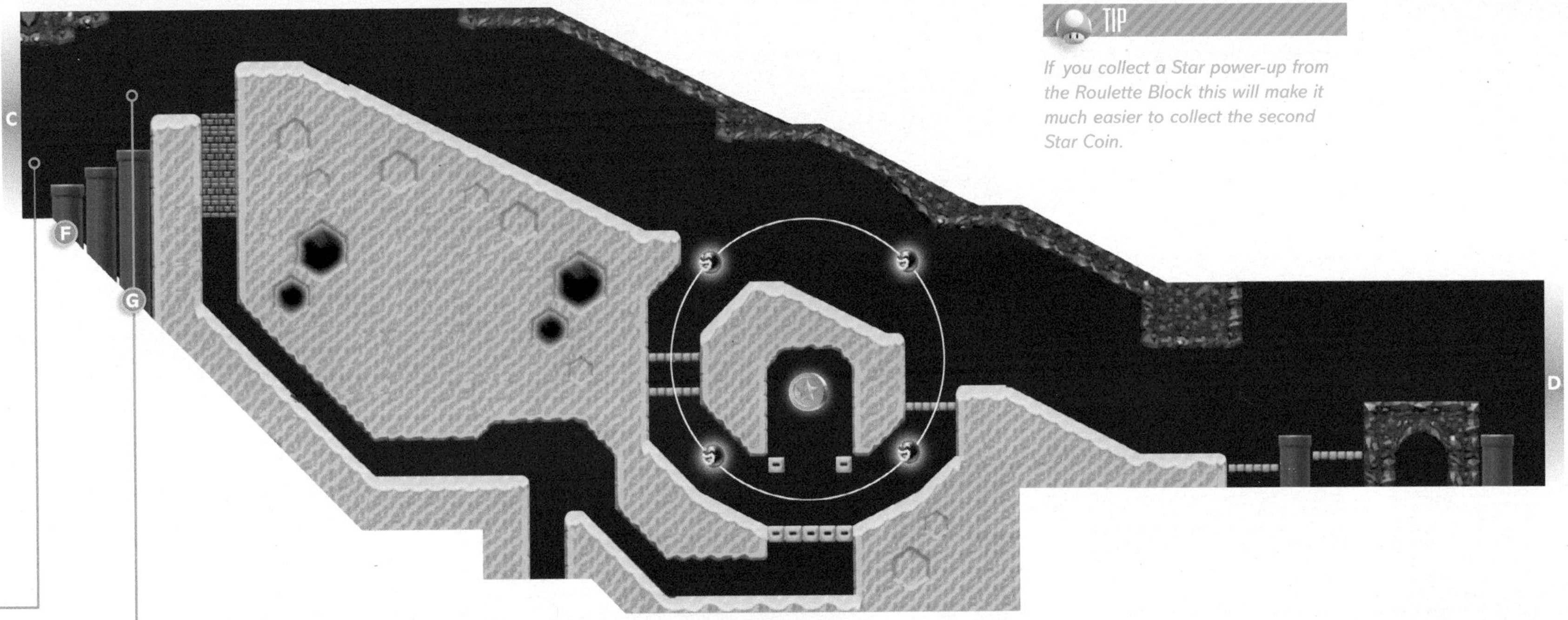

TIP

If you collect a Star power-up from the Roulette Block this will make it much easier to collect the second Star Coin.

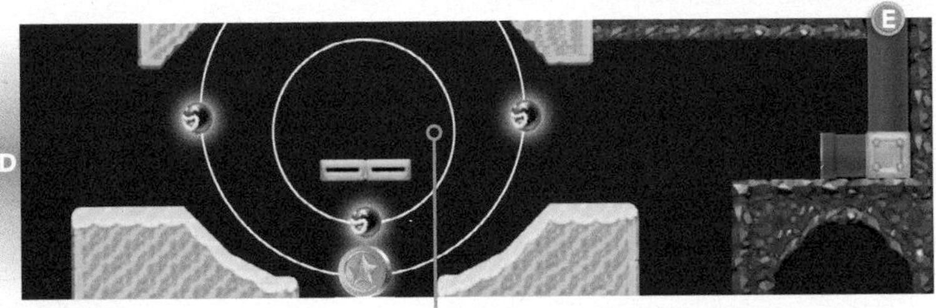

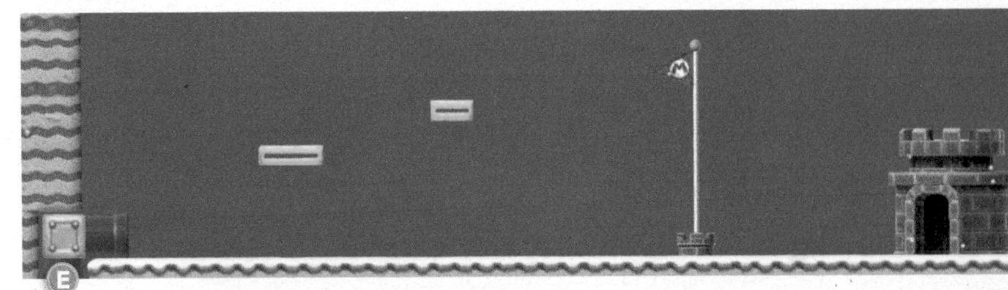

4

The second Star Coin is located under the level's main path. To find it, use an extended ground pound to smash through the Blocks at Point 4.

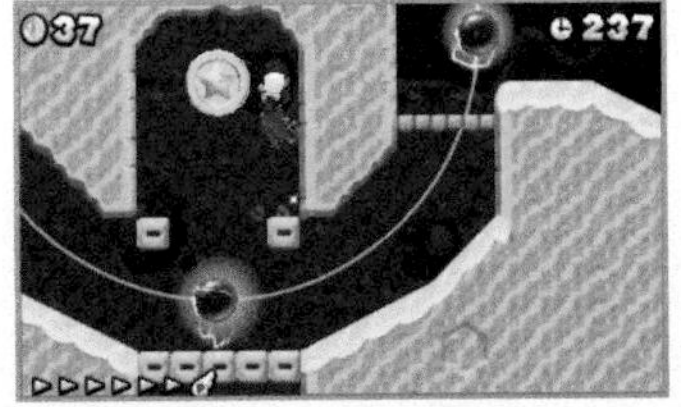

Follow the passage to the right to find an Amp track above a row of Donut Blocks. Wait for an enemy to pass through the area, then jump up to collect the Star Coin above the track.

5

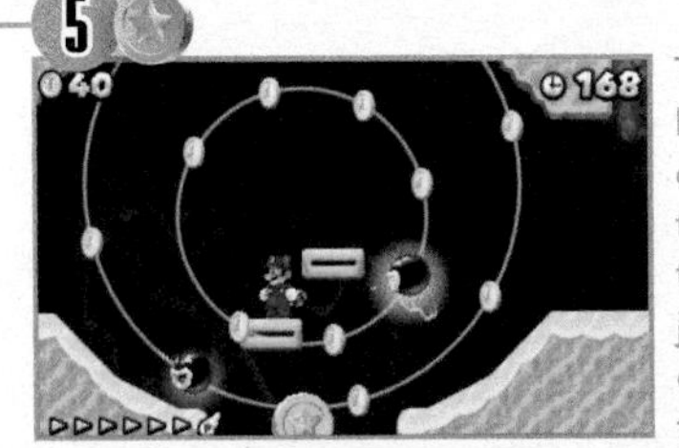

The last Star Coin is located below the Donut Blocks at Point 5. Jump onto one of the Donut Blocks and hop in place to prevent it from falling. When both of the nearby Amps pass below you, stop jumping. Ride the Donut Block as it drops through the Star Coin, then leap to safety before you fall off the screen.

TIP

Throwing a shell to collect the 3rd Star Coin is much easier.

NOTE

To unlock this level, you must find the secret exit in World 4-Tower.

TIP

Hitting a POW Block will defeat nearby Fuzzies. When fireballs aren't an option, look for one of these handy objects.

The first Star Coin is floating above the Fuzzy at Point 1. You'll need the nearby Blocks to reach it, so don't destroy them until you've collected the Star Coin.

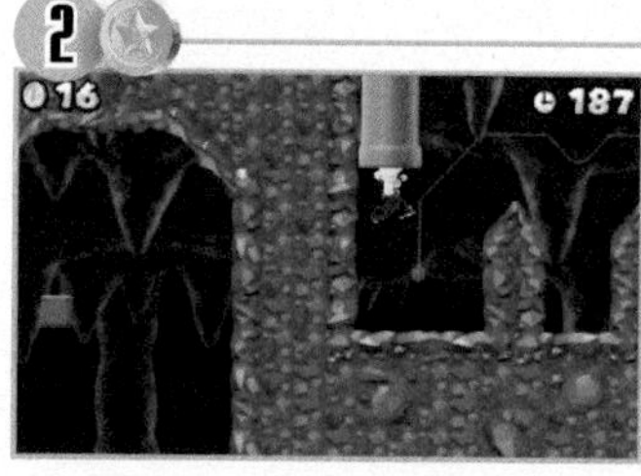

The second Star Coin is located in a hidden room. Defeat or avoid the Big Fuzzy at Point 2, then enter the pipe near the wall to the left.

After you pass through the pipe, move to the middle of the room. Hit the POW Blocks when all of the Fuzzies are in range, then hop onto the used Blocks and jump up to grab the Star Coin.

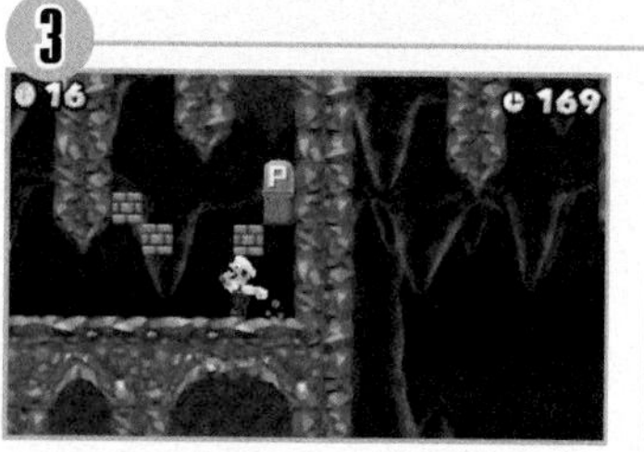

One of the Blocks at Point 3 contains a P Switch. Find and activate the P Switch to reveal the nearby blue coins.

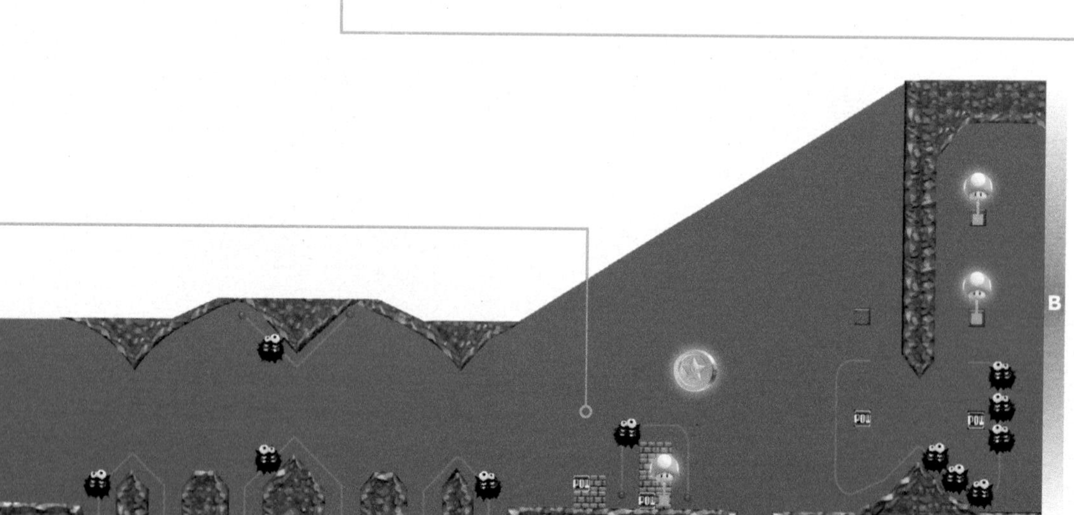

WORLD 4-C

The last Star Coin is hidden near the pipe at Point 4. Use a fireball to defeat the Big Fuzzy to the right, or slip past the enemy when it moves to the left half of its track.

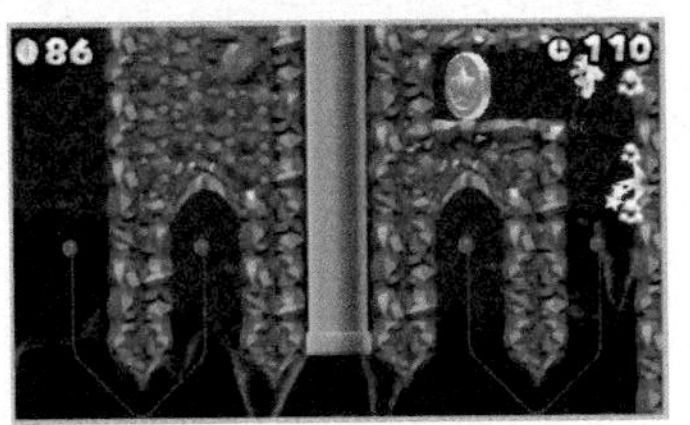

Perform a series of wall jumps to find the Star Coin on a hidden ledge above the track.

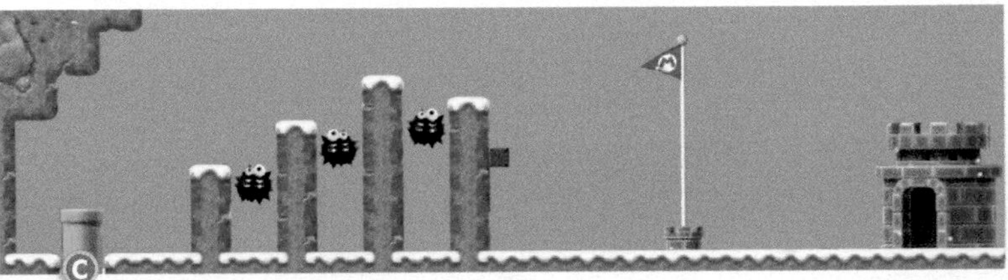

C

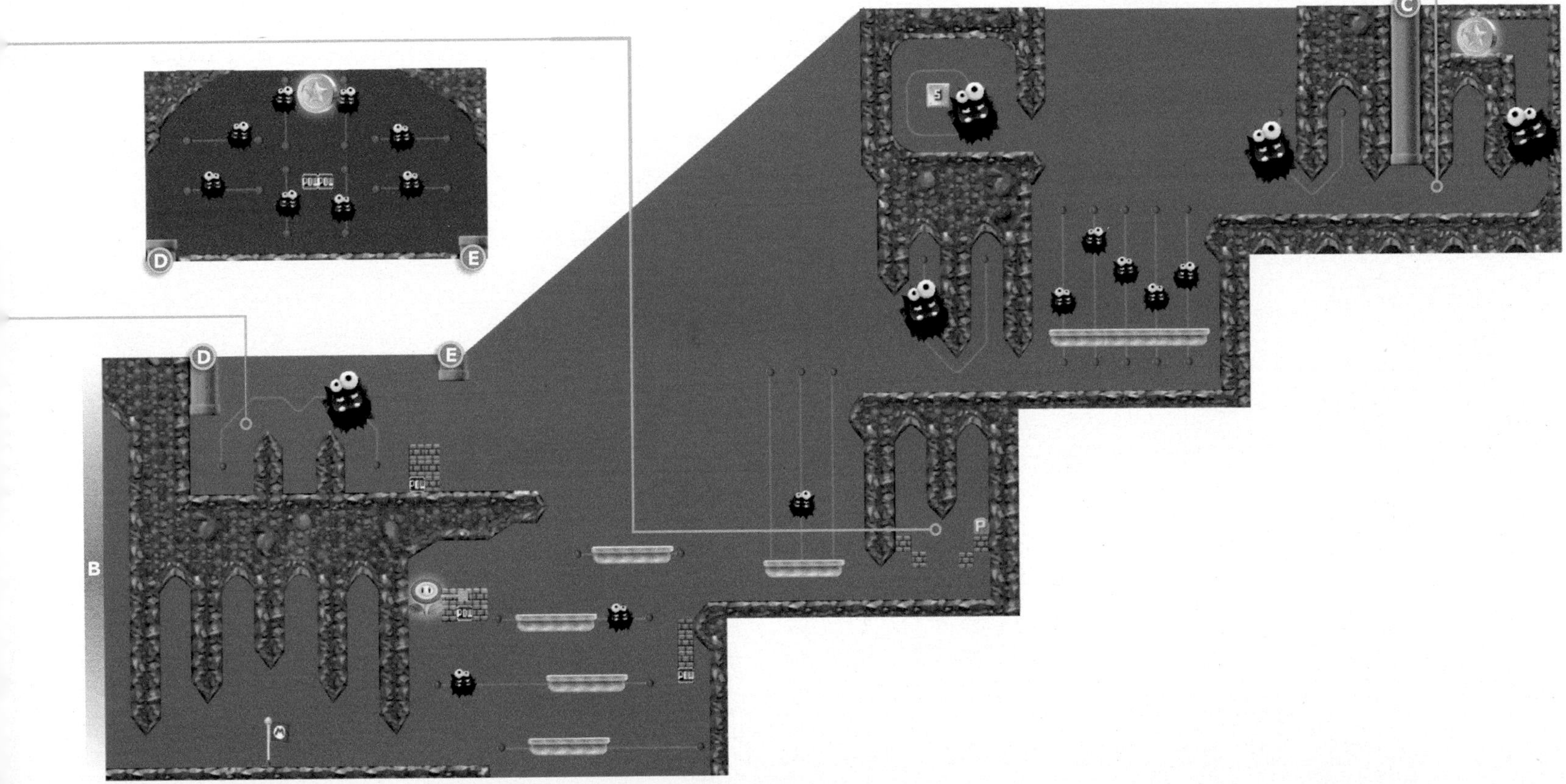

D E

D E

B

P

WORLD FIVE

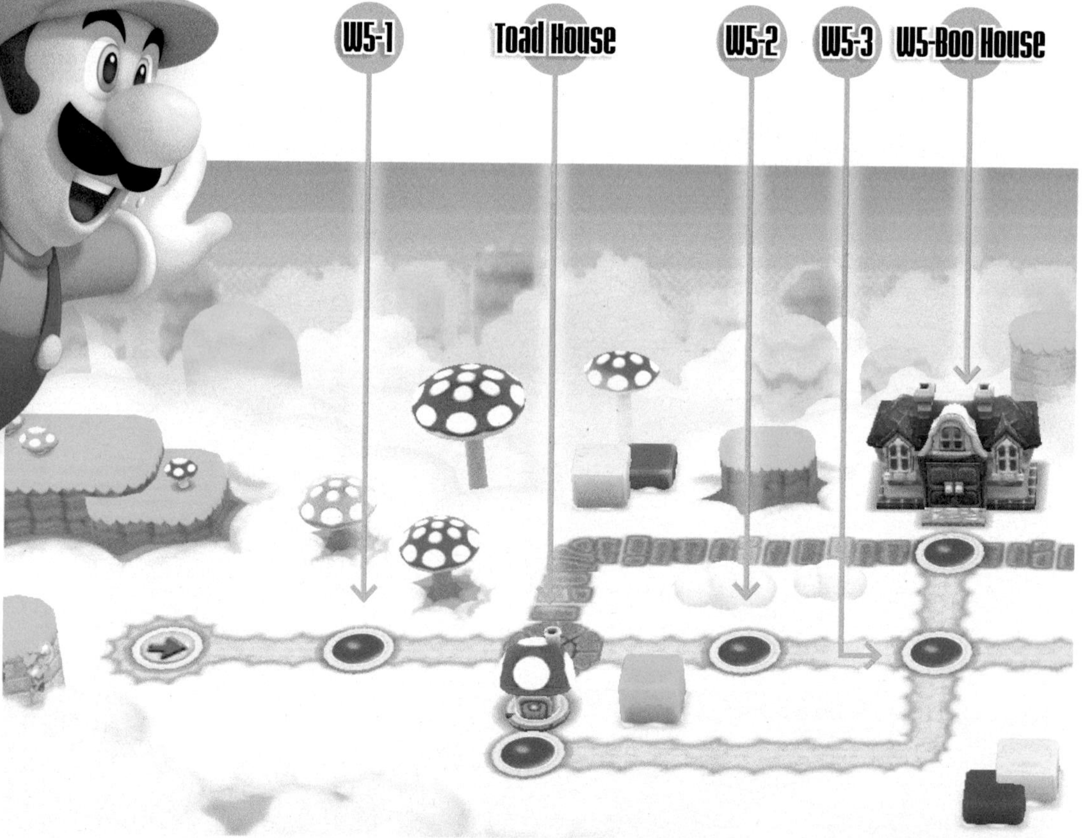

W5-1
Toad House
W5-2
W5-3
W5-Boo House

WORLD LOCATIONS				
Hostile Levels	Toad Houses	Boo Houses	Warp Cannons	Boss
10	4	1	0	Ludwig von Koopa

Main Path Levels:

- World 5-1
- World 5-2
- World 5-3
- World 5-Tower
- World 5-4
- World 5-5
- World 5-6
- World 5-Castle

Alternate Path Levels:

- World 5-Boo House
- World 5-A

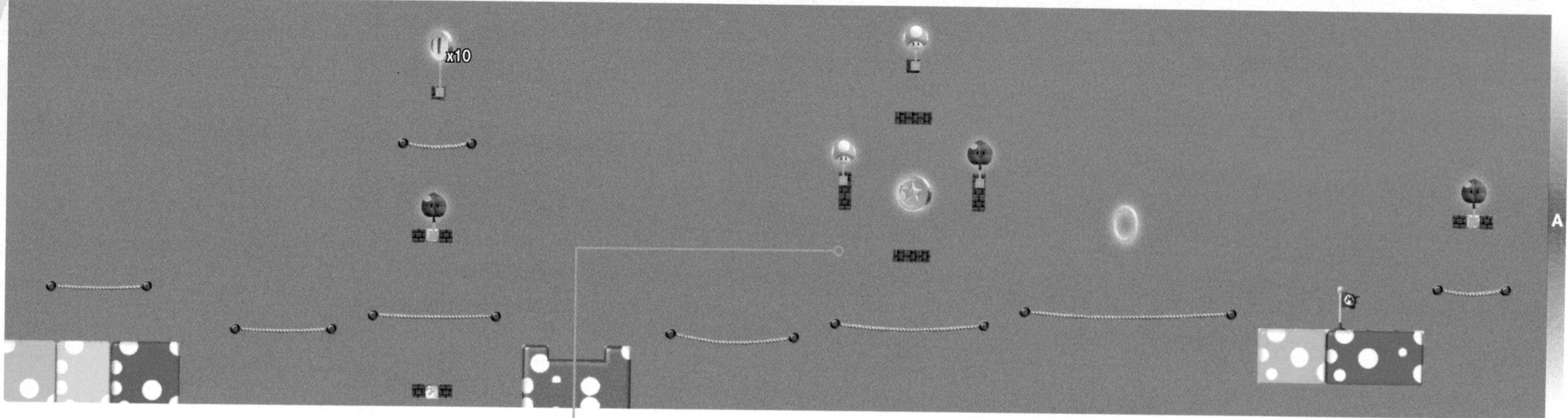

NOTE

To unlock the path to World 5-Boo House, you must find this level's secret exit.

CAUTION

Be careful when moving across tightropes. Mario begins to lose his balance each time he stops moving!

1

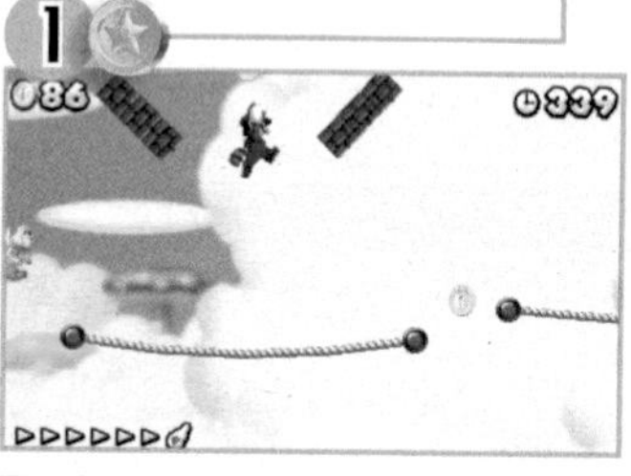

The first Star Coin is floating near the revolving Blocks at Point 1. Wait for a group of Blocks to approach, then jump onto them.

Ride the Blocks up to the Star Coin, or perform a wall jump to collect it.

2

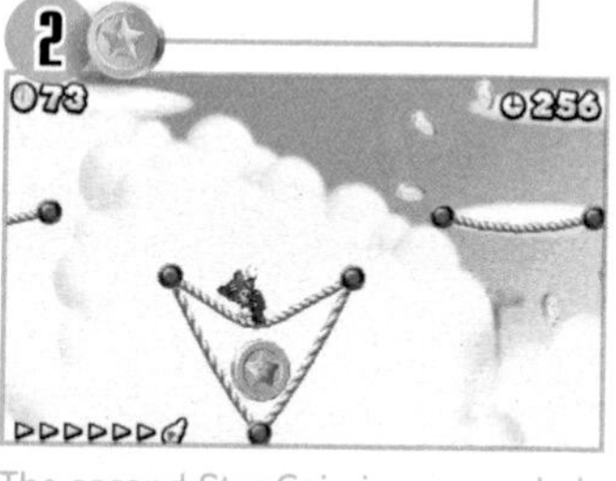

The second Star Coin is surrounded by tightropes. To collect it, simply stand above the Star Coin and wait for Mario to lose his balance.

3

The last Star Coin is located in a hidden area. Jump to the tightrope at Point 3, then jump to find the Invisible Block above you. When the Beanstalk emerges, climb up to the hidden area.

The Star Coin is traveling around a circle of Koopa Paratroopas. As the Star Coin approaches the top of the circle, bounce across the enemies to grab it on your way to the next tightrope.

4

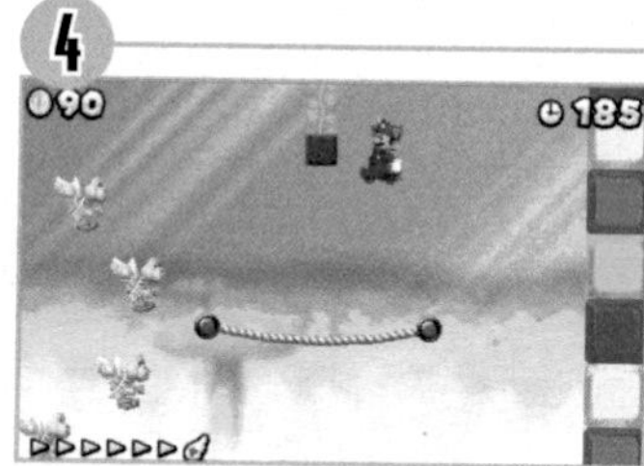

When you reach the tightrope beyond the circle of Koopa Paratroopas, jump up to find the Beanstalk hidden in an Invisible Block. Follow the path to find this level's secret exit. After you reach the Goal Pole, World 5-Boo House becomes available on the Map Screen.

WORLD 5-1

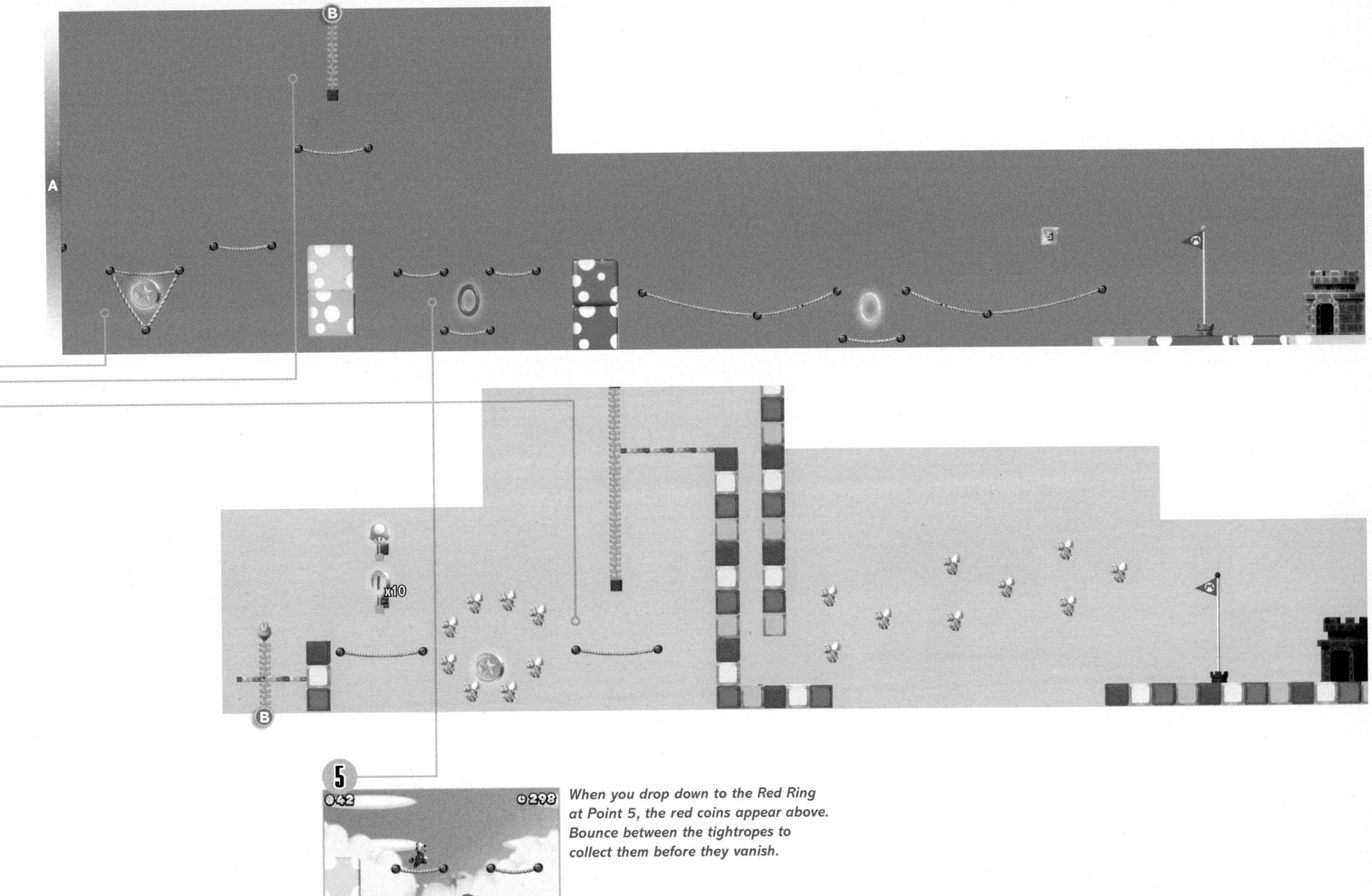

When you drop down to the Red Ring at Point 5, the red coins appear above. Bounce between the tightropes to collect them before they vanish.

1

Many of this level's secrets are hidden high above the ground. To reach them, stomp a Lakitu and use its cloud to explore the surrounding area.

CAUTION

Soon after a Lakitu's cloud starts blinking, it vanishes. Make sure you've got a safe place to land when it disappears.

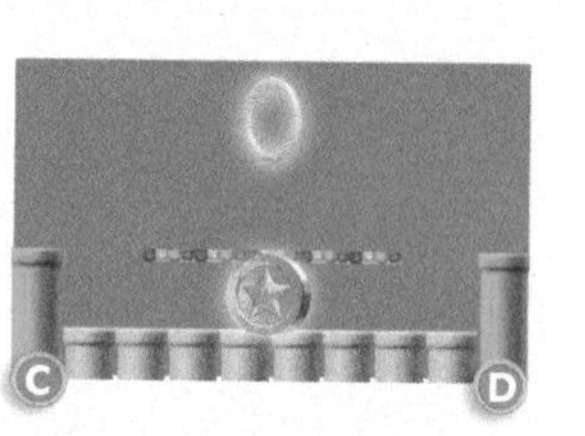

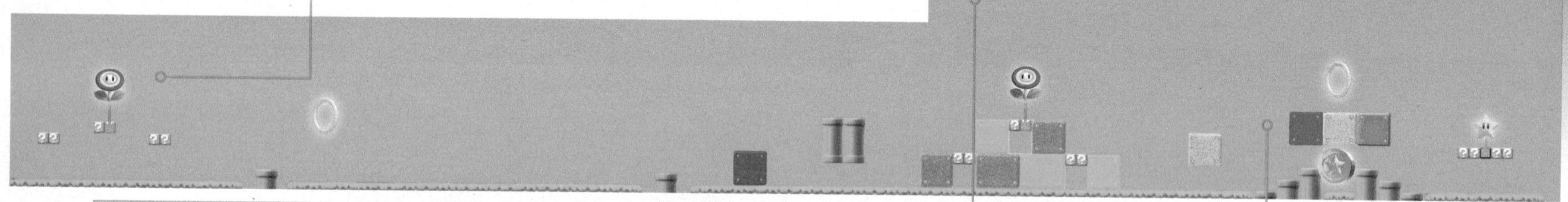

2

Stomp the Lakitu at Point 2 and use its cloud to follow the coins above you. When you reach the ? Switch, use it to initiate a shower of coins from the nearby pipes.

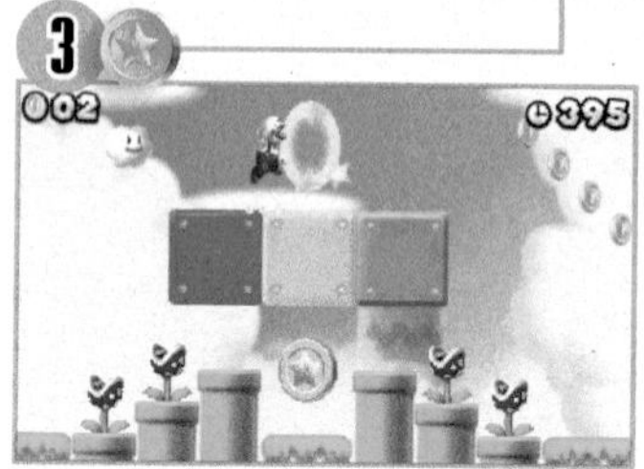

3

It's easier to collect the Star Coin at Point 3 if you defeat the surrounding Piranha Plants first. If you ride a Lakitu's cloud up to the nearby Gold Ring, you can earn some extra coins as you clear a path to the Star Coin.

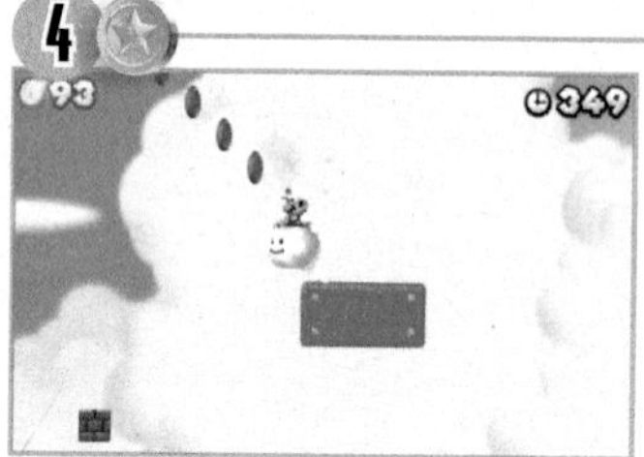

4

The second Star Coin is located in a hidden area. To find it, stomp the Lakitu near the Checkpoint Flag and use its cloud to reach the P Switch at Point 4. Hit the P Switch, then follow the trail of blue coins to find a green pipe.

Enter the pipe to find the hidden area. Stomp the Koopa, grab its shell, then jump through the Gold Ring. Toss the Gold Shell to automatically collect the Star Coin while simultaneously clearing out the remaining enemies.

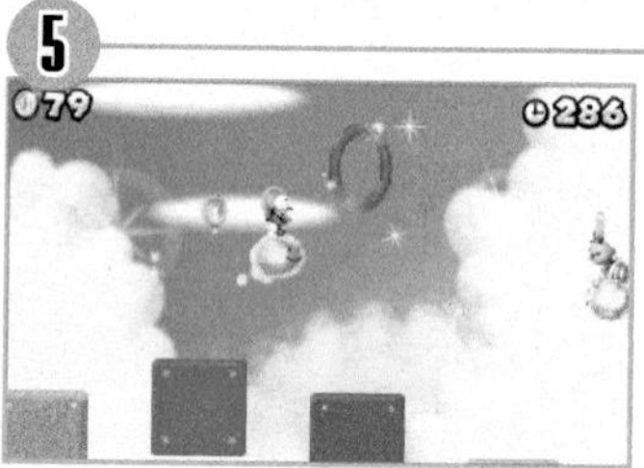

5

There's a Red Ring located at Point 5. Before you pass through it, stomp the nearby Lakitu to gain a fresh cloud—you'll need it to collect the red coins that appear to the right.

WORLD 5-2

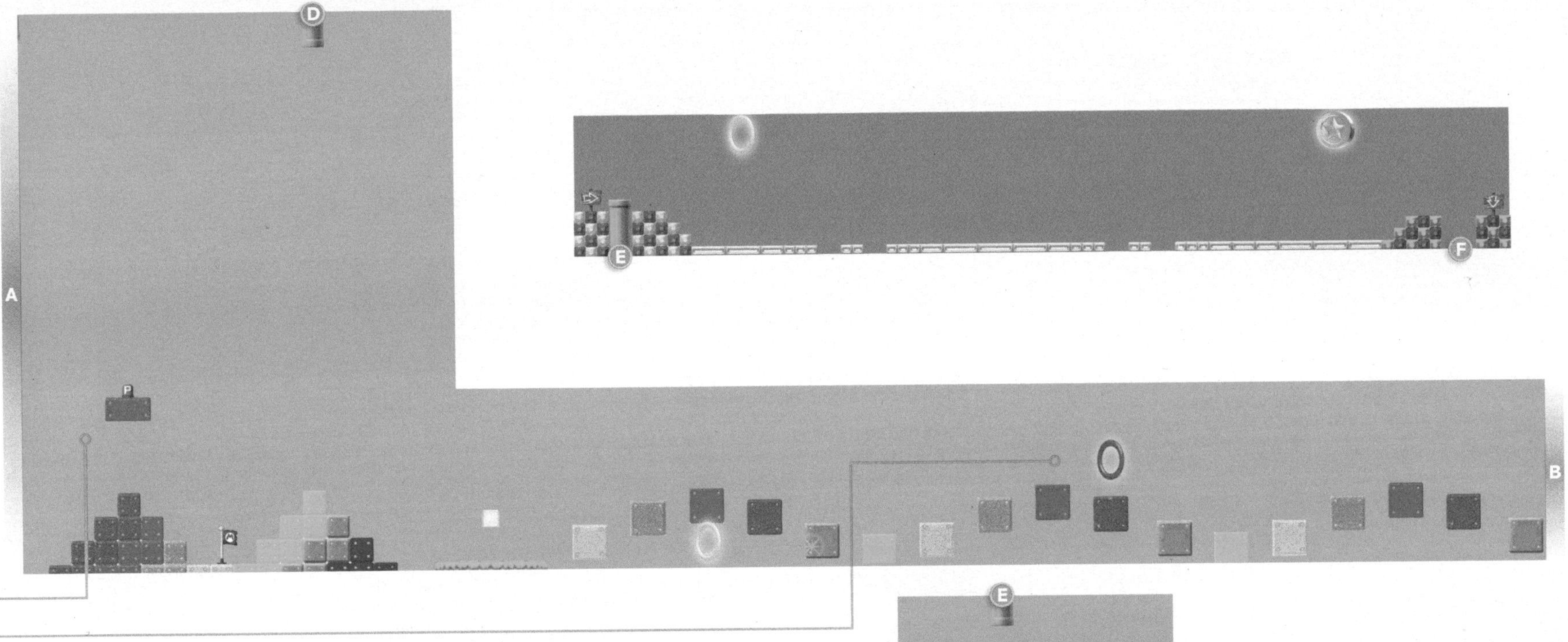

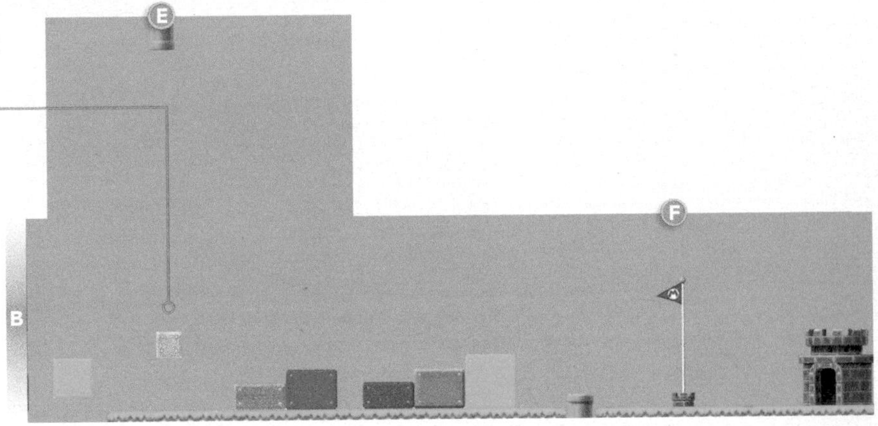

6

The third Star Coin is located in a hidden area. Stomp the Lakitu near the end of the level, then take its cloud to the small yellow platform at Point 6. Fly straight up to find another green pipe.

After you pass through the pipe, stomp one of the Lakitus guarding the hidden area. After you do, use its cloud to reach the Star Coin to the right.

When you drop down from collecting the final Star Coin you will land on top of the Goal Pole.

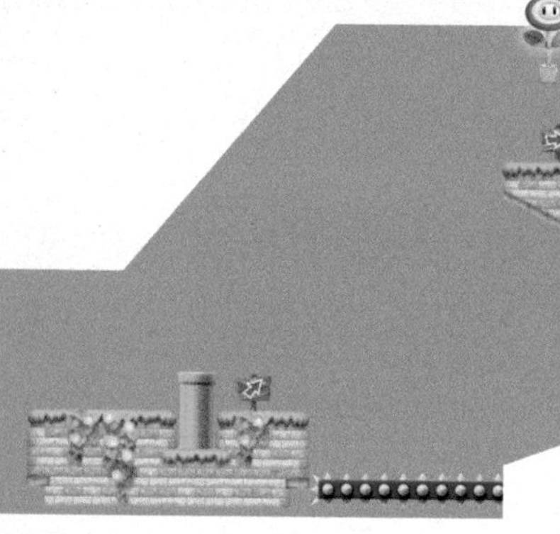

NOTE

Use the many pipes located throughout this level to move between areas. Rather than warp Mario to hidden areas, most pipes will launch him to out-of-reach platforms.

1

Each of the three pipes at Point 1 can launch you to a different location. To collect the first Star Coin, enter the pipe on the right.

After the pipe tilts to the right, it fires you straight through the first Star Coin.

2

When you reach the pipes at Point 2, enter the pipe on the left to launch yourself through the nearby Red Ring.

Follow the red coins as they lead you across the platform and back down the hill. Slide down the decline to build up some speed, then jump for the fifth red coin just before you reach the bottom. If you time this jump properly, you should have no trouble collecting the remaining red coins.

NOTE

To reach Point 3, return to the pipes at Point 1. Enter the pipe in the middle to launch yourself to the platforms high above you.

3

Before you can collect the second Star Coin, you'll need some help from Mini Mario. There are three Invisible Blocks at Point 3. The Invisible Block directly above the ? Block contains a Mini Mushroom.

As Mini Mario, jump along the platforms to the right. The first few platforms each hold three small pipes. The fourth platform, however, has a larger pipe sandwiched between two small pipes. Enter the larger pipe to launch yourself right through the Star Coin.

4

There's a row of five pipes at Point 4. To collect the third Star Coin, enter the pipe in the center of the row. When you do, the pipe launches you back to the left.

WORLD 5-3

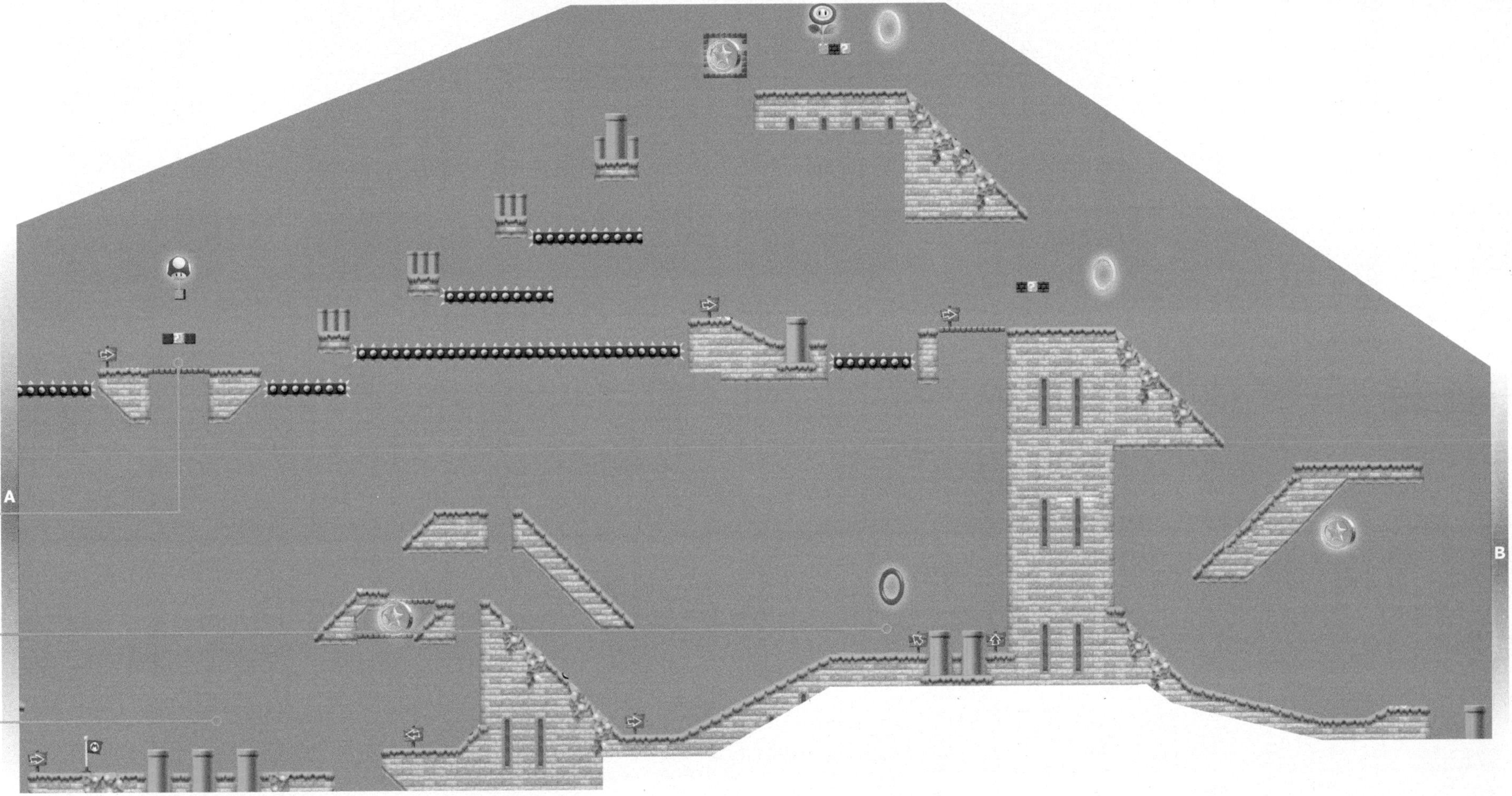

A

B

As long as you entered the correct pipe, you'll soar right through the Star Coin.

When you're ready, return to the row of pipes at Point 4. Enter the fourth pipe to launch yourself to the top of the Goal Pole!

4

If you bring a Mini Mushroom into the level, you can access a hidden room. As Mini Mario, wait for the flames at Point 4 to die down, then enter the pipe to the left. The hidden room contains power-ups, 1-Up Mushrooms, and a P Switch that reveals a stash of blue coins.

3

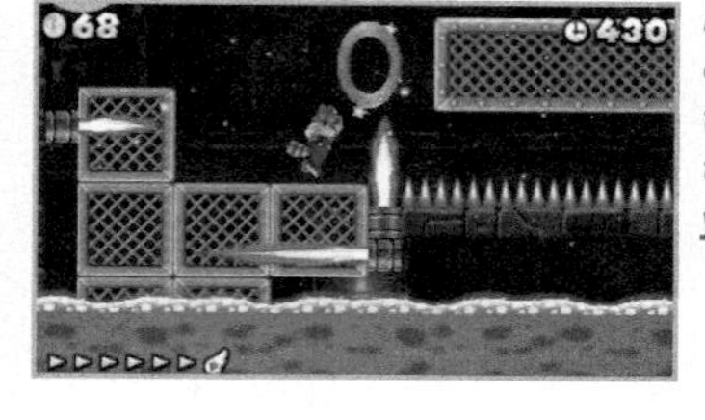

Leap through the Red Ring at Point 3 as soon as you're within range. You must move quickly to stay ahead of the lava. Grab on to the fence to the right, then dodge the Burner flames as you collect the red coins.

2

As you approach the first Star Coin, the fence you're riding rotates counterclockwise. When it does, move to the center of the fence. As the fence moves past the flame at Point 2, make your way to the right.

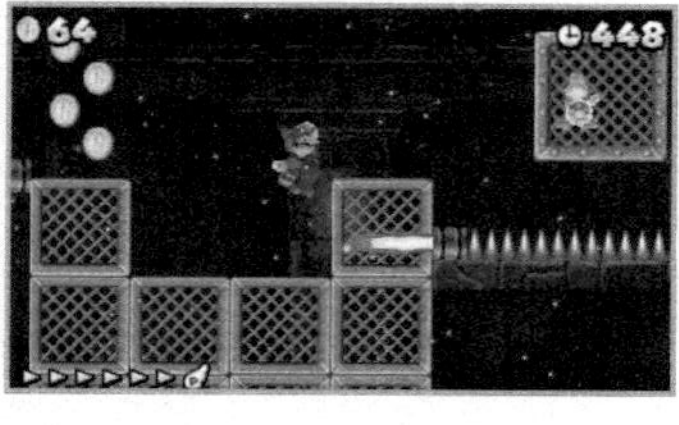

Jump to the small fence below the Star Coin. Defeat or avoid the Koopa that's guarding the area, and climb to the top of the fence. Jump up to grab the Star Coin, then leap back to the moving fence.

1

As you approach Point 1, the room begins filling with lava. Jump between the platforms and fences located throughout the area to stay clear of this creeping hazard.

NOTE

Most fences are stationary, but some of them move when you grab them. While these fences carry you through the area, you must dodge the spikes and flames in your path.

TIP

This level contains several fire-spewing Burners. As you plan your route, pay attention to the size of each flame. The longer flames erupt at regular intervals, but the shorter flames are always active.

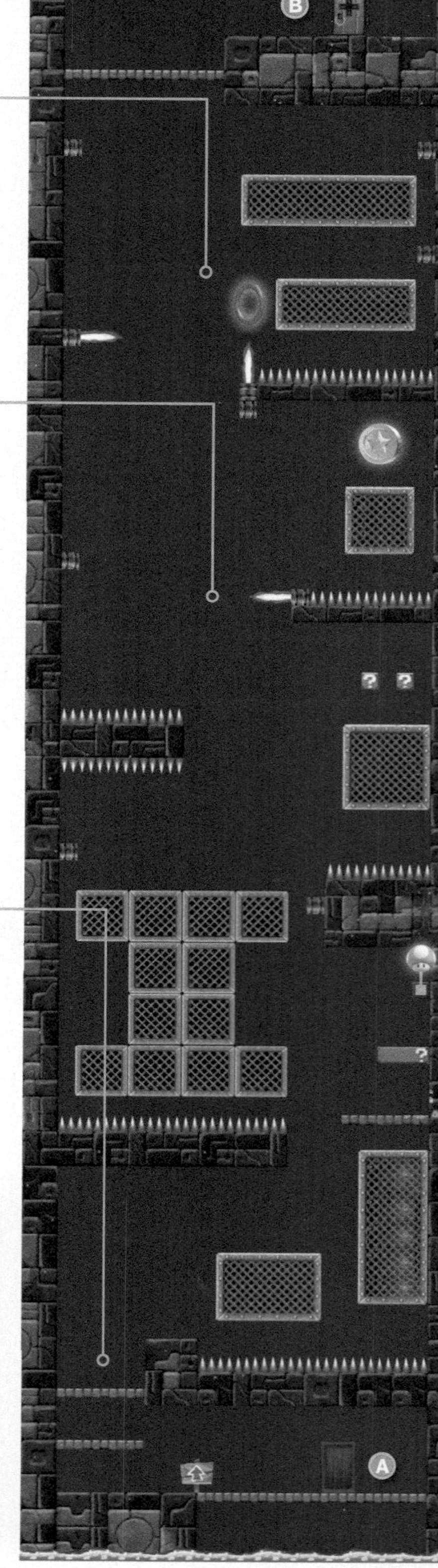

WORLD 5-TOWER

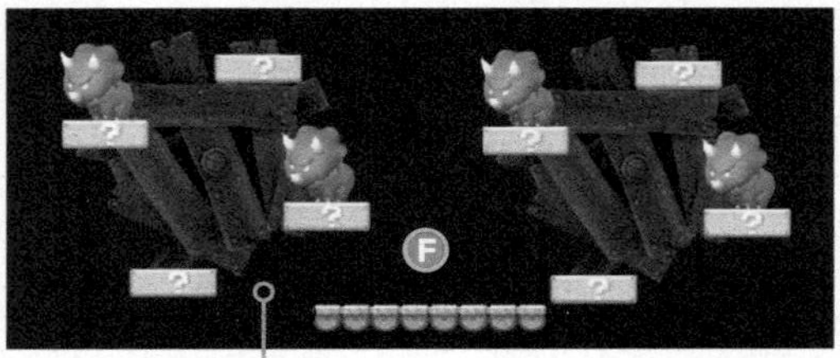

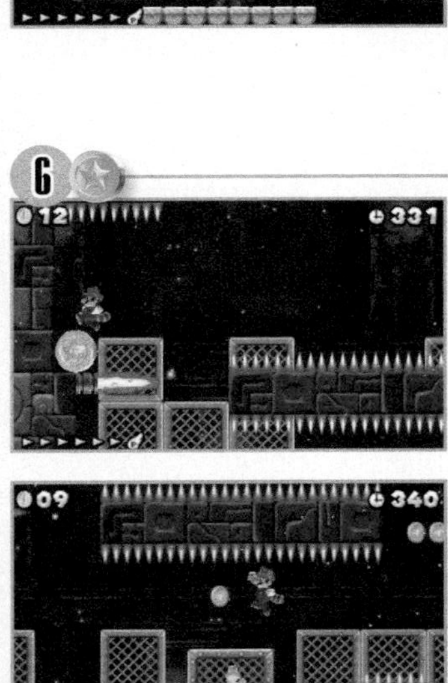

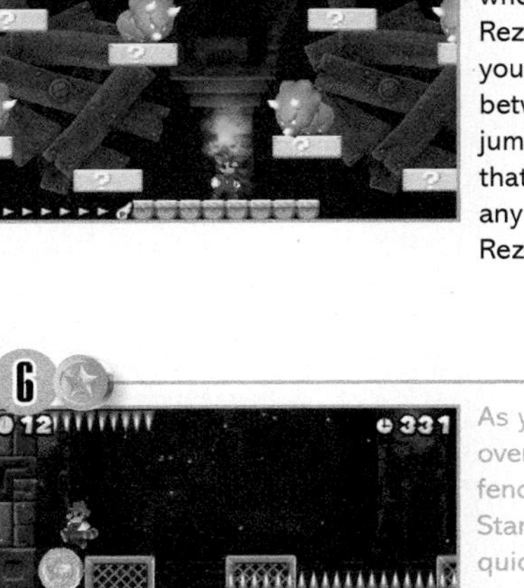

5

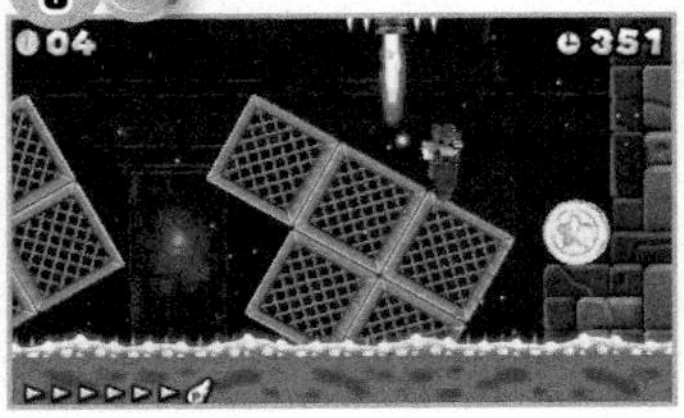

As you approach Point 5, move to the fence's right edge. When the fence splits in half, the section you're riding swings toward the Star Coin along the right wall. Jump over and collect the Star Coin, then hop back to the fence before the lava reaches the ledge.

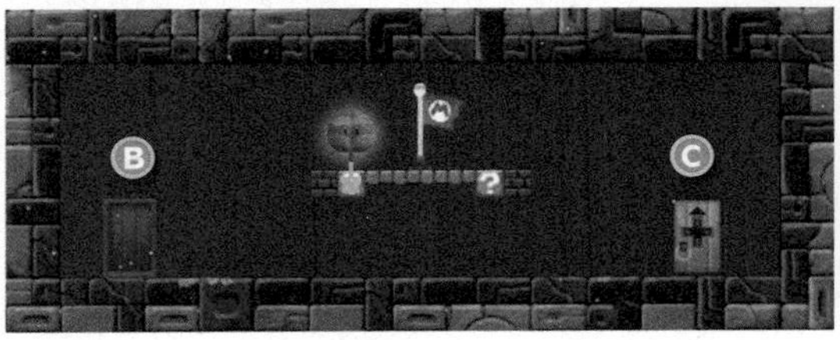

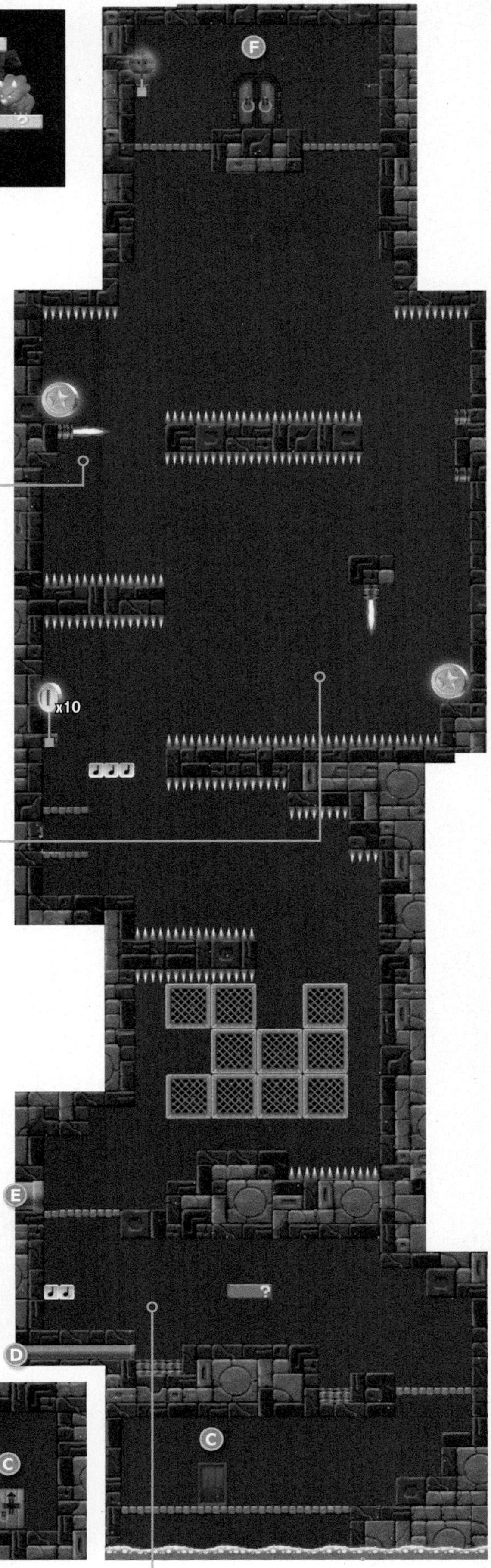

6

As you approach Point 6, jump back over to the left half of the moving fence. It's about to pass by the third Star Coin, so you need to move quickly.

Hop over and grab the Star Coin as the fence moves past the Burner's flame.

7

The final chamber contains two small wheels, each of which holds two Reznors. When you enter the room, you drop down to a small platform between the two wheels. As you jump to a vacant ? Block, remember that fireballs can come from virtually any direction. Clear out all four Reznors to complete the level.

Many of the platforms in this level respond to Mario's body weight. When Mario stands on a blue platform, it drops below its default position; when he stands on a pink platform, it rises above its default position.

1

Stomp the Koopa just past the Gold Ring, then carry its shell to Point 1. Toss the shell onto the pink platform, then follow it as it speeds through the nearby enemies. As you do, each platform reacts to your presence.

If you stay too close to the shell, the blue platforms drop out of position. If you stay too far from the shell, the pink platforms will fail to move into position. If you time it just right, however, the shell will hit the Block just past the platforms to reveal a 1-Up Mushroom.

2

The first Star Coin is floating between the platforms at Point 2. To collect it, stomp the Koopa patrolling the platform to the right, then throw its shell at the Star Coin.

3

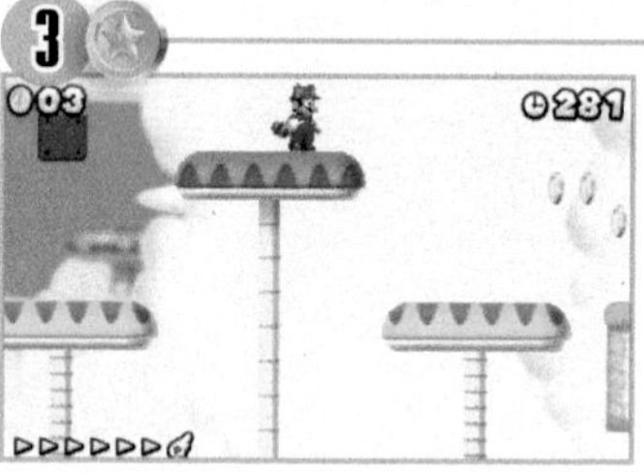

The second Star Coin is located in a hidden area. To find it, hop onto the pink platform at Point 3, and stay put until it carries you off the screen.

WORLD 5-4

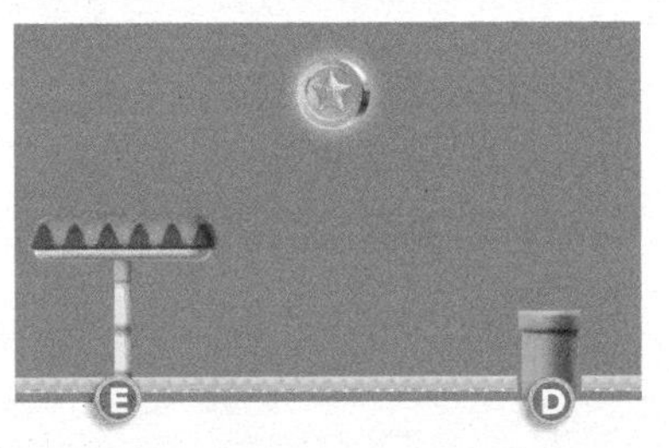

When the pink platform stops, the Star Coin appears to the right. Jump over to grab the Star Coin, then use the green pipe to leave the area.

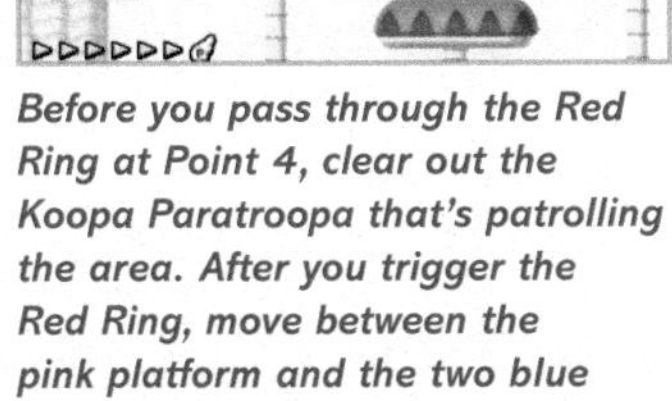

Before you pass through the Red Ring at Point 4, clear out the Koopa Paratroopa that's patrolling the area. After you trigger the Red Ring, move between the pink platform and the two blue platforms to grab each red coin as it drifts down from above you.

The third Star Coin is located below the blue platforms at Point 5. As the patrolling Koopa moves into position, drop down to grab the Star Coin, then stomp the unsuspecting enemy and bounce back up to the platforms.

TIP

Getting to the top of the Goal Pole can be tricky. What you need to do is make sure that you have a Raccoon Tail and jump on top of the Paratroopers. Jump off of the last one and on to the top of the Goal Pole.

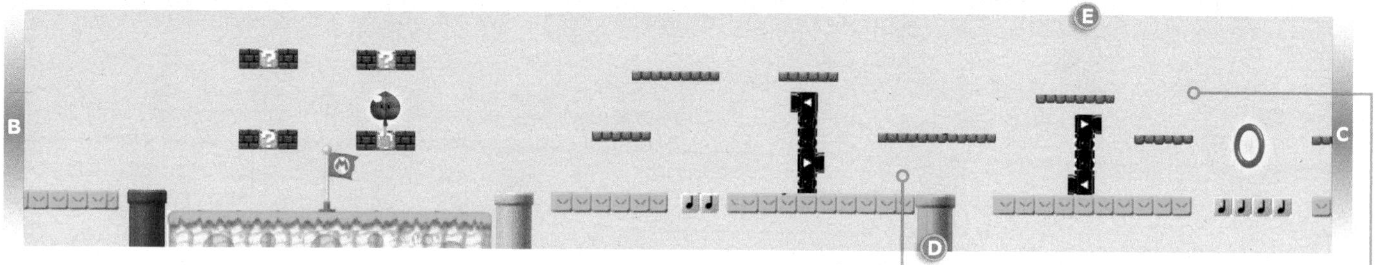

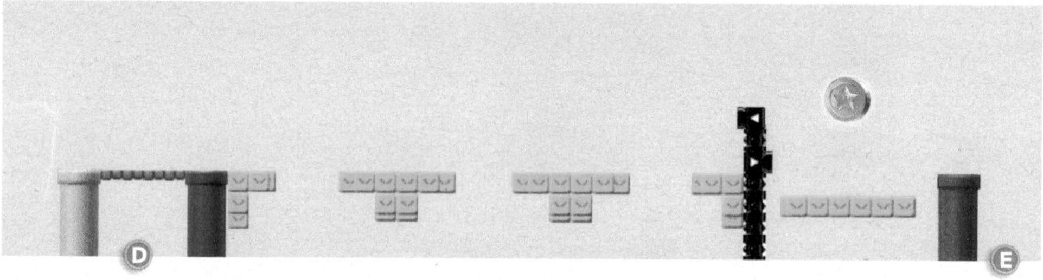

1

To reveal the first Star Coin, jump onto the Bill Blaster Turret at Point 1. Wait for a Bullet Bill to emerge, then stomp the enemy and bounce into position. When you land, the Star Coin appears to the right.

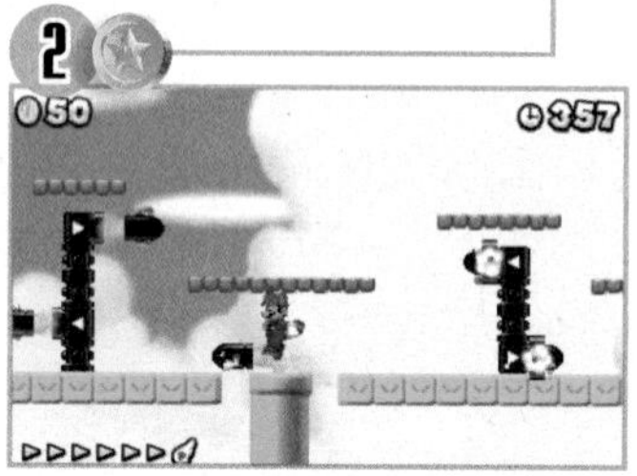

2

The second Star Coin is located in a hidden area. To find it, enter the green pipe at Point 2.

After the pipe launches you to the secret area, jump along the Caterpillar Blocks to the right. The Star Coin is floating just past the Bill Blaster Turret.

WORLD 5-5

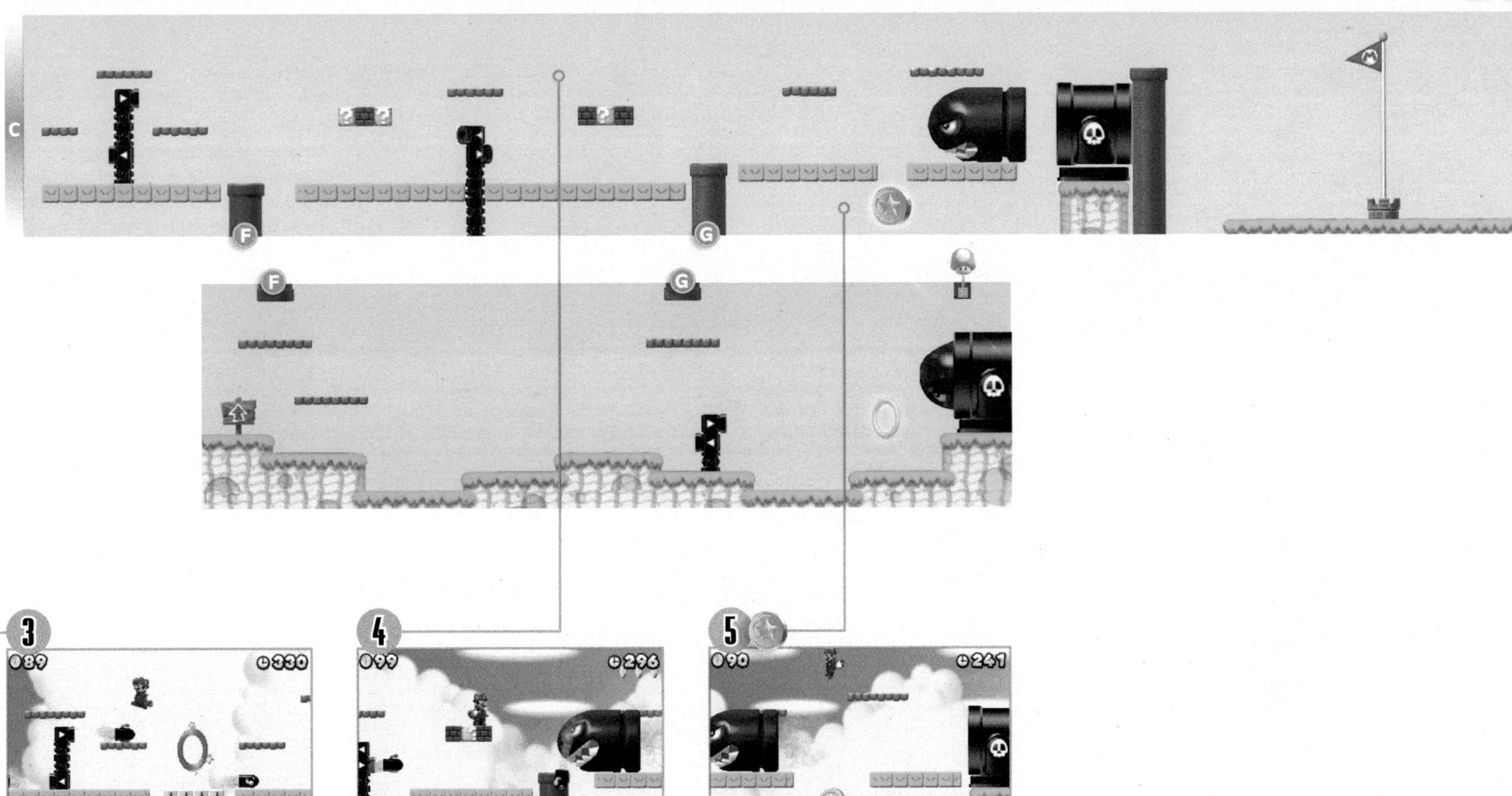

When you pass through the Red Ring at Point 3, eight red coins appear in the area. As you collect them, watch out for the Bullet Bills that emerge from the nearby Bill Blaster Turrets.

When you reach the Blocks at Point 4, a Banzai Bill approaches from the right. Stomp this oversized enemy, then enter the red pipe to find a hidden area containing a Gold Ring.

It takes precision timing to collect the Star Coin at Point 5. Slip between the Banzai Bills as they fly through the area, then drop down and collect the Star Coin just as a Bullet Bill passes under it. Bounce off of the Bullet Bill, then hurry out of the Banzai Bills' flight path.

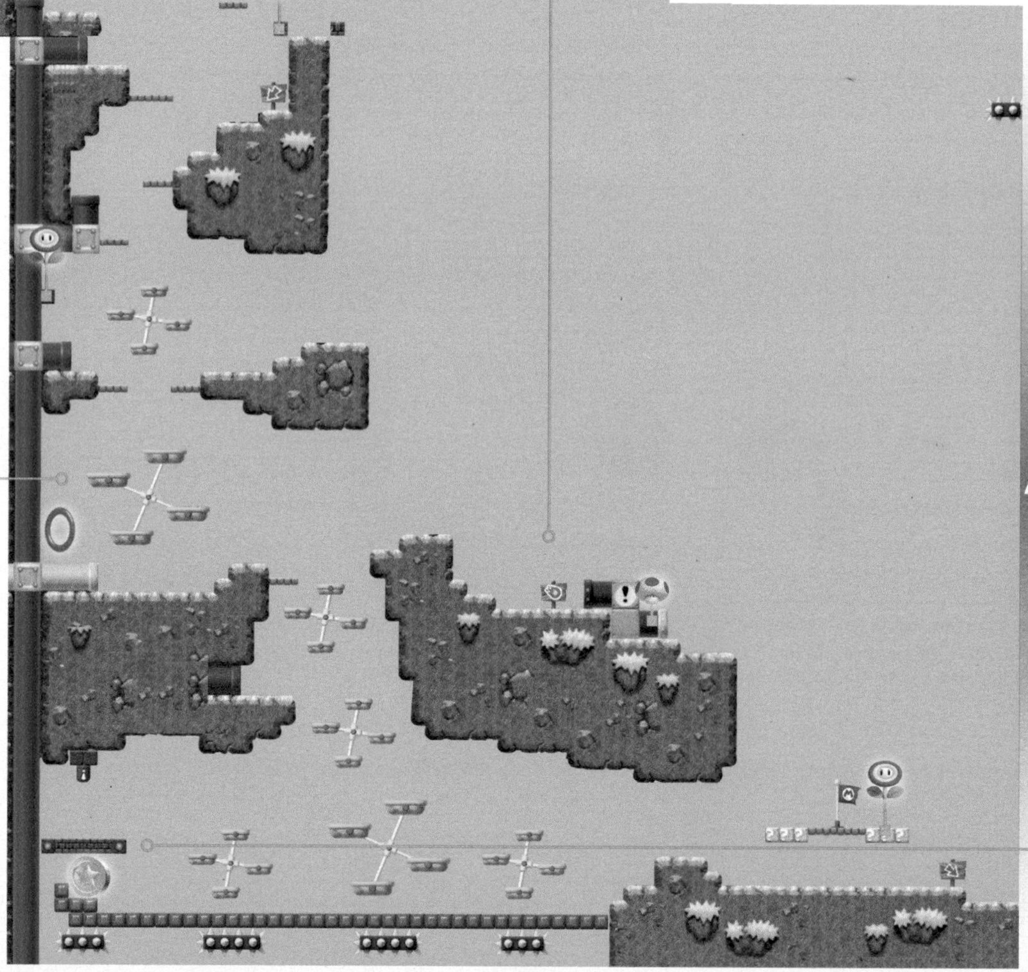

2

The ! Pipe at Point 2 contains a Mega Mushroom. This power-up allows you to collect the third Star Coin, but Mega Mario can cause serious damage to important areas. Unless you plan on revisiting this level, avoid using the ! Pipe until you've collected the first two Star Coins.

TIP

If you start the level as Raccoon Mario, you can jump from the upper platforms and glide right to the Goal Pole!

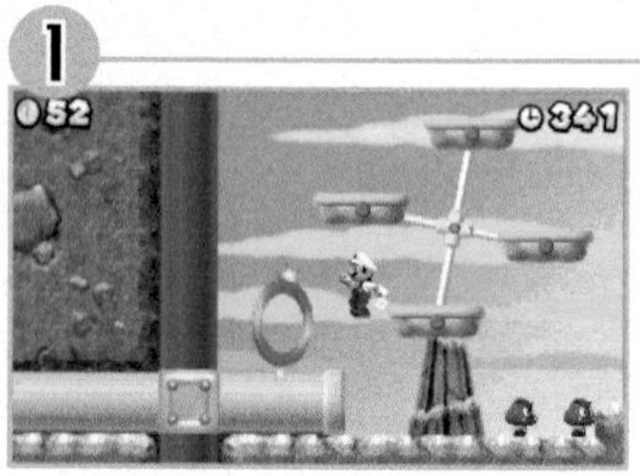

1

Pass through the Red Ring at Point 1, then jump to each of the nearby platforms to collect the red coins.

3

When you hit the ! Switch at Point 3, the Blocks below you swing apart and drop you right onto the first Star Coin. Dash to solid ground before the ! Switch wears off the and the temporary walkway vanishes.

4

The second Star Coin is located in a hidden area. Find the green pipe at Point 4, locate the Invisible Block just above it, then use the pipe to find the hidden area.

WORLD 5-6

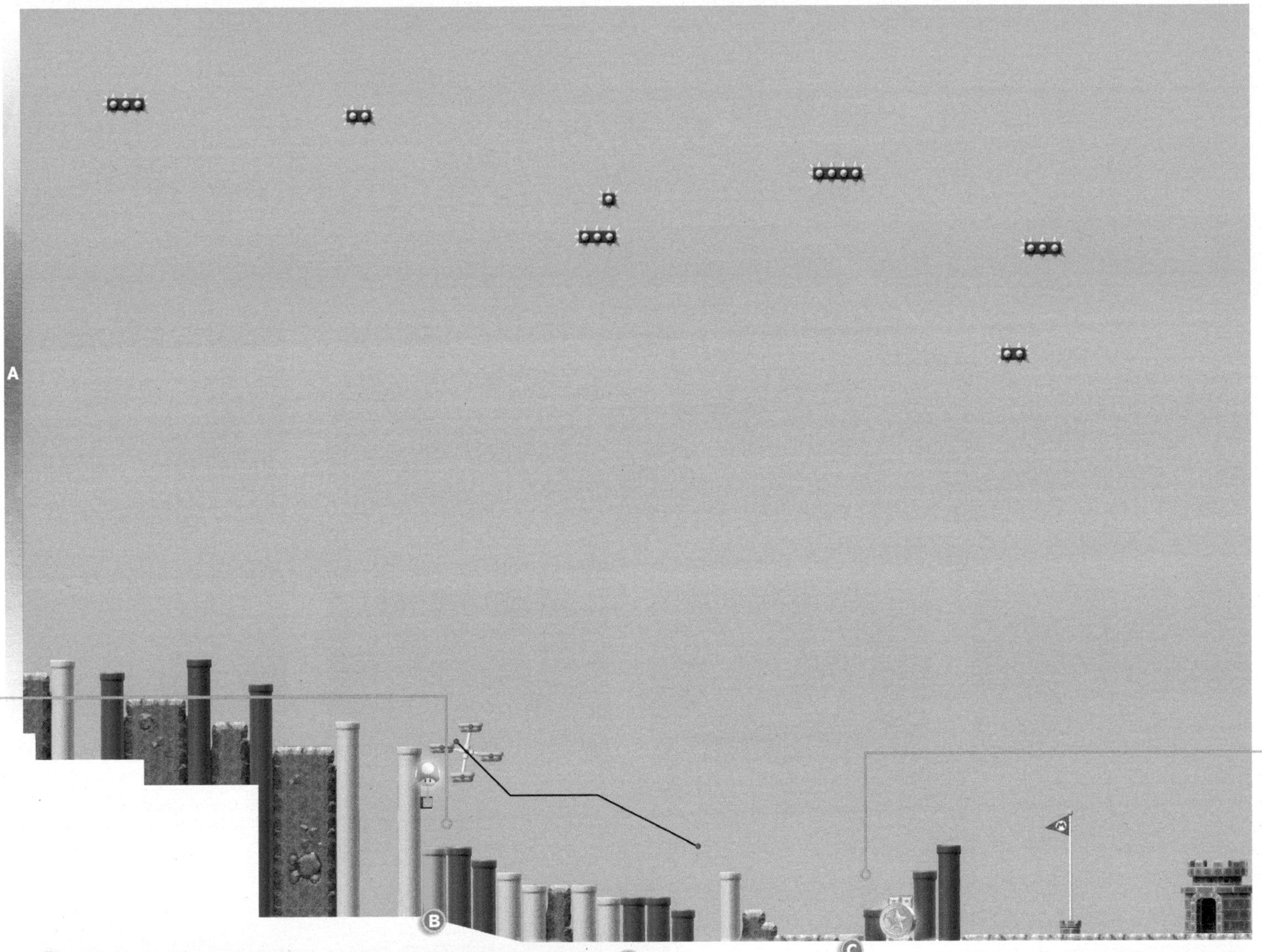

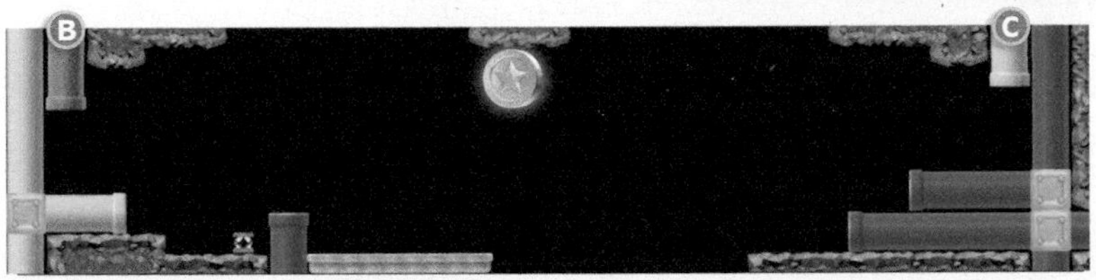

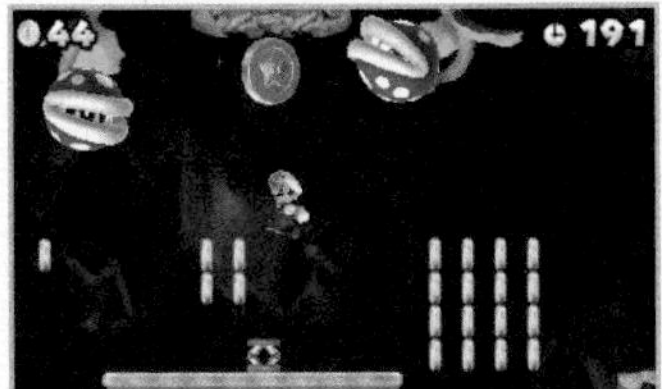

After you pass through the pipe, grab the Springboard and hop onto the platform to the right. As the platform moves back and forth across the gap, use the Springboard to bounce up to the Star Coin.

5

The third Star Coin is stuck in a small enclosure at Point 5. When you're ready, return to the ! Pipe at Point 2, fill it with fireballs until the Mega Mushroom emerges, then use the power-up to clear a path to Point 5. Smash through the enclosure and collect the Star Coin before the Mega Mushroom wears off.

A

B

C

TIP

If you take out the pipes at the end of the level, there are three hidden Blocks to help you get to the top of the Goal Pole. Note: two of these only show up if you take out the pipes.

If you hit the Goal Pole as Mega Mario you will collect three 1-Up Mushrooms.

1

Some of the fences in this level move along tracks. When you hit one of these fences (press the Dash button while latched on to the fence), it moves to the other side of the track. Use this behavior to reach new areas and avoid the obstacles in your path.

2

The first Star Coin is located in a hidden area. Find the Invisible Blocks at Point 2, then use them to reach the red pipe on the ledge to the right.

Enter the pipe to find the Star Coin floating in the center of a small room.

3

The second Star Coin is floating at Point 3. Move over the Star Coin and wait for the small fence to emerge from the lava. When it does, drop down to collect the Star Coin and grab hold of the fence. Jump to safety before the fence drops back into the lava.

4

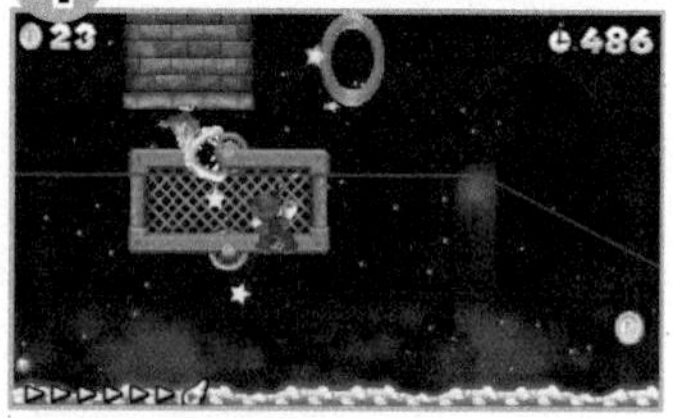

When you reach Point 4, hit the fence to move it toward the Red Ring at the top of the screen. After you pass through the Red Ring, hit the fence to move it toward each of the red coins.

WORLD 5-CASTLE

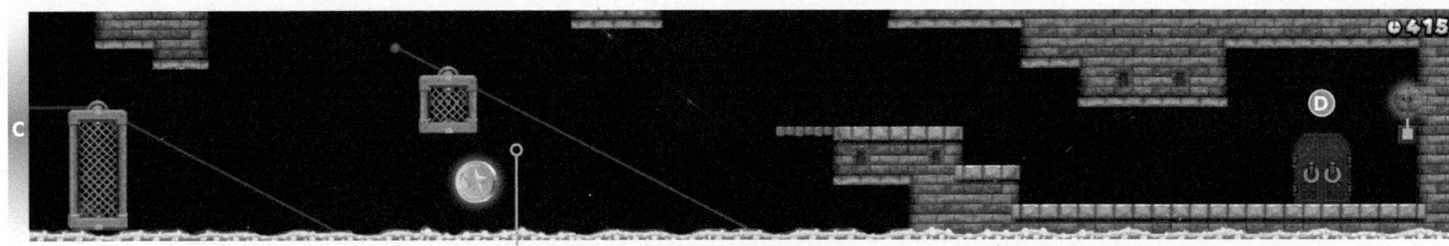

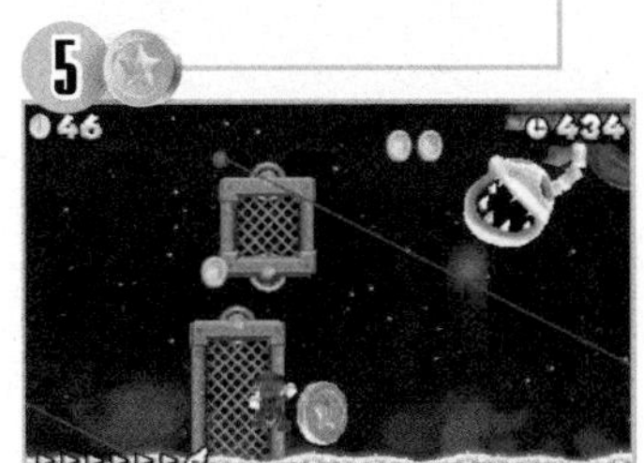

The last Star Coin is at Point 5, floating just above the lava. As you approach it, make sure the fence you're riding is positioned above the track. Grab the Star Coin as the fence sinks into the lava, then jump to the smaller fence above you.

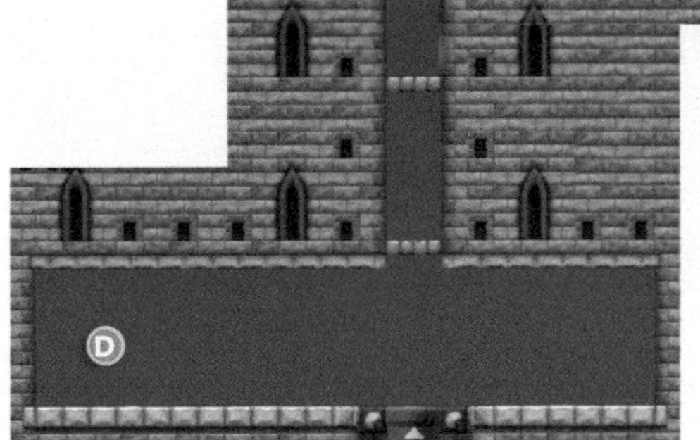

TIP

Once you get the Koopa Kid down from the chains you can bounce on his head before he jumps back up to the chains.

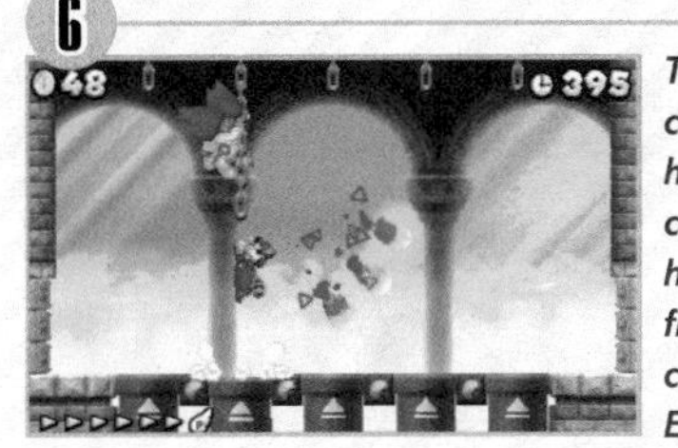

The final chamber has five chains hanging from the ceiling. Each chain is located directly over a pipe. When the battle starts, Ludwig von Koopa jumps to one of the five chains. When he does, enter the pipe directly under him to be launched up, knocking him to the floor. Run over and stomp his head while he recovers. When Ludwig tucks into his shell, avoid him until he leaps to another chain. Repeat the process to stomp him a second time.

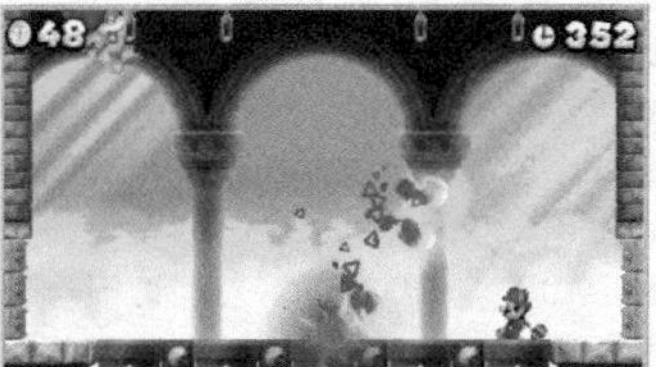

After you stomp Ludwig two times, he uses a chain to swing back and forth across the room. Move to a pipe near one of the walls and dodge Ludwig's fireballs. When Ludwig swings to the opposite side of the room, enter the pipe. This causes you to hit Ludwig as he passes above you. Stomp him one last time to complete the encounter and unlock World Six.

NOTE

To unlock this level, you must find the secret exit in World 5-1.

NOTE

To unlock the path to World 5-A, you must find this level's secret exit.

1

There's an Invisible Block located at Point 1. When the platform swings into position, jump up to reveal the hidden Beanstalk. If you wish to use the level's secret exit, climb the Beanstalk up to the next area.

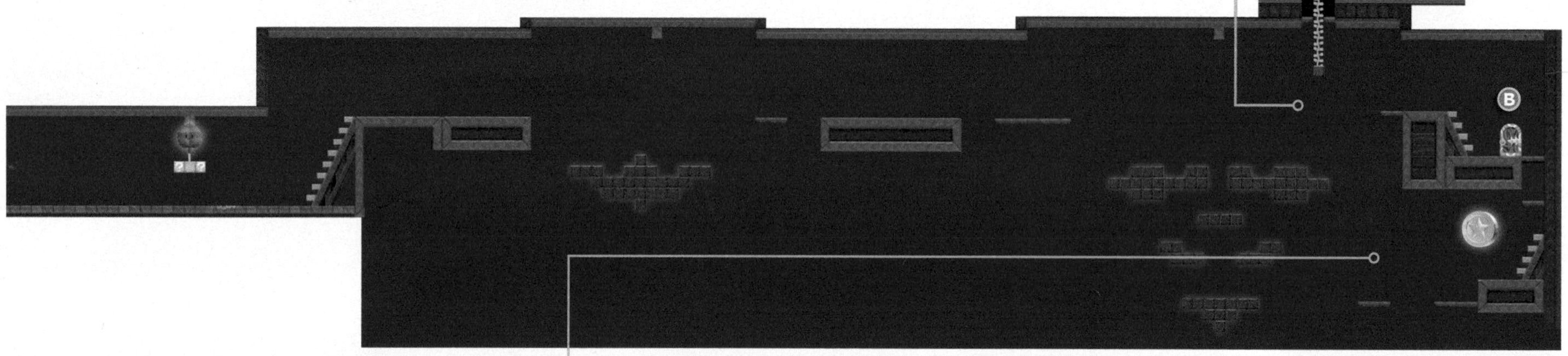

When you reach the top of the Beanstalk, follow the path to find a Big Boo waiting near a ? Switch. Stomp the ? Switch to reveal four doors. The correct door is located behind the Big Boo. Draw the enemy away from the door, then slip past it and head outside. After you reach the secret Goal Pole, World 5-A becomes available on the Map Screen.

2

The first Star Coin is located at Point 2. To find it, drop down along the swinging platforms on the room's right side. Jump over to grab the Star Coin, then climb back up to the top of the room.

3

The second Star Coin is located in a room above the level's main path. As you jump along the swinging platforms, hop onto the pole at Point 3 and climb up to the next area.

When you reach the top of the pole, follow the platforms to the Star Coin at the top of the room.

4

The third Star Coin is located in a room above the level's main path. Climb the pole at Point 4 to find a long set of stairs.

WORLD 5-BOO HOUSE

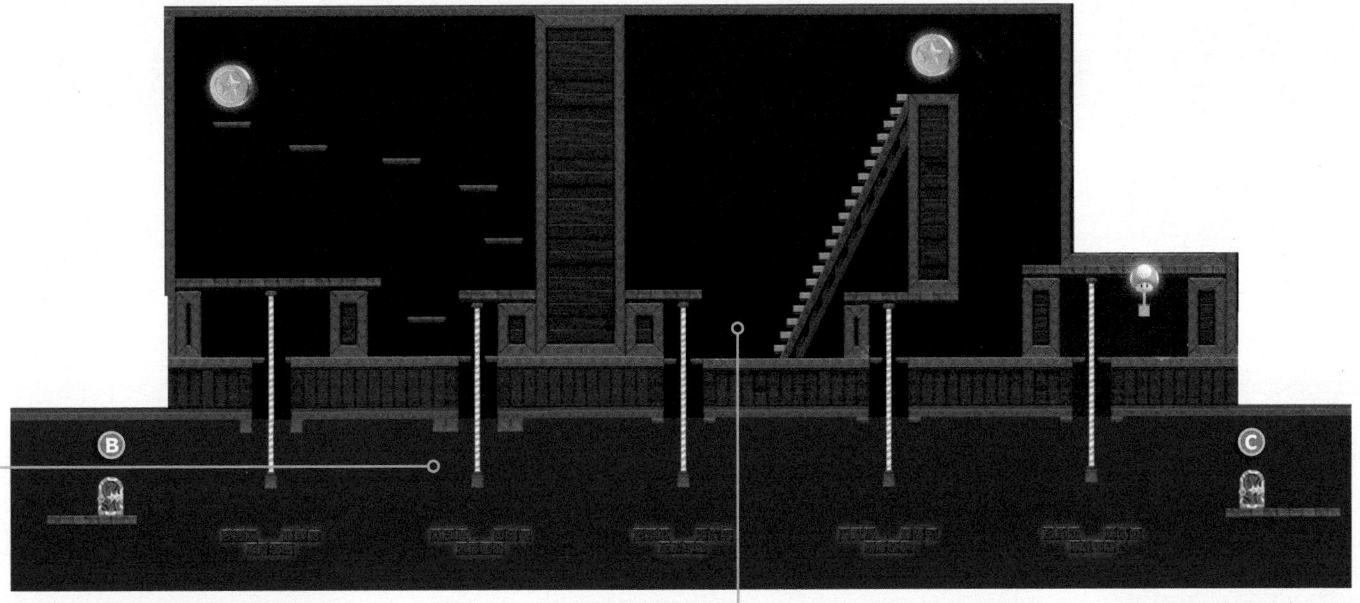

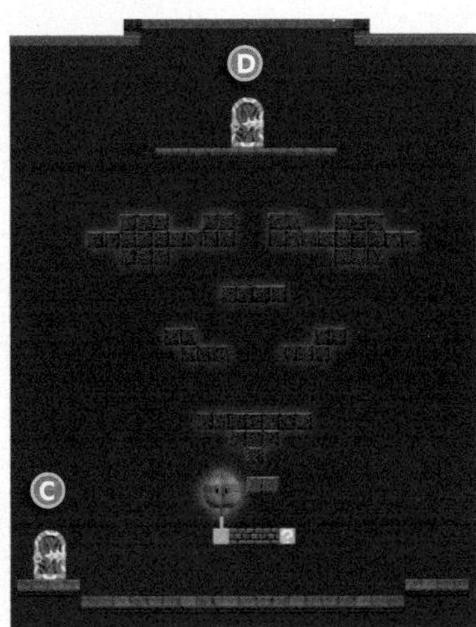

Make your way to the top of the stairs to find the level's last Star Coin.

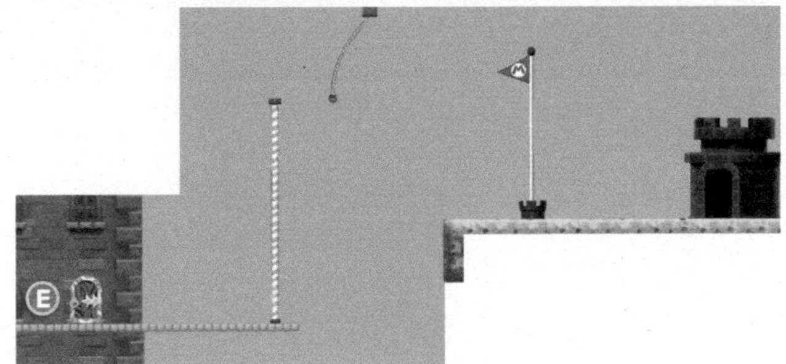

 NOTE

If you take the regular exit this will open up a new path to World 5-3. Though you will have to go through the Boo House again to open the way to World 5-A.

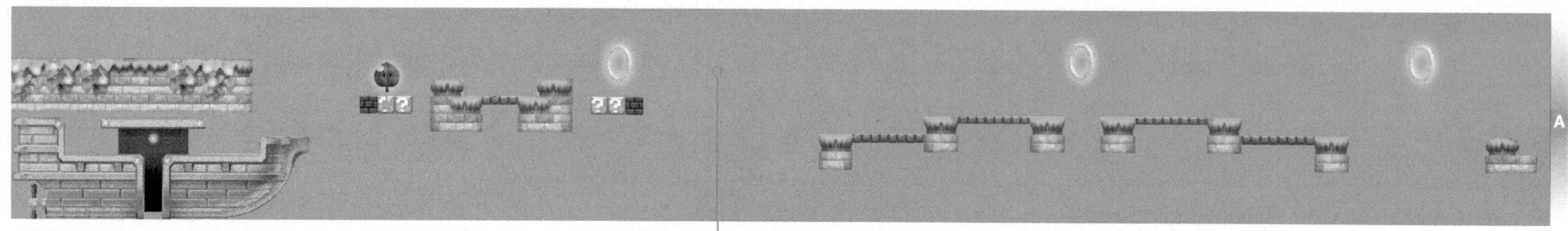

 NOTE

To unlock this level, you must find the secret exit in World 5-Boo House.

 NOTE

You must find this level's secret exit to unlock one of World Five's Toad Houses.

 NOTE

You must use this level's standard exit to unlock one of the paths in World Five.

1

This level contains several Gold Rings. To make the most of each one, stomp the first Koopa Paratroopa you see and throw its shell onto the deck of the airship. Each time you pass through a Gold Ring, the shell will both create and collect coins for the duration of the effect.

2

The first Star Coin is floating at Point 2. To collect it, bounce off of the Koopa Paratroopa patrolling the area.

3

As the airship passes by Point 3, grab the Springboard sitting on the Blocks. You'll need the Springboard to reach the level's secret exit, so make sure you hang on to it.

4

The second Star Coin is atop one of the pillars at Point 4. Use the Springboard to reach it, or bounce off the nearby Koopa Paratroopa.

WORLD 5-A

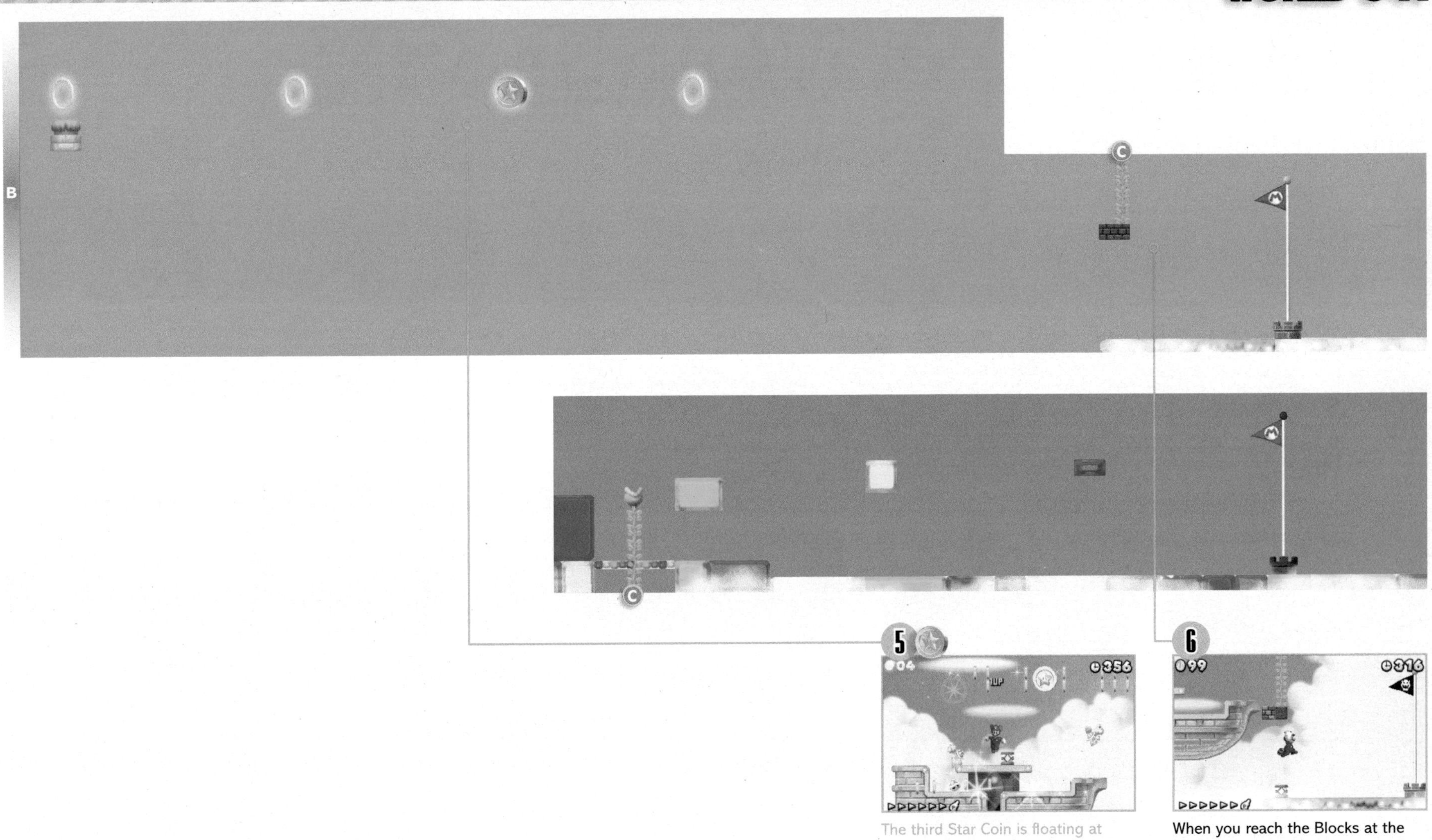

The third Star Coin is floating at Point 5. To reach it, bounce off of the Springboard or one of the nearby enemies.

When you reach the Blocks at the end of the level, use the Springboard to bounce up and hit them from below. One of the Blocks contains a Beanstalk. Bounce up to the Beanstalk, then follow the path to the secret exit. After you reach the secret Goal Pole, a new path appears on the Map Screen.

New SUPER
MARIO BROS. 2

WORLD SIX

W6-1
Toad House
Toad House
W6-Boo House
W6-2
W6-B
Toad House
W6-A

WORLD LOCATIONS				
Hostile Levels	Toad Houses	Boo Houses	Warp Cannons	Boss
10	4	1	0	Bowser

Main Path Levels:

- World 6-1
- World 6-Boo House
- World 6-2
- World 6-3
- World 6-Tower
- World 6-4
- World 6-5
- World 6-Castle

Alternate Path Levels:

- World 6-A
- World 6-B

1

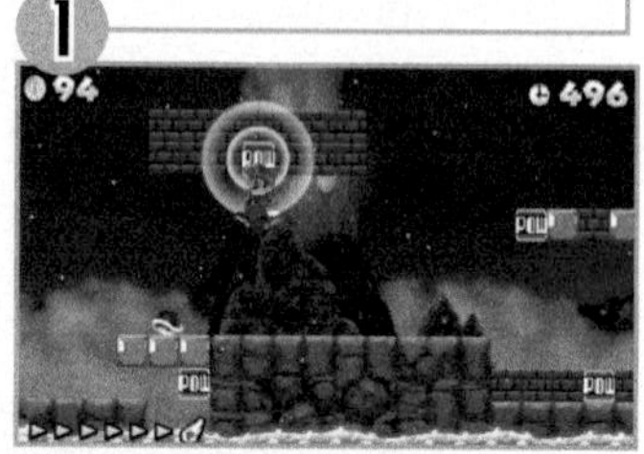

As debris falls down from the sky, it destroys most of the Blocks in this level. If you want to collect the power-ups and coins contained in the Blocks, you'll need to be quick.

2

The first Star Coin is on a stone platform at Point 2. Leap onto the platform to collect it, but watch out—this elevated location doesn't leave you much room to dodge falling debris.

3

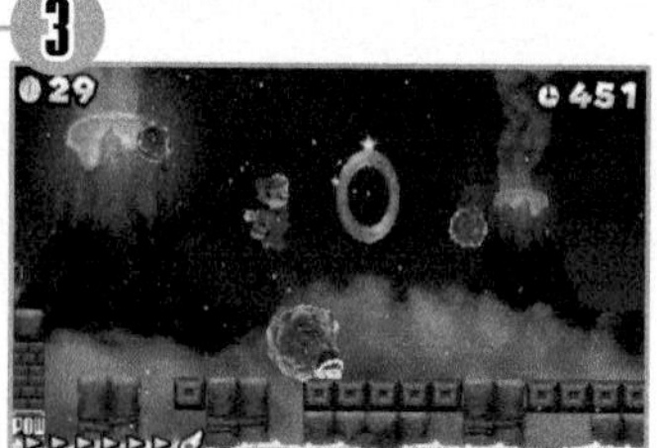

When you jump through the Red Ring at Point 3, the red coins parachute into the area. Be very careful as you collect them. You must not only dodge the volcanic debris as it drops from the sky, you then must avoid falling through the holes it creates in the walkway!

4

The Star Coin at Point 4 is sealed inside of the walkway. To collect it, you must stay in the area until the debris destroys the enclosure.

WORLD 6-1

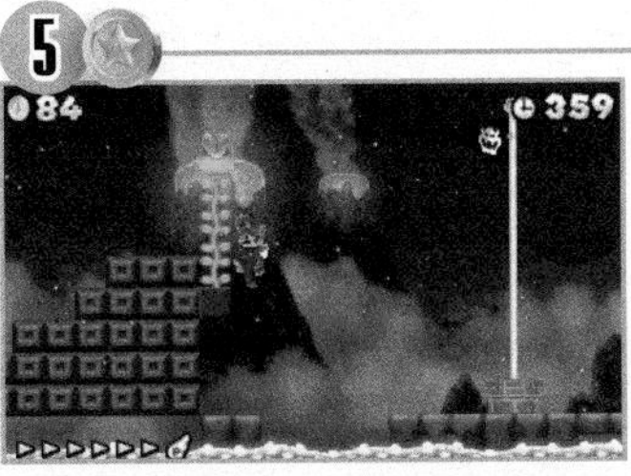

The third Star Coin is located in a hidden area. Find the Invisible Block at Point 5. When you do, a Beanstalk appears.

Climb to the top of the Beanstalk to find the Star Coin. Jump up and grab it, then follow the coin trail down to the Goal Pole.

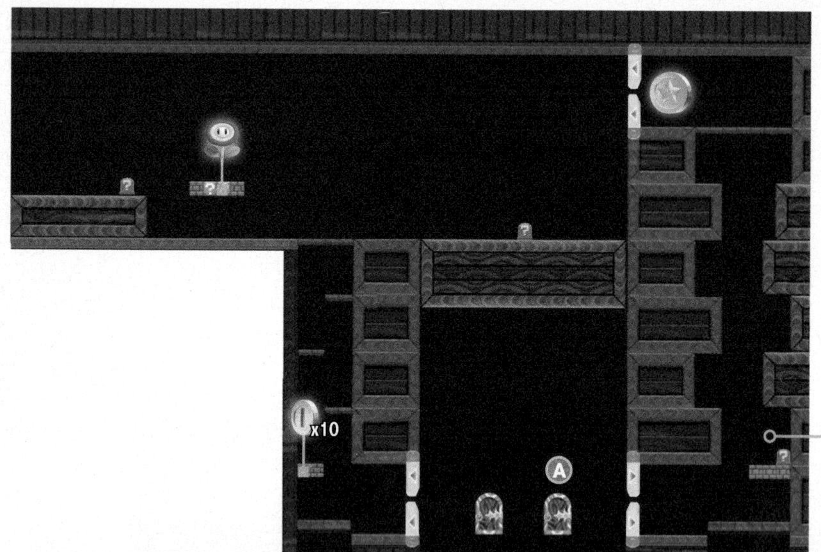

NOTE

To unlock the path to World 6-A, you must find this level's secret exit.

TIP

The ? Switches throughout this level tend to reveal essential platforms, passages, and doors. Don't pass one by without activating it!

1

One of the Blocks at Point 1 contains a ? Switch. When you stomp it, the platforms above you spread apart, revealing the path to the first Star Coin.

Follow the path up to the Star Coin, then pass through the hinged panels and drop back to the floor.

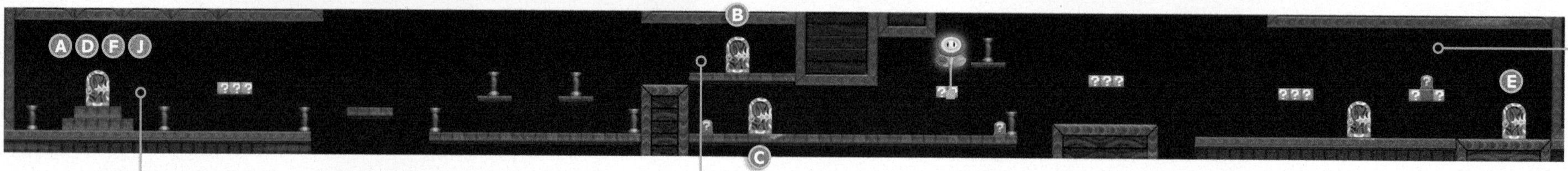

2

The level contains two very similar hallways—one populated by Big Boos, the other populated by normal Boos. As you explore each area, you'll find that multiple doors lead you back to Point 2. The steps below the door and the nearby Big Boo make it fairly easy to recognize this spot.

3

When you first reach Point 3, the raised platform prevents you from exploring the right half of the Big Boo hallway. Enter the accessible door to transition from the Big Boo hallway to the Boo hallway.

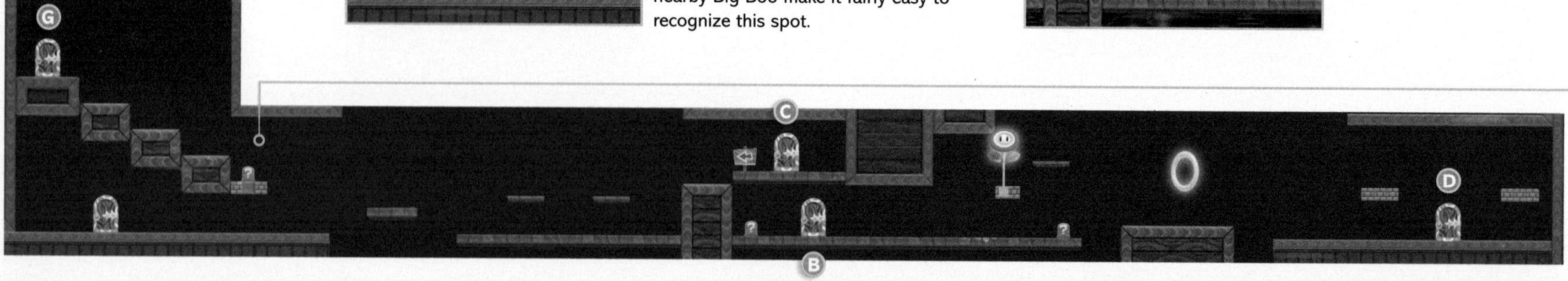

WORLD 6-BOO HOUSE

After you emerge from the lower door in the Boo hallway, use the ? Switch to lower the platform to the left. You can now explore the entire length of the Boo hallway. Enter the door above you to transition to the right half of the Big Boo hallway.

Return to the doors at Point 3 (or the similar doors in the Boo hallway) whenever you need to transition between hallways.

4

To find the second Star Coin, hit the ? Switch at the left end of the Boo hallway. After the platforms drop down from the ceiling, follow them to find a door.

Pass through the door, then drop down and activate the ? Switch below you. The platforms to the right drop down to clear a path to the Star Coin.

The door above the second Star Coin leads to the level's standard exit.

5

To find the third Star Coin, activate the ? Switch at the right end of the Big Boo hallway. After the platform to the right sinks into the floor, pass through the revealed door.

When you reach the next room, stomp the ? Switch to the right to rearrange the surrounding platforms. Perform a series of wall jumps to collect the Star Coin floating directly above you.

6

To find the secret exit, continue performing wall jumps after you collect the third Star Coin. The door at Point 6 leads outside. Head through the door and reach the secret Goal Pole to unlock the path to World 6-A.

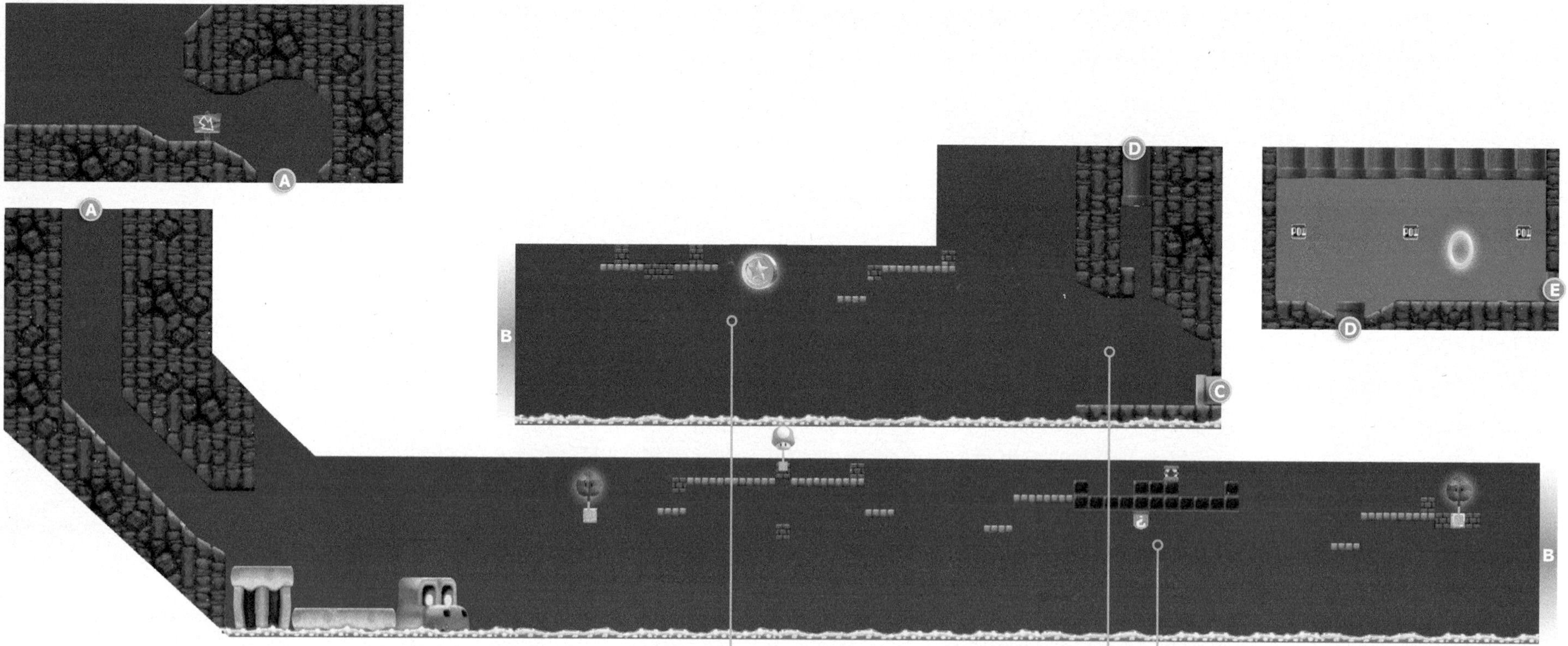

CAUTION

This level contains some segmented platforms that carry you across large pools of lava. While you ride, watch out for enemies that drop down from above and fireballs that spring up from below.

1

There's a Springboard on the platform at Point 1. Leap up to the platform and grab it, or hit the ? Switch below the platform to drop the Springboard down to you.

2

The first Star Coin is floating at Point 2. Use the Springboard to bounce up and grab it.

3

When you reach Point 3, use the Springboard to bounce through the gap in the ceiling. Wall jump to the ledge, then enter the red pipe above you to find a hidden room.

WORLD 6-2

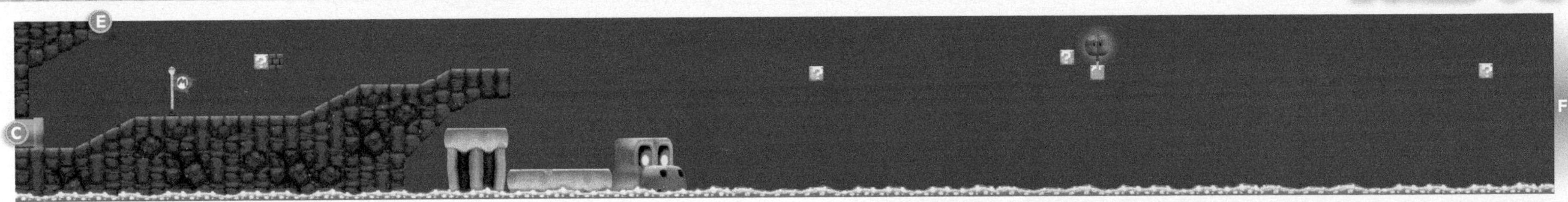

The second Star Coin is surrounded by Blocks. As you pass under it, smash the Blocks to clear a path to the Star Coin.

The third Star Coin is sealed behind a wall. Use a Bob-omb to blast a hole in the wall, then grab the Star Coin before the lava reaches you.

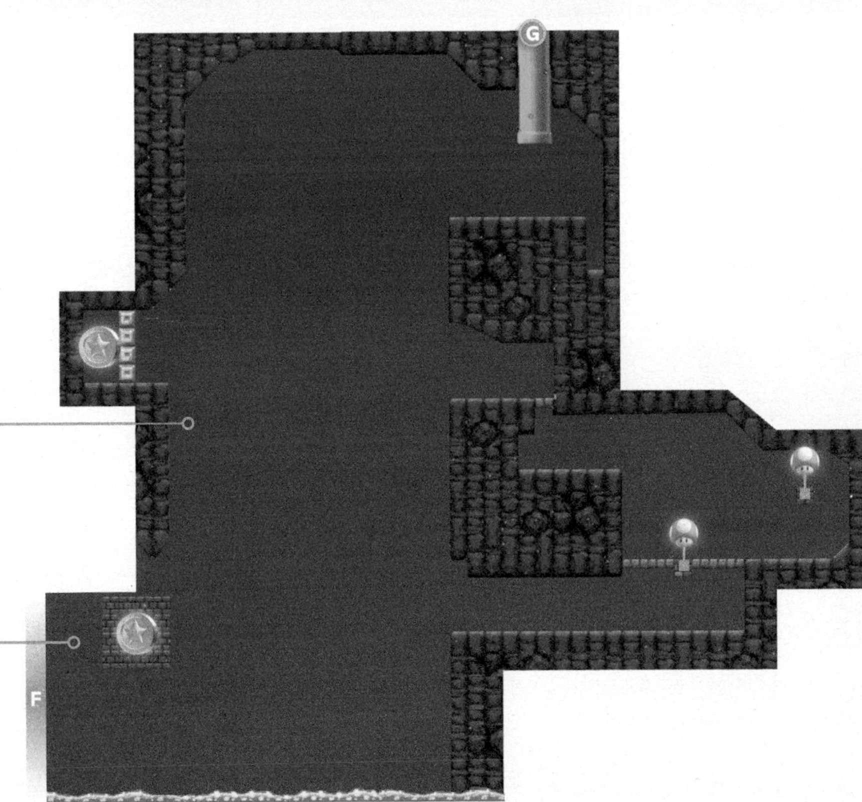

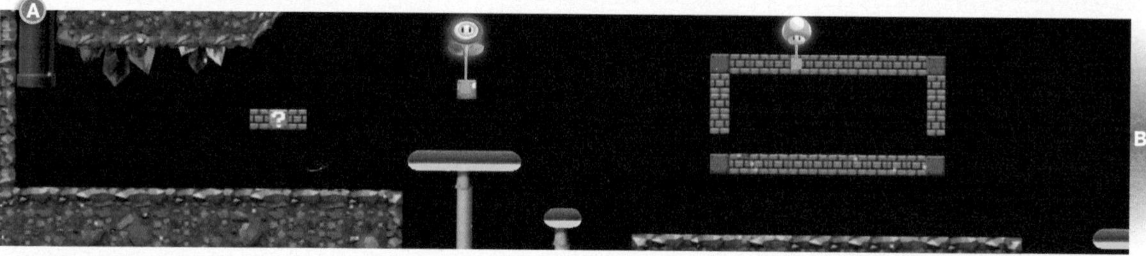

CAUTION

The toadstools in this level expand and contract at regular intervals. Time each jump to avoid falling.

1

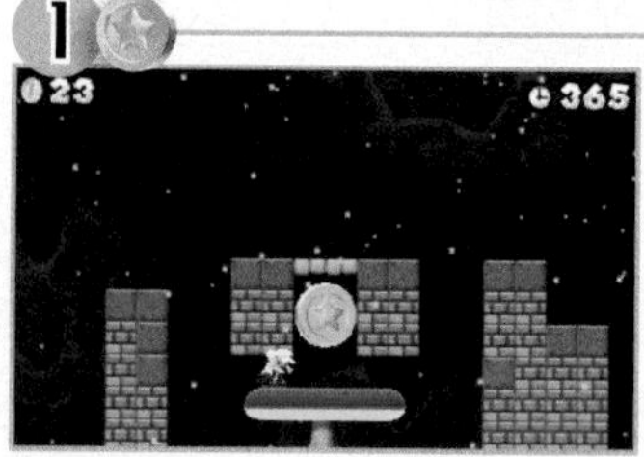

The first Star Coin is located under the platform at Point 1. Stomp the nearby Koopa and use its shell to clear away a few of the nearby Blocks. Wait for the toadstool to expand, then drop to it and crouch down. When the toadstool contracts, it carries you to the Star Coin.

2

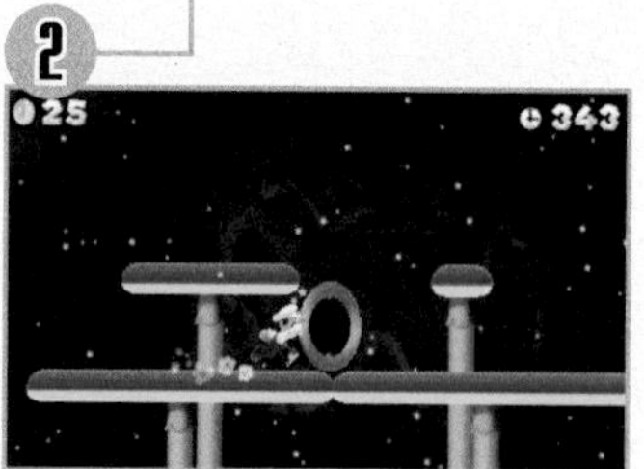

When you pass through the Red Ring at Point 2, eight red coins appear in the area. As the surrounding platforms expand and contract, use them to reach each of the coins.

NOTE

If you make a running leap from the toadstools at Point 2, you can reach the Blocks to the right. This shortcut provides a safe route through the area, but it does bypass some important items.

3

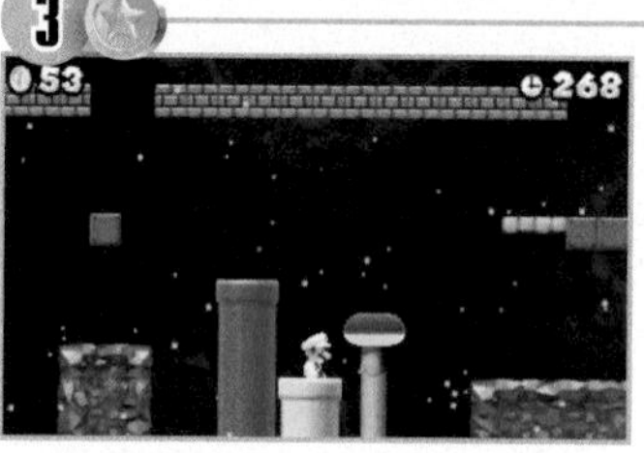

The second Star Coin is located in a hidden area. To find it, enter the yellow pipe at Point 3.

Dodge past the incoming fireballs and pass through the Gold Ring at the top of the room. Clear out the enemies, then collect the Star Coin near the right wall.

WORLD 6-3

If you pass through the red pipe (marked as "F" on the map), look for the Koopa to the right. Jump past the Koopa, then turn back and stomp it as it begins to drop from the ledge. This causes you to stomp the shell each time it bounces back toward you. If you time it right, you can earn a lot of extra lives.

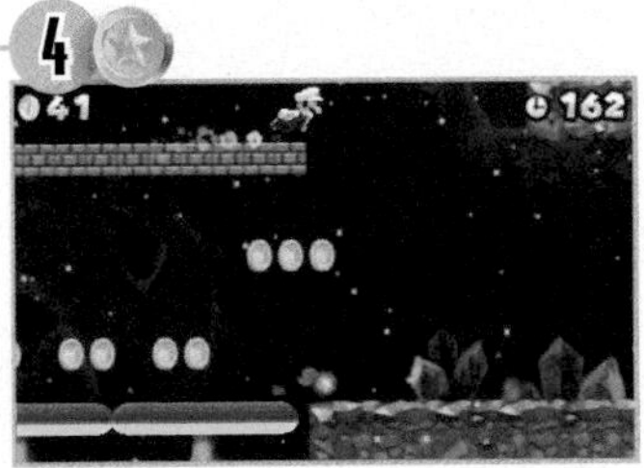

To collect the third Star Coin, you must find the passage hidden at Point 4. If you crossed the toadstools to reach this area, head back and climb up to the Blocks near the top of the screen. Dash to the right, then leap from the last Block to find the hidden passage.

When you reach the end of the passage, drop down and collect the Star Coin.

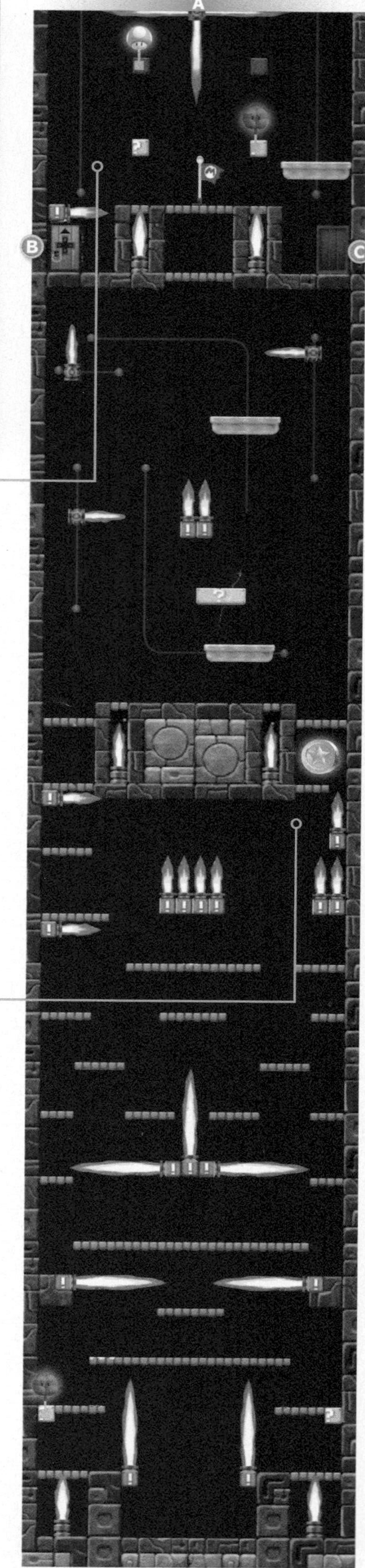

2

The second Star Coin is located through the door at Point 2. Ground pound the burner along the left wall, then drop down and enter the door.

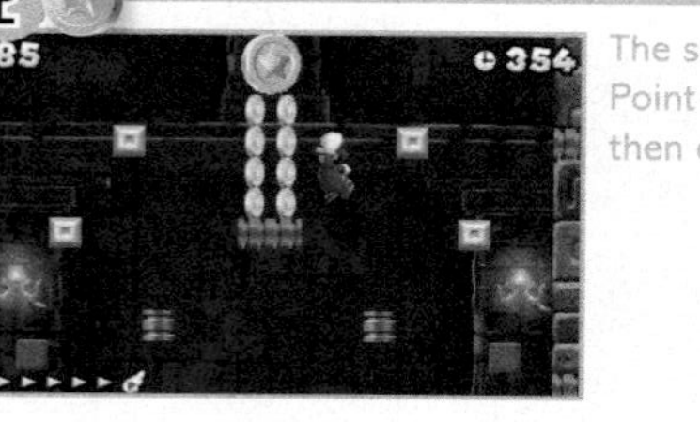

The Star Coin is at the top of the room. To reach it, you must jump up along the scattered Blocks and burners. The burners erupt at regular intervals, so watch out for their flames. Climb up along one of the walls, then hop over to the burners directly below the Star Coin.

1

The first Star Coin is floating at Point 1. Deactivate the nearby burners, then use them to reach the Star Coin.

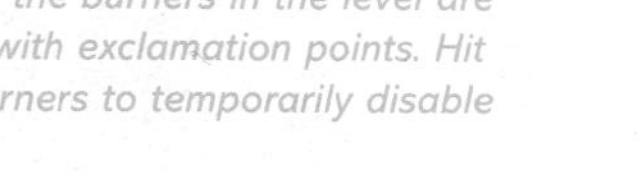

TIP

Many of the burners in the level are marked with exclamation points. Hit these burners to temporarily disable them.

WORLD 6-TOWER

4

The final chamber contains four Reznors on a single large wheel. Stand on the floor and take out each enemy that passes over you. When the floor starts to crumble, jump to a vacant ? Block and finish off the remaining Reznors.

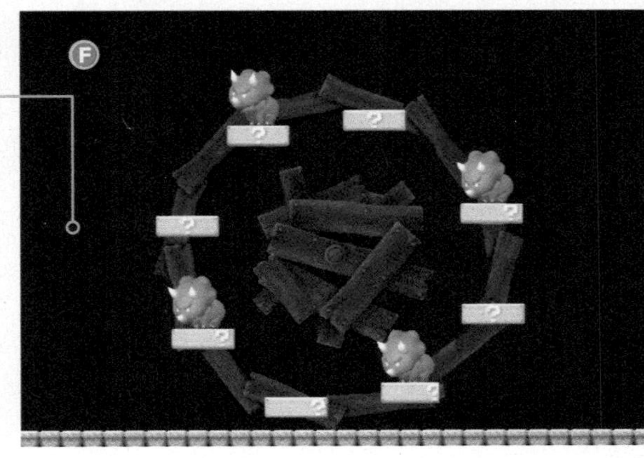

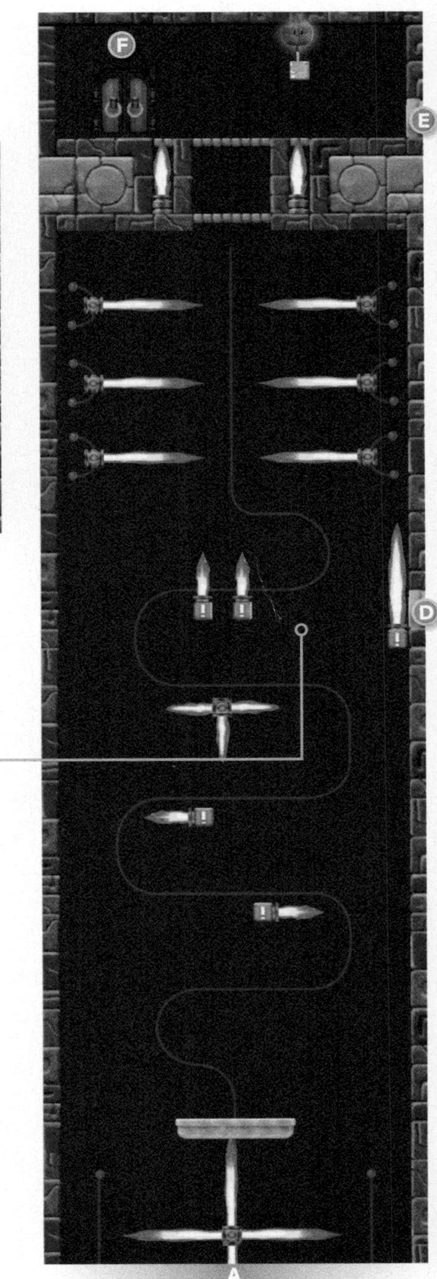

3

The third Star Coin is located in a hidden area. As the platform carries you to Point 3, look for the green pipe embedded in the right wall. Deactivate the burner as you pass below it, then jump onto it and enter the pipe.

The Star Coin is on a ledge at the top of the room. To reach it, you must jump along the burners that fill the room. The burners erupt at regular intervals, and each one moves along a small circular track. Collect the Star Coin from the ledge to the right, then exit through the pipe to the left.

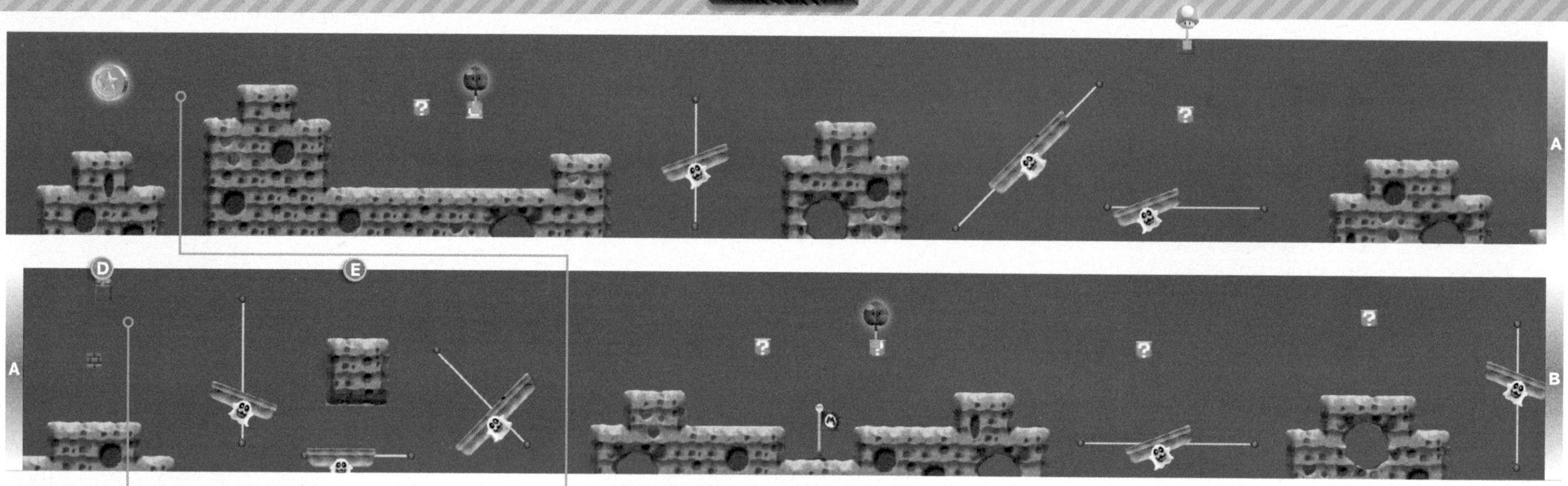

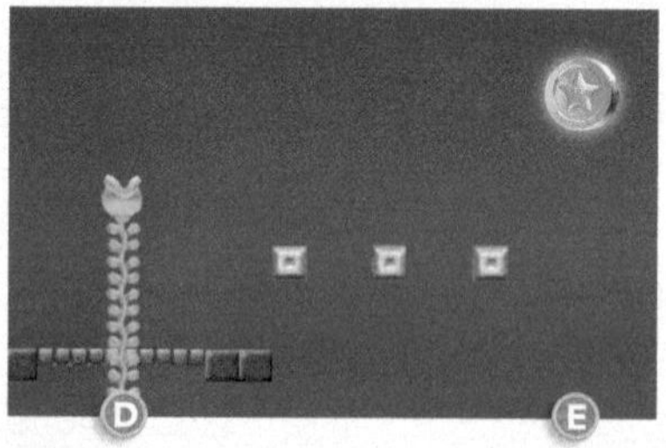

When the level starts, move left to find the first Star Coin floating above a hidden platform.

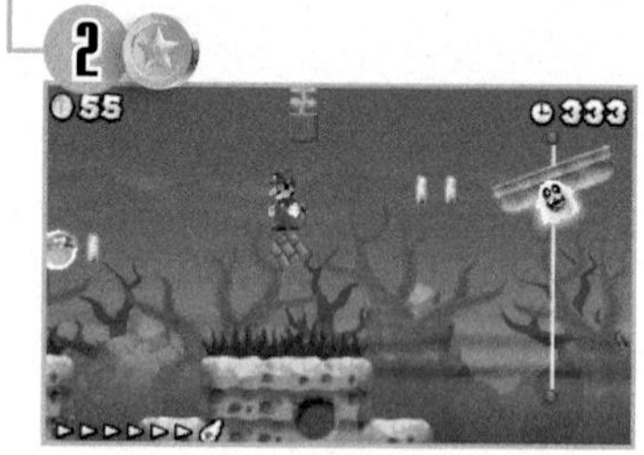

The second Star Coin is located in a hidden area. Hop onto the Block at Point 2, then jump straight up to find an Invisible Block containing a Beanstalk.

Climb to the top of the Beanstalk, then hop across the spinning Blocks to the right. Jump up and grab the Star Coin, then drop out of the area.

WORLD 6-4

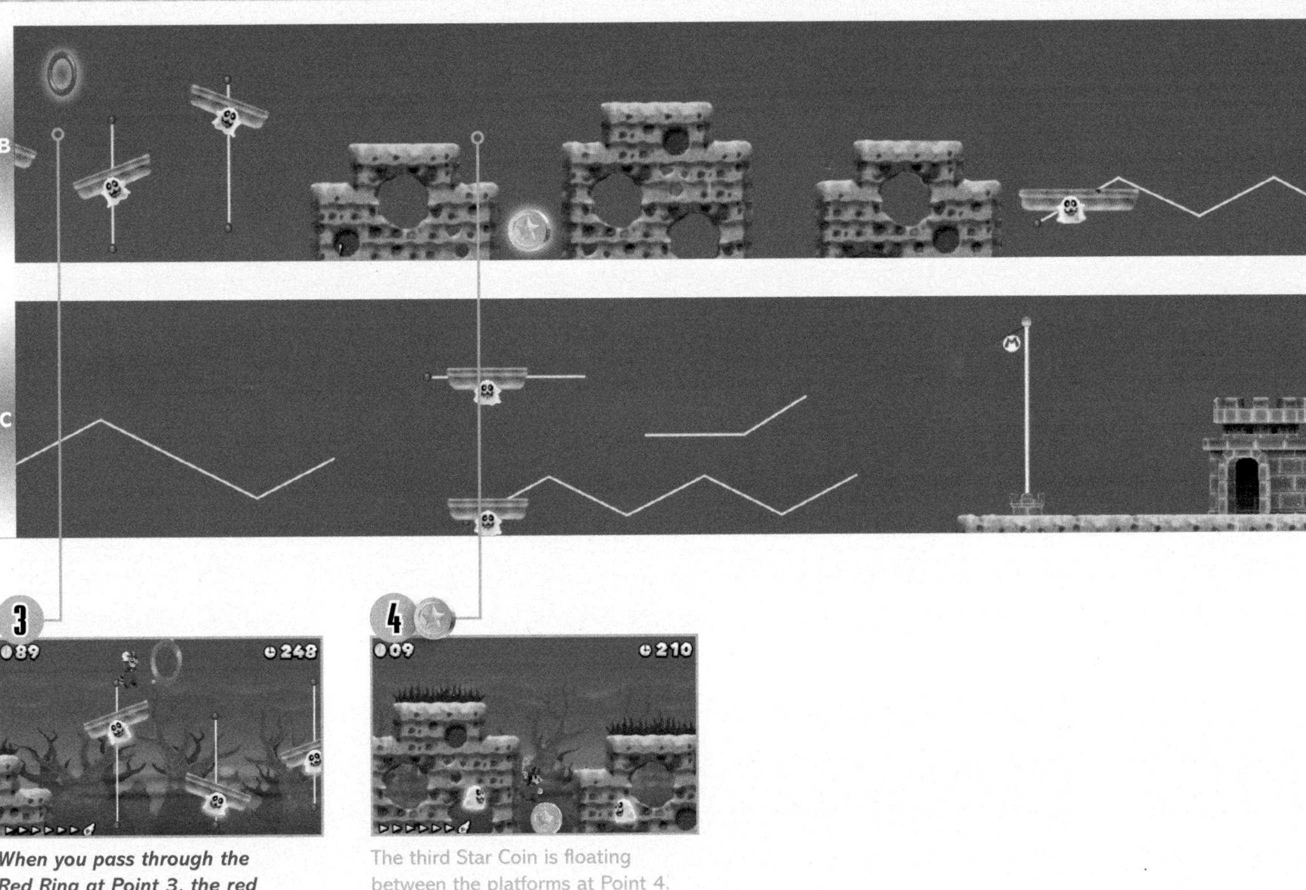

When you pass through the Red Ring at Point 3, the red coins appear above the nearby platforms. Ride each platform to collect all of the red coins before they vanish.

The third Star Coin is floating between the platforms at Point 4. Slip through the gap between the circling enemies, slide down along the side of the platform, then wall jump out of the gap before the next enemy passes above you.

NOTE

The swiveling platforms in this level react to Mario's weight. This allows you to adjust the angle of each platform.

1

Stomp the Koopa at Point 1 and grab its shell. Dodge the incoming fireballs as you continue to the right.

After you drop down from the next platform, face left and throw the shell at the Block on the lava's surface. Grab the 1-Up Mushroom as it emerges to prevent it from falling into the lava.

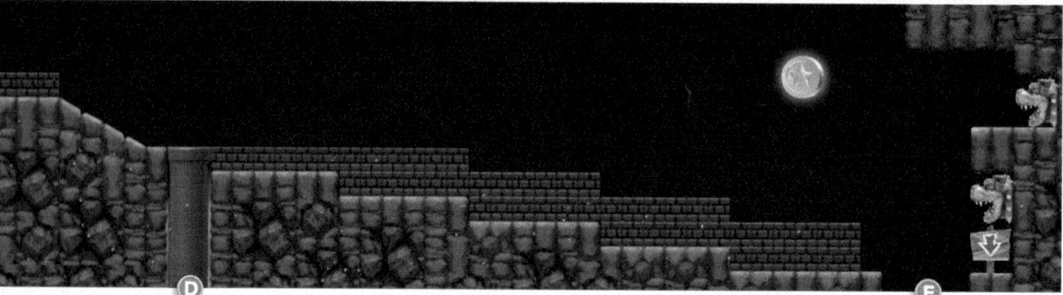

WORLD 6-5

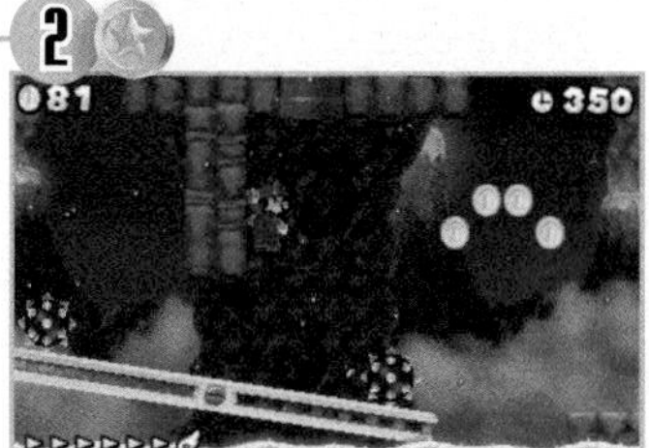

The first Star Coin is located in a hidden area. To find it, wall jump up to the red pipe at Point 2.

Soon after you pass through the pipe, a spiked ball begins smashing all of the Blocks in the area. Dodge the incoming fireballs as you dash along the Blocks to the right, then leap up to collect the Star Coin near the end of the area.

The second Star Coin is sealed in an enclosure at Point 3. Jump up to the edge of the nearby platform to tilt it down toward the Star Coin. This causes the spiked ball to roll toward the enclosure. Just before the spiked ball reaches you, jump out of the way. After the enclosure is destroyed, drop down and collect the Star Coin.

The third Star Coin is floating between the spiked balls at Point 4. Tilt the lower platform toward the Star Coin, then make a running leap to collect it. Try to land directly on the platform's pivot point to avoid disturbing the spiked balls.

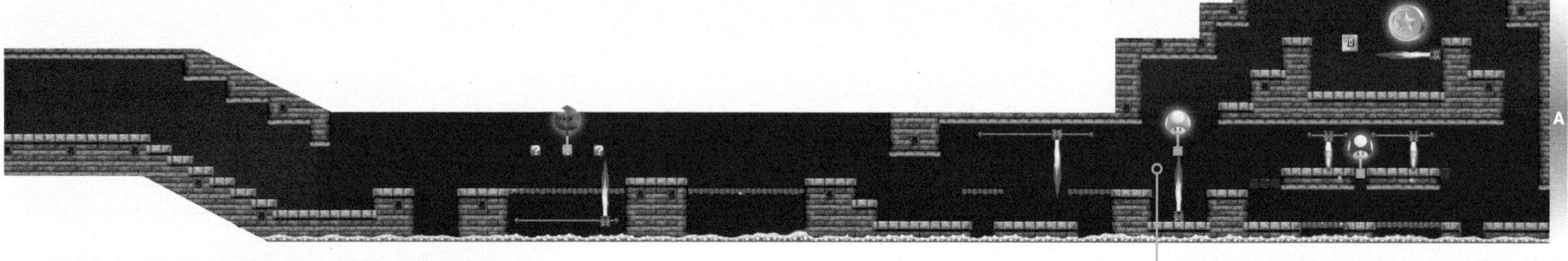

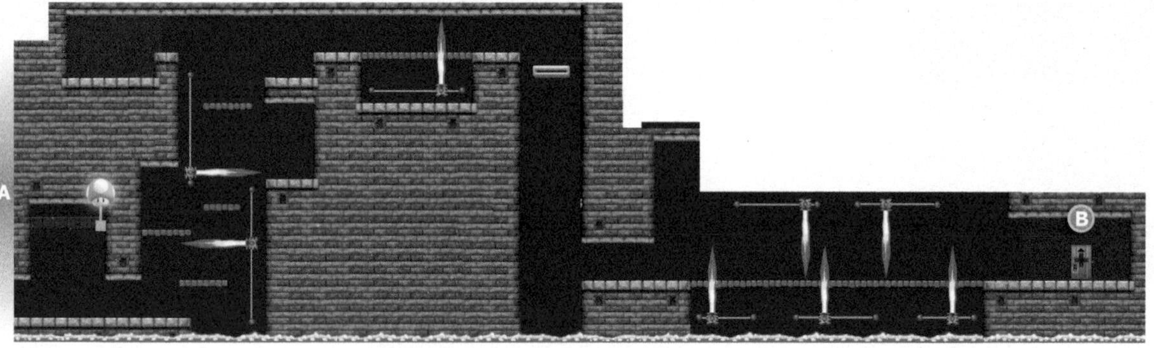

NOTE

The Super Mushroom shown on the map only appears if you hit the indicated Block while playing as Small Mario or Mini Mario.

1

The first Star Coin is located along a secret path. Find the Invisible Block above the burner at Point 1, then use it to reach the hidden ledge to the right.

Follow the path to find the Star Coin near another burner. Wait for the flame to die down, and grab the Star Coin before the burner's next burst.

2

When you step on the Caterpillar Blocks at Point 2, they zigzag past the nearby burner. You only have a short window of time in which to collect the second Star Coin, so you need to move quickly. Wait for the flame to die down, then dash past the burner.

The Star Coin is floating above a small platform. Leap over to collect it, then return to the Caterpillar Blocks before they move out of reach.

WORLD 6-CASTLE

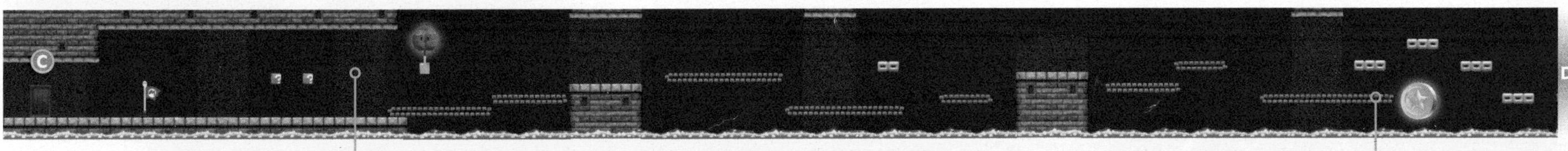

3

Soon after you reach the Checkpoint Flag, the Koopalings arrive in their flying carriage. Each time the lights on the carriage begin to blink, take cover in front of an available wall. The bright flash that occurs after the fourth blink in each sequence will turn you to stone if you're out in the open!

4

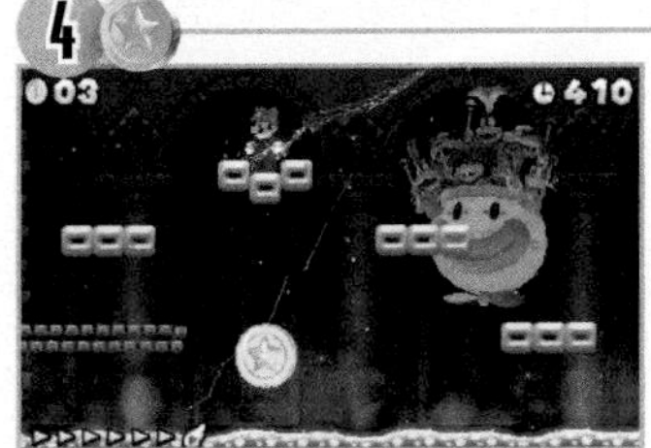

The third Star Coin is floating at Point 4. To collect it, stand on the Donut Block directly above the Star Coin. When the Donut Block falls, it takes you straight to the Star Coin. After you collect it, jump to the nearby treadmill.

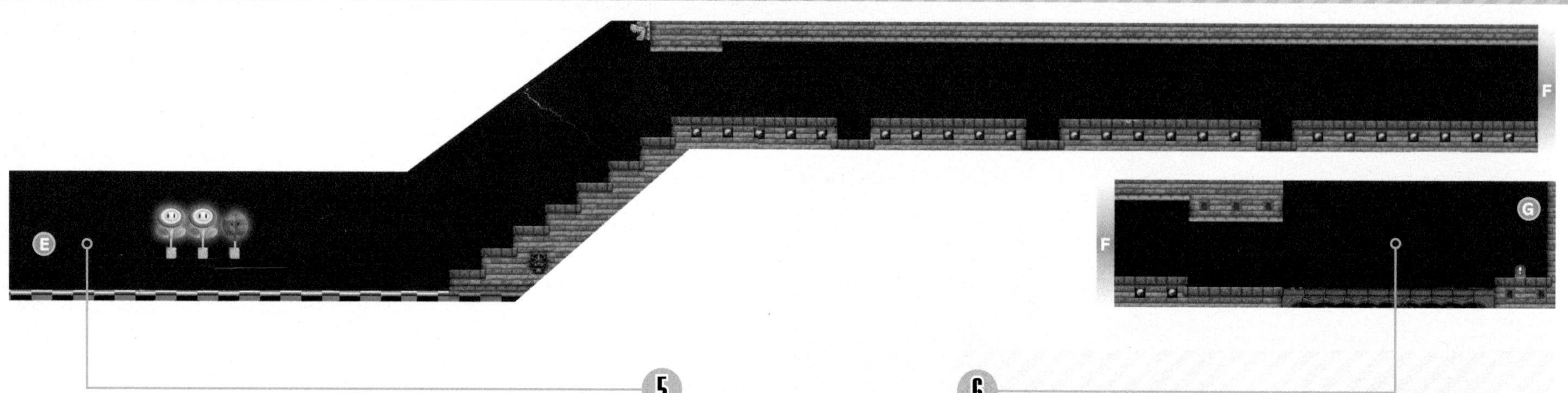

5

Each of the three ? Blocks at Point 5 contains a power-up. The Super Leaf is very useful during the coming encounter—make sure you grab it!

After you collect the Super Leaf, dash to the right to charge your Power Meter, then fly onto the Bowser sculpture at the top of the stairs. This causes several extra coins to appear on the way to Bowser.

6

The first battle with Bowser is fairly simple. Stay back and dodge his projectile attacks. Bowser has a variety of attacks, but they're all fairly easy to dodge.

After a few attacks, Bowser squats down and jumps into the air. When he does, dash under him and stomp the ! Switch near the right wall. The floor gives way and Bowser falls out of the room.

WORLD 6-CASTLE

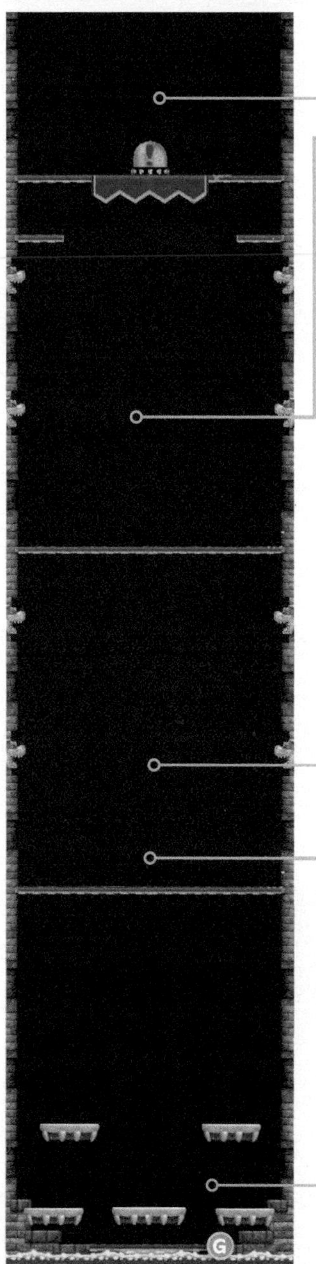

7

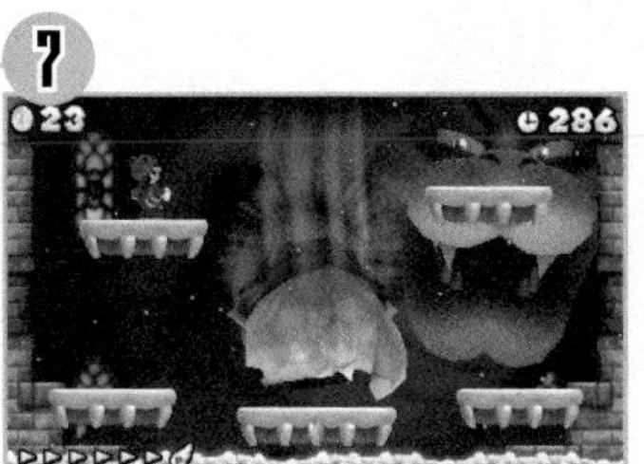

After his initial defeat, Bowser emerges from the lava bigger and angrier than ever. Super Bowser lets out a thunderous roar and the room begins filling with lava. As you jump between the floating platforms to stay ahead of the lava, pay attention to this massive enemy. When Super Bowser's eyes light up, it means he's locked on to you. Jump away from your current platform to avoid his swiping attack.

CAUTION

When you land on a platform, it slows down until it eventually drops into the lava. Each time Bowser swipes at a platform, he destroys any platforms above or below it. Since these platforms are essential to your survival, it's important to conserve them.

8

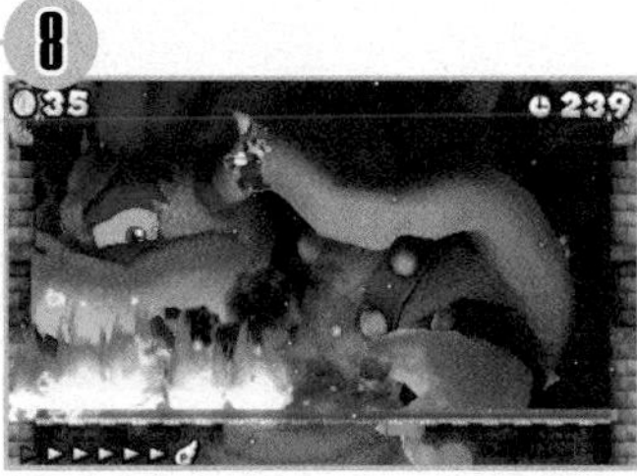

If you manage to stay out of the lava, the platforms eventually carry you to a walkway. When you reach Point 8, Super Bowser attacks with his flame breath. Jump over the flames and wait for the next batch of platforms to appear.

9

After Super Bowser's second roar, you must once again use the floating platforms to stay out of the lava. This time, however, the Bowser sculptures along the walls shoot fireballs across the area. Dodge the fireballs, avoid Super Bowser's swipe attacks, and jump between the platforms until you reach the next walkway.

10

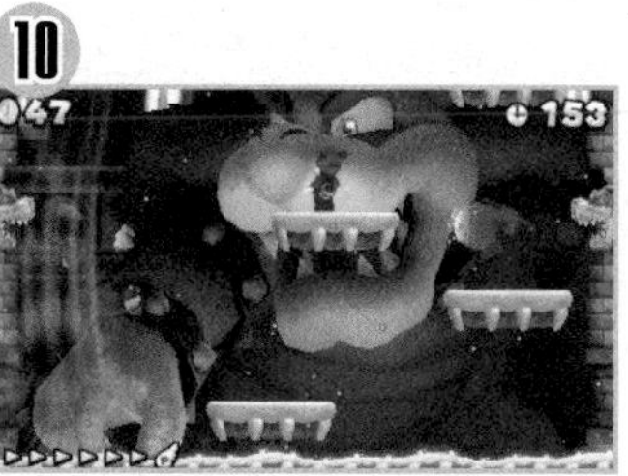

When you reach the second walkway, Super Bowser performs two flame breath attacks. Jump over both attacks and wait for the next batch of platforms to appear. The Bowser sculptures in this area shoot purple fireballs that home in on you, but the same basic tactics should keep you safe.

11

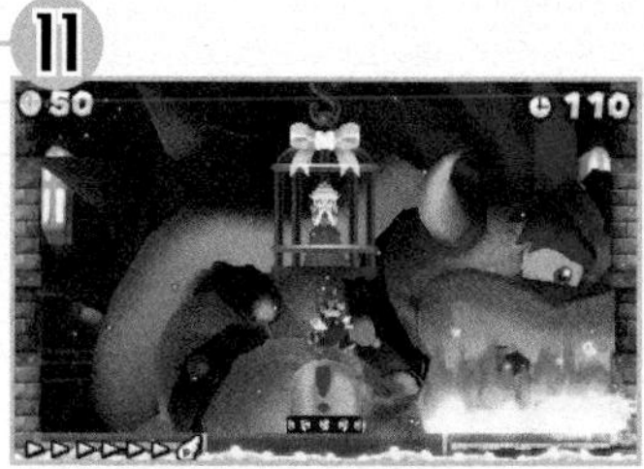

Jump between the platforms to stay out of the lava until you reach the final walkway. Jump over Super Bowser's flame breath, then stomp the large ! Switch in the middle of the room to end the encounter and complete the level.

NOTE

When you complete this level, Star World appears. Although you can visit Star World immediately, you must pay 90 Star Coins to unlock its main path.

To unlock this level, you must find the secret exit in World 6-Boo House.

As you play through this level, the area fills with lava. It happens fairly slowly, but it's best to keep moving!

The first Star Coin is floating high above the ground at Point 1. Stomp one of the nearby Dry Bones and bounce up to collect it.

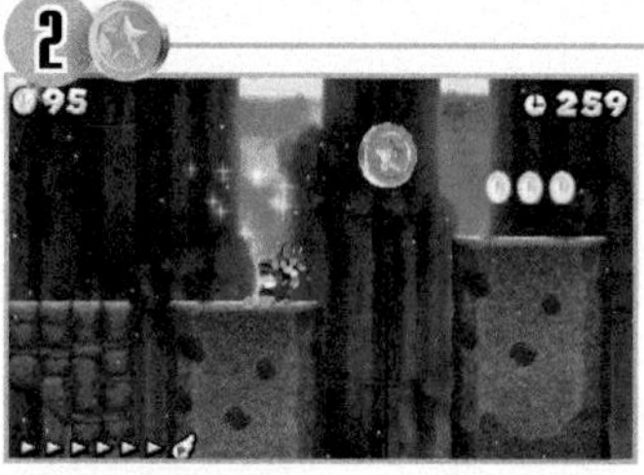

The second Star Coin is floating between the tracks at Point 2. Jump from the edge of the platform to collect it.

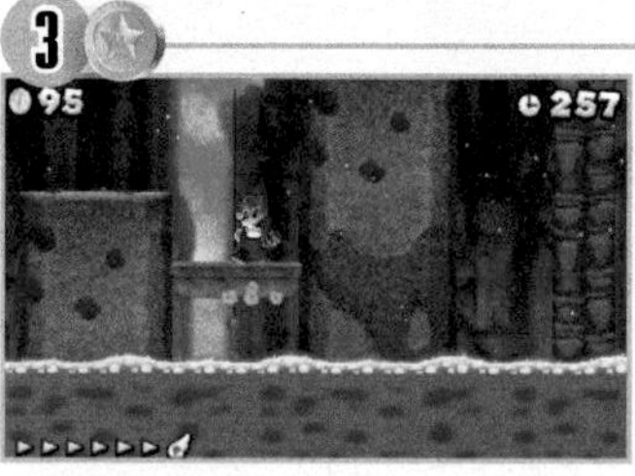

The third Star Coin is located near the cavern ceiling. To reach it, follow the tracks down to the platform at Point 3. When you land, the platform carries you to the upper path.

As you follow the path to the right, jump up to collect the Star Coin.

WORLD 6-A

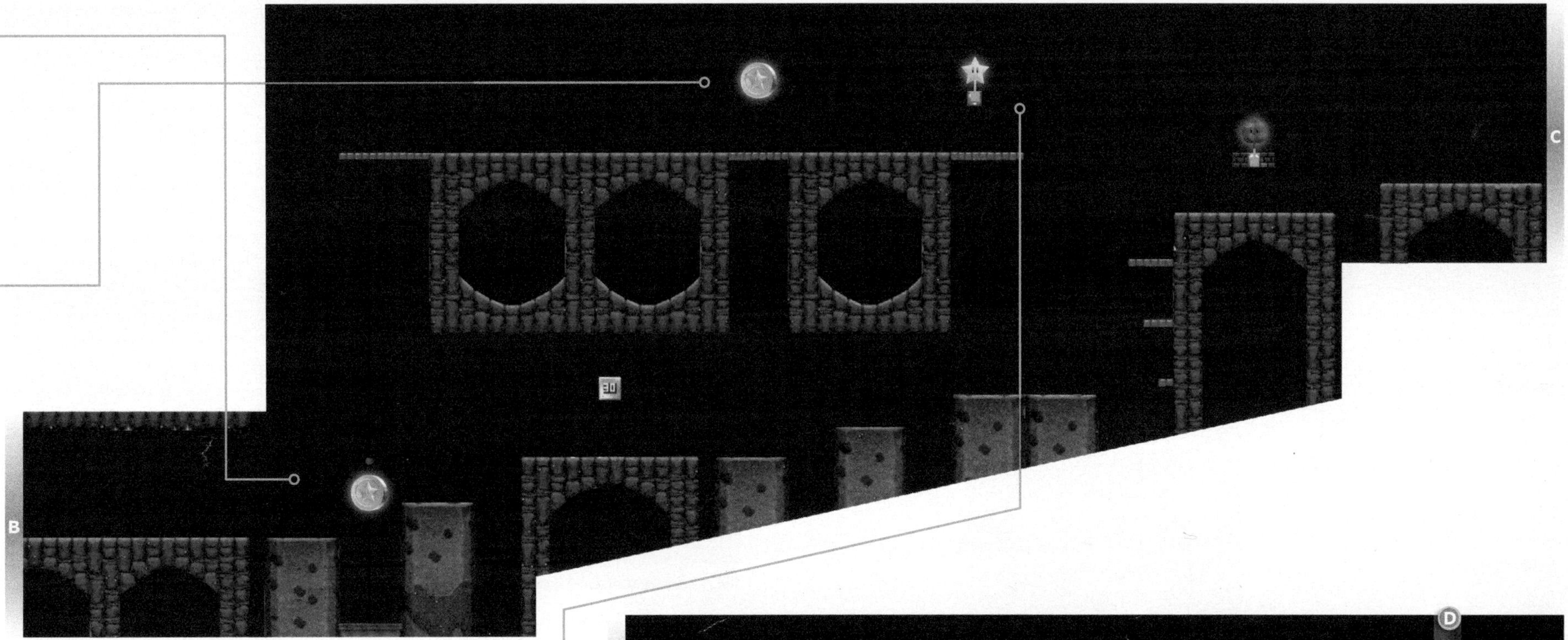

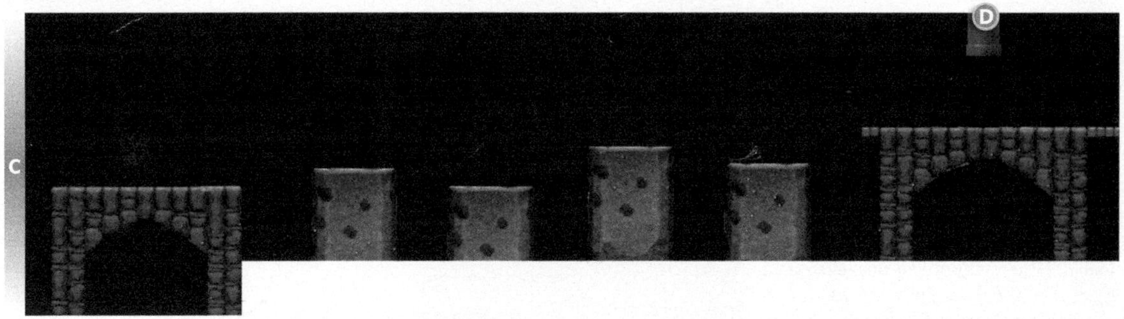

4

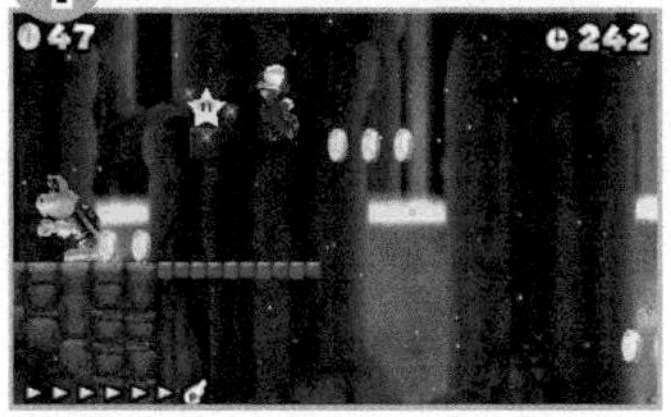

There's a Super Star in the ? Block at Point 4. Grab this power-up, then take out every enemy on the way to the exit to earn an extra life!

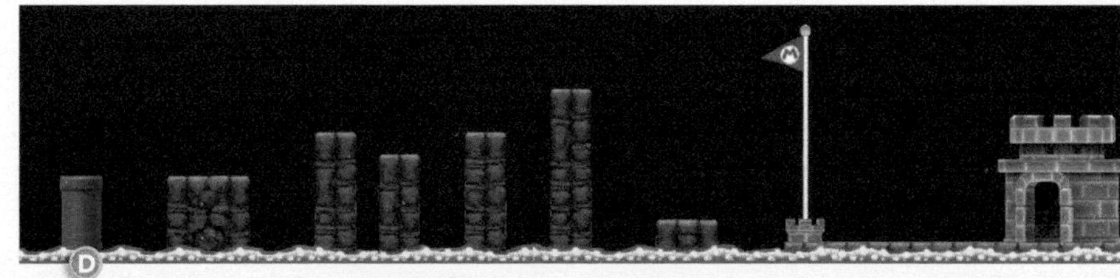

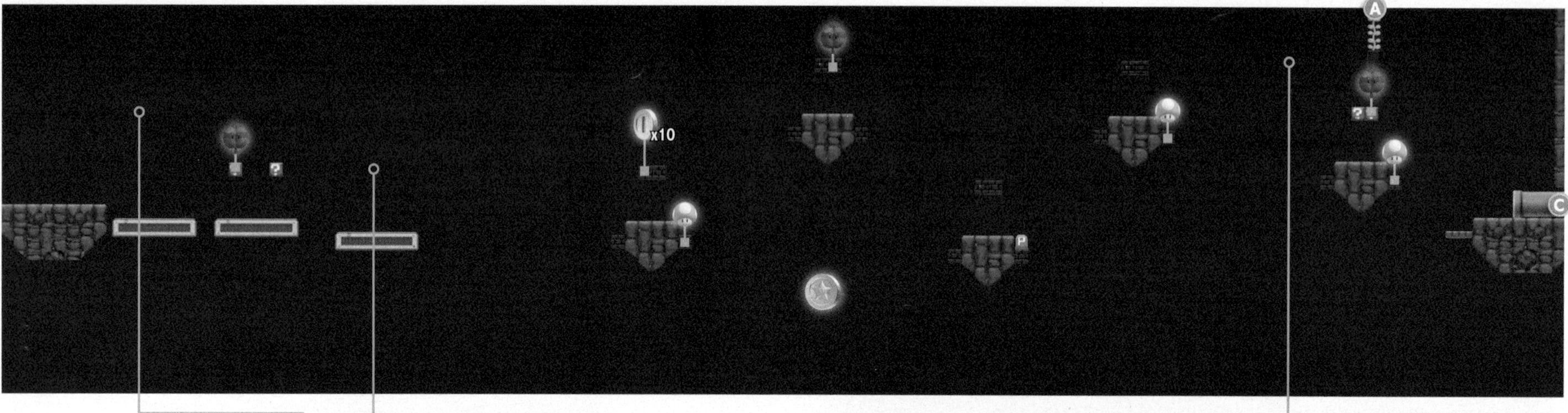

NOTE

Before you can access this level, you must pay five Star Coins to unlock it on the Map Screen.

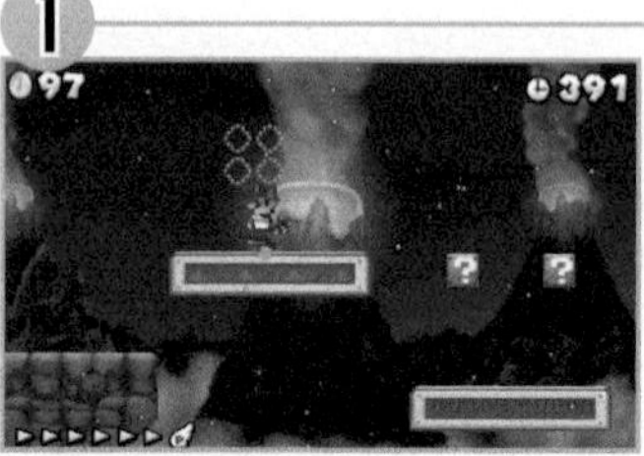

Many of the platforms in this level react to Mario's weight. Once you activate one of these platforms, you can't stop it. However, each time you touch a platform, it switches between two predetermined directions.

The first Star Coin is floating near the bottom of the area. Jump on the platform at Point 2 and move it toward the bottom of the screen.

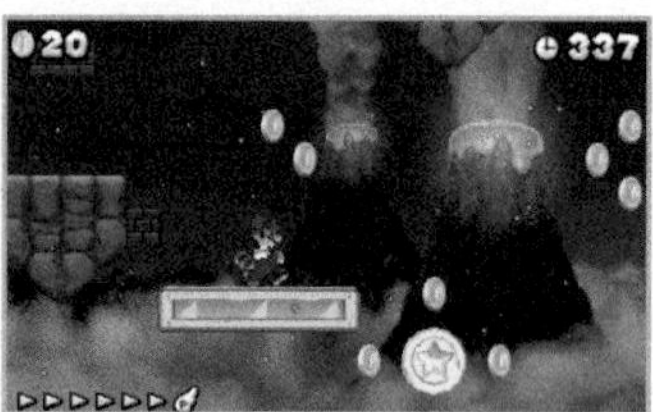

When you spot the Star Coin, adjust the platform as needed. After you collect it, move back toward the top of the screen.

CAUTION

Watch out for the Flame Chomps patrolling the area. These pesky enemies can distract you from steering your platform. Be prepared to make emergency adjustments.

The second Star Coin is located in a hidden area. Stand on the ? Blocks at Point 3, then jump up to reveal the Beanstalk in the Invisible Block above you.

Climb to the top of the Beanstalk, then activate the platform to the right. Steer around the obstacles in your path and collect the Star Coin near the top of the area.

WORLD 6-B

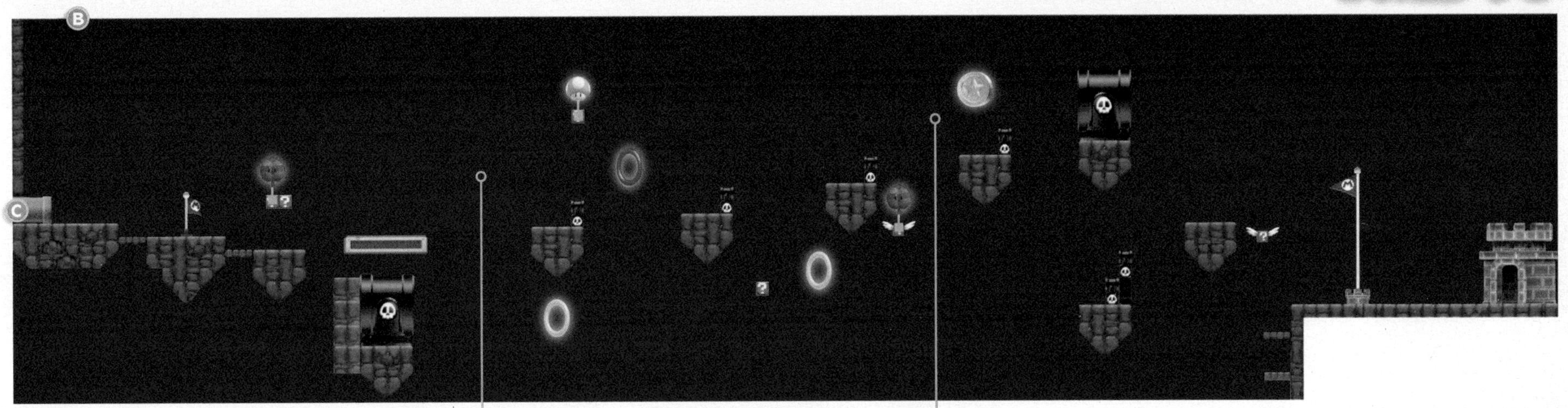

4

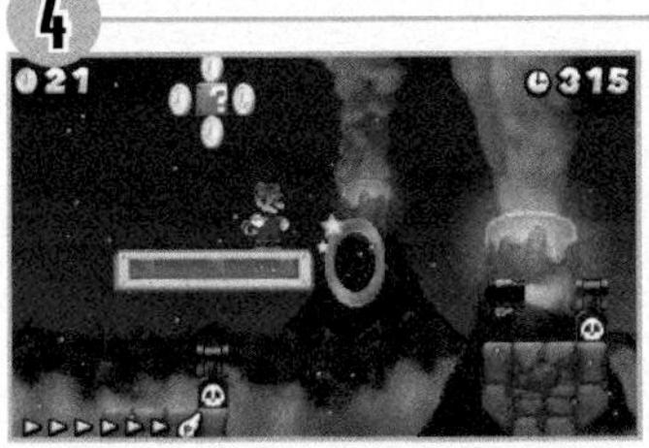

There's a Red Ring floating at Point 4. If you choose to pass through it, watch out for the incoming Bullet Bills. The first red coin appears just above the Bullet Bills' flight path. If you manage to collect it, you shouldn't have any trouble following the trail.

5

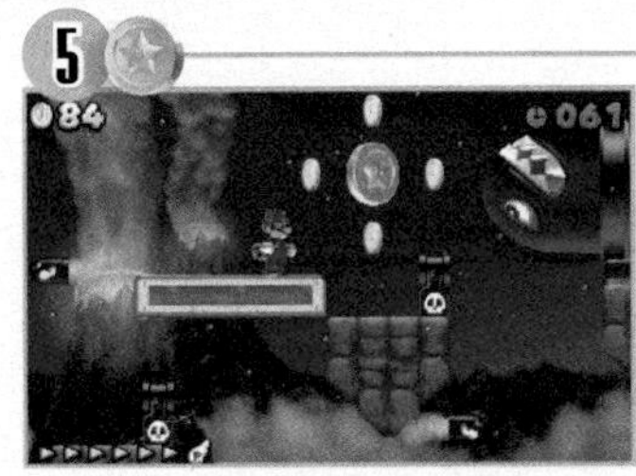

The last Star Coin is floating at Point 5. Follow the trail of Bill Blasters until you spot it. The Star Coin is located in a Banzai Bill's flight path—as you approach it, be prepared to stomp incoming enemies.

MUSHROOM WORLD

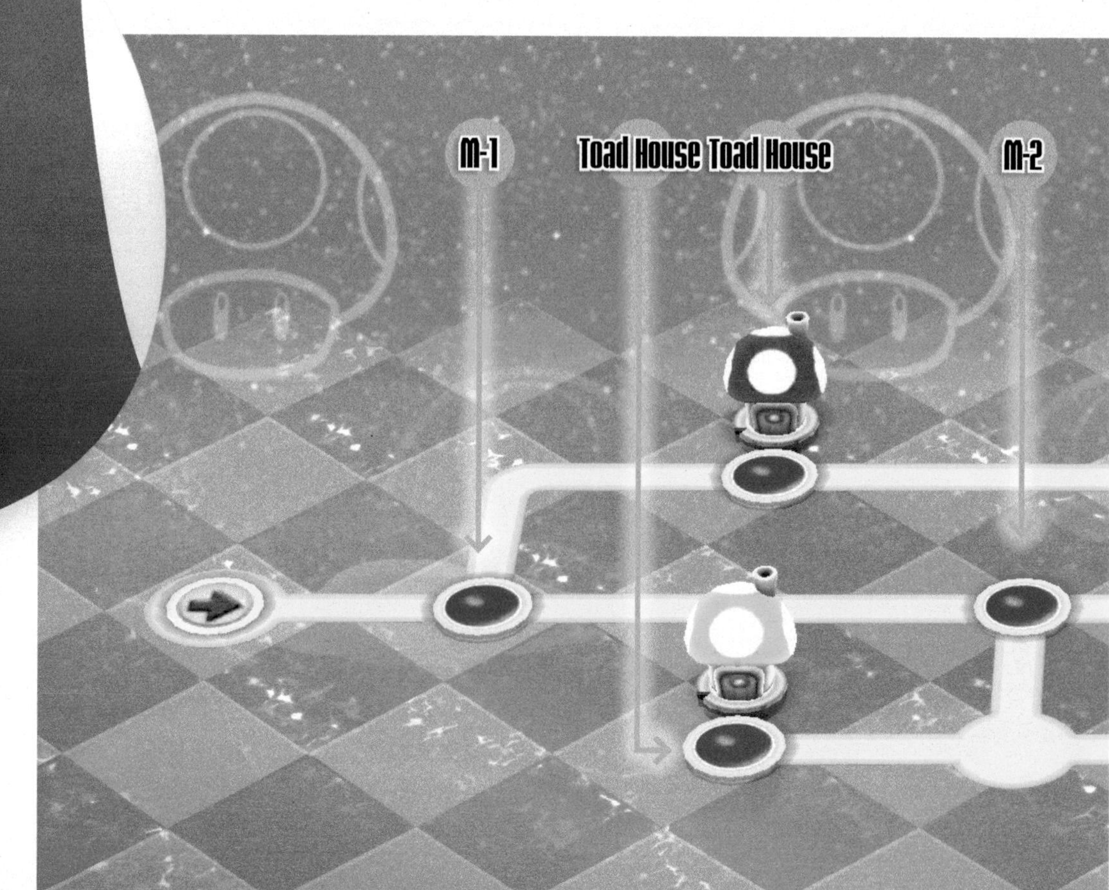

WORLD LOCATIONS				
Hostile Levels	Toad Houses	Boo Houses	Warp Cannons	Boss
8	3	1	1	Larry Koopa

You must complete World 1-Warp Cannon to unlock Mushroom World.

Main Path Levels:

- Mushroom-1
- Mushroom-2
- Mushroom-Boo House
- Mushroom-3
- Mushroom-Castle

Alternate Path Levels:

- Mushroom-A
- Mushroom-B
- Mushroom-Warp Cannon

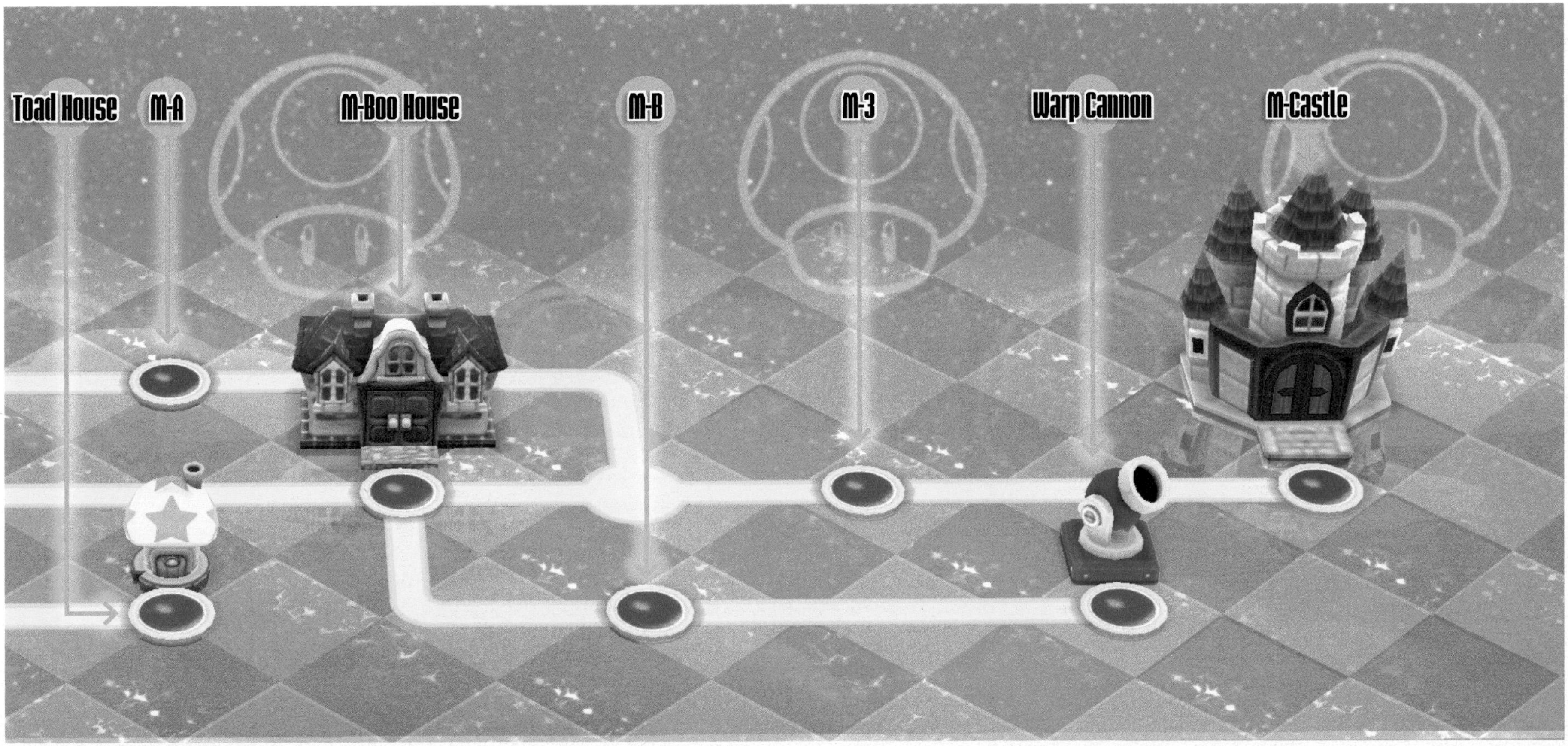

Toad House
M-A
M-Boo House
M-B
M-3
Warp Cannon
M-Castle

NOTE

To unlock Mushroom-A, you must find this level's secret exit.

1

The first Star Coin is located in a hidden area. To find it, enter the yellow pipe at Point 1.

The Star Coin is at the bottom of the room. Use the POW Blocks to clear a path through the area.

2

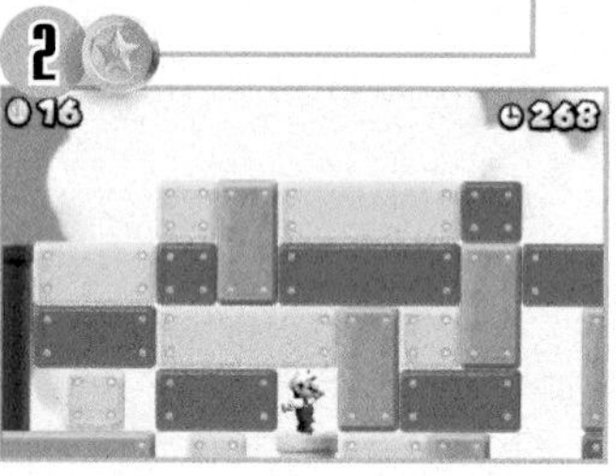

The second Star Coin is located in a secret area. To find it, enter the yellow pipe at Point 2.

After you pass through the pipe, search the nearby ? Blocks to find a Gold Flower. Use this power-up to clear a path to the Star Coin, but be careful! If you destroy too many Blocks, you may not be able to reach the Star Coin.

3

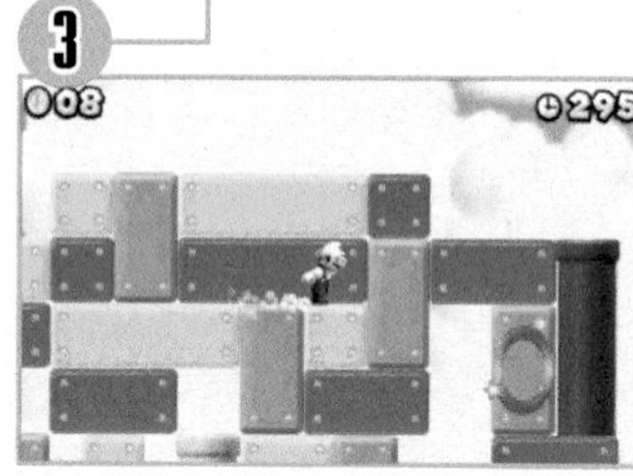

When you pass through the Red Ring at Point 3, eight red coins appear on the platforms to the left.

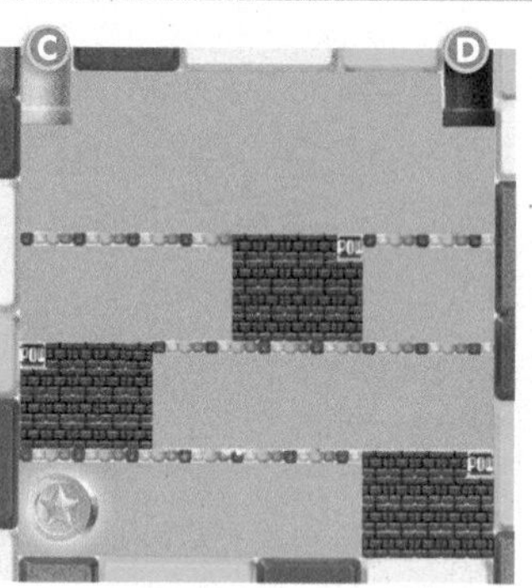

MUSHROOM-1

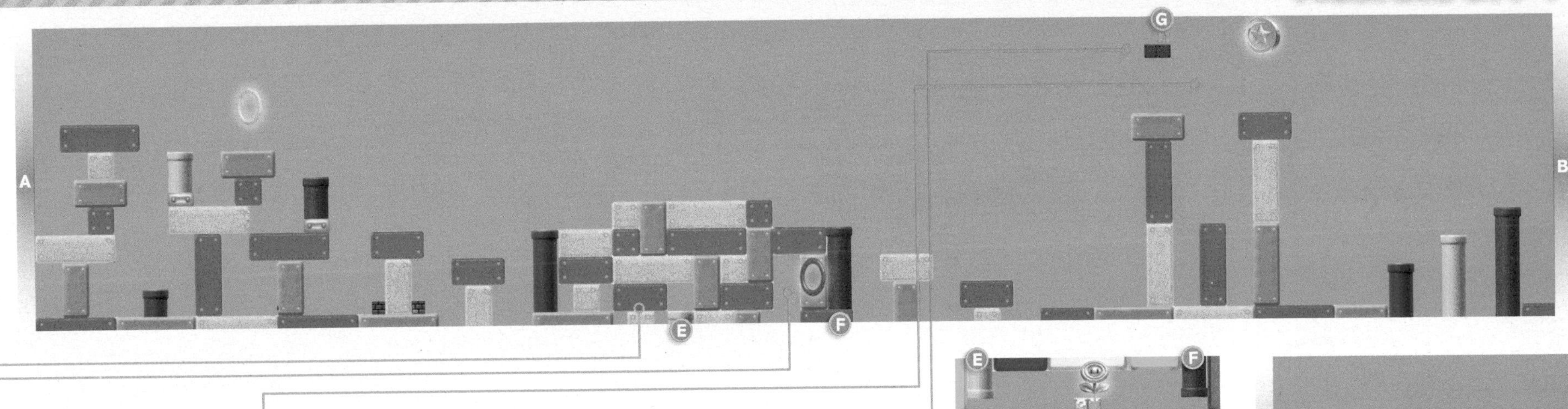

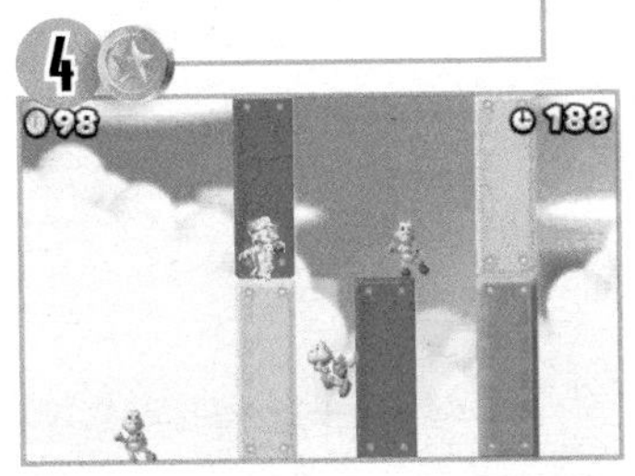

The third Star Coin is hidden above the platforms at Point 4. Stomp the nearby enemies to bounce up to the lower platforms, then repeat the process to bounce to the upper platforms.

When you reach the top of the stack, collect the Star Coin floating above the pink platform.

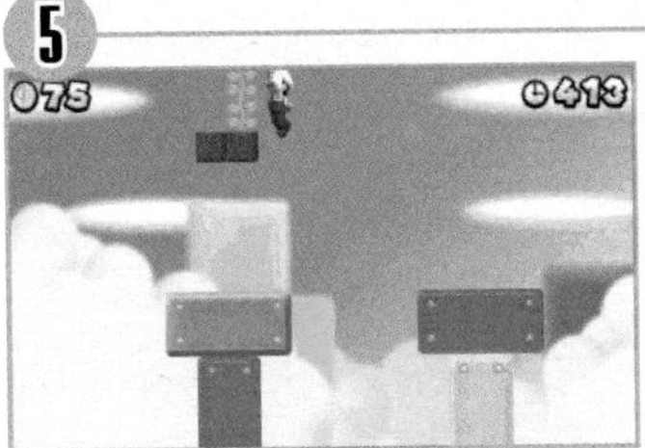

To reach the secret exit, you must locate the Invisible Blocks at Point 5. Stand on the blue platform and jump up to reveal a hidden Beanstalk. Climb to the top of the Beanstalk and follow the path to the secret exit. After you reach the Goal Pole, Mushroom-A becomes available on the Map Screen.

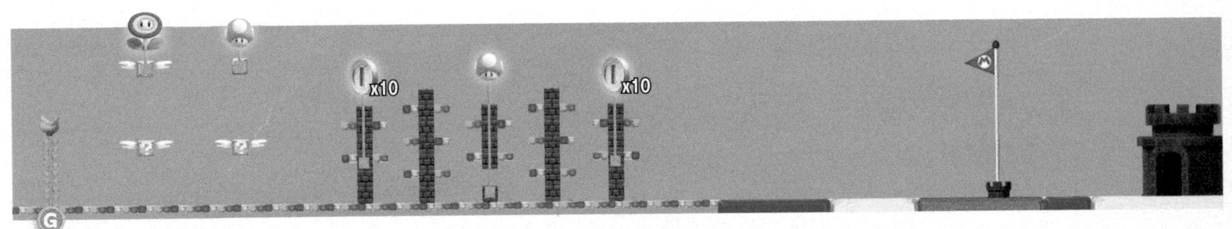

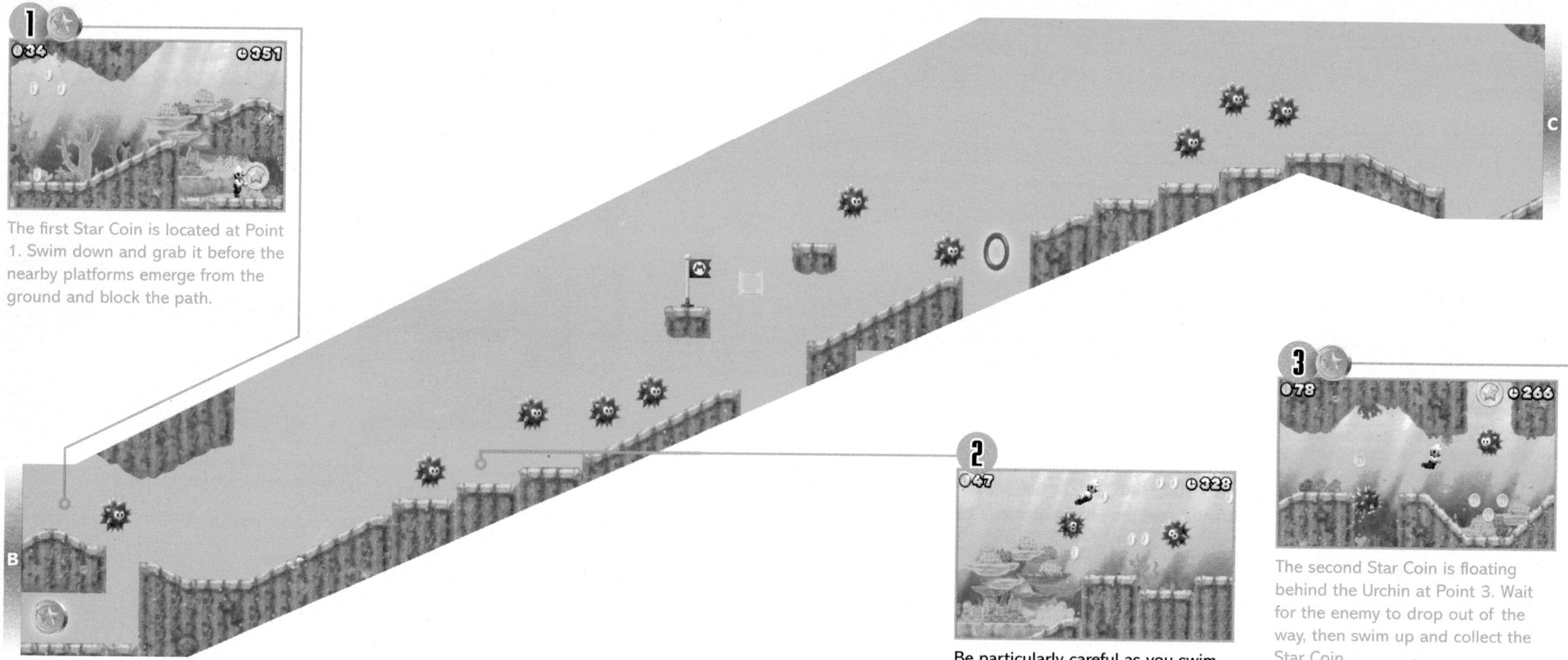

The first Star Coin is located at Point 1. Swim down and grab it before the nearby platforms emerge from the ground and block the path.

Be particularly careful as you swim through Point 2. The platforms below you can knock the nearby Urchins right toward you.

The second Star Coin is floating behind the Urchin at Point 3. Wait for the enemy to drop out of the way, then swim up and collect the Star Coin.

MUSHROOM-2

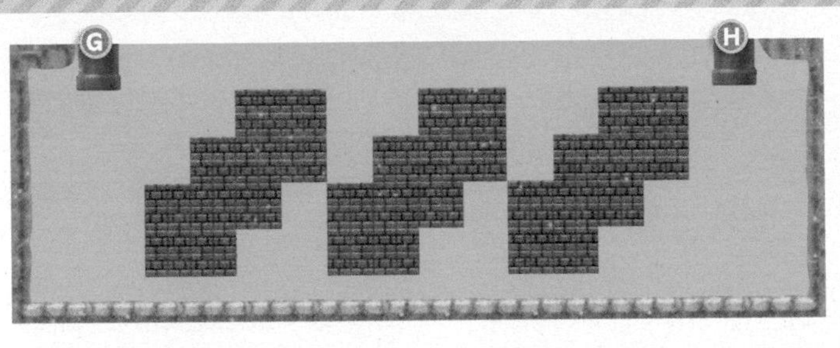

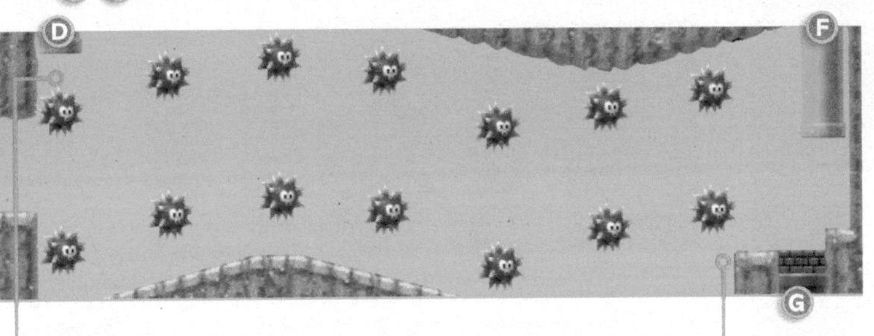

4

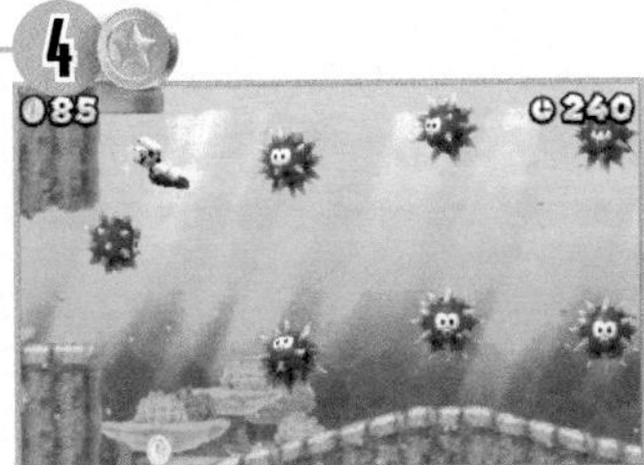

The third Star Coin is located in a hidden area. To find it, enter the green pipe at Point 4.

After you pass through the pipe, swim toward the ceiling. The area is packed with enemies. If you still have a Fire Flower, try to pick off a few of your pursuers, but make sure you keep moving. Collect the Star Coin before it's covered by the coral slab sliding across the ceiling.

5

If you have a Gold Flower, you can use it to destroy the Blocks at Point 5. Enter the exposed pipe to find a room filled with Blocks.

NOTE

To unlock Mushroom-B, you must find this level's secret exit.

1

To find the first Star Coin, enter the door on the left side of the level's first room.

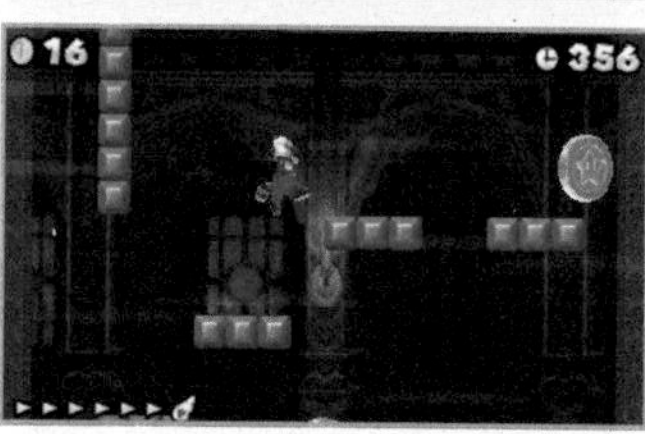

After you pass through the door, you arrive in a room with two ? Switches on the floor. Draw the nearby Boo to the center of the room, then activate the ? Switch near the right wall. Jump along the temporary platforms to reach the Star Coin.

NOTE

After you collect the first Star Coin, activate the ? Switch near the left wall and follow the path out of the room.

2

The door at Point 2 leads to a room with six ? Switches. Each ? Switch triggers a temporary change in the environment—these effects can be combined in various ways.

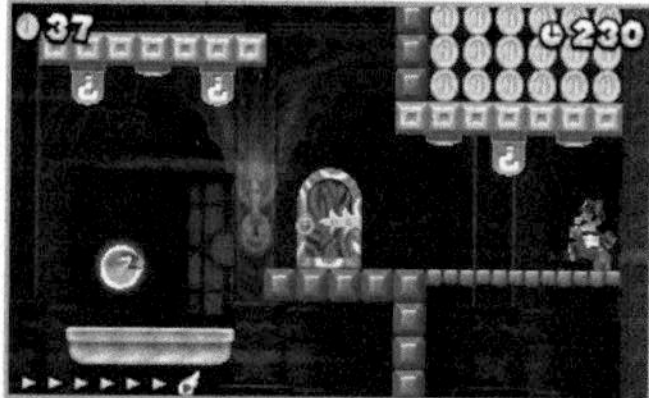

The ? Switches are divided into two groups. Hit the left ? Switch in the right group to reveal a platform below the left group, then try each ? Switch to test its effect. To reveal the path out, hit the right group's left ? Switch and right ? Switch, then hit left group's middle ? Switch.

3

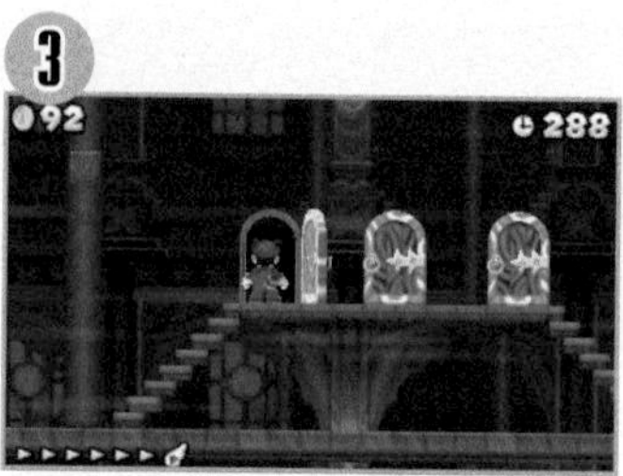

To find the Red Ring hidden in this level, enter the door at Point 3.

As you approach the Red Ring, the trampoline hidden in the floor springs you into the air. Pass through the Red Ring, then use trampolines hidden around the room to bounce up and collect the red coins.

4

To collect the second Star Coin, enter the door at Point 4.

After you pass through the door, use the hidden trampolines to reach the ? Switch at the top of the room. When you hit the ? Switch, a door and a Roulette Coin Block appear near the ceiling, and a Star Coin appears along the room's left wall. Drop down and collect the Star Coin, then exit through the door near the ceiling.

If you have a Super Leaf, use it! Raccoon Mario's glide ability makes it much easier to steer around the trampoline hidden above the Star Coin.

MUSHROOM-BOO HOUSE

5

The door at Point 5 leads to a room filled with hidden trampolines.

One of the Blocks at the center of the room contains a P Switch. Activate the P Switch, then bounce along the hidden trampolines to collect the blue coins.

6

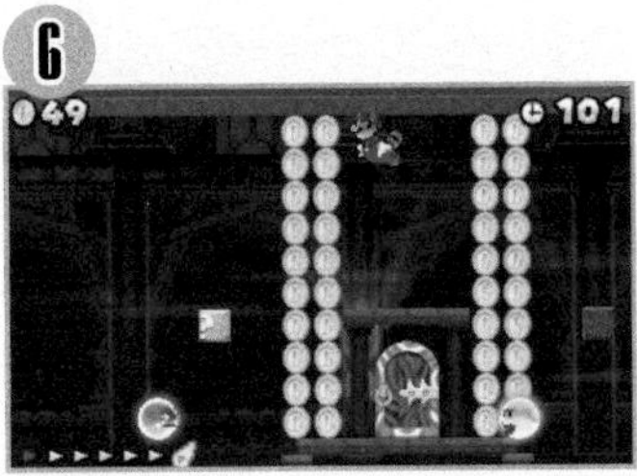

Before you enter the door at Point 6, fly up to the ceiling to reveal a large stash of coins.

7

Use the ? Switches at Point 7 to open a path to the third Star Coin. Hit the ? Switch in the middle and the ? Switch on the right, then jump up and follow the opened path.

As you dash along the path, notice the two openings in the ceiling. Pass by the first opening, then wall jump up through the second opening. When you land, hit the nearby ? Switch to reveal the Star Coin. Return to the first opening and collect it.

8

To find this area's secret exit, activate the same ? Switch you used to find the third Star Coin.

While the ? Switch is active, hop across the gap to the right, slip past the nearby Boo, and enter the nearby door. Reach the secret Goal Pole to unlock Mushroom-B on the Map Screen.

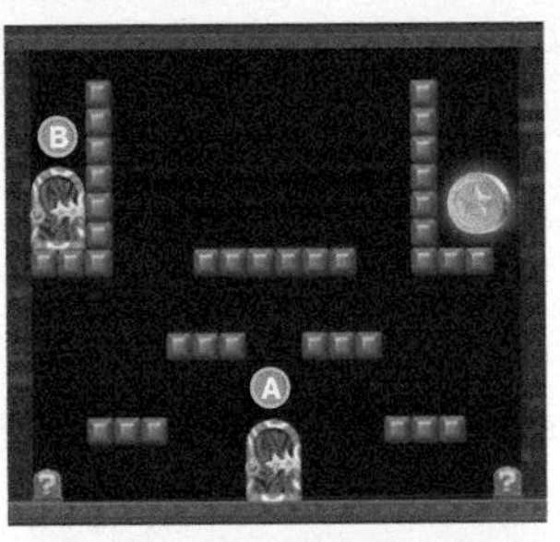

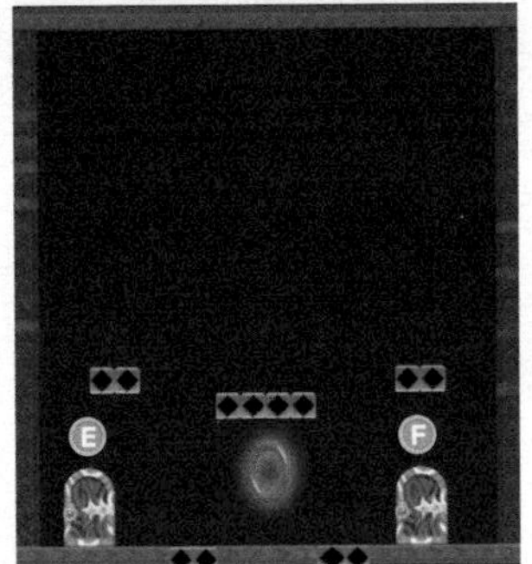

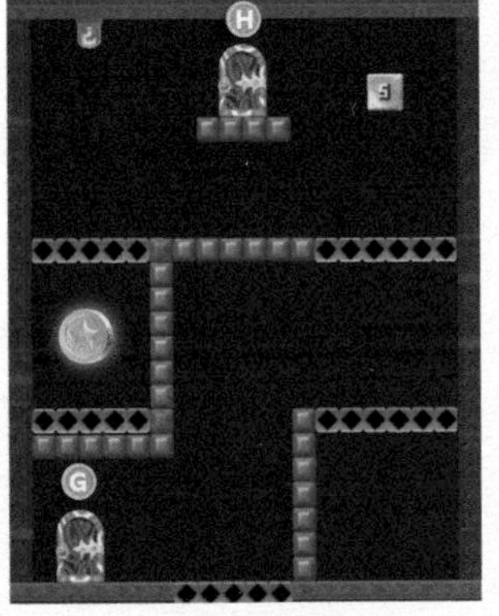

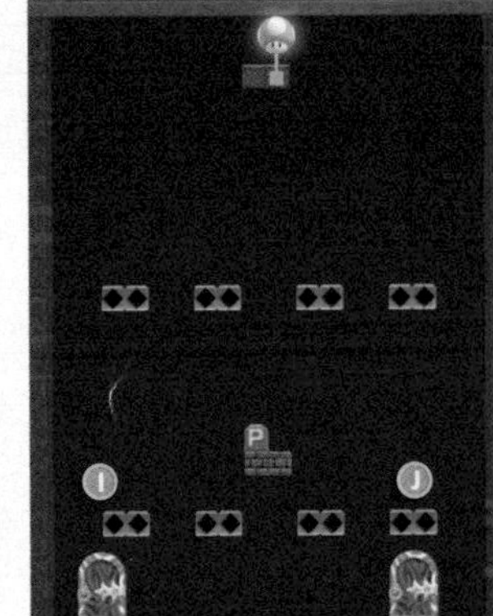

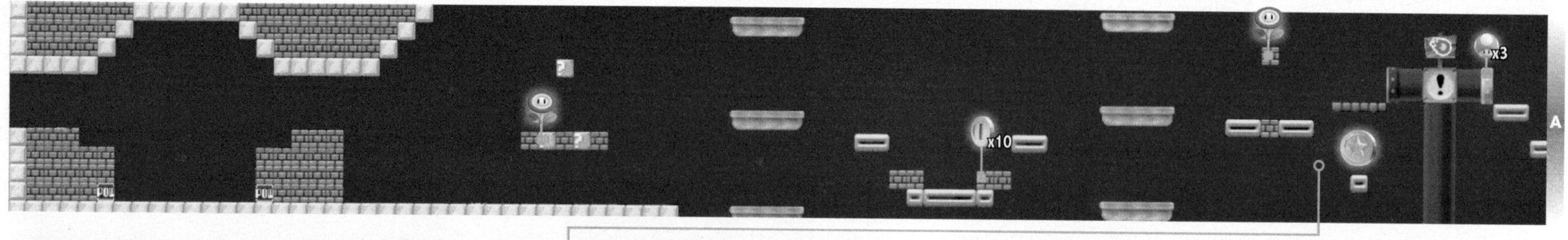

The first Star Coin is on a Donut Block at Point 1. Stand on the Donut Block to the left and wait for it to give way. As you fall, hop over to the Star Coin and jump to the platform above you.

The second Star Coin is on a Donut Block at Point 2. Pass below the Star Coin and jump to the moving platforms. Jump up along the platforms as they drop down from the ceiling, then leap over and collect the Star Coin.

The third Star Coin is surrounded by Blocks. Trigger the nearby POW Block to quickly destroy the Blocks, then grab the Star Coin.

It's easier to collect the Star Coin if you leave the lower Blocks intact. If you destroy them, however, use the platforms to the right to reach the Star Coin before it moves out of reach.

The ! Pipe at Point 4 contains a Mega Mushroom. Collect this power-up to smash a path through the rest of the area.

MUSHROOM-3

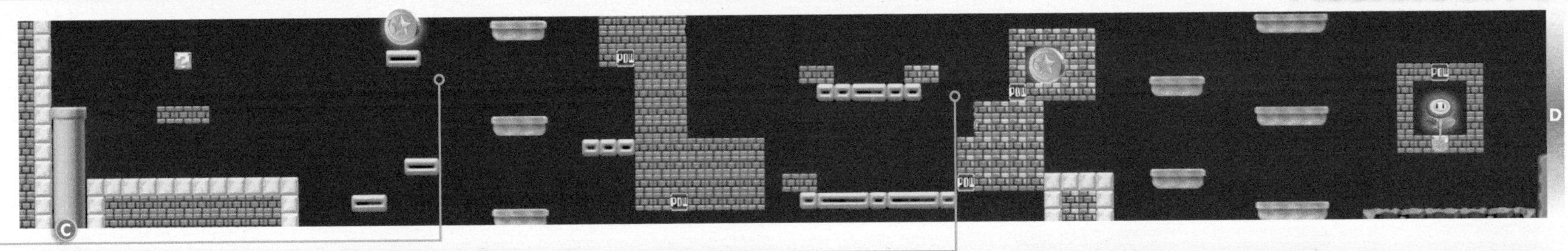

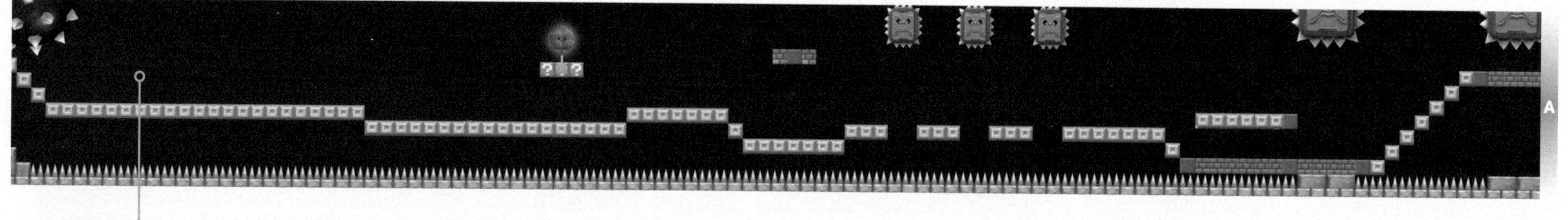

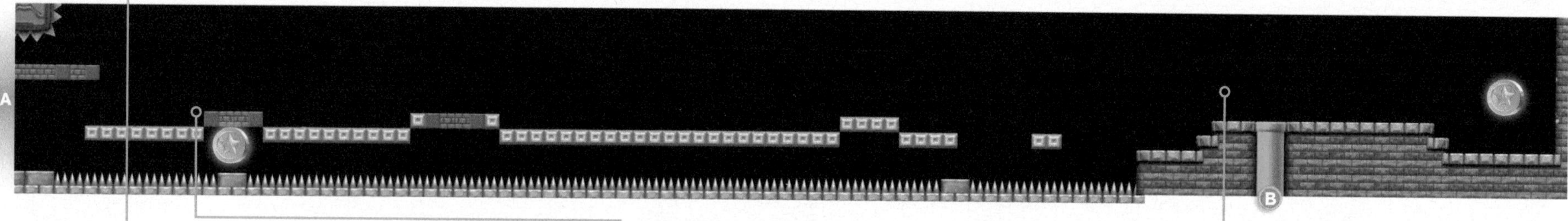

1

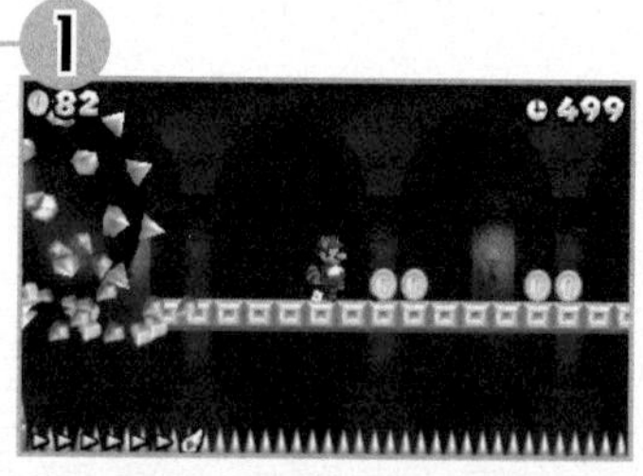

When the level starts, a giant spiked ball begins destroying the walkway. This hazard moves fairly slowly, but it's important to keep moving. Each time you stop to collect items or deal with enemies, watch for the flying debris that signals the spiked ball's approach.

2

The first Star Coin is at Point 2, just below the walkway. Stand above the Star Coin, then perform a ground pound to smash through the Blocks.

3

The second Star Coin is located just past the Big Whomp at Point 3. Coax the enemy into attacking, then use a ground pound to defeat it.

When the path is clear, collect the Star Coin near the wall to the right.

4

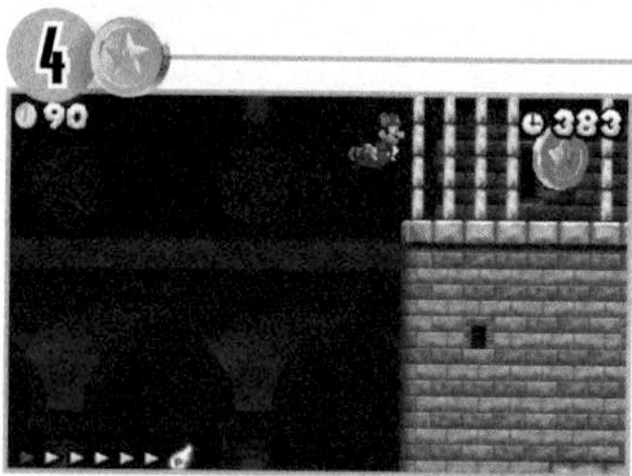

The third Star Coin is in a secret area above the door to Larry Koopa's chamber. If you've managed to hang on to a Super Leaf, use it to fly up and grab the Star Coin.

MUSHROOM-CASTLE

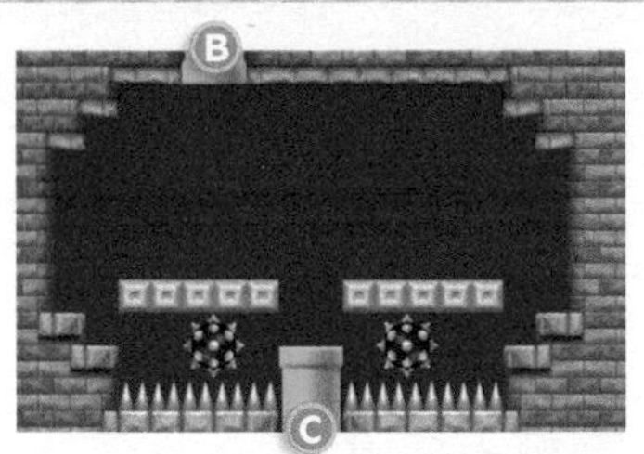

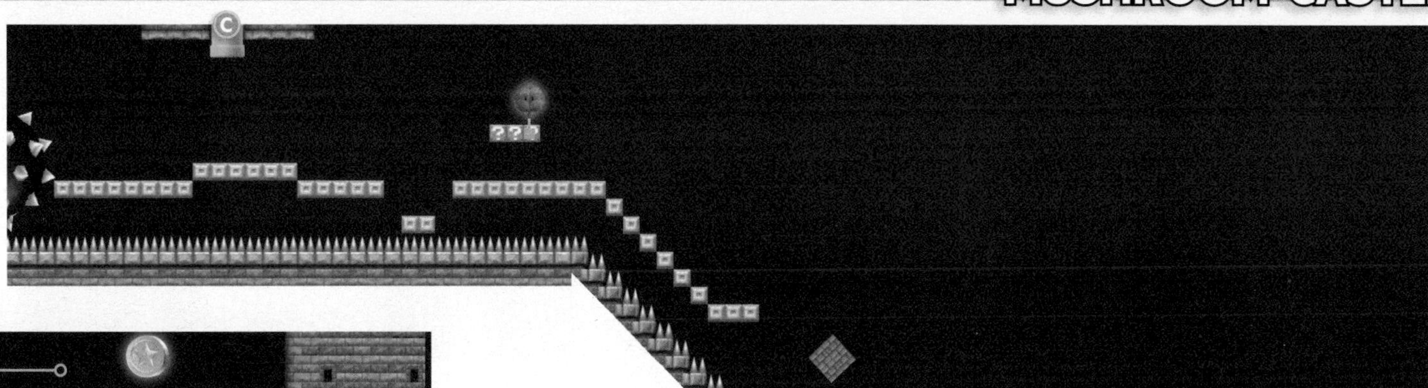

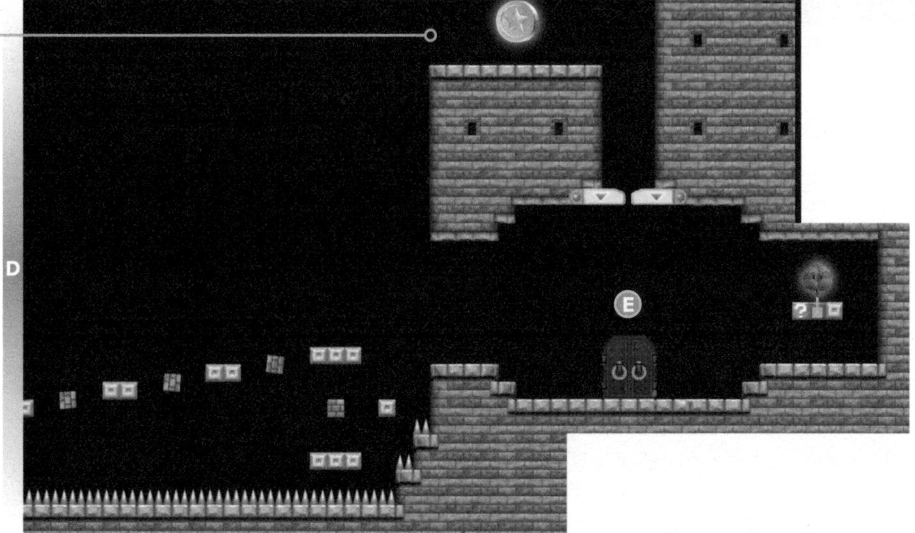

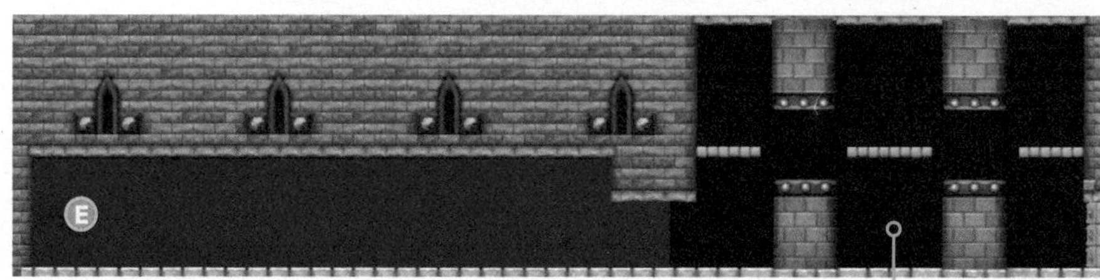

5

The four stone pillars in Larry Koopa's chamber emerge in alternating pairs. As you move around the room, try to anticipate when one of these pillars will move into your intended path. Each fireball Larry conjures bounces around the room for a short time. Avoid his attacks, and stomp Larry's head.

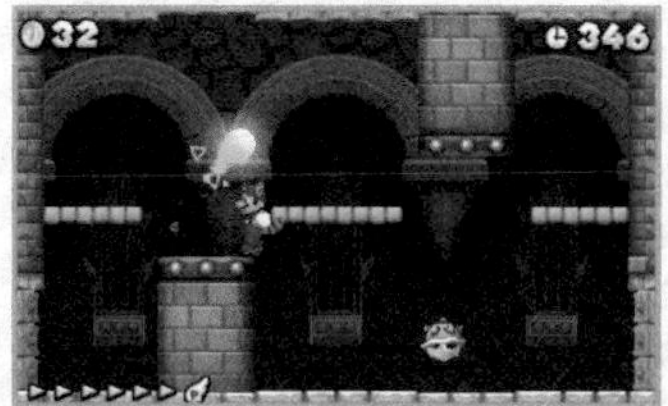

When Larry tucks into his shell, jump to the platforms and wait for him to emerge. When he does, stomp his head again. Repeat the process to stomp Larry a third time and complete the encounter.

If you haven't already unlocked World Three, completing this level will do so.

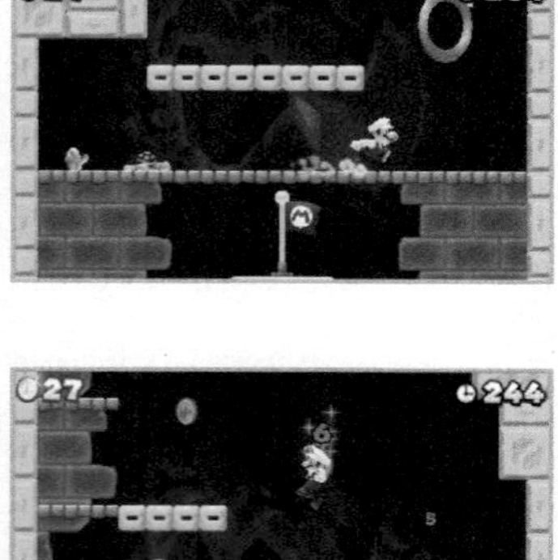

When you pass through the Red Ring at Point 3, the red coins appear above you.

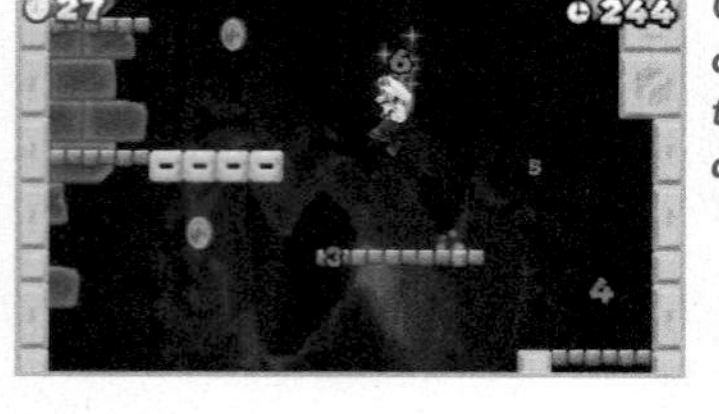

One of the red coins is floating beneath a Donut Block. It takes some time to drop the Donut Block through the coin, so move quickly!

The path splits at Point 2. To collect the second Star Coin, you must follow the path near the right wall.

As you jump up along the platforms, slip past the spiked ball and grab the Star Coin.

There's a spiked ball rolling back and forth near the Star Coin at Point 1. When the spiked ball rolls toward the Star Coin, jump up to the platform above it. When the spiked ball rolls away, drop down, build a bit of speed, and slide through the gap to collect the Star Coin.

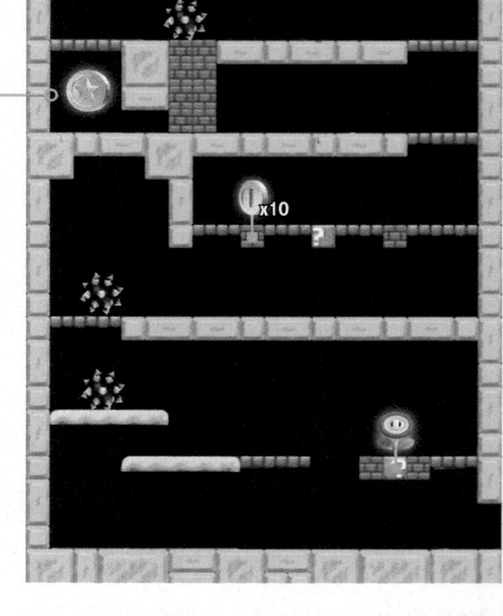

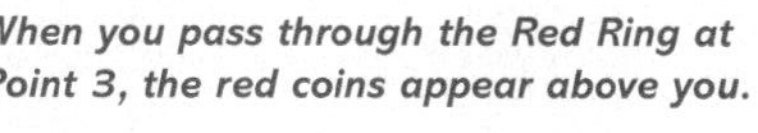

 NOTE

To unlock this level, you must find the secret exit in Mushroom-1.

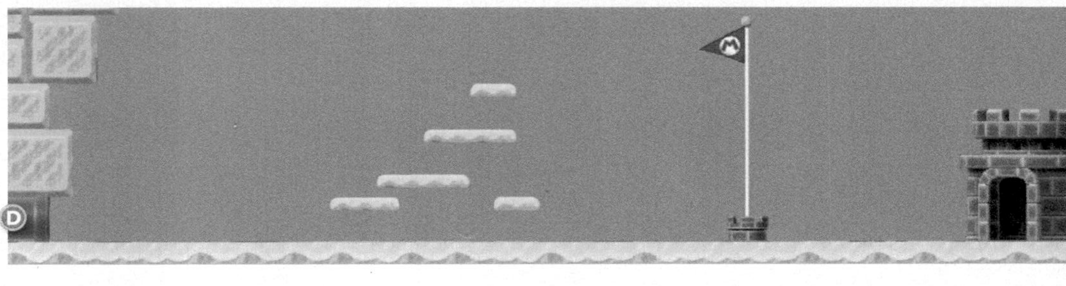

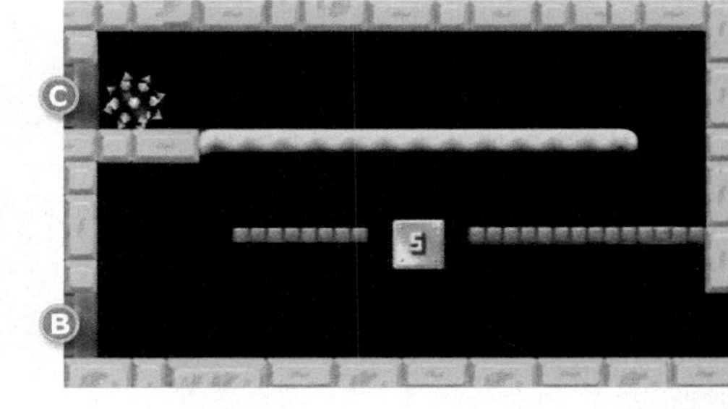

The blue pipe at Point 5 leads to a hidden room. Enter the pipe, then dash over and hit the Roulette Coin Block before it's destroyed.

The two spiked balls at Point 4 prevent you from collecting the Star Coin without taking damage. Jump to the ? Switch near the right wall, then use it to open the enclosure above you. After the large spiked ball crushes the two smaller spiked balls, drop down and collect the Star Coin.

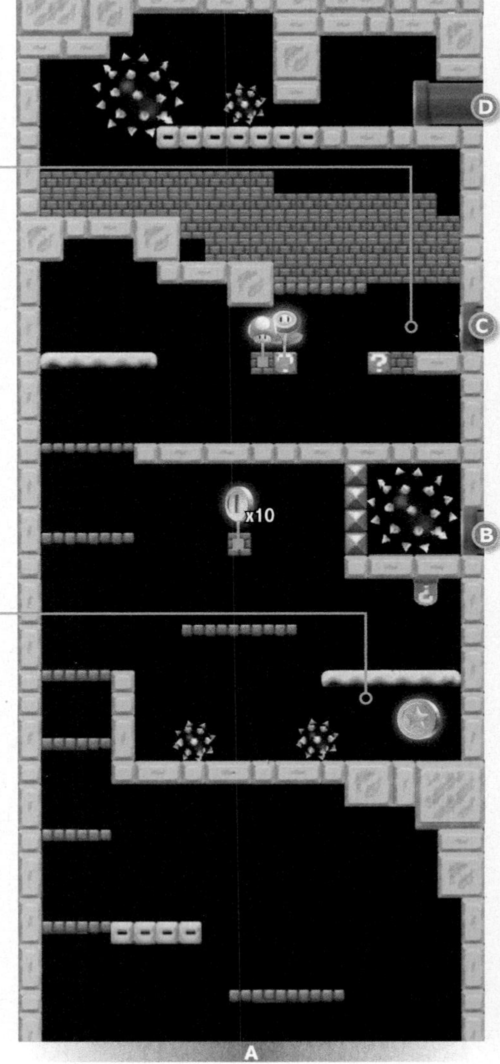

2

The second Star Coin is at Point 2. To collect it, simply jump over to the yellow platform before the Star Coin moves out of reach.

1

The first Star Coin is floating high above the ? Blocks at Point 1. Hit them to reveal the Beanstalks as early as possible, then climb up to the next platform.

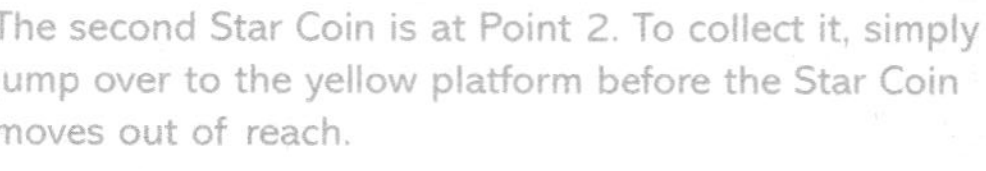

Hop to the Blocks above the Beanstalks, then jump straight up to collect the Star Coin.

TIP

Many of the Blocks in this level contain Beanstalks that allow you to progress through the level. Search as many Blocks as possible, and make sure you activate all available POW Blocks.

NOTE

To unlock this level, you must find the secret exit in Mushroom-Boo House.

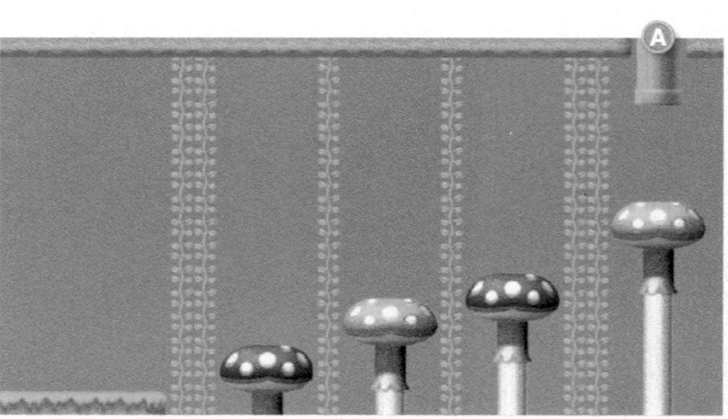

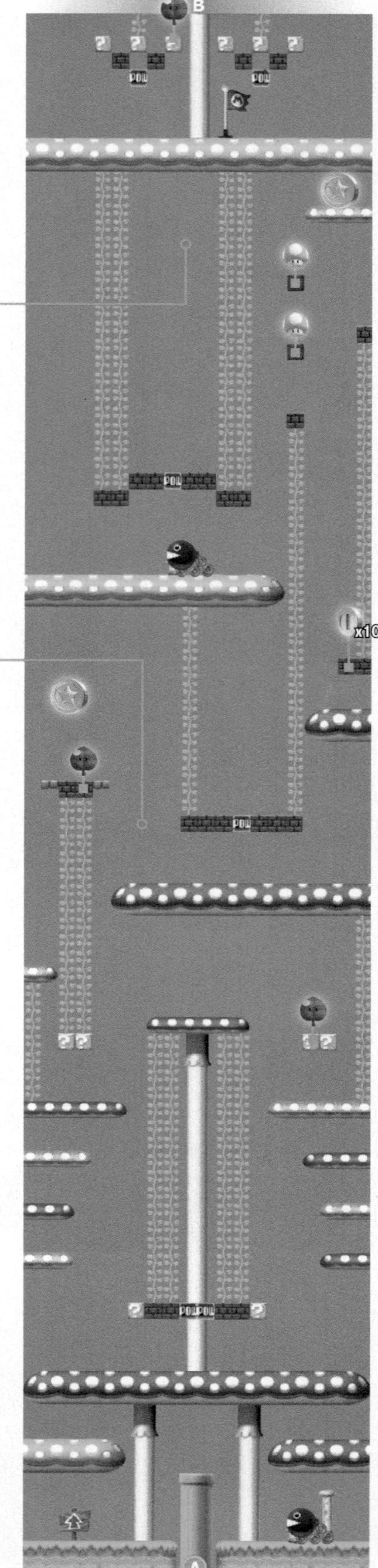

MUSHROOM-B

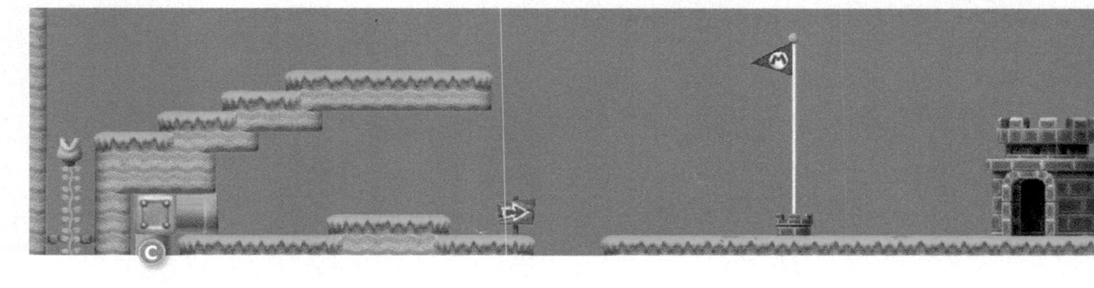

5

There's a Beanstalk hidden inside of an Invisible Block at Point 5. This alternate route makes it much easier to reach the top of the Goal Pole.

4

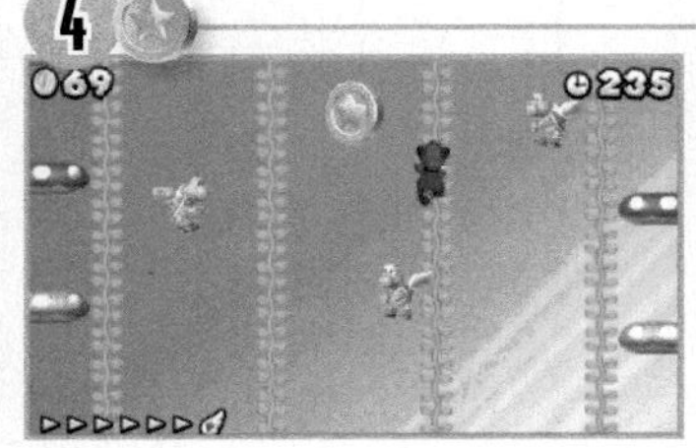

The third Star Coin is floating between the Beanstalks at Point 4. Climb up beside the Star Coin, leap over to grab it, then grab on to the next Beanstalk and continue your climb.

3

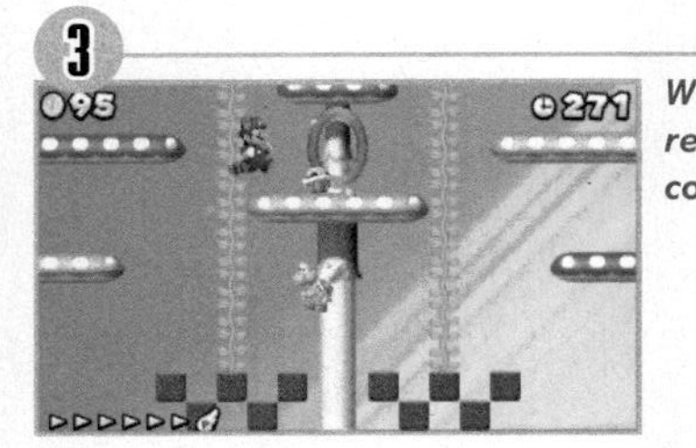

When you pass through the Red Ring at Point 3, the red coins appear above you. Sweep the area and collect them before they vanish.

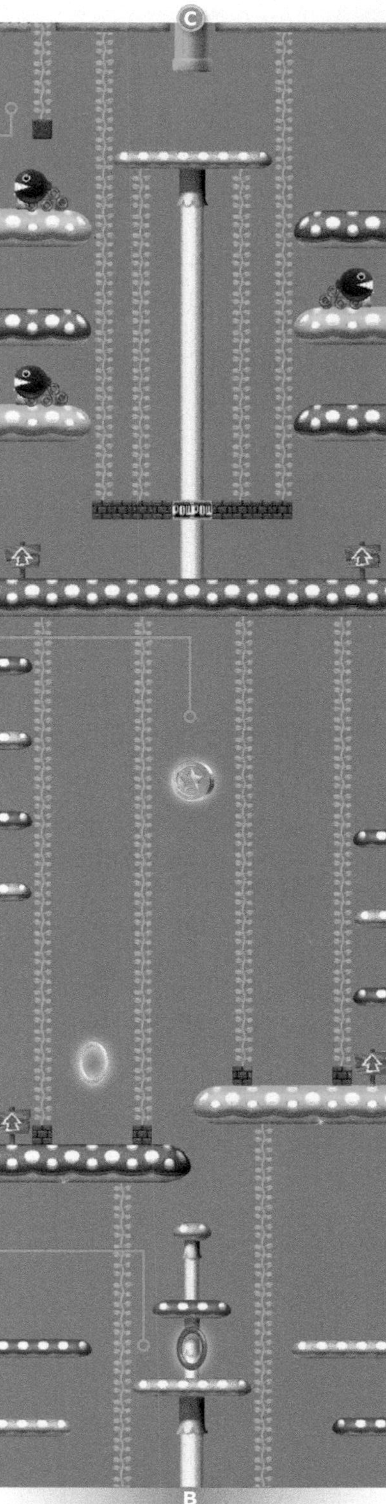

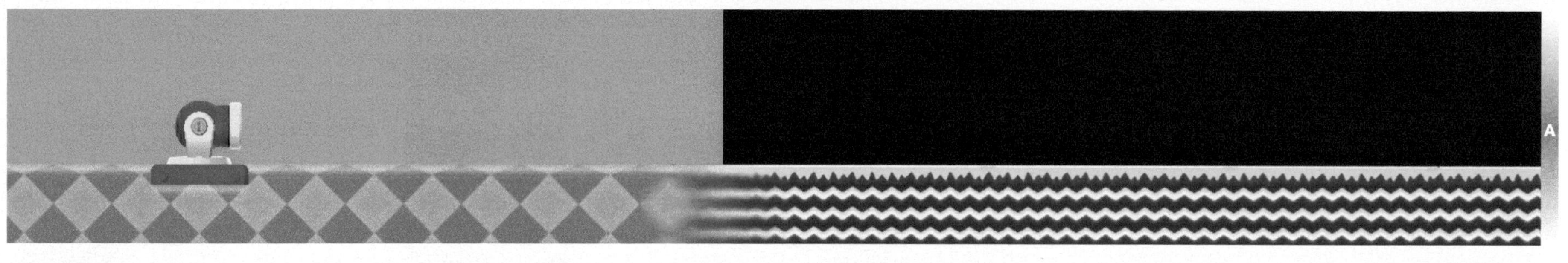

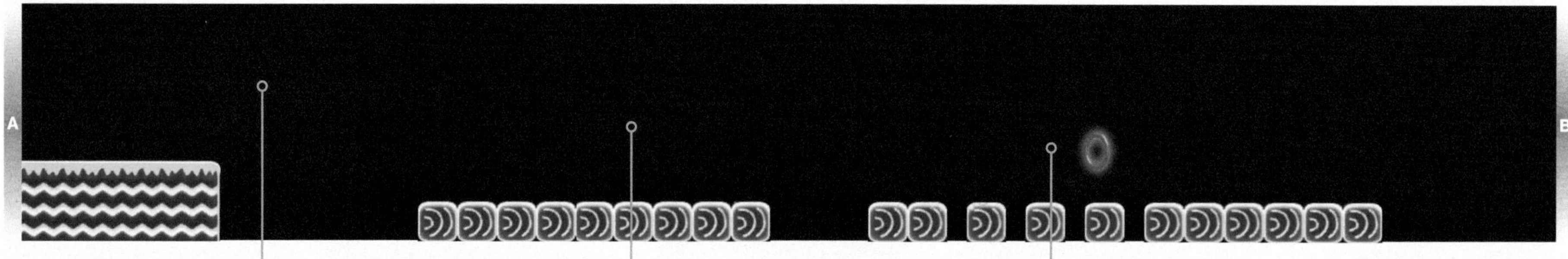

Before you can access this level, you must unlock and complete Mushroom-B.

As with previous Warp Cannons, short coin trails indicate that you should perform a short jump, and long coin trails indicate longer jumps. However not all jumps are marked with coin trails, so it's important to stay alert.

This course involves some fairly tricky jumps. You must not only slip through some very tight spaces, you must make sure you're in exactly the right place when a flock of Crows locks on to you.

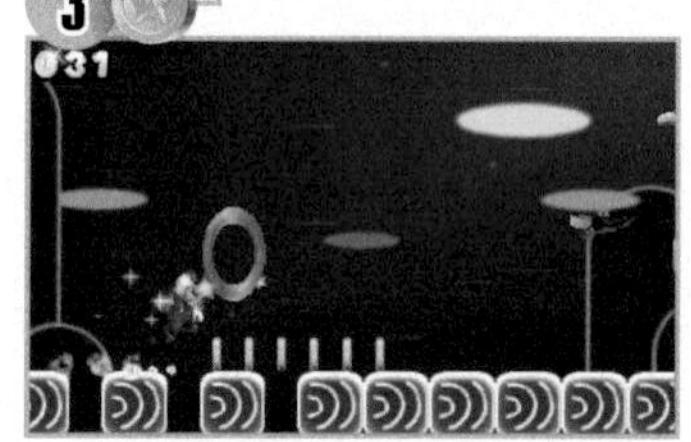

There's a Red Ring floating above the coins at Point 3. To reach it, you must hop up while you dash through the area.

As usual, collecting the red coins requires that you make some significantly more complicated jumps. If you manage to grab them all, you'll be rewarded with a Gold Flower.

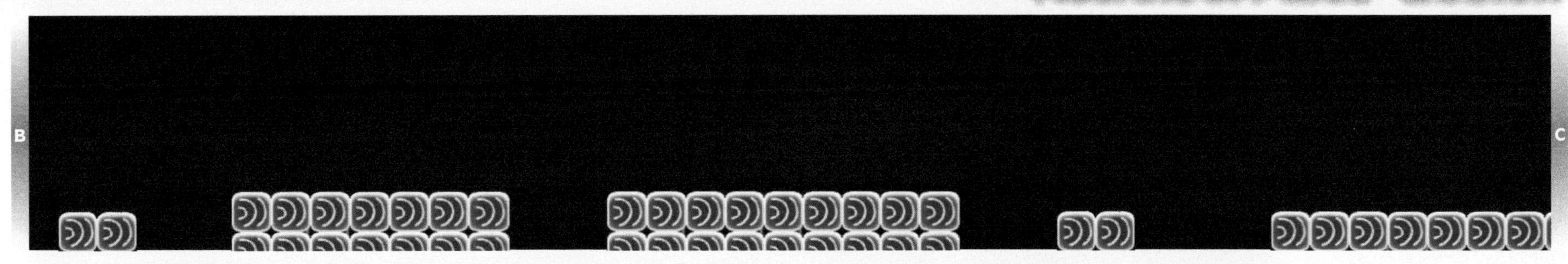

4

If you haven't already unlocked Flower World, simply reach the end of the level to do so.

FLOWER WORLD

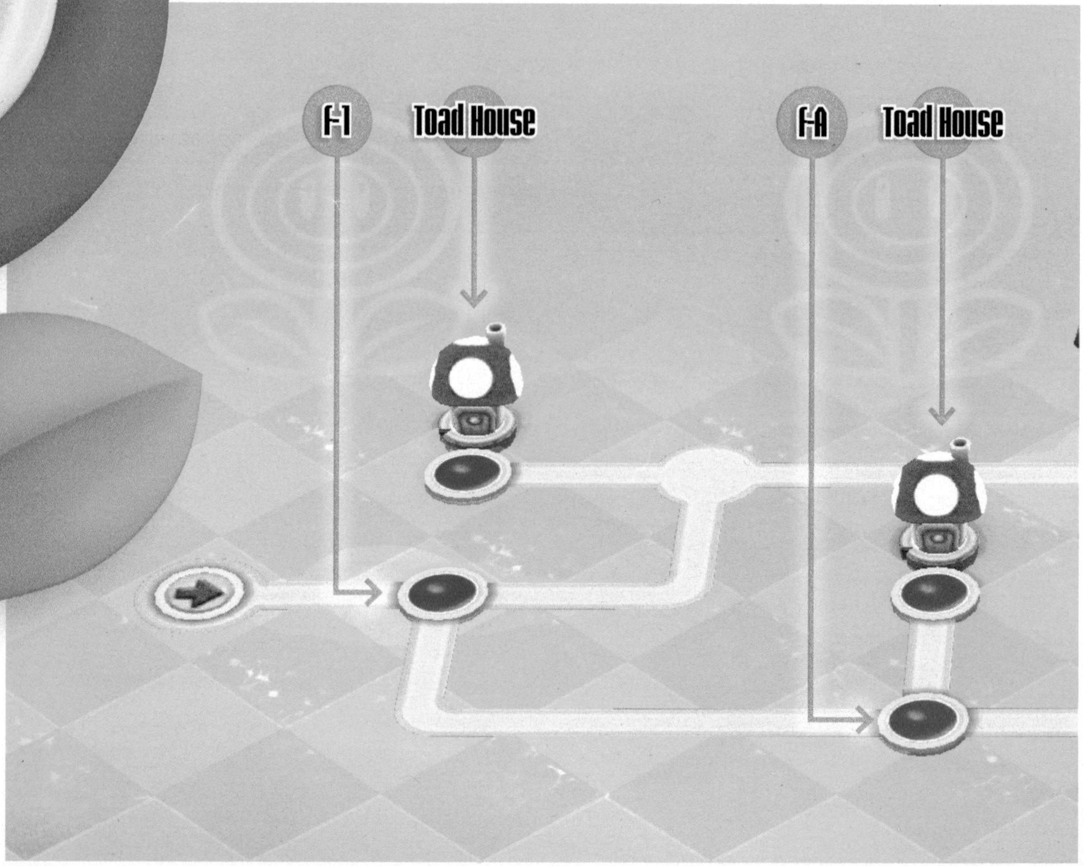

F-1

Toad House

F-A

Toad House

WORLD LOCATIONS				
Hostile Levels	Toad Houses	Boo Houses	Warp Cannons	Boss
8	3	1	1	Lemmy Koopa

To unlock Flower World, you must complete either World 3-Warp Cannon or Mushroom-Warp Cannon.

Main Path Levels:

- Flower-1
- Flower-Boo House
- Flower-2
- Flower-3
- Flower-Castle

Alternate Path Levels:

- Flower-A
- Flower-B
- Flower-Warp Cannon

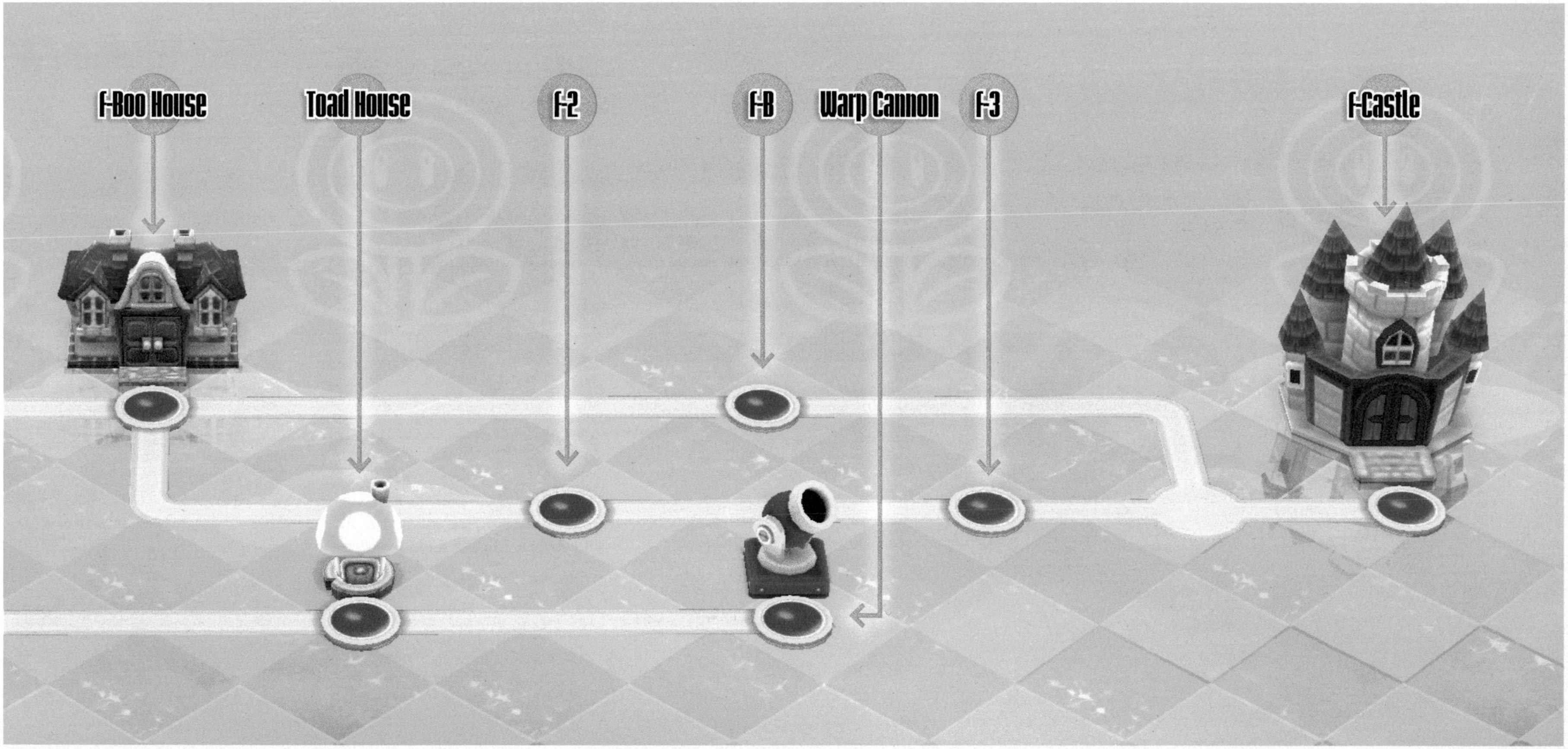

F-Boo House
Toad House
F-2
F-B
Warp Cannon
F-3
F-Castle

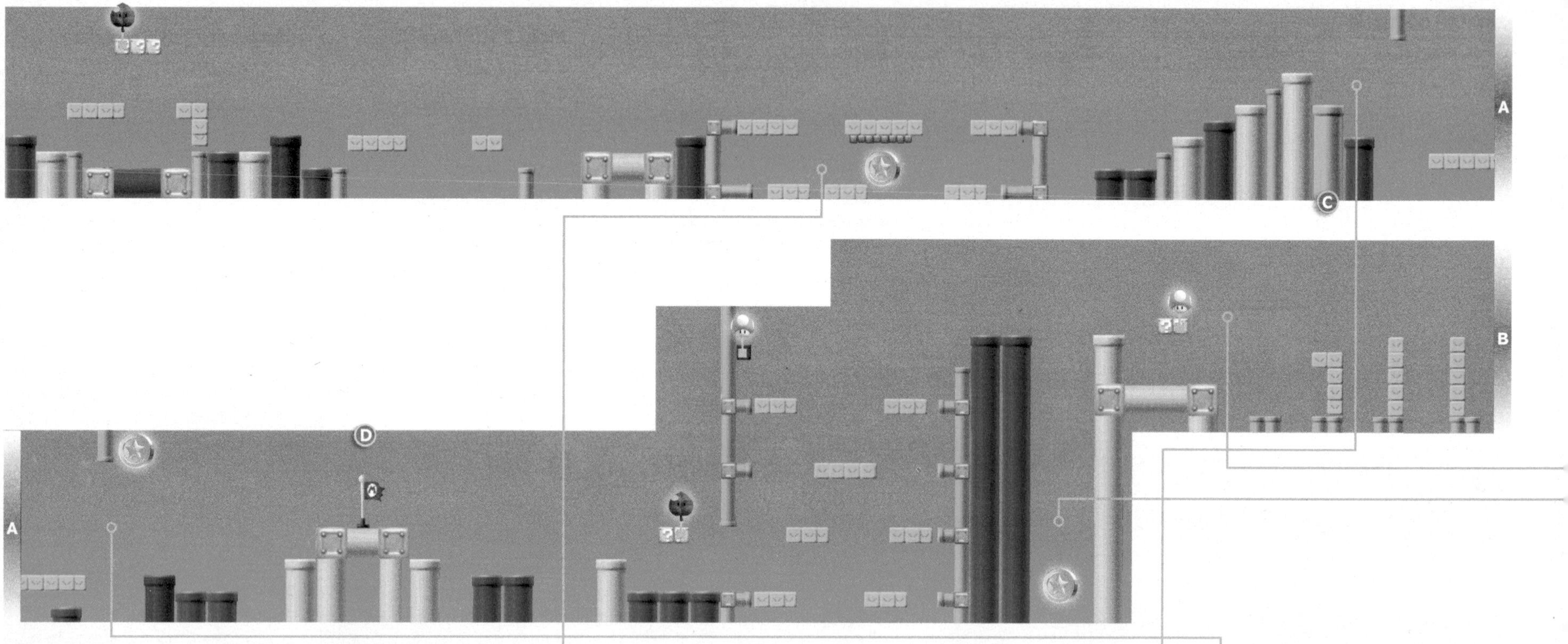

NOTE

To unlock Flower-A, you must find this level's secret exit.

1

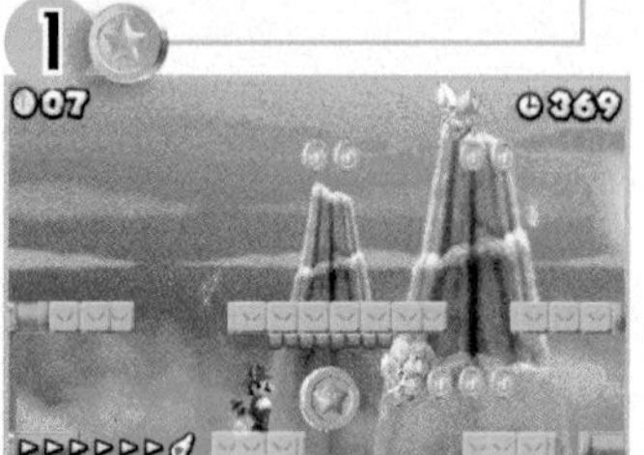

The first Star Coin is located at Point 1. Drop down onto one of the lower Caterpillar Blocks and follow it to the Star Coin.

CAUTION

There's a Koopa Paratroopa patrolling the area. If you're not equipped to defeat it, time your approach so you avoid it.

2

Enter the green pipe at Point 2 to find several coins in a hidden area.

3

To collect the Star Coin at Point 3, ride the Caterpillar Blocks as they head toward the small pipe. At the last second, jump up and collect the Star Coin.

FLOWER-1

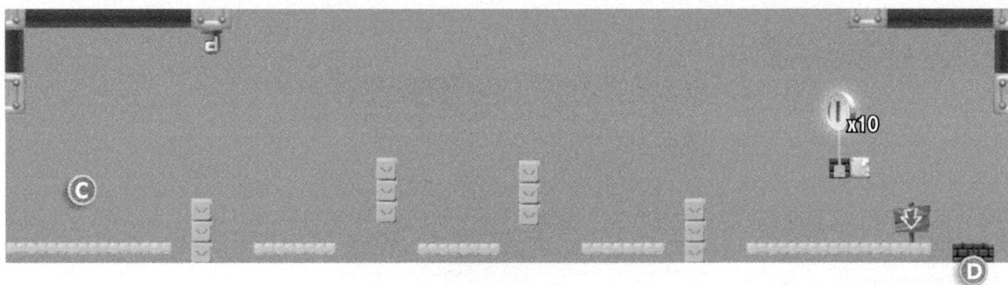

If you prefer, you can stand on the red pipe near Point 3 and wall jump off of the Caterpillar Blocks as they enter the small pipe.

4

The third Star Coin is floating between the pipes at Point 4.

To collect the Star Coin, slide down the side of one of the pipes, then wall jump back to safety.

5

There are two ? Blocks at Point 5. To find this level's secret exit, ground pound the ? Block on the right. After it transforms into a Flying ? Block, allow it to carry you to a hidden area. After you reach the Goal Pole, the path to Flower-A appears on the Map Screen.

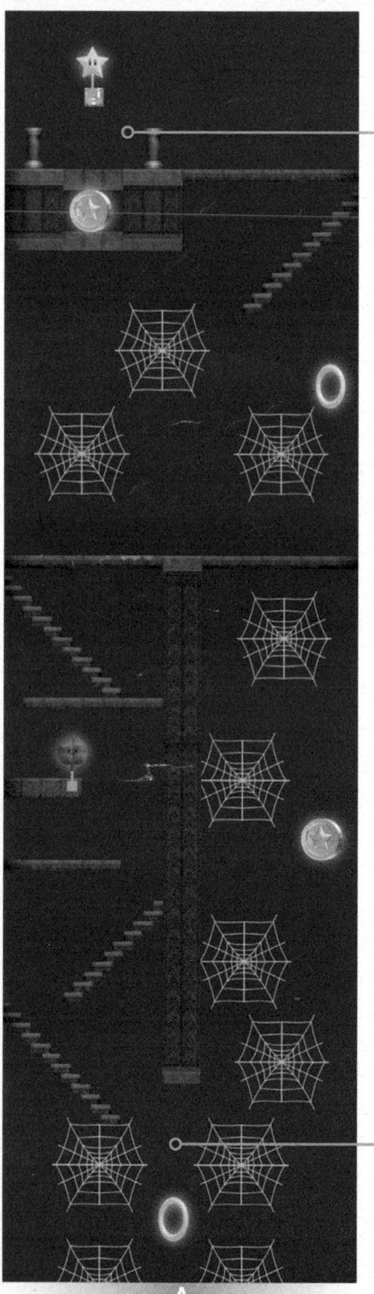

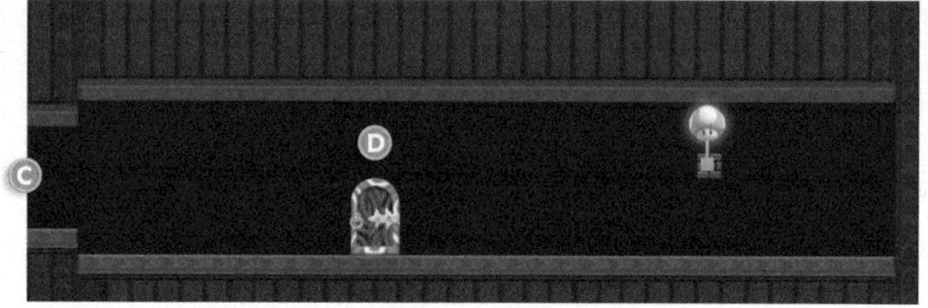

To unlock Flower-B, you must find this level's secret exit.

1

The path splits at Point 1. To collect the first Star Coin, follow the path on the right.

Climb the webs up to the Star Coin, then jump over and collect it.

2

The second Star Coin is sealed between the platforms at Point 2. The nearby ? Block contains a Super Star. When you collect this power-up, all of the platforms and walkways in the area turn into coins. Collect the Super Star while you're standing near the ? Block, then drop though the Star Coin when the environment transforms.

3

To find the secret exit, collect the Super Star at the top of the area, then move to the right wall as you fall through the coins. There's a small ledge at Point 3—stay near the wall to ensure you land on it. Follow the path to the right to find the secret exit. After you reach the Goal Pole, Flower-B becomes available on the Map Screen.

4

When you reach Point 4, a Boohemoth appears to the left. When you slow down to avoid hazards or collect items, remember to face this massive enemy.

5

The third Star Coin is under the stairs at Point 5. To collect it, you must move past the stairs, drop back into the water, and swim back toward the Boohemoth. This puts you in a fairly dangerous position, so be careful when you turn your back on the enemy.

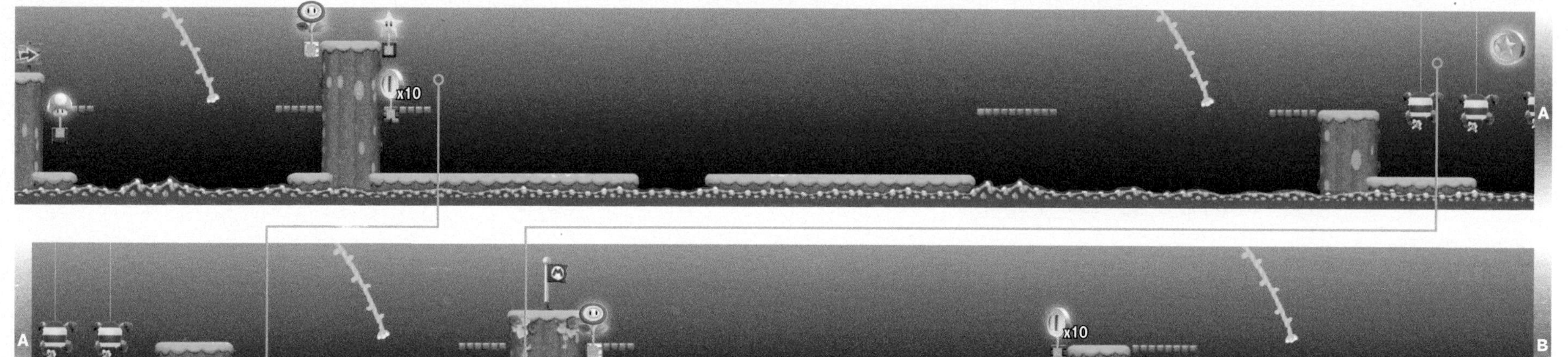

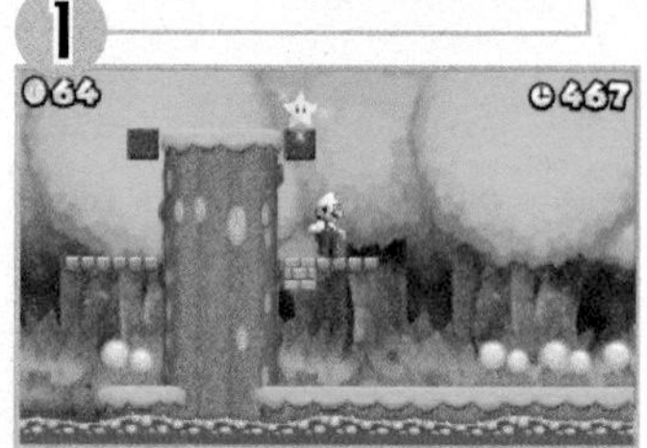

There's a Super Star hidden in an Invisible Block at Point 1.

The first Star Coin is floating above the Spiders at Point 2. When the Spiders move into range, use them to bounce up and grab the Star Coin.

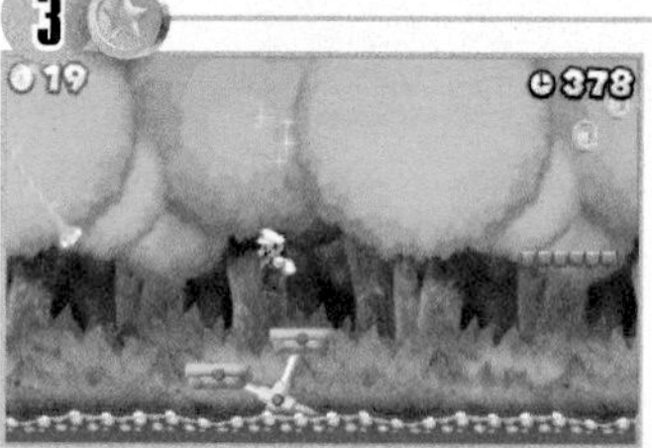

To collect the second Star Coin, you'll need the rotating platforms at Point 3. Swing over to the platforms, then use Mario's weight to move them to the right.

Clear the Spider from your path and move the rotating platforms under the walkway. When you reach the edge of the toxic water, run over and collect the Star Coin to the right.

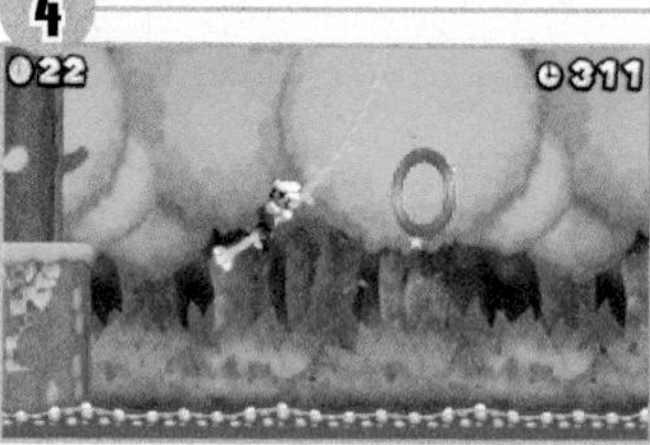

As you swing from the vine at Point 4, pass through the Red Ring floating above the toxic water. After you swing through the first four red coins, leap from the vine to collect the red coins to the right.

FLOWER-2

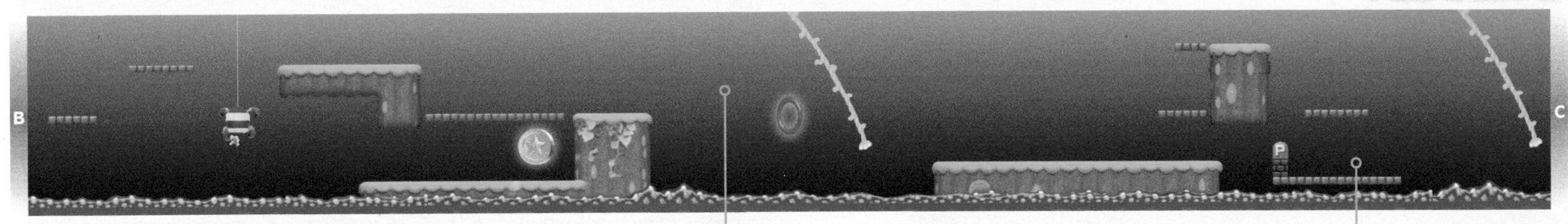

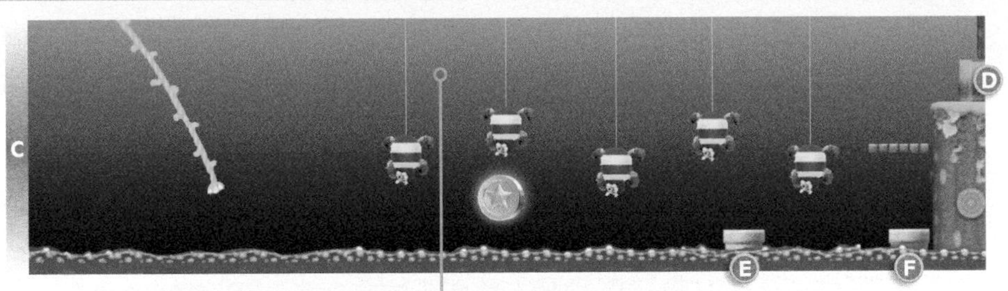

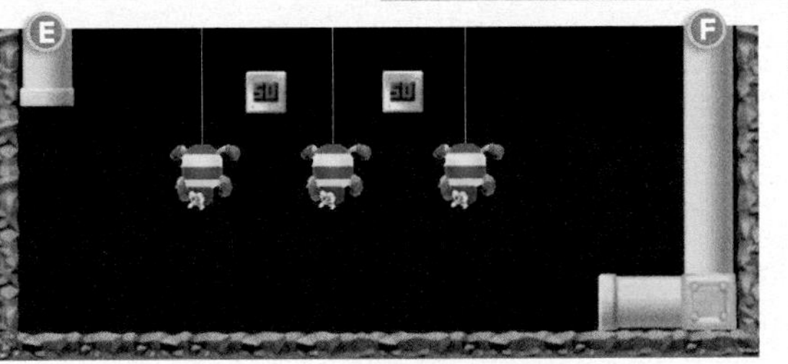

The Block at Point 5 contains a P Switch. Stomp one of the nearby Koopas, then throw its shell at the Block. Activate the P Switch to reveal some blue coins to the right.

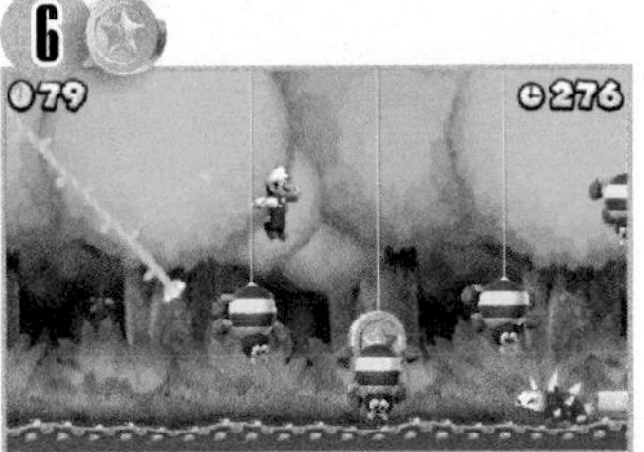

When you reach the Spiders at Point 6, look for the Star Coin floating above the toxic water. Aim for the Star Coin as you leap from the vine, then bounce along the Spiders to avoid falling into the toxic water.

Enter the yellow pipe just past the third Star Coin to find a hidden room containing two Roulette Coin Blocks.

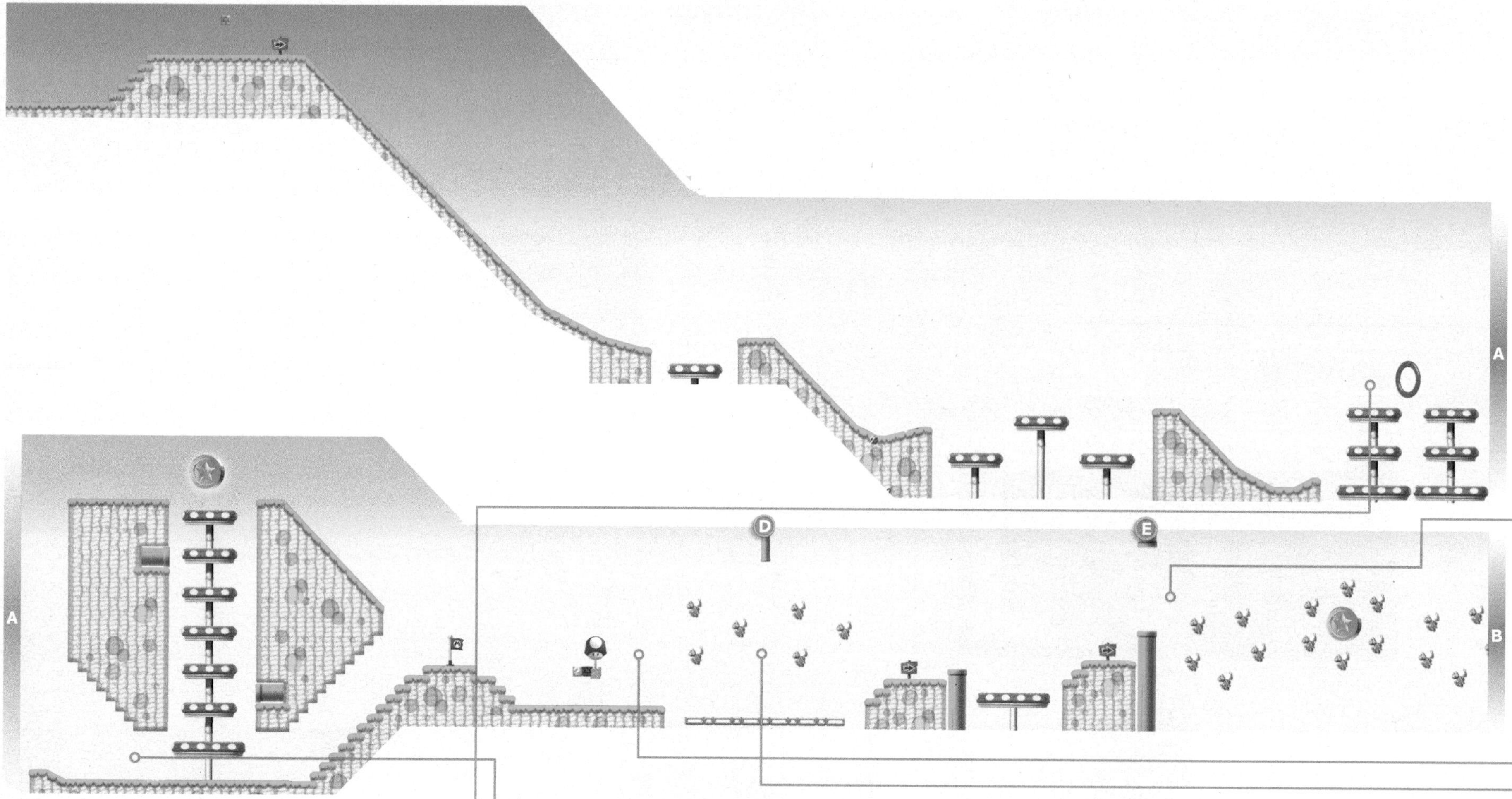

A

B

D

E

1

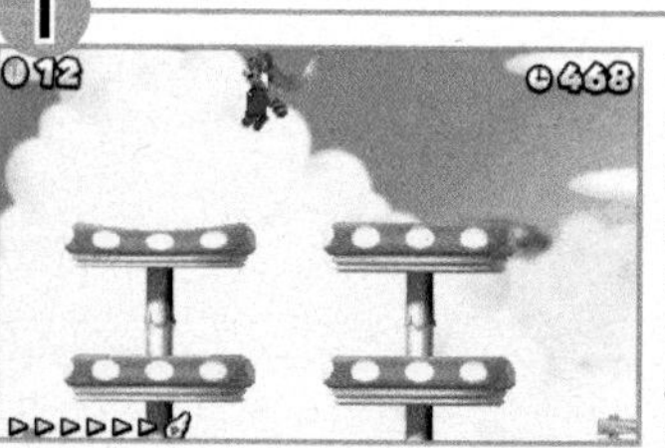

There's a Red Ring floating above the toadstools at Point 1. When you pass through the Red Ring, eight red coins appear in the area. Jump to either side and drop down to the lowest toadstool. Collect the first four red coins as you bounce back up along the toadstools, then repeat the process to collect the remaining coins.

2

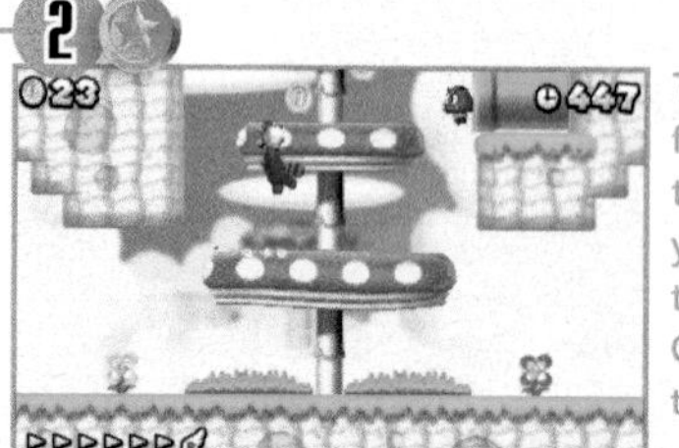

The first Star Coin is floating above the toadstools at Point 2. As you bounce up along the toadstools, dodge any Goombas that emerge from the nearby pipes.

When you reach the top of the toadstools, bounce up and collect the Star Coin above you.

FLOWER-3

3

One of the ? Blocks at Point 3 contains a Mini Mushroom. If you intend to collect the remaining Star Coins, make sure you grab this power-up.

4

The second Star Coin is located in a hidden area. As Mini Mario, jump on one of the Koopa Paratroopas at Point 4, and bounce on its head as it flies toward the small pipe above you. Bounce up and enter the pipe when you're within range.

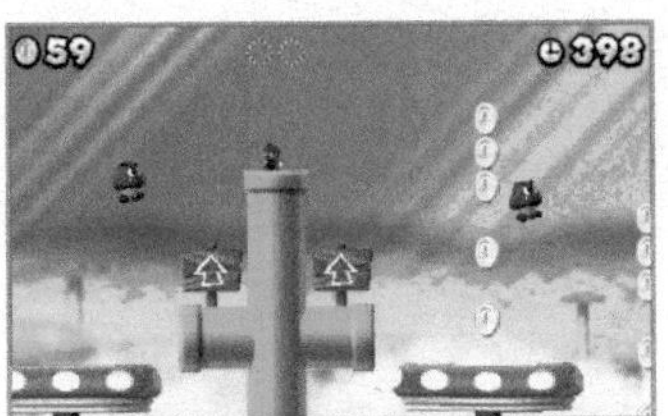

After you pass through the pipe, hit the ? Block to the right. Grab the Super Star, then bounce up to the green pipe at the center of the area. Enter the pipe to launch yourself at the Star Coin above you.

5

The third Star Coin is floating just past the Koopa Paratroopas at Point 5. Jump onto the nearest enemy, and bounce on its head as it circles to the left.

TIP

It may be easier to get the Third Star Coin by using a Raccoon Mario so you can float greater distances.

Hop over to the second group of Koopa Paratroopas, and bounce on one of the enemies as it passes under the Star Coin. Continue to bounce the across the third group of enemies and return to solid ground.

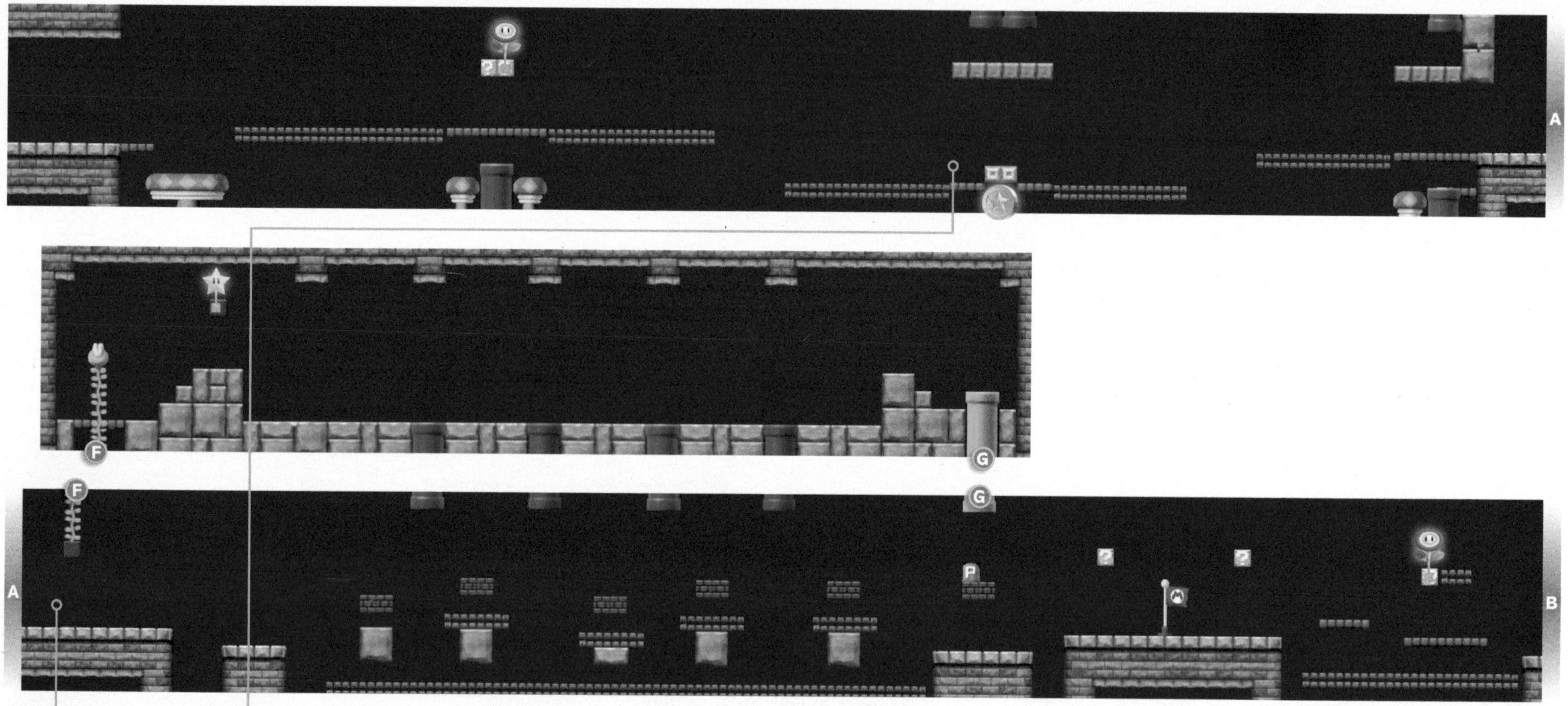

The first Star Coin is located below the walkway at Point 1. Stomp a nearby Bob-omb and use it to blast a hole in the walkway, then throw a second Bob-omb at the Star Coin to collect it.

Hit the Invisible Block at Point 2, then climb the revealed Beanstalk to find a hidden area.

When you reach the top of the Beanstalk, locate the Invisible Block above the steps to the right. Collect the Super Star, then dash through the nearby enemies to gain an extra life.

If you move quickly, you can leave the hidden area and find another ? Block before the Super Star wears off. Doing so will earn you an additional Super Star.

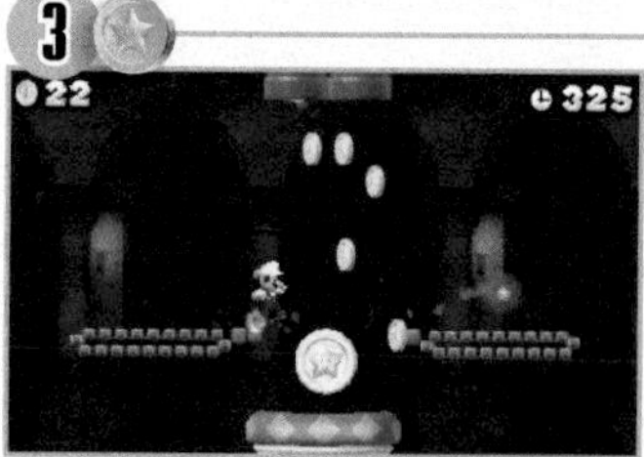

The second Star Coin is located between the conveyor belts at Point 3. When you collect it, watch out for the Bone Goombas that drop down from the pipes above you.

FLOWER-CASTLE

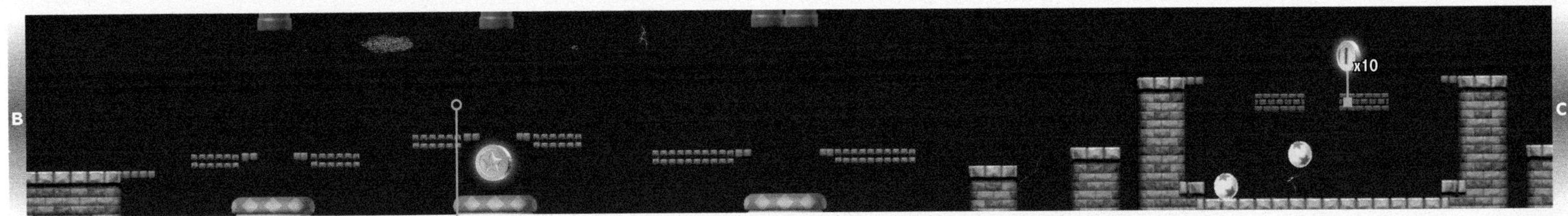

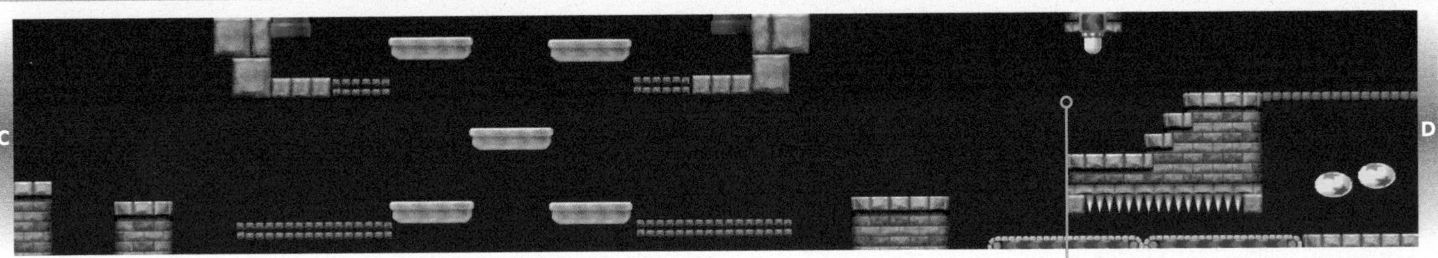

NOTE

If you haven't already unlocked World Five, completing this level will do so.

4

When you reach Point 4, jump up and hit the switch above you. This causes the nearby conveyor belts to change direction. Drop to the first belt and crouch down.

Allow the conveyor belts to carry you under the spikes and into the enclosure. Slip past the balls as they bounce around the area, then grab the Star Coin near the wall to the right.

5

This battle takes place on a conveyor belt, so it's essential that you keep your footing—especially when Lemmy Koopa uses his wand to summon rubber balls. Rubber balls do not cause damage, but they can make it difficult to move around the room. If a rubber ball keeps knocking you out of position, perform a wall jump and leap over it. As soon as you're within striking distance, stomp Lemmy's head.

After you stomp Lemmy, he tucks into his shell and bounces around the room. Avoid the shell as you wait for another chance to attack. The conveyor belt changes direction each time a ball hits the switch on the ceiling, and Lemmy occasionally charges toward you, but this shouldn't affect your basic strategy. Stomp Lemmy a total of three times to end the encounter.

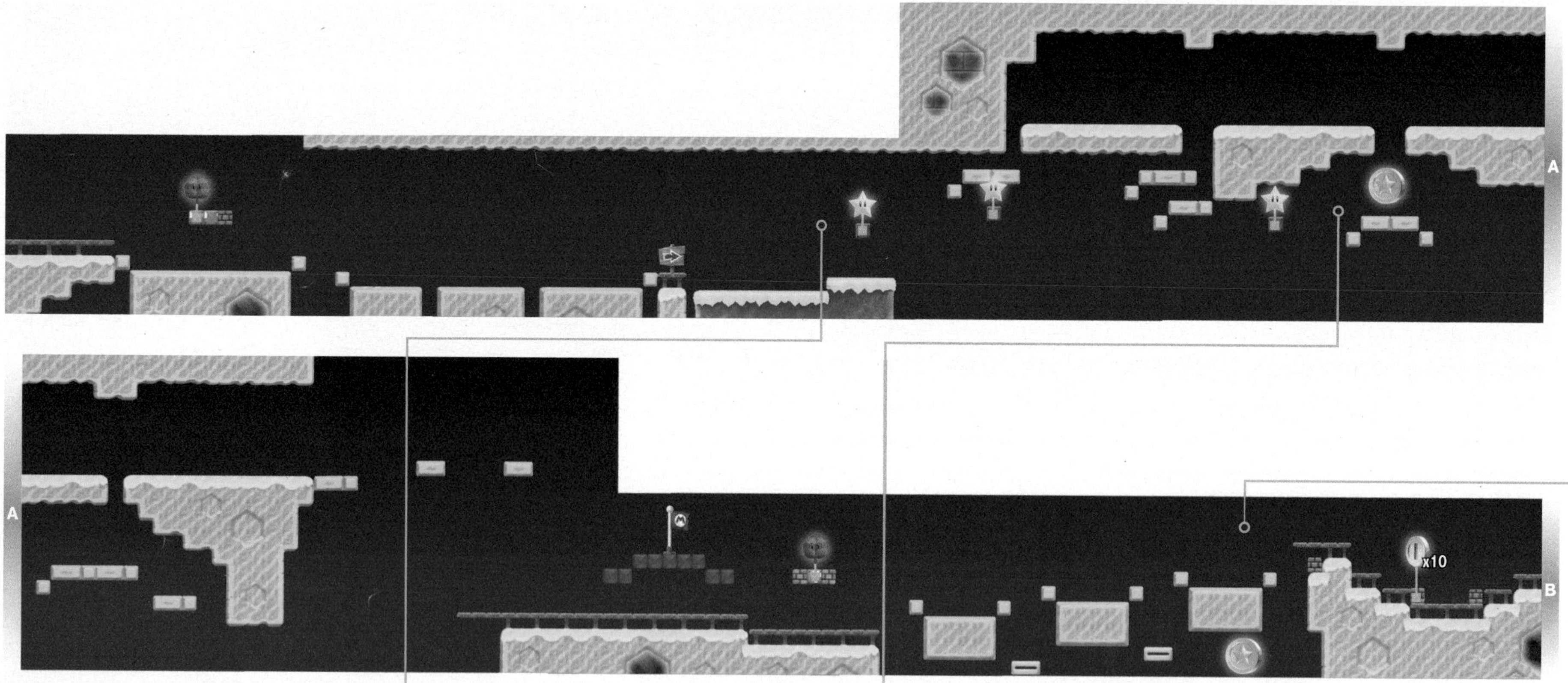

A

A

B

x10

1

There are several Invisible Blocks near the start of the level. Each one contains a Super Star. When you see a cluster of four coins, hit the space in the middle to reveal an Invisible Block.

2

The first Star Coin is above the platform at Point 2. There's a Red Spike Buzzy patrolling the platform—grab the Super Star from the nearby Invisible Block to ensure you clear out the enemy on your way to the Star Coin.

NOTE

To unlock this level, you must find the secret exit in Flower-1.

TIP

After you collect the Star Coin, wall jump up through the gap above you to find a stash of coins.

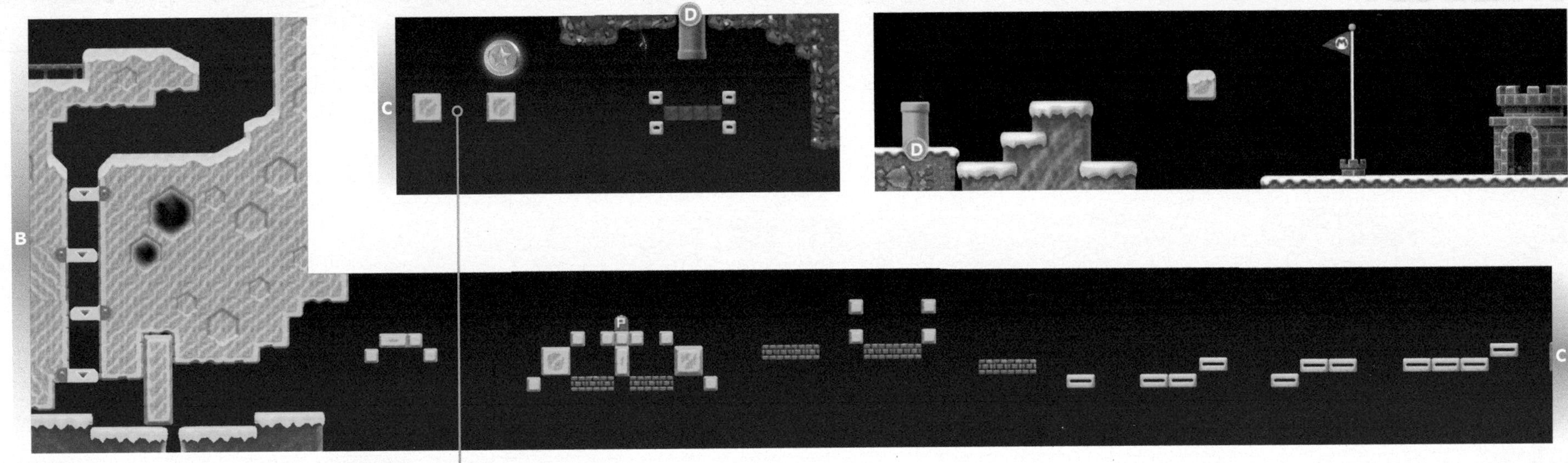

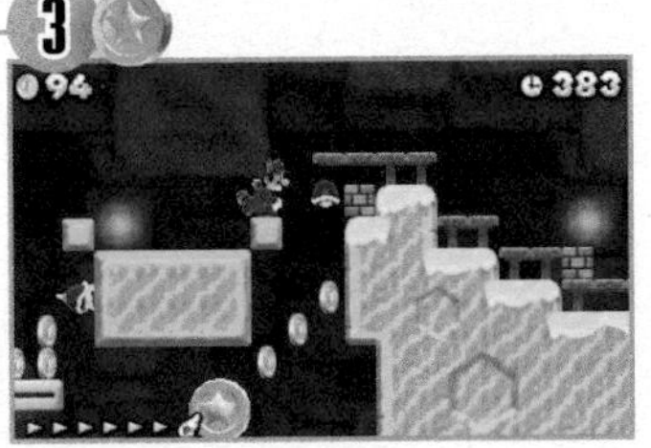

The second Star Coin is floating below the platform at Point 3. To collect it, stomp the nearby Buzzy Beetle and throw its shell at the Block to the right. After a few bounces, the shell passes through the Star Coin.

The third Star Coin is floating above the Red Spike Buzzies at Point 4. Clear the enemies from the nearby platform, then jump across to collect the Star Coin.

To unlock this level, you must find the secret exit in Flower-Boo House.

To reach the first Star Coin, stomp the Lakitu at Point 1 and hop onto its cloud.

Follow the coins to the right of the Gold Ring to find the Star Coin.

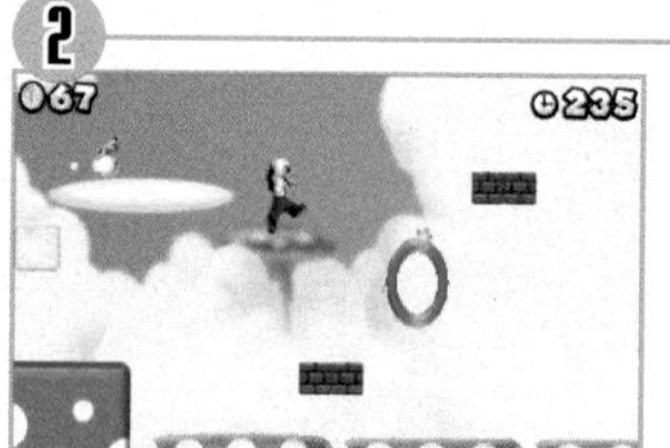

When you approach the Red Ring at Point 2, a Lakitu appears in the background. Either pass through the Red Ring and use the Blocks and toadstools to reach the red coins, or wait for the enemy to arrive and commandeer its cloud.

FLOWER-B

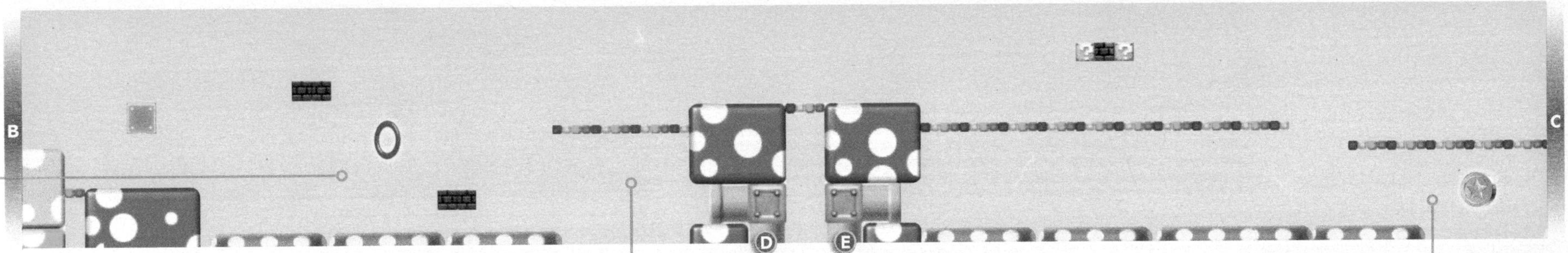

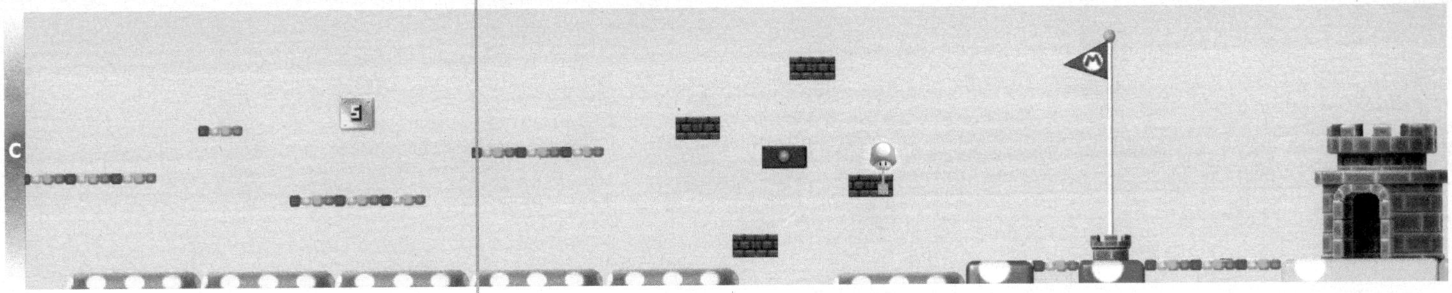

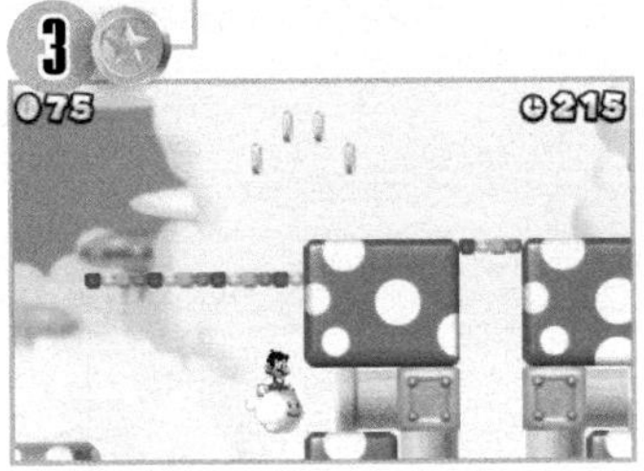

3

The second Star Coin is located in a hidden area. To find it, stomp the Lakitu near Point 3 and use its cloud to fly down to the yellow pipe below the walkway.

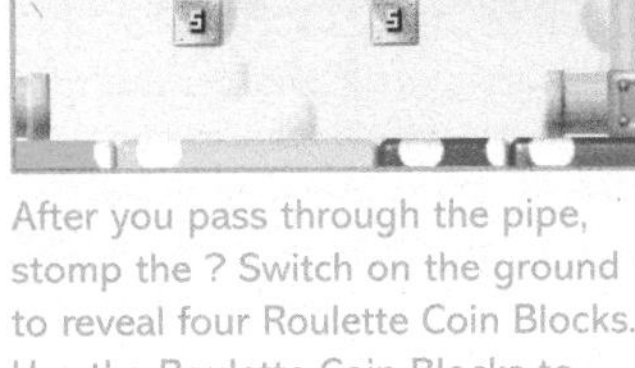

After you pass through the pipe, stomp the ? Switch on the ground to reveal four Roulette Coin Blocks. Use the Roulette Coin Blocks to reach the Star Coin before the ? Switch wears off.

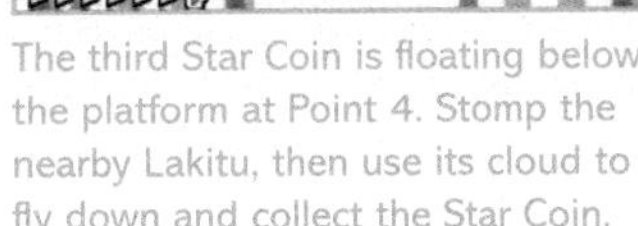

4

The third Star Coin is floating below the platform at Point 4. Stomp the nearby Lakitu, then use its cloud to fly down and collect the Star Coin.

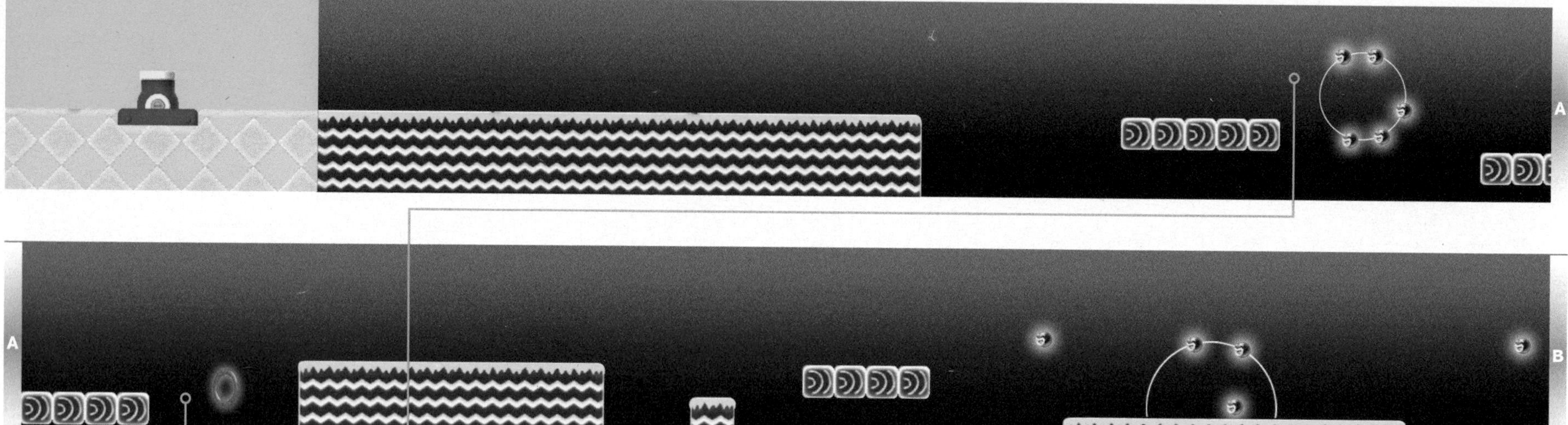

NOTE

To access this level, you must unlock and complete Flower-A.

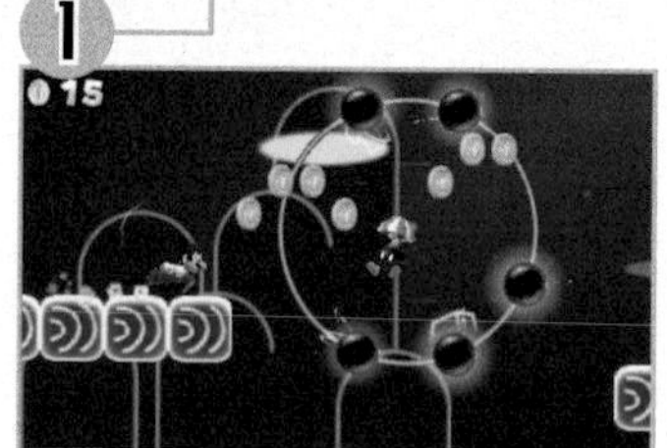

To traverse this level, you must perform some very tricky jumps. Follow the coin trails to make it safely through each group of enemies. The Amps are very dangerous, and since the Bob-ombs sway as they parachute through the area, it can be hard to predict exactly where they'll be by the time you reach them.

There's a Red Ring floating below the coin trail at Point 2. To pass through the Red Ring, you must bounce off of the lower Bob-omb without touching the Bob-omb above you.

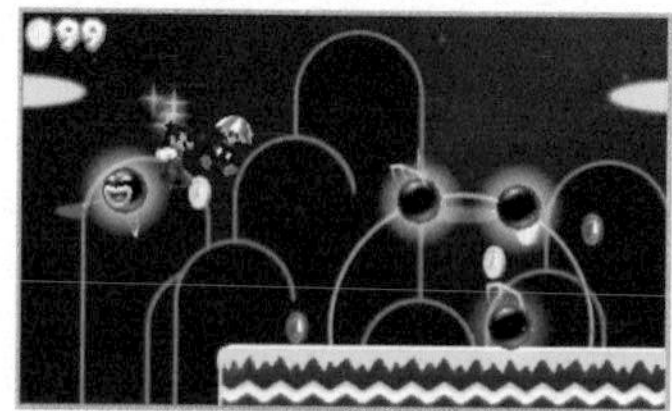

Once again, activating the Red Ring alters the remaining coin trails. To follow them, you must slip through some incredibly tight spaces. If you manage to collect all eight red coins, however, you'll earn a Gold Flower.

If you haven't already unlocked World Six, complete the level to do so.

B

STAR WORLD

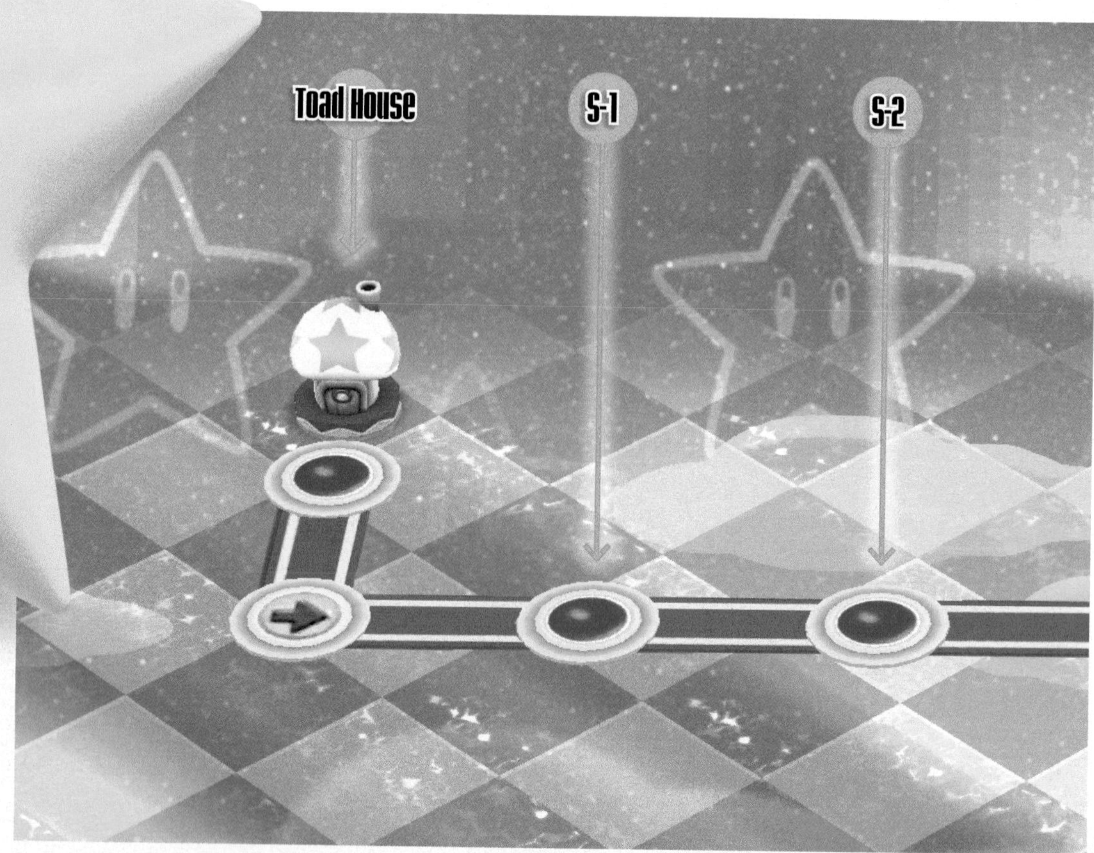

WORLD LOCATIONS				
Hostile Levels	Toad Houses	Boo Houses	Warp Cannons	Boss
8	1	0	0	Dry Bowser

NOTE

To reveal Star World, you must complete World 6-Castle. You must then pay 90 Star Coins to unlock the main path.

Main Path Levels:

- Star-1
- Star-2
- Star-3
- Star-4
- Star-5
- Star-6
- Star-7
- Star-Castle

Alternate Path Levels:

- None

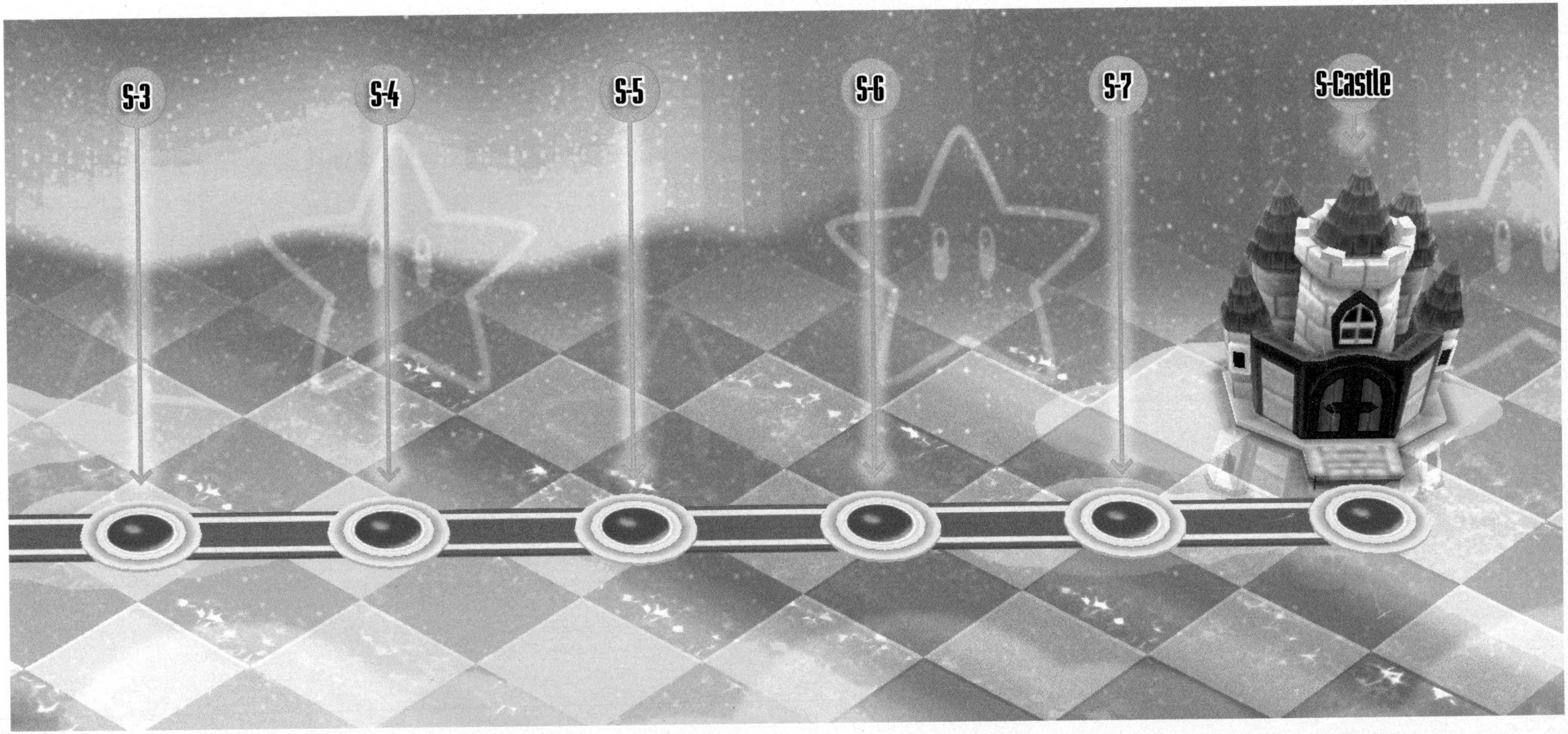

S-3 S-4 S-5 S-6 S-7 S-Castle

1

There's a P Switch hidden in a Block at Point 1. Ground pound through the Blocks just right of the first gap, then move just far enough to the left to hit the Block directly above the gap. Stomp the P Switch to transform all of the nearby Blocks into coins.

2

The first Moon Coin is floating below the walkway at Point 2. Search the Blocks above the Moon Coin to find a P Switch.

Stomp the P Switch to expose the area below the walkway. Gather as many blue coins as you can, then enter the green pipe on the ground. When you do, it launches you through the Moon Coin and back to the walkway.

3

There's a Beanstalk inside the first Block past the rotating platforms at Point 3. Ground pound through the Blocks to the right, then move just far enough to the left to jump up and reveal the Beanstalk.

Climb up and stomp the P Switch near the top of the Beanstalk. If you move quickly, you can use the rotating platforms to collect a Gold Flower from the ? Block at the top of the area.

STAR-1

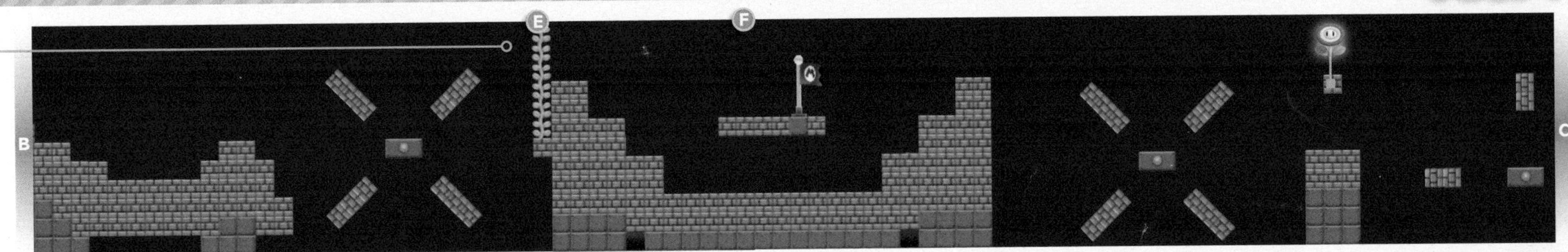

When you reach Point 4, ground pound through the Blocks to create a path to the Moon Coin. Stomp the nearby Koopa, then throw its shell through the opening to automatically collect the Moon Coin.

5

When you pass through the Red Ring at Point 5, a Coin Coffer leaves a trail of red coins for you to follow. Hop along the path to collect all of the red coins before they vanish.

The third Moon Coin is located at Point 6. Search the nearby Blocks for a ? Switch. Activate the ? Switch, drop to the ground, and dash over to collect the Moon Coin.

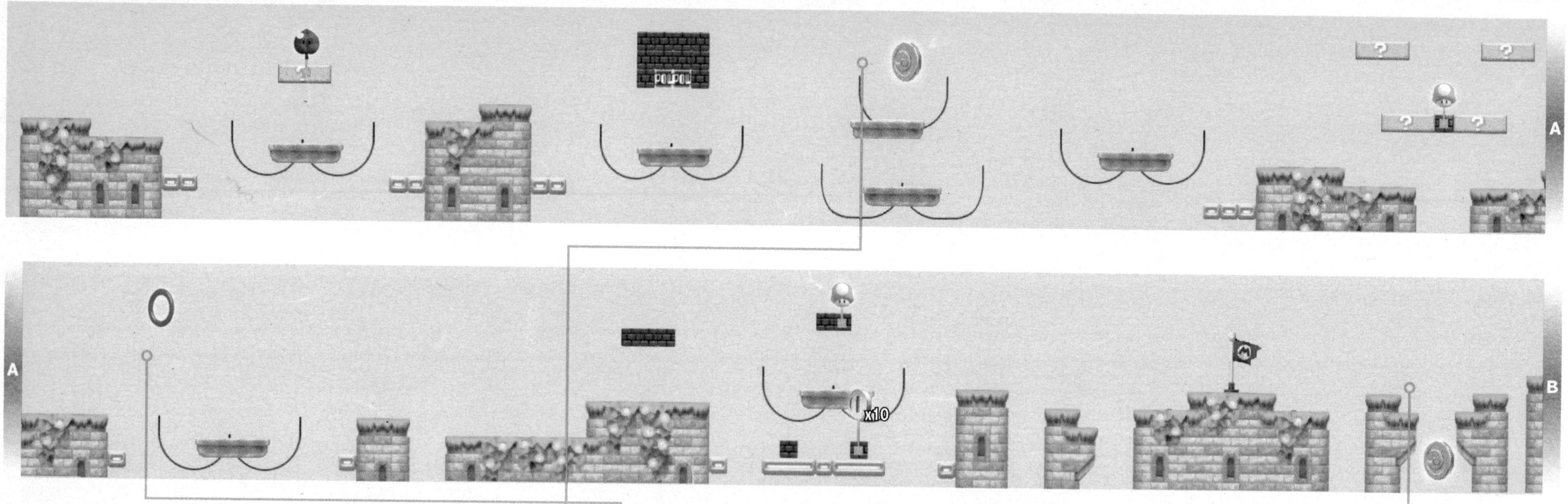

1

The first Moon Coin is floating above the platforms at Point 1. Move to the upper platform and jump up to grab the Moon Coin.

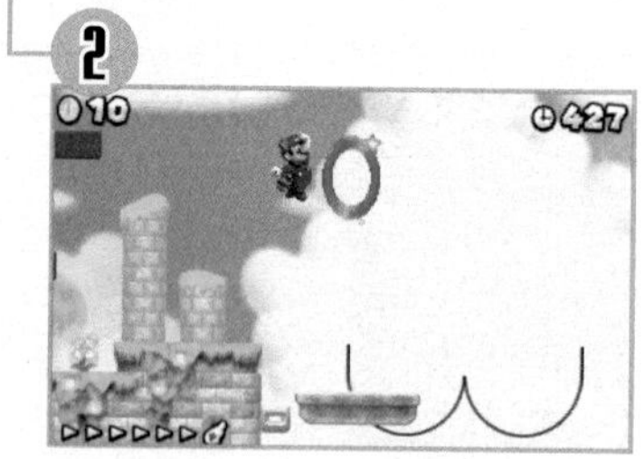

2

When you jump through the Red Ring at Point 2, red coins start parachuting down from above you. Ride the platform as it moves back and forth along its track and collect each red coin before it drifts out of reach.

3

The second Moon Coin is floating between the platforms at Point 3. Stomp the Koopa to the right, then use its shell to collect the Moon Coin.

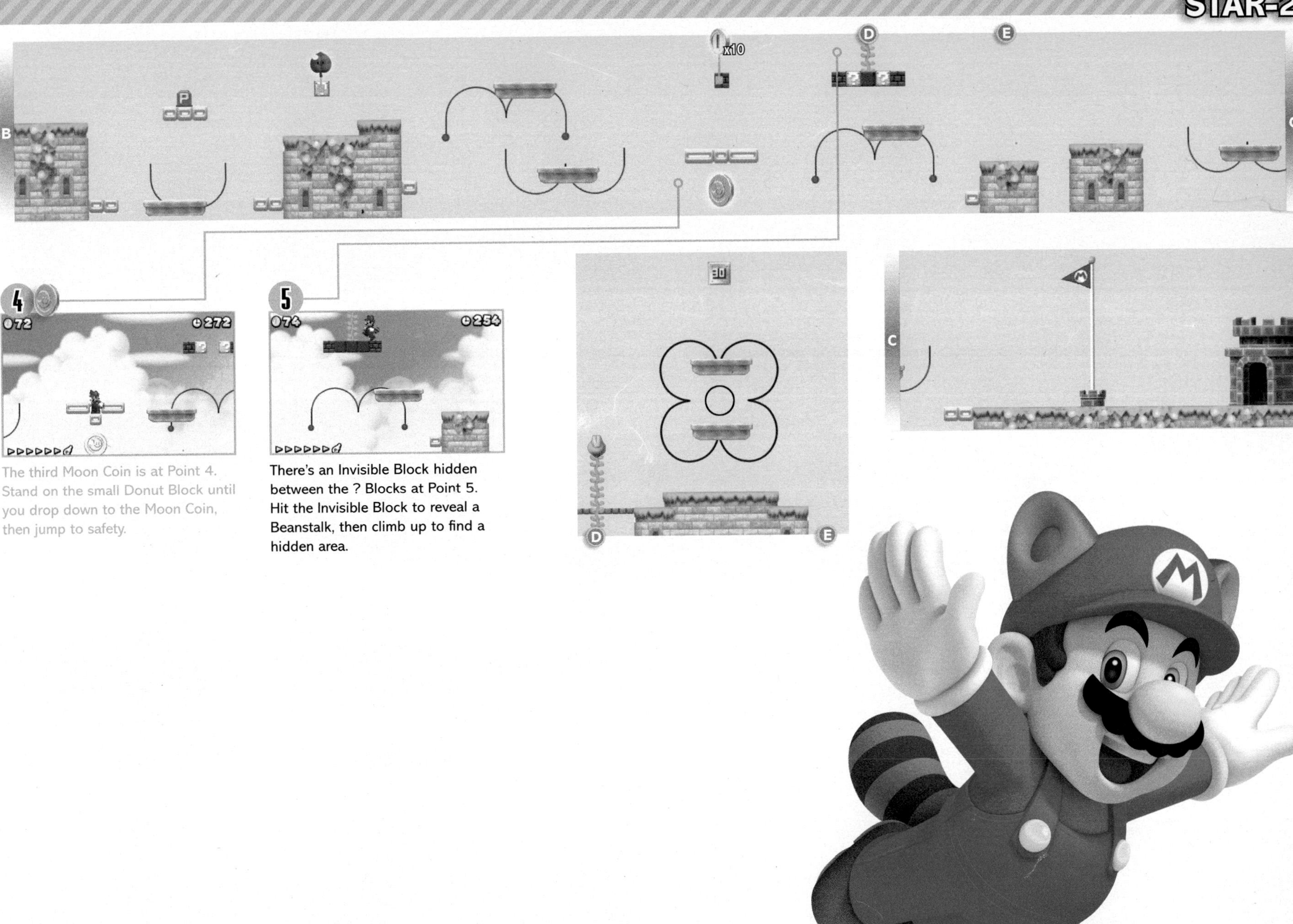

The third Moon Coin is at Point 4. Stand on the small Donut Block until you drop down to the Moon Coin, then jump to safety.

There's an Invisible Block hidden between the ? Blocks at Point 5. Hit the Invisible Block to reveal a Beanstalk, then climb up to find a hidden area.

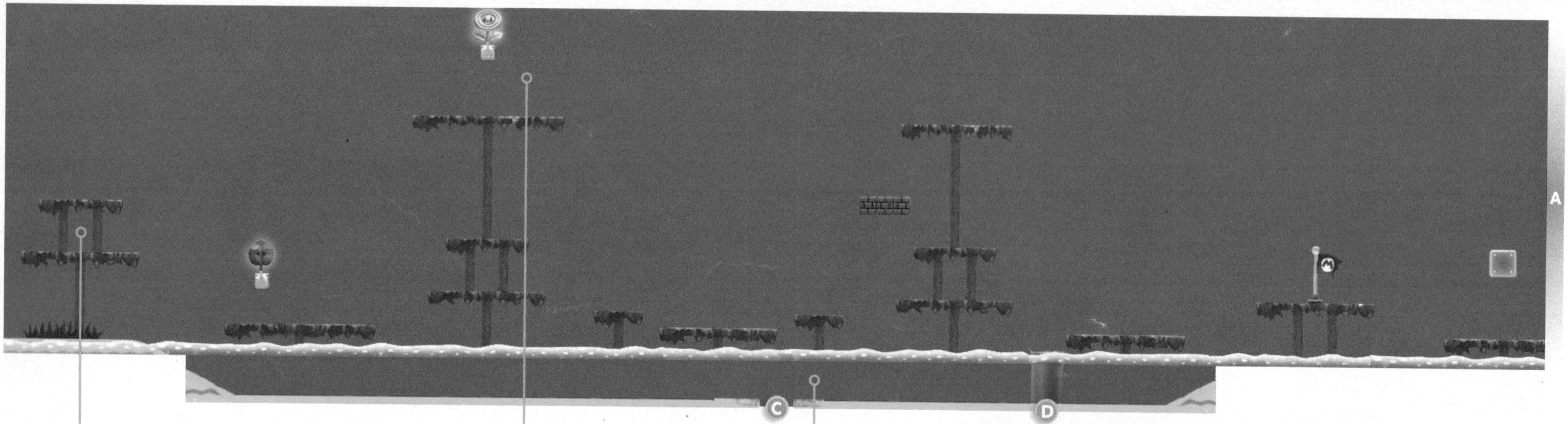

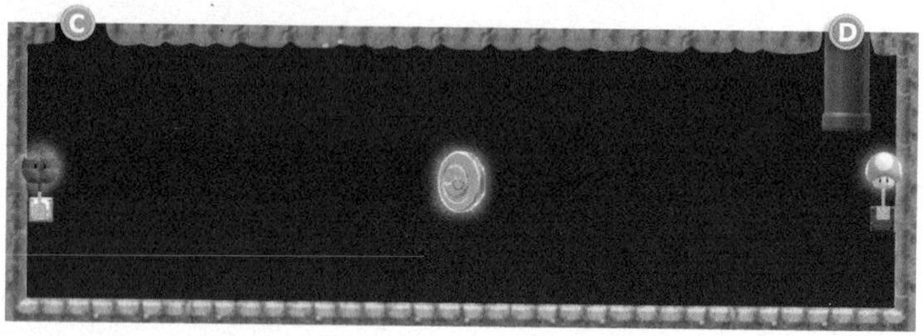

TIP

The Whomps can be advantageous to the player. Instead of defeating them, they can be used as extra obstacles so the player can advance and obtain hard-to-reach Power Ups and hidden blocks.

1

Many of the platforms in this level are supported by two columns. Each time you spot a pair of columns, stand in the gap between them. Doing so will reveal hidden coins or Blocks.

2

The ? Block at Point 2 contains a Gold Flower. To reach this platform, use a Super Leaf to fly up from the ground or glide from the platforms to the right.

3

The first Moon Coin is located in a hidden area. To find it, hop into the water, and enter the passage at Point 3 before the current sweeps you back to the start of the level.

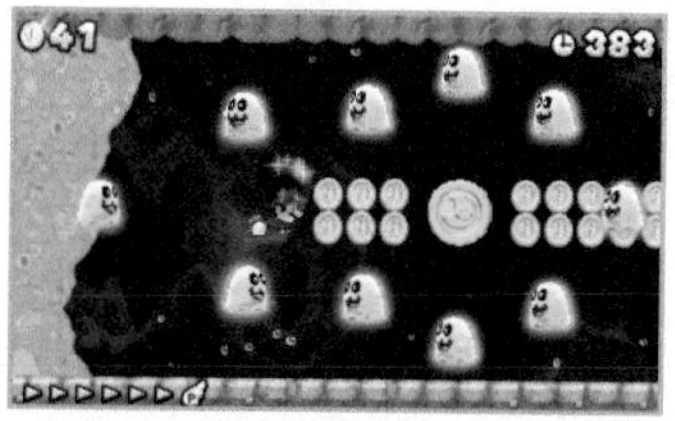

The Moon Coin is floating in the center of the area. Avoid the water currents and circling Peepas as you swim over to collect it.

The second Moon Coin is floating above the platform at Point 4. Search the platforms on either side of this location to reveal two sets of Blocks, then use the Blocks to reach the Moon Coin.

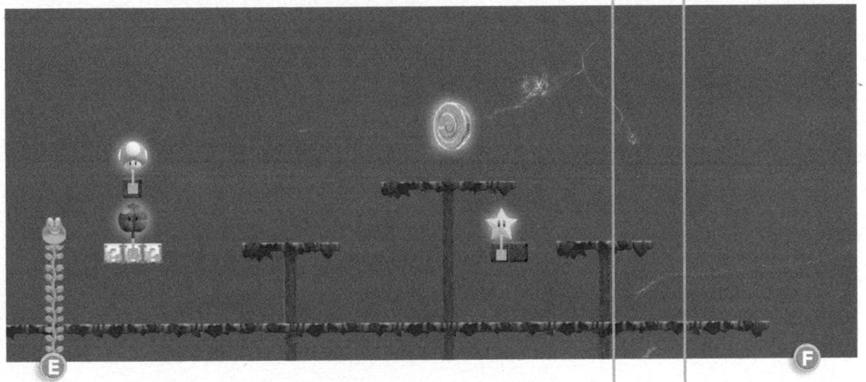

The third Moon Coin is in a hidden area. Use a Super Leaf to fly or glide up to the platform at Point 5. Locate the Invisible Block above you, then climb up the revealed Beanstalk.

The Moon Coin is hidden behind the Big Whomp on the central platform. Dodge the circling Peepas, coax the Big Whomp into attacking, and grab the Moon Coin.

If you clear the enemies from all three platforms, it triggers an eruption of coins.

Before you pass through the Red Ring at Point 6, defeat the Whomps on the nearby platforms. It's much easier to collect the red coins with these enemies out of the way.

There's a Mini Mushroom in the ? Block at Point 1. If you want to collect all of the Moon Coins during a single visit, make sure you grab it.

TIP

Fire Mario is better equipped to deal with persistent Porcupuffers, but Mini Mario isn't defenseless. Each time you reach a Koopa, ground pound it and throw its shell at your attacker.

The first Moon Coin is located above the platforms at Point 2. It doesn't remain on the screen for long, so move quickly if you hope to collect it.

When you pass through the Red Ring at Point 3, the red coins appear along the platforms to the right.

STAR-4

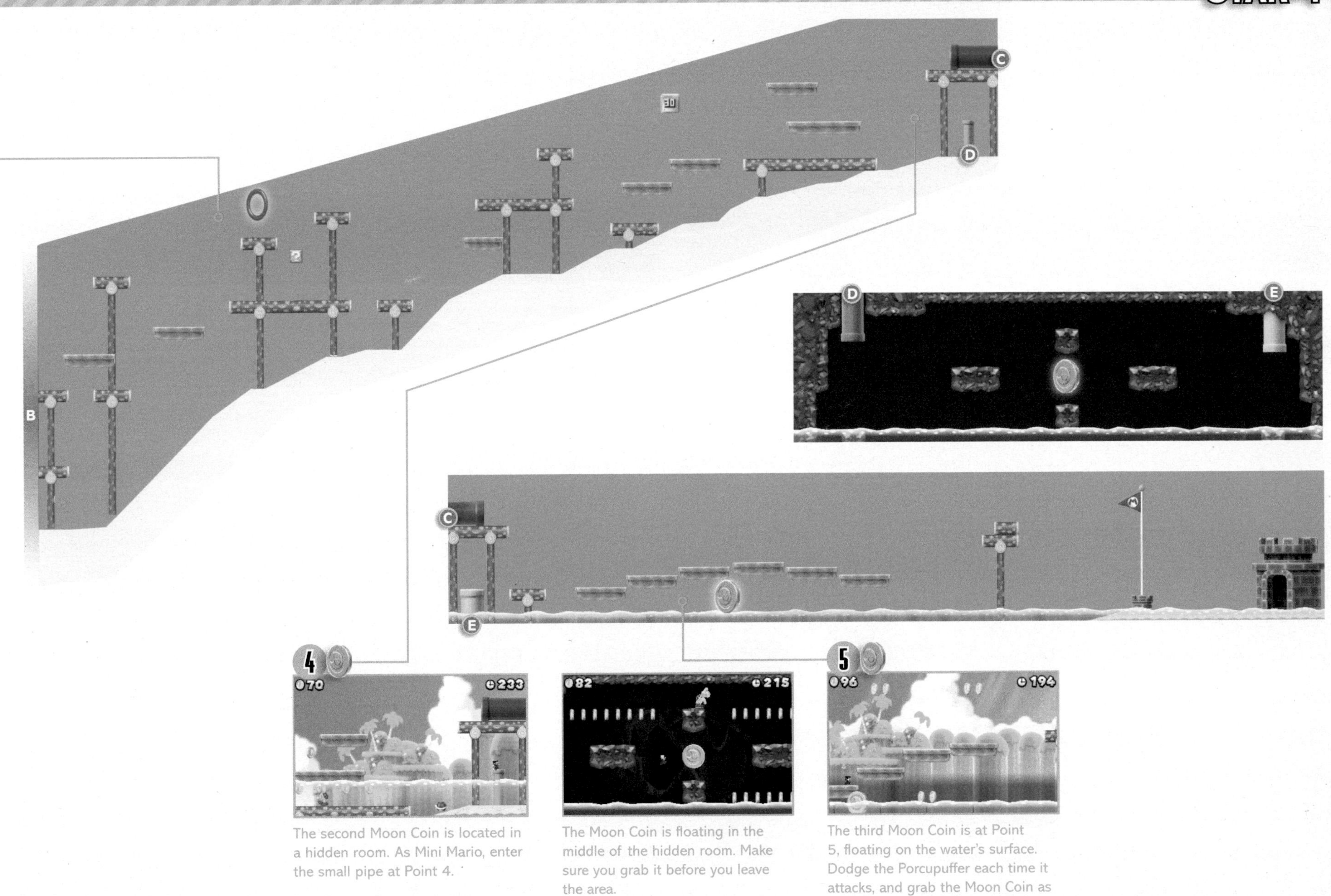

The second Moon Coin is located in a hidden room. As Mini Mario, enter the small pipe at Point 4.

The Moon Coin is floating in the middle of the hidden room. Make sure you grab it before you leave the area.

The third Moon Coin is at Point 5, floating on the water's surface. Dodge the Porcupuffer each time it attacks, and grab the Moon Coin as the platforms drop within range.

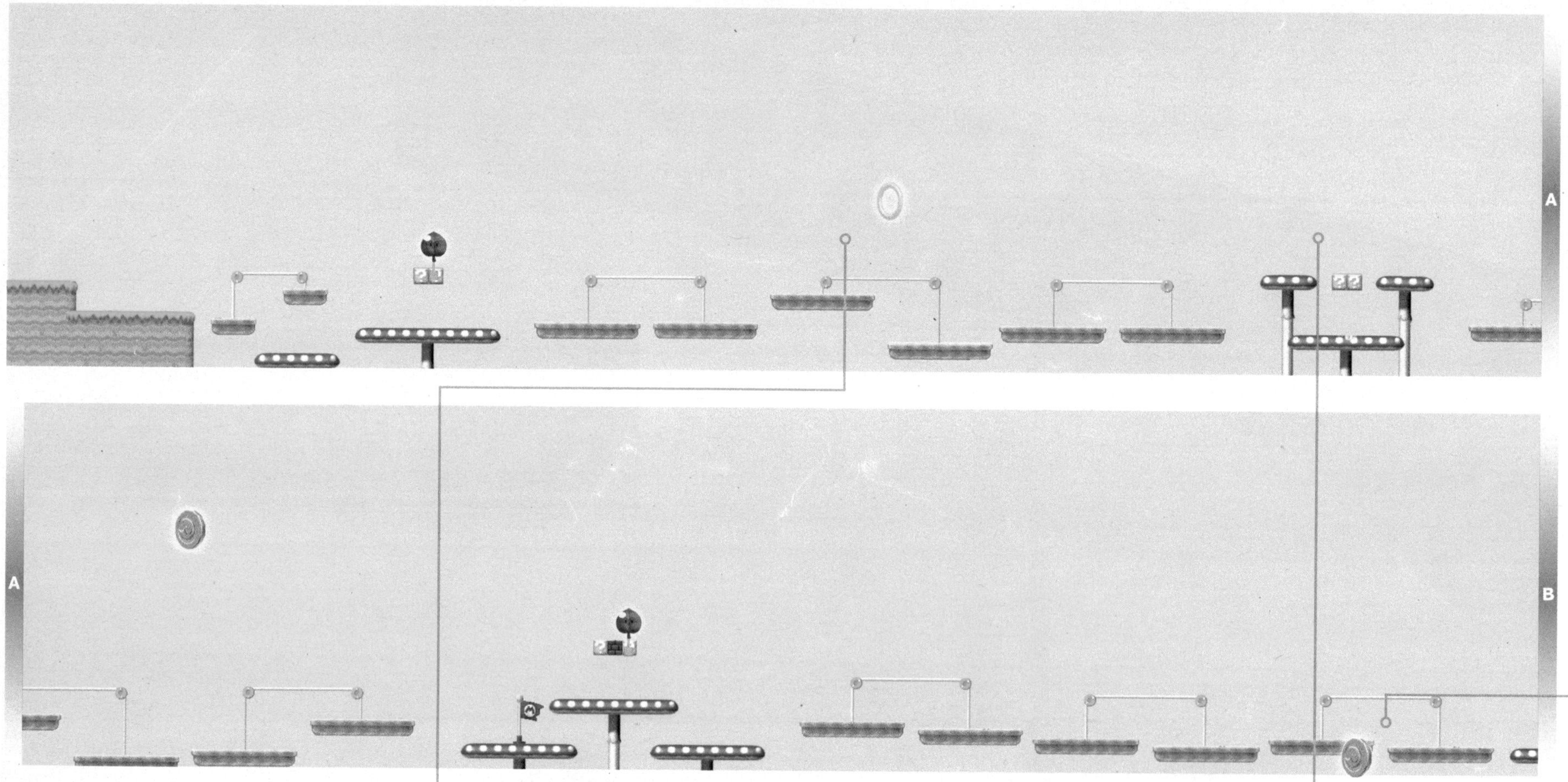

1

As you move across the pulley platforms at the start of the level, a Lakitu appears in the background. Wait for this enemy to move into range, then stomp it and take its cloud. Fly above the platforms at Point 1 to find a Gold Ring.

2

The first Moon Coin is floating high above the platforms. To find it, use a Lakitu's cloud to follow the coin trail above Point 2.

Collect the Moon Coin and return to the platforms before the cloud you're flying vanishes.

STAR-5

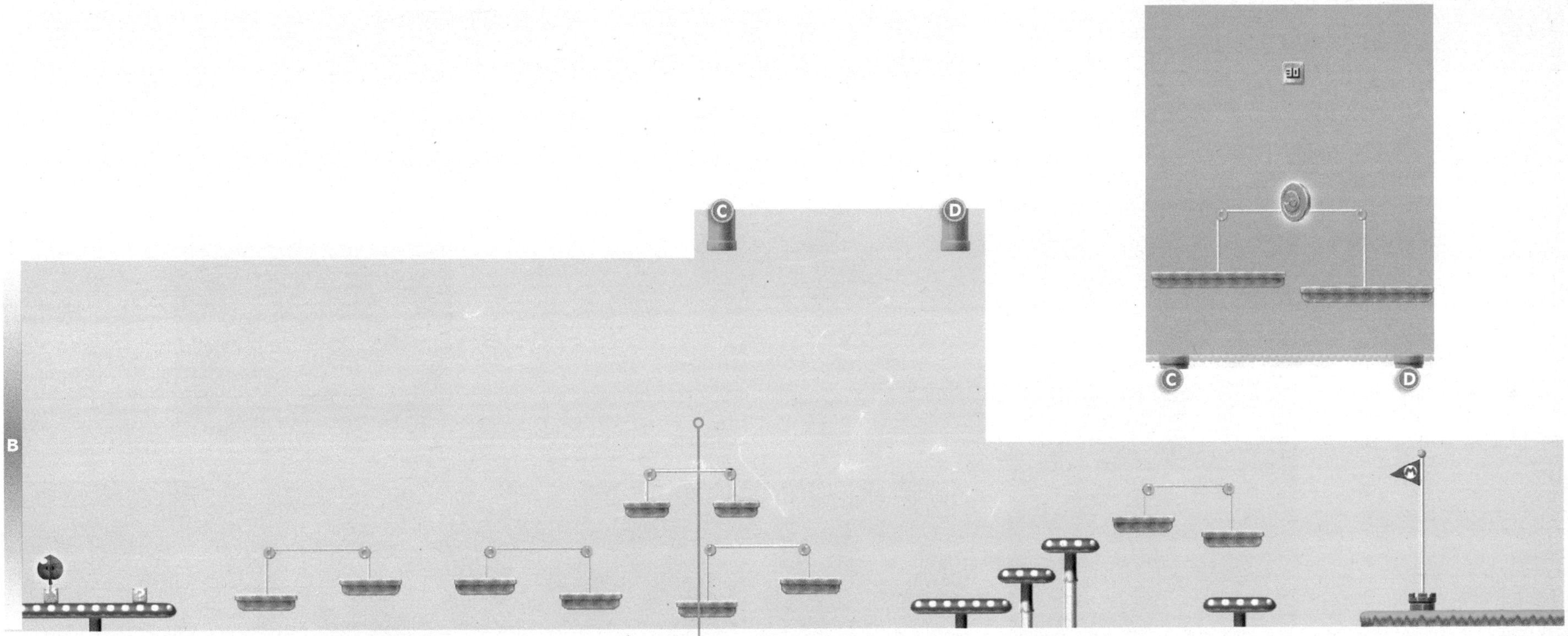

3

The second Moon Coin is just below the platform at Point 3. The nearby enemies can overload the pulley platforms, making it difficult to collect the Moon Coin. Jump to the toadstool just past the Moon Coin and wait for the enemies to break the pulley platforms. As soon as the platforms reappear, hop over and collect the Moon Coin.

4

The third Moon Coin is in a hidden area. Stomp a Lakitu near the pulley platforms at Point 4, then use its cloud to fly up to the green pipe above you.

Enter the pipe, then use the pulley platforms to stomp the Lakitu and collect the Moon Coin.

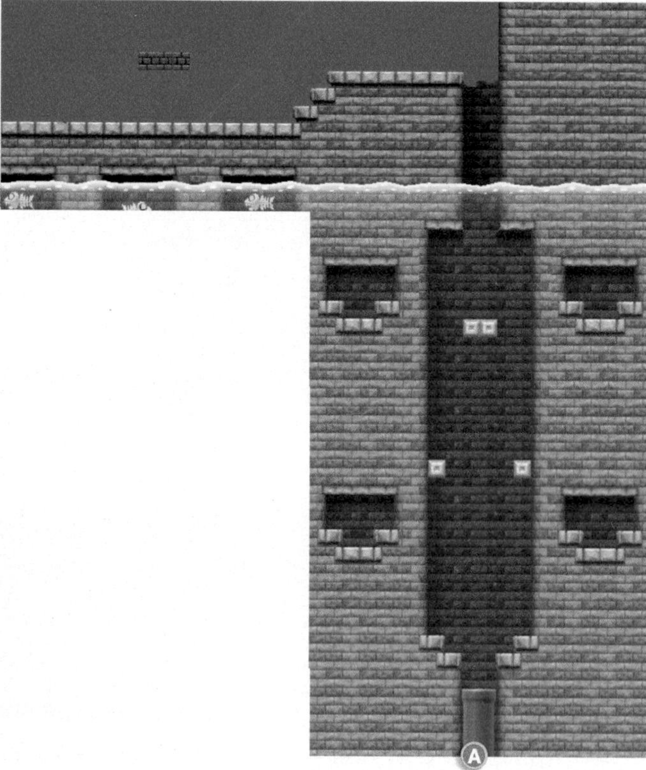

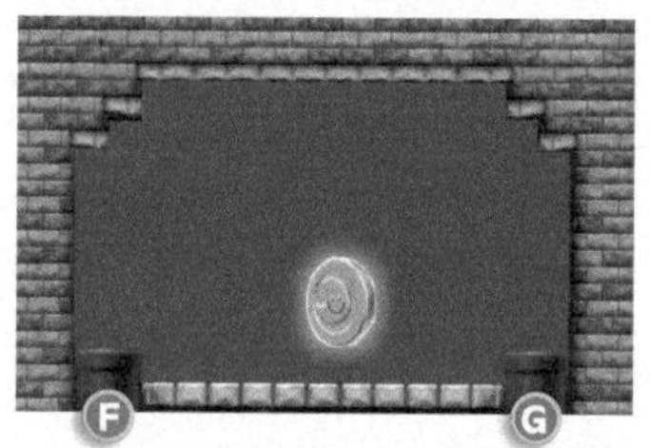

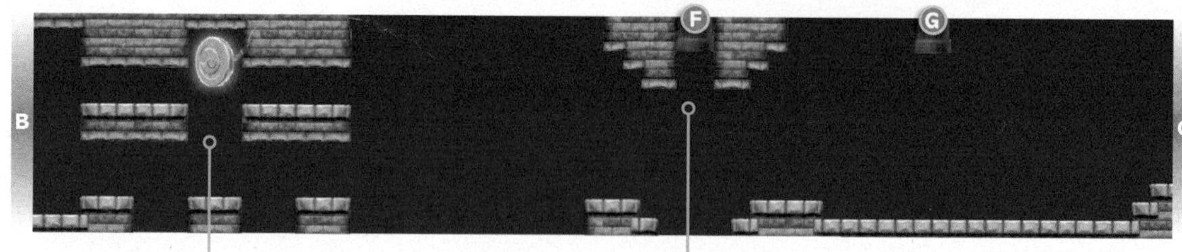

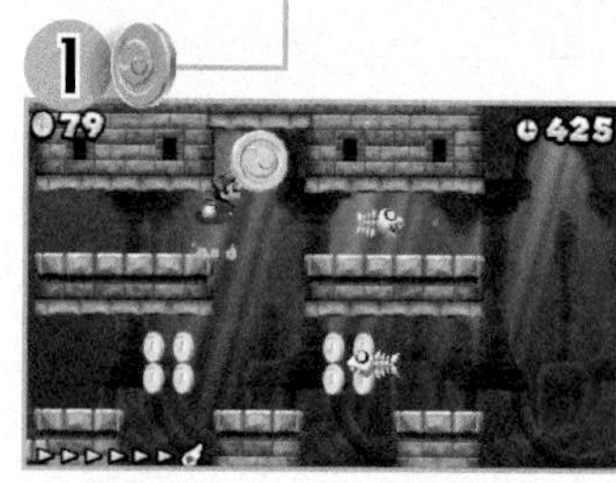

The first Moon Coin is located in a small nook at Point 1. If you have a Super Leaf, use Raccoon Mario's tail whip to clear the Fishbones out of the area. If you no longer have this power-up, approach the Moon Coin from below and dodge the enemies patrolling the area.

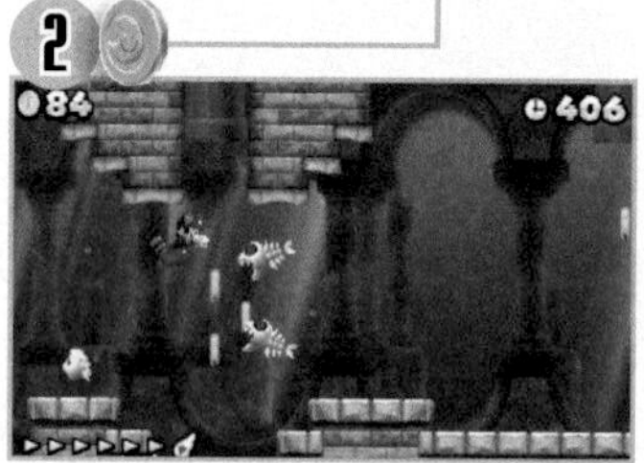

The second Moon Coin is located in a hidden area. To find it, enter the pipe at Point 2.

After you pass through the pipe, grab the Moon Coin to the right.

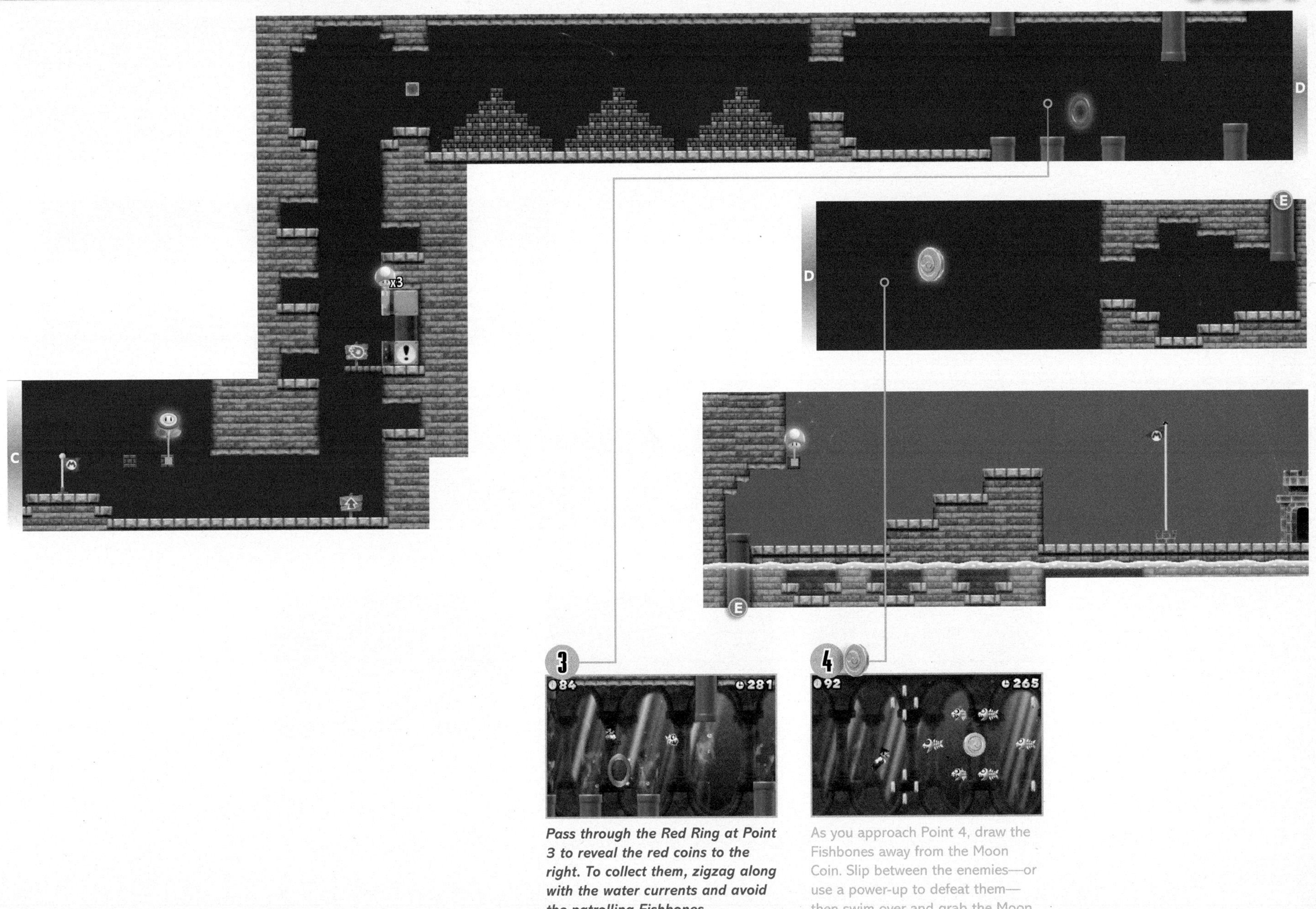

Pass through the Red Ring at Point 3 to reveal the red coins to the right. To collect them, zigzag along with the water currents and avoid the patrolling Fishbones.

As you approach Point 4, draw the Fishbones away from the Moon Coin. Slip between the enemies—or use a power-up to defeat them—then swim over and grab the Moon Coin.

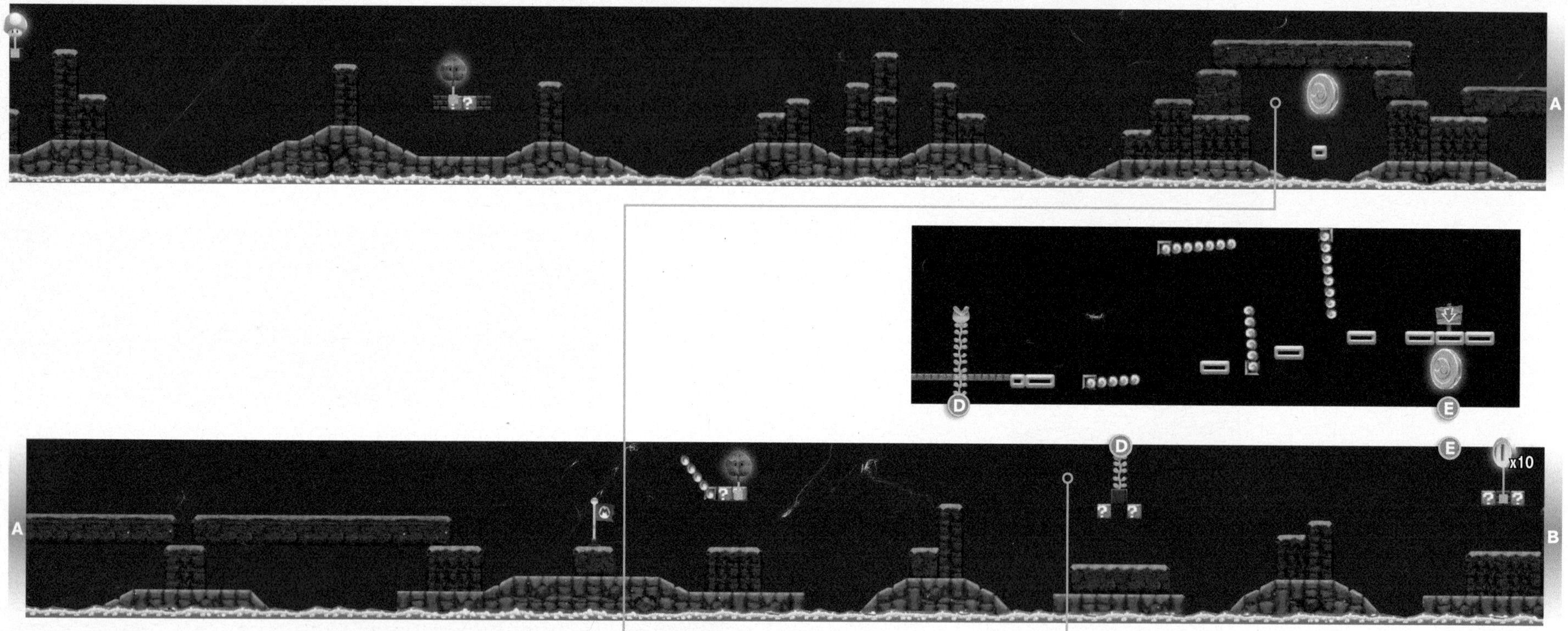

The first Moon Coin is floating above a small Donut Block at Point 1. When you're ready, make a running leap through the Moon Coin just as the Lava Bubble drops out of your path.

The second Moon Coin is in a hidden area. Find the Invisible Block between the ? Blocks at Point 2, then climb up the revealed Beanstalk.

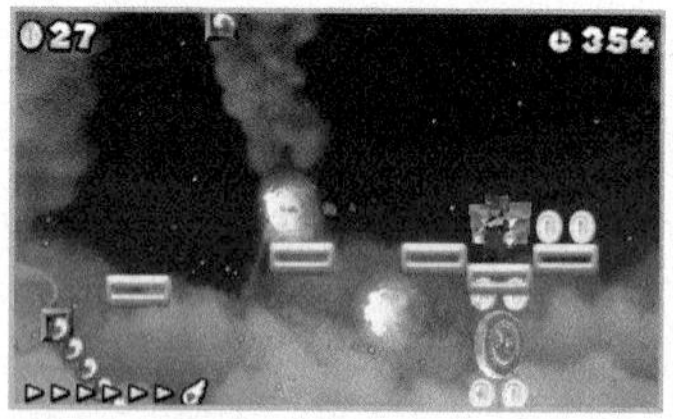

When you reach the top of the Beanstalk, follow the path to the right. Stand on the Donut Block directly above the Moon Coin. Wait for the Donut Block to give way, then grab the Moon Coin as you fall out of the area.

WORLD 3-CASTLE

2

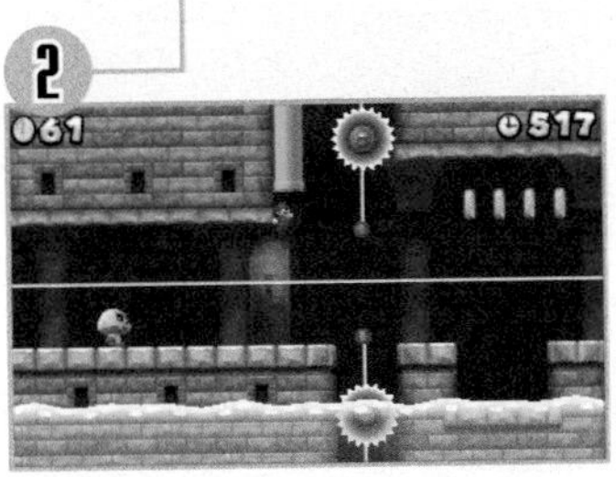

The small pipe at Point 2 leads to a hidden area. To use it, you must bring a Mini Mushroom into the level.

As Mini Mario, pass through the pipe, then hit the ? Blocks to find a Super Star. While the power-up is active, perform a series of wall jumps to destroy the Grinders above you.

If you go through the Pipe for Mini Mario you can gain a 1-UP by destroying the Grinders.

3

The second Star Coin is on a platform at Point 3. Stomp the Dry Bones patrolling the platform, then collect the Star Coin before Grinders appear on the nearby tracks.

TIP

Once the player collects the Star Coin two Grinders appear on either side.

4

The third Star Coin is hidden beyond the wall at Point 4. Locate the Invisible Block near the door, then use it to reach the hidden passage.

5

When the battle starts, Wendy Koopa floods the room with water. Swim away from her as she jumps around the room, and take care to avoid the Cheep Cheeps that emerge from the pipes. Do not attempt to attack Wendy Koopa while the room is flooded.

During the Wendy Koopa fight, you can make the battle go quicker if you hit Wendy right when she is getting out of her shell phase. If the timing is right, this will keep the water from rising.

When the water drains below the floor, stomp on Wendy's head. Wendy pulls into her shell and bounces around the room. Dodge the shell and the Cheep Cheeps that launch out of the water. When Wendy emerges from her shell, stomp her a second time. Keep dodging enemy attacks and stomp Wendy's head a third time to end the encounter and unlock World Four.

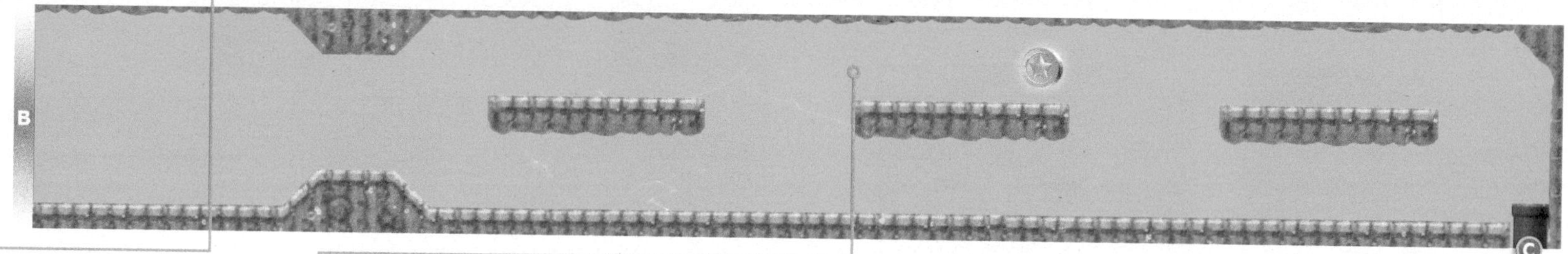

NOTE

Before you can visit this level, you must spend five Star Coins to unlock the appropriate path.

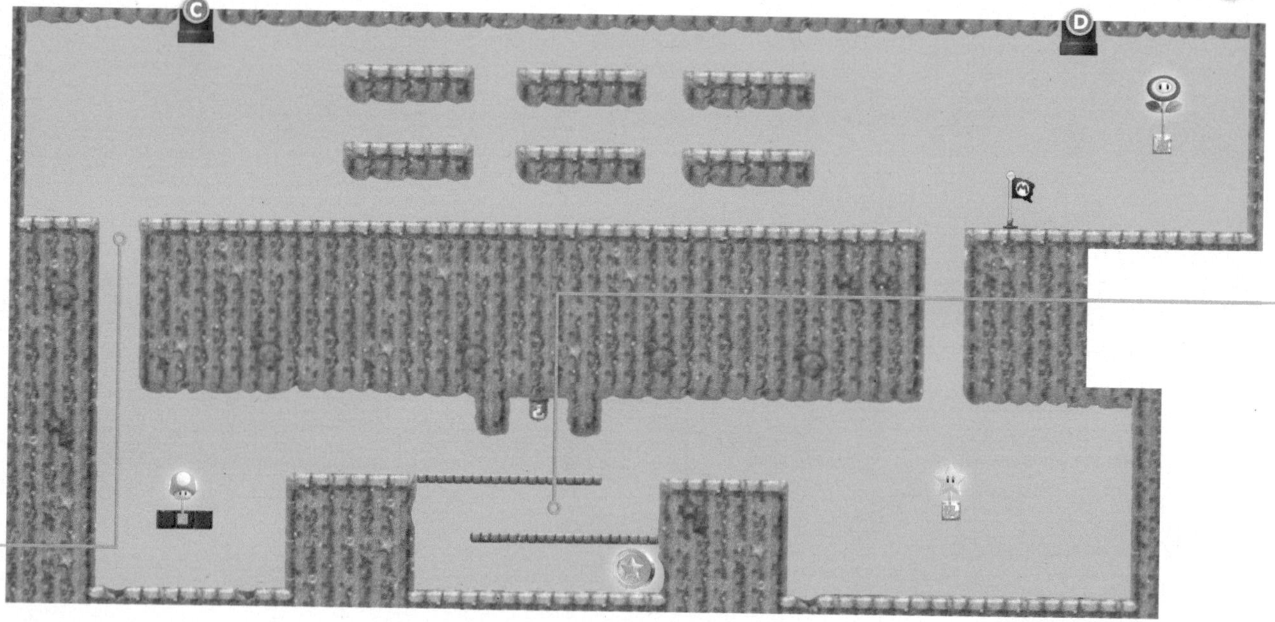

1

When you pass through the first pipe, a strong current sweeps you to the right. As it does, sink down low enough to bump into the platform at Point 1. Slide down and hit the P Switch below you to reveal a trail of blue coins.

2

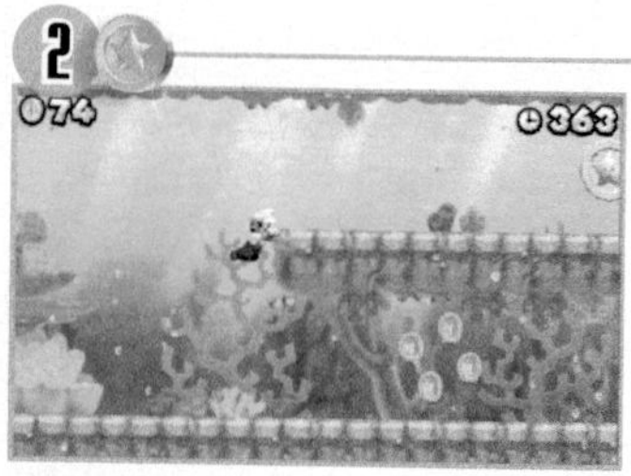

The first Star Coin is located above the platform at Point 2. The current is very strong, so make sure you're in position to grab it on your way through the area.

3

When you reach Point 3, swim through the hole in the floor. This route is a bit longer, but there are some useful items within the hidden area.